CROSSCURRENTS

CONTEMPORARY POLITICAL ISSUES

CROSSCURRENTS

CONTEMPORARY POLITICAL ISSUES

SEVENTH EDITION

EDITED BY

MARK CHARLTON
ST. MARY'S UNIVERSITY COLLEGE

AND

PAUL BARKER
BRESCIA UNIVERSITY COLLEGE

NELSON / EDUCATION

NELSON / EDUCATION

Crosscurrents: Contemporary Political Issues, Seventh Edition
edited by Mark Charlton and Paul Barker

Vice President,
Editorial Higher Education:
Anne Williams

Acquisitions Editor:
Anne-Marie Taylor

Marketing Manager:
Ann Byford

Developmental Editor:
My Editor, Inc.

Permissions Coordinator:
Yvonne Liburd

Content Production Manager:
Claire Horsnell

Production Service:
Cenveo Publisher Services

Copy Editor:
Elizabeth Phinney

Proofreader:
Erin Moore

Production Coordinator:
Ferial Suleman

Design Director:
Ken Phipps

Managing Designer:
Franca Amore

Cover Design:
Sharon Lucas

Cover Image:
Adam Gault/Getty Images

Interior Image Credit:
Robyn Mackenzie/Shutterstock

Printer:
R.R. Donnelley

Library and Archives Canada
Cataloguing in Publication Data

Main entry under title:

Crosscurrents : contemporary
political issues/edited by Mark
Charlton and Paul Barker.—7th ed.

Includes bibliographical
references.
ISBN 978-0-17-650344-4

1. Canada—Politics and
government—1993—Textbooks.
2. Canada—Social policy—
Textbooks. I. Charlton, Mark,
1948– II. Barker, Paul, 1953– III.
Title: Contemporary political
issues.

FC640.C76 2012
971.07   C2011-906392-1

ISBN-13: 978-0-17-650344-4
ISBN-10: 0-17-650344-7

CONTENTS

PART FOUR: POLITICAL ISSUES

CONTRIBUTORS

Michael Adams: Well-known pollster and author of numerous books on Canadian society and politics

Iain T. Benson: Senior Associate Counsel with Miller Thompson LLP and Extraordinary Professor in the Department of Constitutional Law and Philosophy at the University of Free State in Bloemfontein, South Africa

Philip L. Bryden: Wilbur Fee Bowker Professor and Dean of Law at the University of Alberta

Daniel Cohn: Associate professor of political science at York University

Faron Ellis: Political science instructor at Lethbridge College and recently elected alderman of the Lethbridge City Council

Anna Esselment: Assistant professor of political science at the University of Waterloo

Thomas Flanagan: Professor of political science at the University of Calgary

Andrew Heard: Associate professor of political science at Simon Fraser University

John L. Hiemstra: Professor of political science and Dean of the Faculty of Social Sciences at King's University College at the University of Western Ontario

Robert J. Jackson: Distinguished Professor of Political Science at Carleton University, professor of political science at Carleton University, and Fletcher Jones Professor of Government at the University of Redlands in California

Harold J. Jansen: Associate professor of political science at the University of Lethbridge

David Kilgour: Former Member of Parliament for Edmonton-Strathcona

Alex Marland: Assistant professor of political science at Memorial University of Newfoundland

Robert Martin: Professor emeritus at the University of Western Ontario Faculty of Law

Hugh Mellon: Associate professor of political science at King's University College at the University of Western Ontario

Lydia Miljan: Associate professor of political science at the University of Windsor

Paul Nesbitt-Larking: Professor of political science at Huron University College at the University of Western Ontario

Jacquetta Newman: Associate professor of political science at King's University College at the University of Western Ontario

David Olevson: Student at Queen's University Faculty of Law

John H. Redekop: Professor emeritus at Wilfrid Laurier University and adjunct professor at Trinity Western University

Justice Mary Saunders: Member of the British Columbia Court of Appeal

Tim Schouls: Political science instructor at Capilano College

Roger Townshend: Lawyer specializing in Aboriginal issues

Kevin Wiener: Student at the Ivey School of Business at the University of Western Ontario

Nelson Wiseman: Associate professor of political science at the University of Toronto

INTRODUCTION

In the first edition of *Crosscurrents: Contemporary Political Issues,* we stated our desire to develop a collection of readings that would not only challenge students to think through a number of contemporary political issues, but also foster in students an understanding of and tolerance for the views of others. To achieve this, we felt that a text structured in the form of a debate or dialogue on leading political issues provided an ideal format. We find it gratifying that a number of our colleagues have shared this goal and have used the previous editions in their introductory political science or Canadian politics courses.

CHANGES TO THIS SEVENTH EDITION

In preparing the new seventh edition of *Crosscurrents,* we have maintained the basic structure and format of previous editions. The seventh edition addresses fourteen issues, somewhat fewer than previous editions, in response to requests to keep this new edition shorter. For each issue, an introduction provides the reader with the necessary background and places the subject in the context of more general principles of concern to the study of politics. Two essays then present conflicting viewpoints. Finally, a postscript offers a short commentary on the debate and suggests readings for students to explore the topic further.

From the comments of the reviewers, it is clear that *Crosscurrents: Contemporary Political Issues* is used in general introductory courses and in Canadian politics courses to about the same degree. Therefore, we have tried to select topics appropriate to both and have retained the public policy section, which covers a variety of issues. People who use the text in an introductory course may find the public policy section more helpful in the early part of such a course, which often deals with ideologies and concepts relating to rights and the role of the state in society.

A NOTE FOR FIRST-TIME USERS

In introducing the first edition of *Crosscurrents,* we set out our rationale for developing a reader using the debate format. We believe that the rationale for using this format for teaching introductory courses is as strong as ever and bears repeating for those who may be picking up this text for the first time.

There are three good reasons, we believe, for using the debate format. First, studies have shown that students learn and retain more information when they are engaged in an active learning process. Yet the reality in most Canadian universities is that students in introductory courses face ever larger class sizes, which militate against discussion and active student involvement. While students generally come to political science courses with a great deal of interest and enthusiasm, they frequently find themselves slipping into a pattern of simple note taking and passive learning.

Second, most introductory political science courses must of necessity address abstract principles and concepts and cover a great deal of descriptive material concerning processes and institutions. At the same time, students come to these courses expecting that they will discuss and debate what is going on in the chaotic world of politics. Unfortunately, it is often difficult for them to relate the debates of everyday political issues to the broader and more abstract principles encountered in their introductory courses. Without a reference point, discussions of contemporary issues may seem more like interesting "current events" digressions, with little direct relationship to the overall propositions being dealt with in the lectures.

Third, students frequently bring to their readings an uncritical awe of the authority of the published word. When confronted with a series of readings by leading authorities on each subject, there is a strong temptation for students to think that the text presents the "final" word on the subject. They assume that further discussion and debate can add little that is new to the issue.

With these thoughts in mind, we have endeavoured to develop a collection of readings that will serve as a resource for a more interactive style of teaching, whether it be in classroom or tutorial discussion situations or in a more formal debate setting. Because of the flexibility of the format, *Crosscurrents* can be employed in the classroom in several ways.

(i) Some may wish to assign the chapters simply as supplementary readings reinforcing material covered in lectures, and to use them as points of illustration in classroom lectures or discussions.

(ii) The readings may be used as a departure point for essay assignments in the course. To encourage students to develop their critical skills, they could be asked to write an assessment of the arguments and evidence presented in one of the debates. Alternatively, students could select one side of the debate and write an essay developing their own arguments in favour of that view.

(iii) Others may wish to use the readings as a means of organizing weekly discussion sessions into a debate format. On each topic, two students may be asked to argue the case for opposing sides, and these arguments could be followed by group discussion. This format requires students to adopt a particular point of view and defend that position. Because the necessary background material is provided in the readings, this format is very easily adapted to large courses where teaching assistants are responsible for weekly tutorial sessions.

ACKNOWLEDGMENTS

We would like to express our appreciation to the many reviewers who offered very helpful comments and suggestions throughout the years: Tom Enders, Grand Prairie Community College; Karen E. Lochead, Wilfrid Laurier University; Gerry Boychuk, University of Waterloo; Andrew Heard, Simon Fraser University; Susan Franceschet, Acadia University; Darin Nesbitt, Douglas College; Alexandra Dobrowolsky, Saint Mary's University; John von Heyking, University of Lethbridge; Andrew Banfield, University of Calgary; Chris Kukucha, University of Lethbridge; Cheryl Collier, University of Windsor; and Ross Gibbons, University of Western Ontario. We are particularly indebted to those authors who graciously agreed to write original essays or revise earlier ones specifically for this volume, as well as to the authors and publishers who have granted us permission to use their published work. In addition, we want to acknowledge the excellent support of Katherine Goodes of My Editor Inc. in helping us to bring this project to completion. The careful and detailed work of Claire Horsnell, Content Production Manager, and Elizabeth Phinney, Copy Editor, was also much appreciated. Finally, we would be remiss not to mention the support of many others, not named above, who have contributed to this volume in different ways.

Mark Charlton, Calgary, Alberta
Paul Barker, London, Ontario

ABOUT THE EDITORS

Mark Charlton is Vice-President Academic and a professor of political science at St. Mary's University College, Calgary, Alberta. Professor Charlton received his Ph.D. in political science from Laval University, where he studied as an Ontario–Quebec Fellow. He is author of *The Making of Canadian Food Aid Policy* (1992), editor of *Crosscurrents: International Relations* (2005), and co-author of Thomson Nelson's *Guide to Writing in Political Science* (2006). He has also published a number of articles in *International Journal, Études Internationales, Journal of Conflict Studies,* and the *Canadian Journal of Development Studies.*

Paul Barker teaches political science at Brescia University College, London, Ontario. Professor Barker received his Ph.D. from the University of Toronto. He is the author of *Public Administration in Canada* and has written articles on public policy that have appeared in *Canadian Public Administration, Canadian Public Policy,* and the *Canadian Journal of Law and Society.*

PART ONE

Is the Canadian Political Culture Becoming Americanized?

Can Native Sovereignty Coexist with Canadian Sovereignty?

Will Conservatism and the Conservative Party Fail?

Robyn Mackenzie/Shutterstock

Is the Canadian Political Culture Becoming Americanized?

✔ **YES**
PAUL NESBITT-LARKING, "Canadian Political Culture:
The Problem of Americanization"

✘ **NO**
MICHAEL ADAMS, "Canada and the United States—
Separated at Birth"

In the eyes of the world, Canada and the United States are very much alike. The two countries share a language, occupy the same continental space, and support the operation of free markets. The similarities between the two countries also extend to beliefs and attitudes about government—in other words, the political cultures of the two nations are comparable. Canadians and Americans both believe in a modestly sized public sector and exhibit reluctance to offer elected officials much leeway. Other countries may give government a large role, but not Canada and the United States.

However, at the same time, some believe that the two countries are separated by differences in how they approach political life. Americans have been more suspicious of government than Canadians, a view revealed in their determination to ensure that political power is always separated and not concentrated. On the other hand, Canadians have been more positively disposed toward government; since Confederation, when the public sector was crucial to the birth of the nation, Canadians have seen purpose in government. For many Canadians, these contrasting attitudes are fundamental to the uniqueness of Canada. Inherent in the Canadian political culture are a sense of community and an appreciation of the value of collective efforts and public institutions. Such a pose curtails the often rapacious individualism found in the more liberal political culture of the United States.

For those who see and cherish these differences, there are disturbing changes now taking place in the attitudes of Canadians toward government and public life. There is a declining trust in elected officials, and voters have become less attached to traditional parties and more enamoured of new vehicles of representation.

Once-valued public policies are now under attack, and the restriction or even downsizing of government has become an important goal. A belief in individual entitlement, fuelled in part by the Charter of Rights and Freedoms, has emerged as well, pushing aside more communitarian sentiments. For many, these and other developments mean only one thing: the Americanization of the Canadian political culture. The toleration, the sense of collective purpose, the respect for authority—all this and more is being lost. The way Canadians think about politics is changing, and it is a change to be regretted because it threatens to engulf Canada in what has been called the *possessive individualism* of the American political culture.

There are some, though, who believe that important differences in political culture continue to separate the two countries. One has only to look at the size of government today. In Canada, the public sector typically represents a little more than 40 percent of the total value of goods and services; in America, the percentage is almost 10 percent less. And then there are the public policies that emerge from government spending, another reflection of key differences. Canada continues to commit itself to universal health care, while the U.S. struggles to the do the same with a patchwork of initiatives. The same story appears to pertain to other fields of policy, in which Canadians seemingly support aggressive government action and Americans favour little or no action. More generally, there is the perception that Canadians just think differently from Americans when it comes to government. We still seem to prefer peace, order, and good government over life, liberty, and the pursuit of happiness.

In the readings, Paul Nesbitt-Larking argues that, indeed, the political culture of Canada is being Americanized. He also argues that this offers little cause for celebration, for it spells the end of what it means to be Canadian. Michael Adams, in an excerpt from his book *Fire and Ice*, avers that important differences still separate the beliefs of Canadians and Americans about government and the political process.

✔ YES

Canadian Political Culture:
The Problem of Americanization
PAUL NESBITT-LARKING

> Living next to you is in some ways like sleeping with an elephant; no matter how friendly and even-tempered the beast, if I may call it that, one is affected by every twitch and grunt. Even a friendly nuzzling can sometimes lead to frightening consequences.
>
> —Pierre Trudeau, speech to the National Press Club, Washington, D.C., March 25, 1969

For a very long time, and certainly since the American Declaration of Independence in 1776, the destiny of Canada has been shaped through its complex interconnections with the political words and deeds of those other European descendants who live to the south of us. Canada is, and always has been, an American nation. Carved and crafted from a process of "defensive expansionism"[1] in which the harsh wilderness of this northern part of the American continent was stitched together in east-to-west chains of settlement, often "in defiance of geography,"[2] Canada, in its very existence and longevity, is a major North American achievement. Less obviously, political and governmental life in Canada reflects two centuries of an ambivalent relationship with Americans and their way of life during which Canadians have alternately incorporated and rejected American influences. Americans are a self-confident people who share a common heritage grounded in an evolving covenant to sustain the most perfect political system of freedom and opportunity. Through their enterprise and determination, Americans have translated the ideals of their founders into enormous economic, cultural, military, and political achievements. It is no idle boast to claim that the United States of America is the greatest nation on Earth.

When Americans are asked to name their "best friends" in the international community, most name the British; when they are asked with whom they conduct the most international trade, Japan is mentioned most often. These responses strike many Canadians as curious. Canada is in fact America's largest single trading partner,[3] and, when probed, a majority of Americans express a strong and genuine affinity toward Canadians. What these findings reveal is best expressed by former prime minister Pierre Trudeau in the above quotation: a combination of benign ignorance and careless presumption. Americans do not think much about Canada or Canadians at all, and when they do, they think of Canadians as Americans, with some curious characteristics, who happen to live in another place. Over the past two hundred years, Americans have made gracious and consistent overtures to Canadians to join them in their great republic, and they have never been able to understand the apparent stubbornness with which a succession of Canadian leaders has resisted. American leaders have frequently regarded Canada as an odd little anomaly with its monarchical traditions and its chronic French–English tensions. Such Americans approximate Trudeau's elephants: they do not know their own strength and therefore are often unable to appreciate the damage or the offence they cause. Trudeau's tone is mild in its mockery, and it is possible to argue that his choice of animal attributes too much benevolence to the Americans. The American approach to Canada, as the U.S. has crafted its independent foreign policy throughout the past eighty years, might better be described as "bearlike" in its angry malevolence rather than elephantine in its passive tolerance. Whenever it is hungry, hurt, or under a perceived threat, the bear is prone to attack, lashing out against all who offend it or merely get in its way. While the Americans have uttered no serious threats to invade Canada since the late nineteenth century, they have interfered aggressively in our domestic and foreign affairs and, in so doing, have acted in ways that are at best insulting and undiplomatic and at worse in contravention of established international law and precedent. An egregious instance of undiplomatic interference was the ambassadorship of Paul Cellucci. Appointed by President George W. Bush, Cellucci was ambassador to Canada from 2001 to 2005. Using his ambassadorial role as a partisan bully pulpit, Cellucci lambasted Canadian governments for their domestic and foreign policy positions, far exceeding the bounds of normal diplomacy.

While it is possible to argue about the extent to which the American impact on Canada has been elephantine, bearlike, or both, it is indisputable that it has been of great magnitude. Our economy is dominated by American capital. American direct investment in Canada is currently about US$306 billion, and U.S.-based corporations own many of Canada's most profitable industries. Over 50 percent of all foreign direct investment in Canada comes from American corporations.[4] Since the 1950s, Canada's military strategy and structure have been shaped in deliberate synchronization with those of the United States through a series of bilateral and multilateral agreements. Military and geopolitical cooperation with the U.S.A. has intensified since 2006 under the Conservative administration of Prime Minister Stephen Harper. Whether we refer to it as "culture" or the "entertainment industry," Canada is dominated by American material. The vast majority of the movies or TV shows we watch or the magazines we browse through originate in the United States. In political terms, the American influence has also been profound. Many of our major political institutions have been deliberately shaped to reflect, if not entirely replicate, their American counterparts, including federalism, the Senate, the Supreme Court, and the Charter of Rights and Freedoms. Our political practices and processes have also come to approximate the American pattern in certain ways. In the early twentieth century, Canada adopted the American practice of selecting political leaders through holding large-scale party conventions; in recent decades, commentators have referred to the "presidentialization" of the role of Canada's prime minister. Political campaigning and party financing have become more professionalized and Americanized in recent decades, notably under the prime ministership of Stephen Harper. At the deepest level, many Canadians have been enthusiastic followers of the American way of political life and have come to admire American political values and beliefs. These Canadians have attempted to convince other Canadians of the superiority of the American way and to encourage them to incorporate American values into Canadian political parties, institutions, and practices. The struggle between those who value American political ideals and those who wish to preserve a distinctive Canadian set of ideals has been raging since the Declaration of Independence in 1776. In presenting the principal features of this ideological conflict throughout this paper, I shall explain why I believe Americanization is potentially so damaging to Canada and Canadians, and how eternal–or at least periodic–vigilance is the price of remaining Canadian.

POLITICAL CULTURE AND IDEOLOGY

Unlike most concepts in political science, "political culture" has a clear and definite beginning. The term was invented by Gabriel Almond and first used in an article in 1956.[5] Like other American political scientists of his era, Almond was determined to develop political analysis into a more rigorous and scientific discipline than it had been in the early decades of the century. The United States had emerged from the Second World War as the leading military, moral, and economic power in the world, with associated opportunities and dangers. In order to exert a meaningful influence on an unstable and rapidly changing environment, the American state required detailed and accurate analyses of political character in other parts of the world. Aware of the imprecision of existing accounts of political life in other countries, Almond adapted the "structural-functionalist" sociological framework of Talcott Parsons as a basis for developing a systematic understanding of political characteristics. In introducing political culture, he said: "Every political system is embedded in a particular pattern of orientations to political action. I have found it useful to refer to this as the political culture."[6] By this, he meant that it is possible to identify coherent and distinctive patterns of beliefs, values, and attitudes toward political institutions and practices among each of the world's political communities. Almond and his colleague Sidney Verba attempted to identify such political orientations among the citizens of England, Mexico, Germany, the United States of America, and Italy in *The Civic Culture*.[7] On the basis of their analyses of responses to survey data, Almond and Verba produced portrayals of the distinctive political cultures of each country based upon rigorous methodological techniques and consistent quantified measures.

Almond and Verba's study generated great interest and admiration and gave rise to over a decade of research based upon their model. The systematic study of political culture was undertaken in many countries, including Canada.[8] Despite its widespread success and acceptability, the approach also attracted its critics. Prominent among the criticisms were the following: that in its assumption of the civic perfection of the United States of America, the political culture approach provided an arrogant, partial, and distorted image of political values, beliefs, and attitudes in other countries; that there were serious methodological flaws inherent in attempting to capture something as deep, nebulous, and "holistic" as culture merely through adding up a series of quick responses to questions by individuals; and, perhaps most damning of all, that in the increasingly turbulent and conflictual years of the 1960s and early 1970s, the approach could offer little to explain mass discontent, institutional paralysis, sudden change, or socioeconomic breakdown. By the mid-1970s, the huge research industry generated by Almond had dwindled to almost nothing, and political scholars turned their attention to other matters. In the Canadian case, the decline of interest in political culture was marked by a series of influential anti-American articles, reflecting a more general pro-Canadian assertiveness that was prominent at the time.[9]

Regrettably, in turning away from the "Americanized" version of political culture, the Canadian political science community abandoned a very important subfield of enquiry. With all its faults, the path-breaking work of Almond had alerted us to the importance of how people feel about political issues and how they make sense of their political experiences. In criticizing Almond and others for their failure to achieve the exacting standards of full scientific rigour, it is easy to overlook the obscurity of the concept of culture and the difficulties inherent in working with it. Raymond Williams referred to *culture* as one of the two or three most difficult words in the English language.[10] Ongoing disputes at the core of political science over the very meaning of *politics* itself attest to the continued controversies surrounding this concept. When politics and culture are put together in a composite concept, definitional difficulties are multiplied.

Despite these challenges, it is possible to adapt the core of meaning inherent in Almond's approach, adding to it insights derived from other scholars in the field. The central criticisms of Almond pertain to the manner in which the concept was (ab)used—both methodologically and ethically—rather than to the concept itself. In building on Almond, my own definition of political culture incorporates the following additional insights. First, political cultures should be seen as events as well as states of affairs; political cultures are generated, produced, reproduced, modified, and even transformed by people in their daily activities; and people are strongly conditioned through their socialization to the symbolic worlds into which they are born and in which they grow up, but they also, in their turn, contribute to the reproduction of those symbolic orders. Second, political cultures are literally mundane or everyday; many of the political values, beliefs, attitudes, and symbols that we hold most dear are so taken for granted and unquestioned that we are often not aware of them. Third, I define *politics* more broadly than Almond, as the manner in which people come to decide on the appropriate distribution of valued resources, as well as on the making of those rules that govern us. The processes of politics are both cooperative and conflictual; politics happens everywhere there are things to be distributed and rules to be made. To summarize, political cultures happen as people, operating in an already constituted symbolic field of political cultural concepts and practices, convey to each other conceptions of the distribution and uses of valued resources and of the making of decisions and rules.

As I conceptualize them, political cultures are vague, nebulous, and shifting phenomena, and they are difficult to measure in any precise way. One of the most promising ways in which to explore political cultures is through the employment of the related concept of ideology. Political cultures consist of loose and semi-formed ideas, beliefs, and feelings about political institutions and practices. Ideologies are partial appropriations from political cultures, arising from the conscious and deliberate attempts of the intellectual leadership of particular social groups (known as *ideologues*) to achieve a definitional monopoly of the political world that will be accepted by as many people as possible and that accords with the particular interests of their group. Ignoring the complexities and subtleties of political cultures and focusing on a narrow and self-interested band of values and beliefs, ideologues seek to convince others of the way things are, the way they ought to be, and, less obviously, the way it is possible for them to be. In so doing, ideologues hope that their "construction of reality" will convince others to effect political change in their favour. Ideologues employ a range of political movements and associations to achieve their ends, including political parties, political institutions, interest groups, the media, the bureaucracy, and the educational system.

Canadian political culture has provided fertile "clay" for a broad range of ideologues who have attempted to mould and shape it according to their particular interests. Arguably the most important ideological struggle over the past two hundred years has been that between "individualism" and "communitarianism." Canadian political culture, in contradistinction to the American political culture, has managed to sustain a balance between these two principal ideological tendencies. As will become clear in the next section, another way of saying that communitarianism continues to be part of the Canadian equation is to say that Canadians have been consistently seduced by the promise of the American dream but have periodically drawn back in order to develop and sustain distinctive institutions and practices that counter American values.[11]

INDIVIDUALISM AND COMMUNITARIANISM

The quantitative approach to political culture, developed by Almond and his followers, did not recognize the importance of the ideological opposition between individualism and communitarianism. The reason for this is readily apparent: the model of political reality devised by Almond came from an ideological individualism so profoundly entrenched and successful that it had come to dominate the American political culture. It rarely occurred to American students of political culture to think beyond the limits of their individualistic premises. The entire apparatus of methodology, questions, and comparisons among nations was premised upon this unquestioned individualism. It seems hardly surprising that when Almond and his colleagues applied their benchmarks, the United States routinely emerged as the most "perfect" political culture.

Students of political culture in Canada, however, have enjoyed full access to three other approaches to the study of political culture that have enabled them to reflect upon the Canadian experience of individualism versus communitarianism. These are the "fragments" approach, associated with Louis Hartz, Kenneth McRae, and Gad Horowitz;[12] the "historical-developmental" approach, best expressed in the synthesis offered by Seymour Martin Lipset;[13] and the more recent empirical attitudinal surveys of Michael Adams, Matthew Mendelsohn, and Edward Grabb and James Curtis, among others.[14] There are large-scale differences between the three approaches with respect to their theoretical presuppositions and methodological approaches. What unites them, however, is their propensity to portray the evolution of Canadian political culture as an ongoing struggle between the American forces of possessive individualism on the one hand and the European forces of conservative order and socialist collectivism on the other hand. *Possessive individualism*, a phrase originating in the work of C.B. Macpherson, is a distillation of the essence of the pure ideology of individual property rights and freedom from interference, first developed in the work of John Locke.[15] The term *communitarianism* best combines the anti-individualistic impulses of traditional conservatism and socialism. As its name implies, communitarianism is a belief system that stresses both the logical and the moral necessity of thinking about political life in terms of the requirements of the community or the collectivity, rather than in terms of the isolated and abstracted individual. In considering those distinctively Canadian forces that have opposed possessive individualism throughout the past two centuries, communitarianism is best able to convey the alternating right-wing and left-wing critiques of American liberalism.[16]

The fragments approach to political culture argues that the principal "white settler" societies were established by ideologically homogeneous and cohesive colonies of Europeans, whose founding characteristics established the ideological parameters of those societies throughout the succeeding generations. Louis Hartz describes the powerful and pervasive force of liberal individualism in the United States, arguing that, even in the twentieth century, its domination of the political culture can explain the early death of American socialism, the reluctant collectivism and populist character of the New Deal era, and the anticommunist vehemence of McCarthyism.[17] Kenneth McRae illuminates the importance of feudalism in the French-Canadian fragment, as well as loyalty to the British Crown among the English-Canadian fragment, in the establishment of a society in Canada that, while fundamentally sharing in the liberal individualistic ethos of the American political culture, exhibited elements of a political culture of cautiousness, moderation, gradualism, compromise, and order.[18] McRae also makes reference to the incursion of modest doses of left-wing culture with the settlement of parts of the Canadian west by later European fragments ideologically committed to socialism.[19] These themes are further amplified by Gad Horowitz in his seminal account of the development of ideologies in Canada. Horowitz goes much further than Hartz and McRae in pointing out the critical importance of the communitarian elements in Canada's historical development.[20] Horowitz also moves his analysis away from the Hartzian notion that the founding ideologies of the fragments "congealed" early and remained unchanged.

The manner in which historical developments, notably major events, shape the emergence of a political culture was explored in detail in the work of Seymour Martin Lipset. Over a thirty-year academic career from the 1960s to the 1990s, Lipset developed a comparative analysis of the political cultures of Canada and the United States. On the basis of his understanding of comparative patterns of settlement, formative historical events, such as the American Revolution and the Canadian "counterrevolution," and a broad array of sociological data on such matters as crime rates, divorce rates, and church attendance, Lipset came to concur with Horowitz that differences between the Canadian and American political cultures are profound indeed[21]:

> My central argument is that the two countries differ in their basic orga-
> nizing principles. Canada has been and is a more class-aware, elitist, law-
> abiding, statist, collectivity-oriented, and particularistic (group-oriented)
> society than the United States....The United States remained throughout
> the 19th and early 20th centuries the extreme example of a classically lib-
> eral or Lockean society, one that rejected the assumptions of the alliance of
> throne and altar, of ascriptive elitism, of mercantilism, of noblesse oblige,
> of communitarianism.[22]

While Lipset stressed the fundamentally liberal individualist character of both Canada and the United States and argued that, in the global context, "the two resemble each other more than either resembles any other nation,"[23] his frame-work of comparison, like mine, was between the two countries, and the distinctions are substantial enough to be noteworthy.

Recent empirical surveys of Canadian and American attitudes sustain the view that Canada is a more communitarian polity. Michael Adams's data reveal that, over the past decade, both Canadians and Americans have been shifting their attitudes away from support for traditional authorities toward greater individualism. However, Americans have moved strongly in the direction of possessive individu-alism, competitiveness, patriarchy, and exclusionary defensiveness. For their part, Canadians have diverged from the American path and shifted strongly toward socially oriented individualism, self-expression, and fulfillment through altruism and inclusiveness.[24] Both Adams and Edward Grabb and James Curtis highlight the important point that, while the American South skews the United States toward its characteristic values of possessive individualism and exclusionary defensiveness, Quebec skews Canada toward socially inclusive individualism and a comfort with statism, secularism, and communitarianism. In a key table summarizing measures of individualism, Grabb and Curtis's data show that for three out of the four variables that achieve significant national differences, the United States is more individualistic. Moreover, the pattern of American individualism is as strong in the north as it is in the south.[25] Matthew Mendelsohn, in a summary of his findings, remarks that at the beginning of the twenty-first century, Canada remains "more collectivistic, more open to diversity, more supportive of state intervention, more deferential, and more prepared to find solidarity with people in other countries than its southern neighbour."[26] This is despite a decade of globalization, continental economic integration, federal and provincial neoliberal fiscal policies, and the consequent erosion of the Canadian welfare state.

Despite the historical pervasiveness of communitarian elements in Canada's political culture, and the eloquent passion of many of its supporters, possessive individualistic ideology is currently in global ascendancy.[27] If there is a communitarian response to these trends, it is to be found in the reactionary and defensively hostile impulses of religious and nationalistic fundamentalisms. Such social forces have grown in panic response to the rapid onset of a global economy and culture seemingly bereft of morality and meaning. Canadians have worked hard to sustain a more balanced and inclusive communitarian polity that celebrates diversity, openness, and polyethnic traditions. Given the current political landscape in the United States and beyond, such a balance seems increasingly challenging to sustain. In the next section, I turn my attention to the dangers for Canada associated with incorporating too much possessive individualism and narrow defensiveness: the problem of Americanization.

THE PROBLEM OF AMERICANIZATION

To speak of Americanization as a problem is not to adopt a narrowly ethnocentric, anti-American point of view. A large majority of Canadians were horrified at the attacks of September 11, 2001, in which thousands of innocent lives were lost, and chose to express their solidarity in empathetic support and acts of kindness. Canadians continue to express strong bonds of affection for Americans and an admiration for many aspects of the American way of life, notably the exuberant spirit of entrepreneurship. There is even a small minority of Canadians who would welcome a union of the two countries. Equally, not all Americans are defensive, possessive individualists. American scholars, notably Robert Bellah and Robert Putnam, have adopted a critical perspective regarding the consequences of the early and monopolistic domination of individualist liberalism as the American creed and its continuing effects on the American polity. Equating individualism and libertarian freedom with "Americanism" itself has permitted the ideological intolerances of authoritarian populism and "witch hunts" and has discouraged forms of state-led and communitarian solutions to America's problems that have been made possible elsewhere. Globalization, in its economic, cultural, and militaristic forms, represents the universalization of Americanism in the form of global capitalism, global media, and American military presence overseas.

Americanism is rapidly becoming so dominant that communitarian ideological perspectives are in jeopardy. Ideologies in themselves do not die, but given the will and the opportunity, ideologues can so determine and shape political culture that a given people come to believe that only one ideological position is desirable or possible. A political culture can be so imbued with a particular ideological orientation that all others dwindle and fade. Once this is in process, political support for previously existing institutions, practices, and discourses that run counter to the interests of the prevailing ideology falls away. The institutions and practices of the Canadian nation-state have been built on the basis of a political culture characterized by some degree of communitarianism. Once these diminish beyond a certain point, Canada itself is in question. This point was grasped, in a work of brilliant insight, by conservative scholar George Grant in 1965. In his *Lament for a Nation*, Grant understood that the uncritical adoption of American technocratic politics and economics, as well as the culture of populist consumerism, would undermine Canada to the point where its continued existence ceased to be relevant. He noted, "The impossibility of conservatism in our era is the impossibility of Canada."[28] Put simply, Grant was arguing that if nobody loves the country or regards the relationship between the generations as a communitarian trust, then the nation-state itself will become little more than a practical container. The subtitle of Grant's book is "The Defeat of Canadian Nationalism." There has never been a massive Canadian nationalism—at least not in English Canada—but there have been assertive moments of resistance to Americanization. The continued viability of Canada depends upon the capacity and willingness of Canadians to recognize those economic, cultural, and political signs of the eroding Canadian balance, and to work tirelessly in order to redress the imbalances.

For two decades, Canada's principal political parties and political leaders have been actively promoting economic policies of Americanized possessive individualism. At the federal level, with the marginal exception of the early 1980s when the Liberal Party attempted to forge a limited new "national policy," both Liberal and Progressive Conservative governments have driven the ideological agenda toward free-market solutions. As with the construction of any ideological perspective, the politicians have argued that their proposals are not merely sound but that they "have no choice." In the 1970s, the Liberals argued that too many demands had been made on the federal system and that it was impossible to continue to provide the kind of extensive and responsive public service that had been developed throughout the 1950s and 1960s. They promoted monetary and fiscal policies that increased unemployment, facilitated a decrease in the public sector, and squeezed middle-class incomes through higher interest rates and taxes. In the 1980s, the Progressive Conservative Party pointed out that Canadians had been victims of fiscal irresponsibility, and they began to talk of the need to cut the national deficit. They continued the trend against communitarianism in Canada through their modest attempts at public sector cutbacks, their privatizations and deregulations, but mostly through their two free trade agreements and the introduction of the regressive goods and services tax. The Progressive Conservative government hoped that these policies would stimulate noninflationary growth in the economy. In the 1990s, the emphasis on the national deficit intensified, and the Liberal Party perpetuated the trend toward Americanization with its massive cuts to the federal public sector as well as cuts in transfer payments to the provinces. The radical downsizing of the federal government inevitably had an impact on the provinces. In some of them, notably Alberta and Ontario, right-wing governments went even further than the federal Liberal Party in radical reductions to the size and scope of the public sector on the basis of American-style populist individualism, promoting a generalized distrust of government and large-scale tax cuts designed to curtail redistributional policies.

In the 1990s, two new major parties came onto the federal scene. One of them, the Reform Party, which became the Canadian Alliance, was a strong proponent of possessive individualism and committed to further radical cuts in public spending. It advocated reductions in transfers to individuals and regions, large-scale tax cuts, and the diminution of the power of the federal state to enforce national standards. The Canadian Alliance and the Progressive Conservative Party united in 2003 to form the Conservative Party of Canada. Its new platform continued the general thrust of Canadian Alliance policies, calling for tax cuts, deregulation, and greater powers to the provinces. Of all the political parties and politicians in contemporary Canada, very few have been active promoters of policies to enhance the communitarian essence of Canada, or even to slow its decline. The Liberal Party under Prime Minister Paul Martin redressed the balance to some extent, restoring funds to public services, such as health, education, and social assistance; Canadian culture; Aboriginal peoples; and foreign aid. Despite these trends, however, the fiscal strategy of the Martin government simultaneously transferred massive resources and fiscal authority to the provinces while increasing military expenditure and cutting personal and corporate taxes. The combined impact of these measures was to jeopardize the longer-term revenue potential of the federal state, rendering it decreasingly able to act on behalf of Canadians and to devise renewed programs of national scope. Since the Canadian federal election of 2006, the Conservative government has accelerated these trends toward tax cuts, deregulation, and devolution of powers to the provinces. Moreover, the Harper administration has integrated Canada more directly into the

American orbit by bringing Canada's foreign, defence, security, environmental, and trade policies into line with those of the Americans.

Behind the political parties have been the most important special interest groups. Many prominent corporate organizations, such as the Canadian Council of Chief Executives, the Canadian Federation of Independent Business, and the Canadian Taxpayers Federation, have actively promoted greater economic integration into the United States, as well as policies designed to cut the public sector and reduce taxes on the corporate elite. The corporate elite has been strongly supported by most of Canada's leading journalists, intellectuals, and academics. Some of them have, while attacking collectivism, continued to promote the rhetoric of a united Canada, which cherishes its distinctiveness. In this respect, they have offered some resistance to Americanization insofar as they have advocated the old-style orderly and conservative forms of "elite accommodation," through which Canada's distinctive communities are able to achieve a modus vivendi. In other words, they have advocated the kind of political arrangements that the Progressive Conservatives attempted to promote in the 1980s with the Meech Lake and Charlottetown Accords. The ideals of such accords, based upon bilingualism and multiculturalism in a finely balanced Canada consisting of "a community of communities," continue to be supported at the highest levels. In modified form, such is the agenda of the current Liberal and Conservative parties.

The problem for Canada is that the refined and noble politics of cultural pluralism and mutual respect have been promoted through anachronistic and elitist political practices from which most citizens have felt excluded. This is why Michael Adams and others have detected a growing wariness on the part of Canadians regarding traditional authorities. The politics of elite accommodation also runs directly counter to the anticollectivist impulses of economic possessive individualism. The cultural message of economic liberalism stresses narrowly defined rights, absolute freedom from restraint, and a rejection of those virtues associated with family, community, and society, such as love, tolerance, charity, duty, loyalty, and patriotism. There are signs that the hold of such qualities in the Canadian political culture is diminishing. An angry Canadian public rejected the Charlottetown Accord in 1992. The accord had been designed to provide a new compromise among Canadians in terms of their constitutional rights, as well as to restate the commitment of Canadians to a unified nationhood and distinctive national identity. Canadian voters punished the architects of the plan, the Progressive Conservative Party, by almost completely rejecting them in the federal election of 1993. In their place, English Canadians supported the Reform Party, while many Quebeckers turned to the Bloc Québécois; both political organizations did not accept bilingualism and multiculturalism.

The decline in support for the traditional parties, the growing disrespect for politicians, the growth of support for narrowly defined single-issue political movements, and a generalized sense of the atomization of political society all point to a growing individuation of Canada's political culture.[29] The rapidly declining trust in Canada's political institutions, political parties, and politicians is reported in Neil Nevitte's *The Decline of Deference*.[30] Nevitte's data demonstrate that "confidence in governmental institutions is declining while non-traditional…forms of political participation are increasing. In political matters, people are becoming less deferential, less compliant, more inclined to speak out…."[31] Similar findings are reported by Harold D. Clarke and his colleagues in *Absent Mandate*, which also tracks Canadian public opinion in the 1980s and 1990s.[32] Clarke et al. report strong declines in partisan loyalty and attachment over these decades, in conjunction with growing disaffection, detachment, and negativity concerning politicians and parties.[33] Their final chapter is entitled "The Politics of Discontent," and a key feature of that chapter is their characterization of an "angry and cynical" electorate.[34] Concluding their work, Clarke et al. refer to the Canadian political situation as one of "permanent dealignment," by which they mean a consistently fragmented and volatile relationship between citizens and parties.[35] In the context of such permanent dealignment, communitarian attachments to persons and places become strained. Despite the fact that dealignment and disaffection can be dangerous to a political community, blind deference is no better. Deference is always a thin and brittle basis for a political community and is, in the final analysis, as damaging as possessive individualism. Disaffection and the decline of deference are, therefore, in some respects positive forces and represent the kind of assertive enhancement of political efficacy and political participation that Adams refers to as "the balance of individual autonomy with a sense of collective responsibility."[36] However, in contemporary Canada, the principal ideological forces that have picked up on the mood of popular anger and cynicism offer individuated solutions that serve to amplify people's negativity, deepening and broadening their defensive possessiveness rather than encouraging their communitarian imaginations to seek new ways in which to invigorate the body politic. Canadian multiculturalism has come under siege from a barrage of antiterrorist discourses, the rebirth of strands of xenophobia, and the increased securitization of the Canadian state.

Canadians have demonstrated that they are not bound to the traditional political parties and that they are prepared to vote for new "antiparty" parties in numbers large enough to designate them as the Official Opposition in the House of Commons. The Canadian Alliance represented an American-style populism that it made hegemonic in Western Canada. For fourteen years, the Bloc Québécois offered the only true communitarian option in Canada, one that was, of course, grounded in demands for a distinctive and independent Quebec state to reflect the aspirations of the people of Quebec. To some extent, the success of Quebec nationalism is a reflection of the poverty of any true pan-Canadian national vision, either inside French Quebec or in the rest of Canada. The recent election of the New Democratic Party to Official Opposition status, driven by its successes in Quebec in the 2011 federal election, represents a continuation of the communitarian option, even as the party attempts to moderate its "socialist" image to appeal to a broader constituency. Current political discourse in Canada is punctuated by the claims and counterclaims of single-interest groups to which citizens are encouraged to adhere on the basis of their narrowly defined personal and individual desires. Among the most recent crop of such groups are gun owners angry about gun control, victims of crime angry about the lack of compensation in the criminal justice system, and religious traditionalists angry at the right of civil marriage being extended to gays and lesbians. At present there is little to unite the various single-issue groups other than a shared belief in entitlement based on a conception of the state as a repository of goods and legal precedents that are "up for grabs."

The impact of the changing composition of Canada's political culture, as well as of the ideologues of possessive individualism, has been acutely felt. Despite the efforts of small Canadian nationalist groups, such as the Council of Canadians, and an assortment of individuals, including some prominent politicians and journalists, the federal state has been radically Americanized in the past few decades: NAFTA and the GST are accomplished fact; Air Canada, Canadian National Railway, and Petro-Canada, corporations designed with explicit public and nation-building purposes, have been partially or totally privatized; major regulatory agencies, such as the Canadian Radio-television and Telecommunications Commission, have lost much of their regulatory powers; federal Crown corporations, notably the CBC, have suffered enormous budget cuts; and there have been radical reductions in the size and scope of the state, with more to come. The effects of these cuts have reverberated in the quality of life at the provincial level: the "social safety net" has been lowered; universal provision of social services, which nurtures a communitarian ethos, has been rapidly replaced with "means-tested" and limited provision of social services, which targets and stigmatizes the poor; public systems of health care and education are being eroded to the point where partial privatization of so-called core or essential services seems highly probable; the gap between the rich and the poor is increasing as the middle class, which carried much of the burden of redistribution in the 1980s, becomes increasingly reluctant to share.

In furtherance of these trends, the liberal-individualistic message of radical decentralization is currently being hotly promoted by Canada's richest and most influential special interest group, the Canadian Council of Chief Executives. The Canadian Council of Chief Executives and the Conservative Party are both promoting a new Canada in which principal socioeconomic and political control is devolved to the provinces and in which there is little more than some vague sentiment and occasional sports and entertainment extravaganzas to hold the country together. If there is radical decentralization in the future, those ties of common citizenship that bind us will fall away, and the already weak pro-Canada voices will become even weaker. There is growing evidence of parochial assertiveness and a "beggar-thy-neighbour" attitude among opinion leaders in Canada's more affluent provinces, British Columbia and Alberta. As the voices for a pan-Canadian vision diminish, the logic of an independent Quebec state will increase. Once Quebec has gone, the remaining nine provinces and the territories will have very little left to hold them together. As they enter further into the liberal-individualistic ethos of free trade in the North American continent, an ethos buttressed by new World Trade Organization agreements that severely restrict the scope of sovereign states in controlling capital flows, so the patent absurdity of continued independence for a culturally fractured, socioeconomically divided, and geographically split Canada will become increasingly clear. We will have rationalized Canada out of existence.

CONCLUSION

Given the ideological assault of Americanizing possessive individualism on Canada's political culture, and the efficacy of that assault in terms of major changes in public policy, what is the prognosis for Canada? The spirit of self-centred individualism and defensive exclusionism does not bode well for the continued existence of Canada. Traditional conservatives would argue that any nation that has lost its sense of organic connectedness is in poor health. When the sentence "The West wants in" became the rallying cry for the foundation of the Reform Party, it was taken to mean that the western provinces wished to partake of the benefits and burdens of full and equitable citizenship. Regrettably, the sentence has come to be associated instead with a narrowly focused acquisitiveness, opportunistic rent-seeking, and an unwillingness to share natural advantages with those persons and regions less fortunate in the country. Under such circumstances, it seems improbable that the wealthier provinces, such as British Columbia and Alberta, will be able to see much sense in sustaining Canada as a unified nation-state. The deficit-cutting and public sector–gutting economic policies of the Liberal Party and the Conservative Party are actively promoting this fragmentation. And yet some modest signs of Canadian distinctiveness remain. As mentioned earlier, public opinion research reveals Canadians in the late 1990s to be more communitarian, statist, committed to social order, and supportive of public health care than Americans.[37] Moreover, it is always possible that the decline of public provision, the growing inequality, and the increasing immiseration of the poor will so offend the communitarian impulses of our political culture that Canadians will reject further trends toward possessive individualism.[38]

On the cultural front, there seems little evidence of patriotism or spontaneous love of country. There are occasional glimpses of nationalistic pride, such as when Canada won two hockey gold medals in the 2002 Winter Olympics. But other than in these infrequent moments, it simply appears that few Canadians care very much. Over a century ago, the French intellectual Ernst de Renan referred to a nation as an act of will, as "a daily plebiscite." There seems to be very little active will to nurture Canada. While it is possible to be reserved in one's patriotism, our continued silence in the context of accelerated Americanization is deafening. Not only is there an atmosphere of listless apathy about the nation, but also increasing numbers of English Canadians have exhibited an unwillingness to accept the claim of Quebec to be a nation within Canada. Such an uncompromising stance would be welcomed in the radically individualistic melting-pot homogeneity of the United States, but it makes little sense in Canada. It is possible that there are sufficient numbers of French Quebeckers who could be persuaded to remain in a Canada of "two solitudes" united through mutual and distanced respect. The ultimate consequence of the logic of hard-line opposition to distinctive status is to drive those moderate Quebeckers into the welcoming arms of the separatists.

Canada is in jeopardy. Our neighbours to the south have consistently stated that they would welcome Canada as a part of their great country. Such a solution might make sense. Here we might recall the sarcastic and self-pitying vitriol of George Grant, who said: "Perhaps we should rejoice in the disappearance of Canada. We leave the narrow provincialism and our backwoods culture; we enter the excitement of the United States where all the great things are done."[39] Such an eventuality would be a tragic loss to a world that desperately needs the model of polyethnic and multicultural tolerance provided by Canada. Perhaps, given the newfound assertive and anti-elite rebelliousness of Canadians, we will simply reinvent the country and craft something new, authentic, and beautiful. Perhaps, in this globalized, postmodern age in which Canada's greatest claim to international distinctiveness is to be a country that is so tolerant of pluralities of differences among its own citizens that it really has no substantive core, Canada will actually become the first "post-nation": an address with no fixed identity, whose very openness will be an exemplar to the remainder of the world whose new soft tribalisms will gradually infiltrate the remainder of the planet, including America, imbuing them with Canadianism and creating the ultimate global village.

NOTES

1. The phrase comes from H.G.J. Aitken, "Defensive Expansionism: The State and Economic Growth in Canada," in W.T. Easterbrook and M.H. Watkins, eds., *Approaches to Canadian Economic History* (Toronto: McClelland and Stewart, 1967), pp. 183–221.

2. W.A. Mackintosh, "Economic Factors in Canadian History," in Easterbrook and Watkins, eds., *Approaches,* p. 15.

3. United States International Trade Commission, *U.S. Trade Balances, by Partner Country 2010,* available at http://dataweb.usitc.gov/scripts/cy_m3_run.asp. Accessed June 29, 2011.

4. Statistics Canada, *Foreign Direct Investment (Stocks) in Canada (2010)*, available at http//:www.international.gc.ca/economist-economiste/assets/pdfs/FDI_stocks-Inward_by_Country-ENG.pdf. Accessed June 29, 2011.

5. Gabriel Almond, "Comparative Political Systems," *World Politics* 18 (1956), pp. 391–409.

6. Ibid., p. 396.

7. Gabriel Almond and Sidney Verba, *The Civic Culture* (Boston: Little Brown, 1963).

8. See Jon Pammett and Michael Whittington, eds., *Foundations of Political Culture: Political Socialization in Canada* (Toronto: Macmillan, 1976); Richard Simeon and David Elkins, "Regional Political Cultures in Canada," *Canadian Journal of Political Science* 7 (1974), pp. 397–437; John Wilson, "The Canadian Political Cultures: Towards a Redefinition of the Nature of the Canadian Political System," *Canadian Journal of Political Science* 7 (1974), pp. 438–483; Elia Zureik and Robert Pike, eds., *Socialization and Values in Canadian Society: Political Socialization* (Toronto: Macmillan, 1975).

9. Donald Smiley, "Must Canadian Political Science Be a Miniature Replica?" *Journal of Canadian Studies* 9 (1974), pp. 31–42; C.B. Macpherson, "After Strange Gods: Canadian Political Science 1973," in T.N. Guinsberg and G.L. Reuber, eds., *Perspectives on the Social Sciences in Canada* (Toronto: University of Toronto Press, 1974), pp. 52–76; Alan Cairns, "Political Science in Canada and the Americanization Issue," *Canadian Journal of Political Science* 8 (1975), pp. 191–234.

10. Raymond Williams, *Keywords: A Vocabulary of Culture and Society* (London: Fontana, 1976), p. 76.

11. This point is elaborated by Stephen Brooks, *Canadian Democracy: An Introduction*, 6th ed. (Toronto: Oxford University Press, 2009), p. 44, who attributes a range of economic and cultural policies to a series of deliberate "refusals in the face of Americanizing pressures."

12. Louis Hartz, *The Founding of New Societies* (New York: Harcourt, Brace and World, 1964); Kenneth McRae, "The Structure of Canadian History," in Louis Hartz, *The Founding of New Societies*, pp. 219–274; Gad Horowitz, "Conservatism, Liberalism, and Socialism in Canada: An Interpretation," *Canadian Journal of Economics and Political Science* 32 (1966), pp. 143–171.

13. Seymour Martin Lipset, *Continental Divide: The Values and Institutions of the United States and Canada* (New York: Routledge, 1990).

14. Michael Adams, *Fire and Ice: The United States and Canada and the Myth of Converging Values* (Toronto: Penguin, 2003); Matthew Mendelsohn, Canada's Social Contract: Evidence From Public Opinion. Discussion Paper P101 (Public Involvement Network, Canadian Policy Research Networks, November 2002); Edward Grabb and James Curtis, *Regions Apart: The Four Societies of Canada and the United States* (Toronto: Oxford University Press, 2005).

15. C.B. Macpherson, *The Political Theory of Possessive Individualism* (London: Oxford University Press, 1962). The dominance of possessive individualism in the American tradition has been well established in the key political cultural contributions to American society, notably Alexis de Tocqueville, *Democracy in America* (New York: Doubleday, Anchor, 1969); Louis Hartz, *The Liberal Tradition in America* (New York: Harvest, 1955); David Riesman, *The Lonely Crowd: A Study of the Changing American*

Character (New Haven: Yale University Press, 1962); Robert N. Bellah, Richard Madsen, William M. Sullivan, Ann Swidler, and Steven M. Tipton, *Habits of the Heart: Individualism and Commitment in American Life* (New York: Harper and Row, 1986); and Robert Putnam, *Bowling Alone: The Collapse and Revival of American Community* (New York: Simon and Schuster, 2000).

16. Sylvia Bashevkin, "The Politics of Canadian Nationalism," in Paul Fox and Graham White, eds., *Politics: Canada* (Toronto: McGraw-Hill, 1995), pp. 40–47.

17. Hartz, *The Founding of New Societies,* pp. 107, 111–112, 119.

18. McRae, "The Structure of Canadian History," p. 239.

19. Ibid., p. 270.

20. Horowitz, "Conservatism, Liberalism and Socialism in Canada," p. 148.

21. General interpretations of the comparatively communitarian character of Canada, proffered by McRae, Horowitz, and Lipset, are rejected by Janet Ajzenstat and Peter J. Smith, "Liberal-Republicanism: The Revisionist Picture of Canada's Founding," in idem., eds., *Canada's Origins: Liberal, Tory, or Republican?* (Ottawa: Carleton University Press, 1995), pp. 1–18. Not only do they claim that there is little Tory conservatism in the Canadian political tradition, but they go further in regarding the Upper and Lower Canadian establishments of the nineteenth century as fundamentally "liberal," and their principal rebel opponents, such as Mackenzie and Papineau, as "civic republican." While this is not the place to engage in detailed debate with Ajzenstat and Smith, I am in fundamental disagreement with their characterizations. Not only do they ignore the abundant evidence of elitist, ascriptive, affective, and particularistic practices on the part of the governing classes, but they also promote the idea that "civic republicanism" is "antiliberal." The ideology is better interpreted, by Louis Hartz among others, as "left" or radical liberalism. While it is true that Mackenzie and Papineau "scorn...the nineteenth-century liberal constitution" (p. 8), the basis of their opposition is not antiliberalism, but antiauthoritarianism. There is little evidence to support the claim that the nineteenth-century rebels were against the basic principles of possessive individualism. Their rallying cry was not for the abolition of capitalism but for responsible government and genuine democratic rights.

22. Lipset, *Continental Divide,* p. 8.

23. Ibid., pp. 214, 219, 225. Neil Nevitte has recently produced comparative survey data to illustrate the fact that, in the context of the advanced industrial nations, Canada and the United States are often closer to each other than to any other nations. He goes further and argues that Lipset's claims that Canadians are more deferential, law-abiding, and passive than Americans are not supported in his data. See Neil Nevitte, *The Decline of Deference* (Peterborough: Broadview Press, 1996), pp. 105–106.

24. Adams, *Fire and Ice,* pp. 39, 97, 123.

25. Grabb and Curtis, *Regions Apart,* p. 181.

26. Mendelsohn, Canada's Social Contract, p. 1.

27. The historical tradition of communitarianism and collectivism is mentioned in numerous sources, including Rand Dyck, *Canadian Politics: Critical Approaches* (Toronto: Nelson, 1996), p. 286; and Michael Whittington and Richard Van Loon, *Canadian Government and Politics: Institutions and Processes* (Toronto: McGraw-Hill Ryerson, 1996), p. 99; and Brooks, *Canadian Democracy,* pp. 52–55.

28. George Grant, *Lament for a Nation* (Toronto: McClelland and Stewart, 1965), p. 68.

29. Peter Dobell and Byron Berry, "Anger at the System: Political Discontent in Canada," in Fox and White, *Politics: Canada,* pp. 4–9; and Maclean's/Decima polling data, *Maclean's,* January 2, 1995.

30. Nevitte, *The Decline of Deference,* pp. 56, 79, 267, 291. Nevitte uses his data to interpret recent changes in the Canadian political culture as evidence of a general move toward postindustrial, postmaterialist, and postmodern values, pervasive throughout the West, and he specifically downplays the "Americanization" thesis. Nevitte's method of calculating the degree of "Americanization," outlined in footnote 2 on page 314 of his book, is designed to assess the "cultural lag" thesis that Canadian value changes lag behind those of the United States. Nevitte takes a series of dimensions in which he measures the change in both Canadian and American values from 1981 to 1990. One of these dimensions is "confidence in government institutions." According to Nevitte's data, "confidence in government institutions" declined from 49.6 percent in 1981 to 31.8 percent in 1990 in the United States, a decline of nearly 18 percentage points. In Canada, the comparable change was from 36.9 percent in 1981 to 29.4 percent in 1990, a decline of 7.5 percentage points. Using his calculus of "cultural lag," Nevitte declares Canada to be the leader of the trend in 1990 (Table 9-2, p. 292). The fact that the U.S. figure in 1990 more closely approximates the Canadian figure in 1981 than the Canadian 1990 figure approximates the American 1981 figure—Nevitte's criterion for Canada as the cultural leader—is, in my opinion, inadequate as a measure of the degree of Americanization. It is, of course, possible to argue that the Americans are becoming more like Canadians. However, it seems equally plausible to postulate that the profound loss of confidence, tracked in the American data, has a more moderate, yet still substantial, echo effect in Canada.

31. Ibid., p. 267.

32. Harold D. Clarke, Jane Jenson, Lawrence LeDuc, and Jon H. Pammett, *Absent Mandate: Canadian Politics in an Era of Restructuring,* 3rd ed. (Vancouver: Gage, 1996).

33. Ibid., pp. 22, 61, 65, 67.

34. Ibid., pp. 176–180.

35. Ibid., p. 185.

36. Adams, *Fire and Ice,* p. 123.

37. Footnote 12. See also George Perlin, "The Constraints of Public Opinion: Diverging or Converging Paths," in Keith Banting, George Hoberg, and Richard Simeon, eds., *Degrees of Freedom: Canada and the United States in a Changing World* (Montreal and Kingston: McGill-Queen's University Press, 1997), pp. 71–149.

38. For data in support of these claims, refer to Statistics Canada, *Canada at a Glance, 2000* (available at http://www.statcan.ca), "Persons with Low Income after Tax." The percentage of Canadians with low incomes declined only marginally from 3,744,000 in 1993 (13.1%) to 3,163,000 in 2001 (10.4%). Given the economic boom of this era and the conservatism of the measure (*after*-tax income), the failure to deal with poverty is troubling. The failure was particularly pronounced among children. In 2002, 35 percent of female-headed sole-parent families had low incomes according to Statistics Canada. A United Nations report on *Child Poverty in Rich Nations* (2000) calculated the Canadian child poverty rate at 15.5 percent. More detailed—and disturbing—data on child poverty

are contained on the Campaign 2000 website (http://www.campaign2000.ca), which states in its 2004 report that more than a million Canadian children continue to live in poverty and shows an increase in child poverty between 1989 and 2000. This is despite pledges made by all major Canadian political figures in the late 1980s to eradicate child poverty by 2000.

39. Grant, *Lament,* p. 8.

✗ **NO**

Canada and the United States— Separated at Birth
MICHAEL ADAMS

Canada's history has been dominated by three great themes: building a nation and holding it together, providing a growing list of services to the Canadian people, and managing our relations with the United States.

At the time of the American Revolution, Canada was a collection of British colonies that remained under the protection of the British crown rather than join the republican experiment launched by the thirteen colonies to the south. Thanks to that revolution, we even inherited some American Tories who stood loyal to the British Empire and migrated north.

To put it in a social values context, the American colonists rejected the traditional authority of the British crown while the Canadian colonists deferred to it, or, in the case of Quebec, fashioned a pragmatic compromise between the authority the British won on the Plains of Abraham in 1759 and that of the Roman Catholic Church.

From the late eighteenth century until 1867, the northern colonies remained under British rule, although increasing numbers of colonists demanded that their governments be more responsible to them than to the colonial administrators in Britain and their agents here. Some firebrands even instigated rebellions—one in Upper Canada (Ontario) in 1837 and another in Lower Canada (Quebec) in 1837 and 1838. These were revolts against an elite of appointed officials, not revolutions against the British regime, and in neither case was there significant loss of life. Early Canadians valued a liberty based on order over a freedom derived from the chaos of mob rule, which they believed prevailed in the new republic to the south.

Whereas America was conceived in violent revolution, the Canadian colonists were counter-revolutionaries whose cautious leaders were unable to negotiate the compromises necessary for their reluctant Confederation until 1867, nearly a century after the American colonies broke from Britain. While the Canadian colonies were slowly and laboriously brokering a larger union, America was deadlocked over slavery, lurching unrelentingly toward—and ultimately embroiled in—a bloody civil war that took the lives of 620,000 soldiers representing 2 percent of the population at that time, or nearly 6 million Americans in today's terms.

In his Declaration of Independence, Thomas Jefferson dedicated his country to the ideals of life, liberty, and the pursuit of happiness. Not to be outdone in the evocative slogan department, a century later Canada's Fathers of Confederation could see no higher pursuits than peace, order, and good government.

The early experience of the two countries also differed in a way that haunts America still. The southern colonies had developed an economy based on slavery, an institution the United States retained (with increasing reluctance in a number of quarters) until the Civil War in the 1860s. The Canadian economy had little use for slaves or indentured workers on plantations for cotton or any other crop. As a result, the gradual abolition of slavery by Upper Canada's first governor, John Graves Simcoe, after 1793 and later by the British government was a non-issue for Canada, except to make this country a refuge for American slaves who were able to escape their servitude via the Underground Railroad prior to Abraham Lincoln's Emancipation Proclamation of 1863. The American Dilemma, as Swedish sociologist Gunnar Myrdal aptly termed that country's legacy of slavery in his 1944 book of that title, continues to express itself today—often tragically for the large proportion of African-Americans who live in poverty and under threat of violence even amid the affluence of the world's richest country.

The American Constitution also infamously guaranteed the right of its citizens to bear arms. The Second Amendment was once understood to be a provision granting militias the power to overthrow illegitimate governments through the use of force, but it has recently been recast as the codification of the God-given right of every man, woman, and toddler to pack heat. Canada's Constitution contained no such right, and the consequences for each country are palpable to this day. Americans kill themselves and each other with the use of firearms at ten times the rate Canadians do.

America's revolutionaries, many of whom were Deists, agnostics, or even atheists, separated Church from State. Their forebears, the Puritans, had departed Britain in search of freedom to practise their religion. In founding their own communities in the New World, the Puritans were not in turn overly generous to those with dissenting theologies: Tocqueville notes that the criminal codes of some early communities included long passages copied verbatim from Leviticus and Deuteronomy. Nevertheless, 150 years later, the U.S. Bill of Rights enshrined the principle of religious freedom for Puritans and all others, declaring in the First Amendment that "Congress shall make no law respecting an establishment of religion, or prohibiting the free exercise thereof."

The Canadian colonies, on the other hand, inherited the British tradition of direct state involvement in religion. After the British conquest of Quebec in 1759–60, the British not only allowed Roman Catholics to practise their religion, but, with the 1774 Quebec Act (designed to keep Quebeckers loyal as the American colonies threatened open revolt), ceded to the Church the responsibility for the education of Catholic children. Meanwhile in Upper Canada, Governor John Graves Simcoe attempted to implement Anglicanism as the state religion, but failed in the face of religious pluralism in the colony. The British North America Act of 1867 entrenched in Canada's Constitution the Catholic Church's control over the education of Catholics in Quebec and elsewhere in the country. This provision sought to reciprocate similar rights granted to Protestants. America's constitutional separation of Church and State and its more market-driven approach to religion has contributed to much higher rates of religious belief and practice than we now see in countries like Canada and the United Kingdom.

Another difference in the founding ideologies of the two countries was the orientation to citizenship. The American revolutionaries envisioned their country as the Biblical "City upon a Hill," a shining beacon for all who shared the Enlightenment ideals of free speech, religion, and commerce as well as progress, science, and rationality. People from all nations of the world would be welcome to cast off the chains of feudalism and migrate to the home of the brave and the land of the free. Out of many, there would be one, *E Pluribus Unum,* a proud American living in one nation, and, since the 1950s when the Pledge of Allegiance was updated, "under God." Some might argue that this ideal of unity and ultimate sameness has not been honoured from the outset, beginning with the exclusion of all but property-owning Caucasian males from the voters' list in America's first presidential election in 1789, a group that formed less than 10 percent of the population.

In spite of many gaps between the ideal and the reality that seem obvious to us today, Americans have generally honoured their self-evident truths by welcoming migrants from around the world to join their melting pot, to become unhyphenated Americans willing to join the struggle for success and to send their sons to fight and if necessary die for their new country even against their former homelands.

Canada, by contrast, had no aspiration to mould an archetypal Canadian out of its three founding nations—French, English, and Aboriginal—or subsequent waves of newcomers from every corner of the planet. Each of the founding groups found themselves in their own enclaves. In the case of the Aboriginals, relocation was often forced and to be followed by various abuses; in the case of the French in Quebec, the enclave has always enjoyed considerable sovereignty. Sociologist John Porter characterized Canada in 1965 as a Vertical Mosaic, with the descendants of the English and the Scots at the top of the socioeconomic hierarchy. According to Porter, all groups lived more or less peaceably in their communities, whatever their position in the pyramid, but had little to do with one another—a place for everyone and everyone in his or her place. In 1945 novelist Hugh MacLennan characterized English- and French-speaking Canada as Two Solitudes; this even in his native Montreal, where each comprised about half the population of what was then Canada's largest metropolis. The ethnic hierarchy of Canada today bears little resemblance to the descriptions of 1945 or even 1965, and the ideology of multiculturalism has promoted more positive attitudes toward racial and ethnic minorities north of the border than the melting pot creed has in the republic to the south.

The seeds of this compartmentalized but generally peaceful society are to be found in large part in the gradual decision by the British after their defeat of the armies of France on the Plains of Abraham in 1759 to allow 60,000 French habitants to retain their language and religion rather than attempt their assimilation into what were then very small Anglo-Saxon colonies in Canada. By the mid-nineteenth century, when the English-speaking Canadian provinces were more populous, so too, thanks to the "revenge of the cradle," was Quebec's French-speaking minority, which was able to successfully resist further calls for assimilation (most famously that of Britain's Lord Durham in 1839, who saw the absorption of the French as a solution to the "two nations" that he found "warring within the bosom of a single state"). The subsequent union of Canada East (Quebec) and Canada West (Ontario) ultimately proved unworkable. But the Confederation of those two colonies, as well as New Brunswick and Nova Scotia in 1867 and subsequently six others, has proven more lasting (although certainly not without its shaky moments).

When Quebec awoke in the 1950s from its traditional deference to the Church and Anglo-Saxon commercial hegemony, it launched a "Quiet Revolution," with the election of Jean Lesage's Liberals in 1960, to assert greater political control within its own borders. The response by the federal government was a Royal Commission on Bilingualism and Biculturalism, the latter concept soon extended to Multiculturalism when the one-third of Canadians whose ancestors had come from countries other than France and the United Kingdom demanded acknowledgement. The result was the official recognition of Canada's linguistic duality and multicultural heritage—the political birth of modern Canada—and the formal entrenchment of one of the most significant differences between Canada and the United States, one that has become more, not less, important over the past half-century. No government in the United States has ever adopted a policy of bilingualism (except the commonwealth of Puerto Rico, where English-Spanish bilingualism was imposed through military force in 1902), even though up to a third of the population in states like California, Texas, and Florida are Spanish-speaking. Nor is it conceivable that a state could negotiate separation from the other forty-nine. Canada, like the former Soviet Union, has acknowledged in its 1999 Clarity Act that a province can legally secede under certain conditions.

Federalism is the political institution that accommodates the centrifugal forces of Canada's regions, allocating responsibility for education and the delivery of social and health services to the provinces. In contrast, the parliamentary system that Canada inherited from the British has become hierarchical and quasi-authoritarian. Canadian governments rarely get a majority of the votes, but our first-past-the-post, single-member district electoral system usually gives the party with the most popular support across the country the majority of the seats, and a majority government can pretty well do what it wants: increase taxes, negotiate a free trade agreement with the United States, put in place a tax on goods and services, privatize Crown corporations, implement strong gun control legislation, legalize abortion, establish a national medicare program.

Canada now spends 45 percent of its gross domestic product on government services, which is close to the average for the countries of the European Union. The United States, by contrast, spends 35 percent—including double the amount spent by the entire European Union on defence.

Part of the reason Canada has more activist government than does the United States is our governments' ability to act decisively within their areas of jurisdiction when they have parliamentary majorities—which is most of the time. Canada's British parliamentary system gives majority governments the power to do things that are popular, but more importantly to implement policies they believe to be necessary but unpopular—policies that may cause their defeat in the next election, but that are rarely reversed by the next government. The infamous Goods and Services Tax imposed by the Conservative government in 1990 was a major factor in its defeat in 1993, but the Liberals elected on the promise to rescind the tax recanted and were rewarded with re-election in 1997 because the voters had become inured to the new tax on consumption.

The Americans, in contrast, devised a system of government designed to balance power among the executive, legislature, and the judiciary so as to limit government. In times of national crisis, the president and commander-in-chief could wage war, but for the most part the government of the United States operates by consensus and compromise. It takes an extraordinary domestic crisis like the Great Depression of the 1930s or a reform-minded surge of idealism as in the 1960s for the country and its institutions to coalesce around national programs like Social Security (income support for the elderly), the 1964 Civil Rights Act, Medicare (health care for the elderly), and Medicaid (health care for the poor). Often in America it is the judiciary that initiates significant change, as in *Brown v. Board of Education* (1954), which desegregated schools in Topeka, Kansas, and *Roe v. Wade* (1973), which guaranteed a woman's right to abortion. Much of the rest of the time, the country seems content that politics be a game played in an opaque world of behind-the-scenes tradeoffs between politicians who are constantly running for re-election and the lobby groups who fund their campaigns.

Canadian democracy is certainly vulnerable to the charge of elitism, even authoritarianism, but it is more democratic than the U.S. system if judged on the basis of predictable policy outcomes. Despots too can deliver predictable outcomes, of course, but with no democratic recourse. In Canada, majority governments can quickly adapt to reflect public opinion, or can dare to resist public opinion, making unpopular decisions in the hope that their judgments will prove wise over the long term—and that today's risky policy initiative will be the seed of tomorrow's public consensus (and hopefully "tomorrow" rolls around before the next election). If a government makes an unpopular decision that remains unpopular for long enough to bring about its electoral defeat, a subsequent government can always rescind the decision. The Canadian system of government, I would claim, does a better job of reflecting the considered judgment of the people and therefore keeping them engaged in the political process than does that of the United States.

The United States is renowned for the direct democracy that the Progressives inspired at the turn of the twentieth century and that is given expression in the myriad plebiscites and referenda we see on state-wide ballots every two years. But these forms of democracy have not proven themselves to be superior to or more democratic than representative democracy; they overly simplify political choices (forcing yes/no binaries) and are often preceded by impenetrable preambles that are so complex voters turn off and don't vote at all. Furthermore, plebiscites and referenda tend to align majorities against minorities and invite private corporations and interest groups to spend lavishly when their self-interest is threatened. Such direct democracy looks to me more like mob rule than the considered judgment of the people that one would hope for in a democracy. American practice is a far cry from the occasional use of referenda in Canada on major constitutional issues like secession.

Canadian parties have platforms and policy positions that they usually try to implement once in office. The Mulroney Conservatives ran for re-election in 1988 on the single issue of implementing the historic free trade agreement they had negotiated with the United States. They were re-elected, albeit with only 43 percent of the popular vote, and then proceeded to carry out one of the most important policy initiatives, certainly from a symbolic point of view, in modern Canadian history. Can there be a better case for the legitimacy and effectiveness of Canada's system of representative government than the election of 1988, an election that truly represented the future to the present? By the mid-1990s, three-quarters of Canadians told pollsters they supported North American free trade that by then included Mexico.

Limited government is a cornerstone of America's political institutions and is tightly yoked to the country's founding ideology. The periods of activist government—at the turn of the twentieth century, in the 1930s, and in the 1960s and early 1970s—should be seen as aberrations. The neo-conservatism of the past two decades, beginning with Ronald Reagan's inauguration, should be viewed as a return to the norm. "New" Democrat Bill Clinton was least successful when he tried to be a liberal activist, as in the case of gays in the military or when pushing his wife's leftist notions of universal health insurance. He was at his zenith when, in league with "moderate" Republicans, he dismantled "welfare as we know it," the 1996 reform reducing American welfare rolls by one-third—a literal triage of America's poor. Americans have far less tolerance for state-sponsored dependence than do Canadians and Europeans, with the curious exception of the elderly, whose Social Security entitlement (kept cozy in its much ballyhooed "lock box") is a sacred cow that even the most right-wing conservative Republican dare not question.

Orientation to religion, government institutions, and founding ideology. These three factors fundamentally differentiate Canada and the United States, and this has long been the case. But these foundations have expressed themselves in the latter part of the twentieth century in some unanticipated ways. First let us look at the present realities that we or a French count might have anticipated 200 years ago. The United States has become the greatest nation on earth. It is the world's dominant economic and military power, and the leading innovator in the new information and biotechnologies. It is still the only nation on earth capable of mounting a concerted effort in exploring at the same time the human genome and the solar system. Its citizens have, on average, the highest standard of living on the planet, nearly half of the world's billionaires (242 out of 538 cited by Forbes in 2002) even after the dot-com/telecom implosion, and 60 percent of its millionaires, the largest elite ever known in history.

Certainly the growing gap in social values between our two countries during the 1990s (see Figure 1) must be at least partly attributable to America's emerging, after the collapse of the Soviet empire, as the world's only superpower, perhaps the most powerful ever to have existed on earth. This unique new status has reduced America's need to forge multilateral alliances against a powerful and threatening state adversary and encouraged the U.S. to revert to the more aggressive unilateralism it demonstrated in its conquest of the American West and in President Monroe's nineteenth-century doctrine proclaiming America's right to control affairs in the western hemisphere, a doctrine that came to seem implicitly writ large over the entire planet. Toward the close of the last century, American exceptionalism was becoming the realpolitik of globalization. Although the foreign-policy swagger that was evident during George W. Bush's first term has been checked by the chaos in Iraq (and the obvious overstretching of the

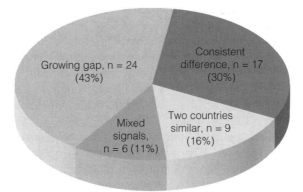

FIGURE 1

CANADA–U.S. COMPARISON OF 56 COMPARABLE VALUES 1992–2000

Reprinted with permission of Michael Adams, Environics Research Group Limited.

U.S. military), America remains uniquely powerful both militarily and culturally. This exceptional position, I believe, will act to further differentiate the values of the United States from those of the rest of the developed world.

History is very much with us. The violence that was America is America. The moralism—good guys, bad guys, right and wrong, you're either with us or against us, establish moral superiority, wait for provocation, and then blow them away—that was America remains America. In the first decade of the twenty-first century, we have an American government that, however challenged by the consequences of its actions in Iraq and Afghanistan, retains a sense of righteous zeal that is not up for negotiation. America's allies are not its counsellors; they are relegated to toeing the line, some enthusiastically, others resentfully.

Canada and the countries of Europe try to balance market forces with public policy, to reconcile the tendency for the rich to get richer and create an all but impenetrable elite with a social welfare state and policies to redistribute income from the haves to the have-nots. Such countries recognize individual rights but try to balance them with the rights of collectivities. These societies are more likely than Americans to realize that individuals can have too much freedom and that freedoms can be exercised irresponsibly by individuals to their own and others' detriment. Canadians put greater value than Americans on peace, order, and good (read activist) government. This is the aspiration of a conservative people, as opposed to the eighteenth-century liberalism that appealed to the American revolutionaries.

The diseases of an all but untrammeled individualism are, of course, not without their desirable counterpoints. America is a more dynamic society than Canada, more creative, more innovative, more exciting, and more fun. According to *The Economist* 700 of the world's 1,200 leading scientists work in the United States; these are the people we rely on to find the cure for cancer, the antidote for AIDS, and the key to Alzheimer's, and to best the long list of diseases that afflict people in every part of the planet.

Some of the sites at which Canada's difference from the U.S. is most apparent are, somewhat surprisingly, our cities. In examining the size and density of the communities in which we live, we find that a counterintuitive evolution has taken place. Canada, as any schoolchild knows, is the world's second largest country after Russia, but in terms of population contains a modest 30 million or so. The U.S. is a large country too, the world's fourth largest, but numbers roughly 300 million people.

What is astonishing is that in spite of all this vast northern space, Canadians are huddled in relatively few large urban centres, mostly a few kilometres north of the Canada–U.S. border. More than a third of Canadians live in one of three metropolitan areas: Toronto, Montreal, or Vancouver. In contrast, America's three largest metropolitan areas, New York, Los Angeles, and Chicago, represent only 16 percent of the United States population.

Canada is a more urban country than the United States. It is also more multicultural. Whereas 11 percent of Americans are foreign born, the figure for Canada is 18 percent. Moreover, a large proportion of America's foreign born are from Mexico; in Canada they are drawn from virtually everywhere on the planet, with very large populations being East and South Asian.

As in the United States, first- and second-generation immigrants tend to congregate in cities where entry-level jobs, now often in the service sector, are located and where they are more likely to find support from previous waves of immigrants from their homelands.

What is fascinating about Canada's cities is their cosmopolitan livability, their relatively low rates of crime and interracial and inter-ethnic conflict. Toronto is arguably the world's most multicultural city, but has a murder rate only slightly higher than fifty years ago when it was predominantly Anglo-Saxon. The homicide rate in Metro Toronto has increased slightly from 1.4 per 100,000 in the 1959-61 period, when its population was approximately 1.5 million, to 2.2 per 100,000 in the 1999-2001 period, when its population had grown to approximately 2.6 million. Compare this with murder rates in major U.S. cities: in 1999 rates per 100,000 in New York City, Chicago, and Los Angeles were 8.9, 22.7, and 11.6 respectively. In the U.S. capital of Washington, D.C., the rate was a whopping 46.4 per 100,000, in contrast to only 0.36—three murders—in 2001 in Canada's capital of Ottawa where, thankfully in this case, nothing much ever happens.

Canada's history of multiculturalism and the pattern of development that led to its urbanism have rendered its three great cities as models of vibrant and peaceful multicultural coexistence throughout the world.

It is interesting indeed that these two New World nations have each won the sweepstakes in two international competitions: the Americans for the highest standard of living on the planet and the Canadians for the best quality of life. The Americans have done this by being motivated by the notion of individual achievement; the Canadians by balancing individual autonomy with a sense of collective responsibility. We are each twenty-first-century expressions of the ideas of our ancestors and the institutions they built. America honours traditionally masculine qualities; Canada honours qualities that are more traditionally feminine. America honours the lone warrior fighting for truth and justice, the father who is master of his lonely house on the prairie, and a few good men planting the Stars and Stripes on a distant planet. Canada honours compromise, harmony, and equality. Americans go where no man has gone before; Canadians follow hoping to make that new place livable.

The founding ideas and institutions of each country have given rise to unanticipated consequences. I have found Americans to be more deferential to institutions than Canadians. This is counterintuitive. I have found Canadians to be less anomic, aimless, and alienated from their society than are Americans, who are nominally a more religious people. This too is counterintuitive. And, perhaps most surprising, I have found Canadians to be a more autonomous people than Americans, less outer-directed and less conformist. This too is contrary to the stereotype of Americans as a nation of individualists.

Canadians, however, have found themselves throughout their history to be in an interdependent world. After the Conquest of the French by the British army on the Plains of Abraham in 1759, it was decided by the authorities not to vanquish or assimilate the Quebec colonists but to accommodate their collective aspirations to preserve their religion, language, and culture. In the nineteenth century, when America suffered a bloody civil war over slavery, Canada experienced a few rebellions, but in the end negotiated compromises that eventually led to Confederation in 1867. Good never triumphed over evil in Canada. Rather, opposing forces, often more than two, fighting over geography, religion, language, or the spoils of power, eventually came to some sort of accommodation—usually with little loss of life, especially when compared with the U.S. Civil War and the near annihilation of Aboriginals as Americans settled the West.

Our founding ideas, our institutions, and then the experience of building our two nations have been very different: one by conquest, the other by compromise. This Canadian penchant for going halfway rather than fighting it out to see who's left standing expressed itself in the twentieth century with the recognition that Canada was not only bilingual but also multicultural. And now, with the establishment of the new northern jurisdiction of Nunavut (one of whose official languages is Inuktitut), Canada is formally recognizing multilingualism as well.

Thus, in Canada, the culture of accommodation that has been our socio-historical tradition expresses itself today as social liberalism, multiculturalism, multilingualism, multiple faiths and spiritual paths, and sometimes even as cultural fusion or hybridization. In its most postmodern form, it can exist as an openness to flexible, multiple expressions of individual personality, the leading edges of which are the flexibility of gender, age, and cultural identities. Demography as destiny is the vestige of a bygone era.

It is fascinating to see a country evolve from such deep deference to hierarchical authority to such widespread autonomy and questioning of authority—yet in the process not descending into chaos. Canadians are no longer motivated by duty, guilt, noblesse oblige, or fear of social sanction if they do not conform to group norms. Their kinder, gentler balance of freedom and equality, and of the public and the private domains, has created a tolerant, egalitarian society that enjoys freedom from potential catastrophe, danger, and violence that many on this planet envy, including many Americans.

In my nightmares, I may see the American fire melting the Canadian ice and then dream of the waters created by the melting ice drowning the fire, but this will not happen—at least not in our lifetimes. The two cultures will continue side by side, converging their economies, technologies, and now their security and defence policies, but they will continue to diverge in ways that most people in each country, I believe, will continue to celebrate.

POSTSCRIPT

In his essay, Nesbitt-Larking paints a picture that must be familiar to many. Government restraint, strident interest groups, growing public intolerance and anger—these are signs of the times. And Nesbitt-Larking argues, convincingly, that these are all manifestations of the growing Americanization of Canadian political life. Canada has always battled the threat of Americanization, and now it faces the prospect of finally losing this protracted war. Yet, it may be possible that Nesbitt-Larking exaggerates his case. Canada still has a coherent national health care program; the United States does not. Canada still has a disciplined political process; the United States does not. And Canada still has a sense of community; the United States does not. Moreover, recent surveys reveal that Canadians remain different from Americans in their basic attitudes.

Nesbitt-Larking can be challenged in another way. Perhaps the changes taking place are what Canadians want. One of these changes is a weakening of the deferential attitude Canadians hold toward leaders and political elites. As Nesbitt-Larking admits, this development can be seen in a positive light. Perhaps the costs of Americanization are acceptable in view of the development of a more vibrant and democratic polity in Canada. What is happening is not really the Americanization of Canada but rather the democratization of a nation held back by the vestiges of traditional conservatism.

Michael Adams nicely reminds readers of the differing origins of Canada and the U.S. and their impact on political culture. He also presents evidence that permits one to hold that the effects of these differences largely remain: government is still larger in Canada, the political process still reflects the British heritage, and Canadians still resist the attempt to build a monolithic polity built on strictly liberal beliefs. But doubts linger. Adams likens Americans to lonely warriors fighting for justice, and Canadians to a peaceful people in search of compromise. This may have been true in earlier years, but Canada has committed men and women to fighting a counterinsurgency war in Afghanistan. The peacekeeper has become literally a warrior, possibly a signal that Canadians now view political life in a different—a more American—light.

Before pursuing further readings relating to the debate, students should first read Adams' update on his thoughts about Canada and the United States in Michael Adams, "Canadian and American Value Differences: The Narcissism of Small Differences," in David M. Thomas and Barbara Boyle Torrey, eds., *Canada and the United States: Differences That Count*, 3rd ed. (Peterborough: Broadview Press, 2008). With this completed, the next step is to gain a general overview of Canadian political culture. For this, one would do well to read David V.J. Bell, *The Roots of Disunity: A Study of Canadian Political Culture*, 2nd ed. (Toronto: Oxford University Press, 1992) and Nelson Wiseman's more recent *In Search of Canadian Political Culture* (Vancouver: UBC Press, 2007). Shorter treatments of Canada's beliefs about politics include David V.J. Bell, "Political Culture in Canada," in Michael S. Whittington and Glen Williams, eds., *Canadian Politics in the 21st Century*, 7th ed. (Scarborough: Thomson Nelson, 2008) and Stephen Brooks, "Canadian Political Culture," in James P. Bickerton and Alain-G. Gagnon, eds., *Canadian Politics*, 5th ed. (Toronto: University of Toronto Press, 2009). An examination of the American political culture is also appropriate, for which Herbert McCloskey and John Zaller's *The American Ethos: Public Attitudes toward Capitalism and Democracy* (Cambridge: Harvard University Press, 1984) would be suitable. A text that gives a more nuanced view of the possessive or competitive individualism of Americans is Richard J. Ellis, *American Political Cultures* (New York: Oxford University Press, 1993).

Students should then consult comparative studies of American and Canadian political cultures. Such studies include Gad Horowitz, *Canadian Labour in Politics* (Toronto: University of Toronto, 1968), ch. 1; Seymour Martin Lipset, *Continental Divide: The Values and Institutions of the United States and Canada* (New York: Routledge, 1990); and Richard M. Merelman, *Partial Visions: Culture and Politics in Britain, Canada, and the United States* (Madison: University of Wisconsin Press, 1991). More recent works include Michael Adams, *Fire and Ice: The United States and Canada and the Myth of Converging Values* (Toronto: Penguin, 2003); David M. Thomas and Barbara Boyle Torrey, eds., *Canada and the United States: Differences That Count*, 3rd ed. (Peterborough: Broadview Press, 2008); and Edward Grabb and James Curtis, *Regions Apart: The Four Societies of Canada and the United States*, new ed. (Toronto: Oxford University Press, 2010). Another recent text of some relevance is Andrew Cohen, *The Unfinished Canadian: The People We Are* (Toronto: McClelland and Stewart, 2007), which contains a critique of Adams's thesis on the differences separating Canadians and Americans.

A large part of the debate revolves around changes in the political culture of Canada. For an important work on this subject, students should read Neil Nevitte, *The Decline of Deference* (Peterborough: Broadview Press, 1996) as well as Neil Nevitte, ed., *Value Change and Governance in Canada* (Toronto: University of Toronto Press, 2002).

Can Native Sovereignty Coexist with Canadian Sovereignty?

✔ **YES**
ROGER TOWNSHEND, "The Case for Native Sovereignty"

✘ **NO**
THOMAS FLANAGAN, "Native Sovereignty: Does Anyone Really Want an Aboriginal Archipelago?"

In Canada, the subject of Aboriginal rights has generally never been high on the political agenda. Most Canadians have a vague awareness of the deplorable living conditions on many Indian reserves, but that is about all. The demands of Native people for land, greater autonomy, and even self-government have received little sustained public attention. More "immediate" issues such as constitutional reform, Quebec separatism, western alienation, free trade with the United States, or economic recovery from recession have usually pushed Native issues off the list of urgent public issues, especially at election time.

However, dramatic events will occasionally push Native issues to the forefront of media attention. One such case was the Oka crisis of 1990, which, at the time, probably did more to change the public perception of Native issues than any other single event. Reacting to municipal plans to expand a local golf course onto traditional Native lands, armed Mohawk Warriors began erecting barricades in an effort to stop the work. The protest soon escalated into a full-scale confrontation between the Quebec provincial police and the Mohawk Warriors, in which one police officer was killed. Soon a second set of barriers was erected on the Kahnawake reserve near Montreal as a demonstration of support. As the situation appeared to become more violent, Quebec Premier Robert Bourassa called in the Canadian armed forces to restore order to Oka. For the first time in twenty years, Canadian troops were deployed against fellow citizens.

For federal and Quebec officials, the issue was straightforward. The Mohawks, in using arms and barricades to press their case, had broken the law and needed to be brought to justice like any other citizens who had committed illegal acts. Land claims and other grievances would be settled only when arms were surrendered and the lawbreakers brought to justice. But the Mohawks rejected this view. It was not just the matter of land claims that was at stake. It was, the Warriors claimed, a question of sovereignty. The Mohawks occupied sovereign territory that had never been surrendered to any British or Canadian government. Thus, the Mohawks had every right, as any other sovereign nation, to take up arms to defend themselves. It was the police and army who were acting illegally.

At the heart of Native grievances is the *Indian Act*, 1876, which set the tone for successive federal government dealings with Native people. Under this act, elected Indian band councils, not traditional political institutions, deal with the Department of Indian Affairs and Northern Development. Band councils are granted limited powers, but all financial decisions are ultimately subject to the approval of the minister responsible for Indian Affairs. Thus, sovereignty remains undivided and concentrated in the hands of Ottawa. Band councils are like fledgling municipal governments, able to exercise only those powers specifically delegated to them.

Native leaders have long argued that this relationship is humiliating and paternalistic. The real aim of the *Indian Act*, they argue, has been to use the band councils as an instrument for destroying traditional Native institutions and for assimilating and integrating Native people into the larger Canadian society. For moderate Native leaders, the solution has been to negotiate some greater delegation of powers to the band councils. But for a growing number of Native leaders, this is not enough. Only when the full sovereignty of Indian nations is recognized will Native people be able to overcome their degrading colonial status.

In the wake of the Oka crisis, Native issues were suddenly given a more prominent place on the Canadian political agenda. The government of Brian Mulroney appointed a Royal Commission on Aboriginal questions and gave Native leaders an increasingly prominent role in discussions leading up to the constitutional proposals of 1992. The Charlottetown Accord appeared to address many Native concerns. The accord included a recognition of the inherent right of Aboriginal people to self-government and the commitment to make these Aboriginal governments one of three orders of government along with Ottawa and the provinces. Federal and provincial governments committed themselves to negotiating self-government agreements with those Native bands that wished to do so, while a series of future First Ministers' Conferences were promised to give ongoing consideration to Aboriginal constitutional issues.

However, many remained skeptical of the accord. Non-Native critics wondered what a third order of government meant. What form would Native self-government take? How would it mesh with the notion of a sovereign Canada? At the same time, many Native people felt that the accord had not gone far enough. After all, the accord stated that Aboriginal laws could not be inconsistent with those Canadian laws that are deemed essential to the preservation of peace, order, and good government. This was hardly a recognition of Native sovereignty.

With the defeat of the referendum, many of the questions surrounding the issue of Native sovereignty were left unresolved. In October 1996, the Royal

Commission on Aboriginal Peoples published its five-volume report. Although the commission made more than four hundred specific proposals, the report has quietly passed from public attention. This complacency was due in part to the lukewarm response of the Liberal government, which stated that the estimated $30 billion cost of implementing the report's recommendations was too great to accommodate in the present economic circumstances. Instead, the Liberal government introduced the *First Nations Governance Act,* which the government stated was designed to ensure financial and political accountability and to "modernize" the old *Indian Act.* Many Native groups opposed the pending legislation, arguing that, rather than being a step forward, the legislation would in fact turn Aboriginal communities into the equivalent of municipalities and open the door to the expansion of provincial powers in Native affairs. When Parliament was prorogued in December 2003, the *First Nations Governance Act* was allowed to die on the order paper and has not since been reintroduced. In 2010, the Conservative government of Stephen Harper proposed making some amendments to the *Indian Act,* but these too died when Parliament was prorogued. However, in 2011 the Assembly of First Nations released a document proposing the replacement of both the department of Aboriginal Affairs and the Indian Act. In response, Peter Penashue, the Conservative government's Minister of Intergovernmental Affairs, suggested that the Harper government was willing to consider scrapping the *Indian Act* if that were the wish of the First Nations chiefs.

In the following essays, two specialists in Native issues debate the meaning of Native sovereignty and its relationship to the concepts of a sovereign Canada. Roger Townshend, a lawyer who has done extensive work on Native land claims and Aboriginal constitutional issues, sets out the case for Native sovereignty. Thomas Flanagan of the University of Calgary argues that the demand for Native sovereignty as it is posed by Native leaders is incompatible with the continued existence of Canada.

✔ **YES**

The Case for Native Sovereignty
ROGER TOWNSHEND

There is a great divide in perceptions between Aboriginal people in Canada and non-Aboriginal people. The average non-Aboriginal Canadian takes as self-evident the legitimacy of the Canadian state and its jurisdiction over Canadian territory. The average Aboriginal person, on the other hand, views much of the power exercised by the Canadian state as illegitimate, oppressive, and infringing on Aboriginal governance powers. To the extent that non-Aboriginal Canadians are aware of this perception among Aboriginal people, they are likely bewildered by it and have trouble seeing either a reasonable basis for it or any practical ways in which such a view could be acted on. Yet it is precisely this divergence of views that has caused and will continue to cause confrontations in the political arena, such as those regarding constitutional amendments, and confrontations on the ground, such as at Kanesatake (Oka), Ipperwash, and Caledonia.

Although non-Aboriginal Canadians rarely question the legitimacy of the Canadian state, most thoughtful people would likely be distressed at how flimsy the logical justification for Canadian sovereignty indeed is. There is no question that, prior to European contact, Aboriginal nations in North America had stable cultures, economies, and political systems, and that many (if not all) of these were of amazing sophistication in adaptation to their environment. What is sometimes not recognized is that different Aboriginal nations had cultures and economies that were vastly different from one another. They still are.[1] However, European peoples were often blinded by preconceived notions of Aboriginal culture and mistook difference from European lifestyles for inferiority. Some Euro-Canadians still do. But to view as inferior cultures that, for example, had the technology and organization to hunt whales on the open ocean, build large permanent houses, or create sophisticated political confederacies is surely untenable.[2]

Pre-contact Aboriginal nations unmistakably exercised full control or "sovereignty" over their traditional lands, although in somewhat different ways than did European nations. It would be arrogant and ethnocentric to recognize only a European model of political organization as capable of possessing sovereignty. It would also be deeply ironic, since European political theorists took a significant interest in the Haudenosaunee (Iroquois) confederacy and its structure influenced the drafters of the U.S. Constitution (the latter was acknowledged by the U.S. Senate in 1987).[3]

In their initial contact with Aboriginal nations, Europeans generally treated them as allies or as enemies, but in any event, as nations to be treated as equals with European states. How then did this change? International law then and now recognized changes in sovereignty based on conquest, discovery and settlement, or treaty. There is nothing in Canadian history that could qualify as a conquest in the international law sense. Treaties with Aboriginal nations fall into two rough categories. There are "peace and friendship" treaties, which, if anything, reinforce the concept of the equal nationhood of Aboriginal nations. There are also treaties that read as land transactions, which by their silence concerning matters of jurisdiction would seem to provide little help in rooting a claim that they are a source of Canadian sovereignty. Furthermore, there are vast areas of Canada where there are no historic treaties whatsoever. Thus, the invocation of treaties is wholly unsatisfactory as a foundation of Canadian sovereignty. What is left is the doctrine of discovery and settlement. The difficulty with this is that it was intended to apply only to lands that were vacant. Its initial application to a claim of European jurisdiction required the step of considering the Aboriginal people as legal nonpersons. In fact, the "discovery" of the Americas sparked lengthy theological and judicial debates in Europe about whether indigenous people indeed were or should be treated as humans. Thus, the only justification for Canadian sovereignty (inherited from British sovereignty) that has an air of reality to it requires, as a precondition, a judgment that Aboriginal people are not really human for legal purposes. This is surely repugnant to thinking Canadians.[4]

Despite the logical flimsiness of its assertion of sovereignty, the British (and later the Canadian) state, after an initial period of nation-to-nation dealings, has treated Aboriginal people as subjects and indeed as less than equal subjects. Since the onset of European settlement, Canadian "Indian" policy has been aimed at assimilating Aboriginal people into Canadian society. This integration was to be achieved on an individual level and preferably by entry into the working-class level of society. Efforts of Aboriginal people to interact as a group with Canadian society or to integrate at a non-working-class level of Canadian society met with suppression. For example, for many years an Aboriginal person who graduated from university automatically ceased to be an "Indian" in the eyes of the federal government. The policy of assimilation came to a head in 1969 with the notorious White Paper, which called for the termination of "Indian" status. This document was resoundingly rejected by Aboriginal people and in fact became the catalyst for the creation of Canada-wide Aboriginal political organizations. This policy of assimilation has been a complete and utter failure. The political resistance of Aboriginal peoples to assimilation into Canadian society has never been stronger. Most Aboriginal people, in a fundamental way, view the Canadian government as a foreign government and not one that is "theirs." This should hardly be shocking, since it was only in 1948 that the Inuit gained the right to vote in federal elections and in 1960 that status Indians living on reserves were given this right. Neither have Aboriginal communities lost their social, cultural, and economic distinctiveness. The Canadian government has tried long and hard to change this, but it has failed. Its attempts have only created much human misery. The residential school system, where Aboriginal children were separated from their families, forbidden to speak their language or practice their religion and culture, and were physically, psychologically, and sometimes even sexually abused, is one of those attempts. Another attempt was the criminalizing of traditional Aboriginal religious ceremonies. Also, the Aboriginal traditional economy has in many parts of the country been seriously impaired both by the environmental effects of development activities and directly by legislation restricting hunting rights. Yet the attachment of Aboriginal people to the land remains unbroken.[5]

So what options are open? The dismal social conditions in which many Aboriginal people in Canada live are the result of failed assimilationist policies of the Canadian government. Most Aboriginal people firmly believe that the political key to a better future is the recognition of jurisdiction of Aboriginal governments. This must be a jurisdiction that goes well beyond a municipal-government type of jurisdiction, which would allow and encourage the development of new types of structures that would reflect the distinct cultural, political, economic, and spiritual aspects of Aboriginal society. This must be a jurisdiction that is provided with sufficient resources to be viable. It would indeed mean a fundamental restructuring of the institutions of the Canadian state or, perhaps more accurately, a rolling back of the jurisdiction of the Canadian state to allow Aboriginal institutions to flourish. It is this approach that could allow for a just and peaceful coexistence of Aboriginal peoples in the Canadian state.

The defeat of the proposed constitutional amendments in 1992 was a missed opportunity to begin to pursue this path. These amendments were rejected by the majority of both non-Aboriginal and Aboriginal people. However, it must be realized that they were rejected for very different reasons. The rejection of the Charlottetown Accord by non-Aboriginal people seems to have little to do with the Aboriginal proposals in the accord. To the extent that these were a factor, non-Aboriginal Canadians were probably disposed to view them as giving too much to Aboriginal peoples. Most Aboriginal people, on the other hand, rejected the accord because it was too small a step in the direction they wanted to go.

It is puzzling that the idea of Aboriginal sovereignty should be so threatening to non-Aboriginal people. The very nature of the Canadian political system involves a division of powers between federal and provincial governments. It is but an easy step in theory to implement another order of government and provide for an appropriate division of powers. This would not be a challenge to the very essence of Canada, since the sharing of jurisdictional powers between different government institutions is already part of the essence of the Canadian state. Canadian sovereignty is also leaking at the other end with increasing globalization and trade agreements. It becomes confusing, then, why Canada should be unwilling to share jurisdiction with Aboriginal governments if it is indeed willing to modify its sovereignty with relation to the provinces and also at the international level. Nor would the idea of Aboriginal sovereignty within a federal state be an uncharted course. In the United States, a country hardly known for being progressive, it is an established legal doctrine that Indian tribes are "domestic dependent nations." The implementation of this concept extends to separate tribal justice and court systems.

Many non-Aboriginal Canadians may be troubled by the idea of Aboriginal sovereignty, since they feel that Aboriginal people should be able to achieve their social and economic goals by participation as individuals within Canadian society. This misses the entire point of Aboriginal difference. Most Aboriginal cultures have a distinctive and tangible collective nature that goes well beyond the sum of the individuals that constitute them and that would be destroyed by assimilation on an individual basis. The failure of many non-Aboriginal Canadians to appreciate this reflects only that liberal individualism is such a pervasive ideology in Canadian society that it is barely recognizable as an ideology at all and often viewed as ultimate truth. This appears to be the position taken by Thomas Flanagan in the opposing article. He uses "liberal democracy" as a touchstone. The definition of "liberal democracy" has contentious points, but the sense in which Flanagan appears to be using it, and in which I am using it for the purpose of this article, is a political system in which individual rights are considered paramount and equality is measured as formal equality of agency (that is, as the lack of state restraint on an individual's actions) rather than measured by whether the result of political and economic forces leads to substantively equal results. The economic aspect of a "liberal democracy" in this sense is an unrestrained free market, which by this definition is the pinnacle of economic equality, despite resulting in extremes of wealth and poverty.

By definition, a group with a culture that differs in significant points from liberal individualism cannot be accommodated within a purely individualistic framework, particularly when any integration with a larger society can take place only on an individual basis. It is true that a society that permits or encourages interaction on a collective basis is not a "liberal democracy" in the sense explained above. In this sense, many Canadians are not "liberal democrats" and few nations are "liberal democracies."[6]

The point is, a "liberal democracy" is not an acceptable political structure for most Aboriginal people. Fortunately (in my view), Canada has never been a "liberal democracy" in a strong sense. As Flanagan notes, French–English duality and ethnic diversity (both of which include collective aspects) challenge the basis of "liberal democracy." For that matter, whether or not "liberal democracy" is a meaningful term is questionable, since the concepts of liberalism and democracy can come into sharp conflict (for example, when a majority wishes to suppress rights of a minority).

Others may view the kind of structural diversity advocated in this article to be impractical. As Flanagan admits, it is not unprecedented—he cites the Ottoman Empire as an example. There are also analogies less unfamiliar to Canadians—the position of Indian tribes in the U.S. system is one.

The practicality of political structures that could accommodate Aboriginal diversity was studied extensively by the Royal Commission on Aboriginal Peoples. The commission operated from 1991 to 1996, collected thousands of briefs, generated tens of thousands of pages of transcripts of hearings, and commissioned an extremely comprehensive set of research papers. The commissioners included a retired Supreme Court judge and a Quebec Superior Court judge. The report of the commission is more than 3,200 pages long. The underlying research papers are many times that long.

The commission recommended sweeping changes to relations with Aboriginal peoples. The report sets out the following:[7]

- First, Aboriginal nations have to be reconstituted.
- Second, a process must be established for the assumption of powers by Aboriginal nations.
- Third, there must be a fundamental reallocation of lands and resources.
- Fourth, Aboriginal people need education and crucial skills for governance and economic self-reliance.
- Finally, economic development must be addressed if the poverty and despondency of lives defined by unemployment and welfare are to change.

The commission emphatically saw the needs for political restructuring and social initiatives as mutually dependent—neither could succeed without the other. The commission also went into great detail about processes and structures. For example, it saw the right of self-determination as vested in Aboriginal nations, not individual local communities (e.g., First Nations). The commission made detailed recommendations about how such nations could be encouraged to reconstitute, for example, as aggregations of local communities. It also suggested a number of options for the integration into this structure of off-reserve and urban Aboriginal people. This vision of fairly sizable Aboriginal nations having the right of self-determination responds to concerns about the practicality of hundreds of First Nations or similar communities, some very small, having powers similar to those of provinces. With the issuance of the commission's report, it should no longer be enough for those opposing Aboriginal self-determination to simply object that hundreds of small Aboriginal communities could not possibly be able to be self-governing, except perhaps in the municipal sense. To be made fairly, any such objections need to engage with the many and detailed recommendations of the commission about how to make Aboriginal self-determination work.

The alternatives to recognizing Aboriginal jurisdiction must be examined realistically. The commission also looked at this question in considerable detail and concluded that the economic cost of doing nothing exceeded, in the long term, the cost of implementing its recommendations.[8] Flanagan's alternative is to do more consistently what the Canadian government has been trying to do for a century. This has failed utterly and has created much suffering and resentment in the process. What is there to lose in trying something different? Demands for the recognition of Aboriginal jurisdiction are not going to go away. If "legitimate" avenues for advancing these demands are shut down, other means may be sought. The continued peace and security of Canada may well depend on accommodating Aboriginal jurisdiction.

Respect for the cultural distinctiveness of Aboriginal people requires the recognition of institutional forms of Aboriginal governments, with sufficient resources to exercise jurisdiction meaningfully. The sad history of the treatment of Aboriginal people by the Canadian state also cries out for redress in the form of recognition of Aboriginal sovereignty. Such recognition should not be viewed as completely impractical or as entailing the very destruction of the Canadian state.

NOTES

1. See, for example, the descriptions of five distinct pre-contact Aboriginal cultures in *Report of the Royal Commission on Aboriginal Peoples* ("RCAP") 1 (Ottawa: Minister of Supply and Services, 1996), pp. 46–90.

2. For whaling practices, see, for example, G. Monks, A. McMillan, and D. St. Claire, "Nuu-chah-nulth whaling: Archaeological insights into antiquity, species preferences, and cultural importance," *Arctic Anthropology,* 2001. Aboriginal nations on the Pacific coast built large permanent houses (*RCAP* 1, p. 73). The Haudenosaunee (Iroquois) had a sophisticated political confederacy (*RCAP 1*, pp. 52–61). Thomas Flanagan, in the article opposite, characterizes pre-contact Aboriginal cultures as "Neolithic" hunting–gathering societies, incapable of possessing sovereignty. "Neolithic," if understood in the technical anthropological sense of agricultural peoples settled in large villages with domesticated plants and animals, fairly accurately describes the economies of some pre-contact Aboriginal cultures. "Hunting–gathering" (if interpreted to include fishing) describes the economies of some others. However, "Neolithic hunting–gathering society" is a contradiction in terms. See, for example, P. Driben and H. Herstein, *Portrait of Humankind: An Introduction to Human Biology and Prehistoric Cultures* (Boston: Pearson Custom Publishing, 2002), pp. 347–351. Further, Flanagan appears to be using anthropological vocabulary in a value-laden way to disparage Aboriginal cultures and has ignored the fundamental rejection by anthropology of any kind of ethnocentrism, including conceptual ethnocentrism (Driben and Herstein, p. 359).

3. See *RCAP* 1, p. 53 and related endnotes, and Dale Turner, *This Is Not a Peace Pipe: Towards a Critical Indigenous Philosophy* (Toronto: University of Toronto Press, 2006), p. 34.

4. For more detail on the international law aspects of this, see, for example, O. Dickason, "Concepts of Sovereignty at the Time of First Contact," in Dickason and Green, eds., *The Law of Nations and the New World* (Edmonton: University of Alberta Press, 1989). See also a brief summary in *RCAP* 1, pp. 43–46.

5. For more examples of the failure of the policy of assimilation and Aboriginal resistance to it, see, for example, Diane Engelstad and John Bird, eds., *Nation to Nation: Aboriginal Sovereignty and the Future of Canada* (Concord: House of Anansi Press, 1992), and the revised edition by John Bird, Lorraine Land, and Murray MacAdam, eds. (Toronto: Public Justice Resource Centre and Irwin Publishing, 2002).

6. The U.S. would amount to a liberal democracy in this sense, although "liberal democrat" in U.S. political parlance means something completely different.

7. *RCAP* 5, pp. 2–3.

8. *RCAP* 5, pp. 23–89.

✗ NO

Native Sovereignty: Does Anyone Really Want an Aboriginal Archipelago?
THOMAS FLANAGAN

"... words are wise men's counters, they do but reckon by them: but they are the money of fools...."

—Thomas Hobbes, *Leviathan* (1651), I, 4

In the spirit of Hobbes, we should be clear on what we are talking about before we try to debate Native sovereignty. I have elsewhere defined *sovereignty* as "the authority to override all other authorities." More specifically, it is

... a bundle of powers associated with the highest authority of government. One is the power to enforce rules of conduct.... Another is the power to make law, [also the power of] raising revenue, maintaining armed forces, minting currency, and providing other services to society. In the British tradition, sovereignty also implies an underlying ownership of all land.... Finally, sovereignty always means the power to deal with the sovereigns of other communities as well as the right to exercise domestic rule free from interference by other sovereigns.[1]

That is the abstract meaning of *sovereignty* in the vocabulary of political science. In this sense, it is a conceptual property of the states that make up the international state system. Almost all of the entities that possess sovereignty are members of the United Nations (192 members in 2007).

In this frame of reference, sovereignty can pertain only to states. It makes no sense to speak of sovereignty unless there is, as in the classical definition of the state, an organized structure of government ruling over a population within defined territorial boundaries. Native societies in what is now Canada did not possess sovereignty before the coming of the Europeans; neither the concept nor the underlying institutions were part of the Neolithic cultures of their hunting–gathering societies. Of course, hunting–gathering societies have political processes that assign rank and dominance within communities and involve conflict between communities, but the political processes of stateless societies are not the same thing as statehood and sovereignty.

As a way of increasing their political leverage in contemporary Canada, Native political leaders have adopted the classical language of statehood to describe their communities. What used to be called bands or tribes are now called "nations," and these nations are said to have possessed sovereignty from the beginning and to possess it still.[2] This strategic use of language has served Native leaders well in their struggle for greater power within the Canadian polity, but politically effective assertions should not be confused with intellectually persuasive analysis.

When Native leaders in Canada now claim to possess sovereignty, they typically mean one of two things, each of which is related to a particular political situation. In what follows, I will argue that both of these meanings are incompatible with the continued existence of Canada and the maintenance of essential Canadian political traditions. It is not that words alone can destroy Canada; words in themselves do not accomplish anything. But words such as *Native sovereignty* are the verbal symbols of political projects that cannot be reconciled with Canadian institutions.

1. Some Native leaders, for example those from the Mohawk communities of Kahnawake and Kanesatake in Quebec, speak of sovereignty in the robust sense described above, that is, the international sense. They hold that the Mohawks on their territory constitute a sovereign, independent state not part of Canada or the United States. This sovereign state should be admitted to the United Nations and in other respects become part of the international community. A Mohawk elder told the Royal Commission on Aboriginal Peoples in March 1993, "You have no right to legislate any laws over our people whatsoever. Our lands are not yours to be assumed. You are my tenant, whether you like it or not."[3] Many times since then, some (not all) Mohawks have acted as if Canadian law did not apply to them, as in the occupation, beginning in 2006, of a construction project in Caledonia, Ontario.[4]

   While I respect the honesty of this position, I do not take it seriously as a political proposition. In the ten provinces, Canada has over six hundred Indian bands living on more than 2,200 reserves, plus hundreds of thousands of Métis and non-status Indians who do not possess reserves. These scattered pieces of land and disparate peoples are not going to be recognized as independent sovereign states, now or ever. They are simply not viable as sovereign states paying their own way and defending their interests in the international community. Nor is there any practical way to weld them into a single sovereign state. Native peoples are deeply divided by language, religion, customs, and history and in no way constitute a single people. They are not seeking emancipation from the tutelage of Indian Affairs in order to lose their identity in some supra-tribal bureaucracy.

2. The concept of sovereignty, as originally formulated by the philosophers Jean Bodin and Thomas Hobbes, was thought to be a set of powers located in a single seat of authority—perhaps the monarch, perhaps the parliament, but in any case one sovereign. However, sovereignty can also be divided. Indeed, the classical definition of *federalism* implies a system of divided sovereignty, in which two levels of government each have shares

of sovereign power guaranteed in a constitution that cannot be changed unilaterally by either level of government acting alone. In such a context, it is at least verbally meaningful to speak of giving Native peoples a constitutionally entrenched share of sovereign authority.

This is more or less the political theory contained in the failed Charlottetown Accord. According to that document, "[t]he Constitution should be amended to recognize that the aboriginal peoples of Canada have the inherent right of self-government within Canada," and Aboriginal self-governments should be recognized as "one of the three orders of government in Canada."[5] Although the terms *federalism* and *sovereignty* were not used, the most straightforward way to interpret the scheme proposed by the Charlottetown Accord was as an extension of divided sovereignty in a federal system from two to three levels. Although none of the details were worked out, the accord would have endowed Aboriginal self-governments with many of the attributes of provinces: an entrenched constitutional basis of authority, participation in constitutional amendment procedures, representation in the Senate, a role in fiscal federalism, broad legislative jurisdiction, and so on.

Even though the Charlottetown Accord was defeated in a 1992 referendum and never adopted, its proposal for a limited form of Aboriginal sovereignty cannot be dismissed on a priori grounds. There is no self-evident reason that federalism must be based on only two levels of government. Why not a "third order"? There are in fact many reasons why not, but they are more practical than conceptual.

As mentioned above, there are in Canada over 700,000 status Indians belonging to more than six hundred bands on more than 2,200 reserves scattered across all provinces. No one has proposed a workable mechanism by which this far-flung archipelago could be knit together into a single level of government. On the contrary, it was widely assumed in the debate on the Charlottetown Accord that the focus of self-government would be the band, or perhaps small clusters of closely related bands organized into tribal councils. Indeed, one of the widely touted advantages of the third order of government is its alleged flexibility, which would allow different bands or groups of bands to have their own institutions of government, criminal justice systems, schools, and so on.

But surely realism must intervene at some point. We are talking about six hundred bands with an average population of little more than a thousand, many located on small, remote pieces of land without significant job opportunities, natural resources, or economic prospects. There would be virtually no revenue base, let alone a pool of human skills necessary to operate modern public services. How are such small, isolated, and impoverished groups of people supposed to support and operate an untried system of government incorporating a degree of complexity not seen since the Holy Roman Empire of the Middle Ages?

This is only the initial objection. Hard as it would be to harmonize 2,200 reserves into a workable third order of government in a multi-tiered federal system, the problem is actually much more difficult than that. At any given time, about half of Canada's status Indians live off reserve. They reside almost everywhere in the rest of Canada, from remote wilderness areas to the city centres of Vancouver, Toronto, and Montreal. In addition to status Indians, there are several hundred thousand (the true number is impossible to ascertain) Métis and non-status Indians, that is, people of partly Indian ancestry who are not registered under the *Indian Act* but have some degree of identity as Native people. A small number of Métis live in territorial enclaves (the Métis settlements of northern Alberta), but most are mixed in with the general population of Canada. Again, there is every conceivable kind of social situation. There are Métis hunters, trappers, and fishermen in the northern forests; Métis farmers on the Prairies; and Métis business owners, professionals, and workers in Winnipeg and other major cities.

How could one create a third order of government embracing all Aboriginal people, as the Charlottetown Accord purported to do, when most of these people do not live in defined territories? Since no one, thank God, was talking of forcibly relocating populations to create separate territories, the only other approach would be to create a racially defined system of government for Aboriginal people no matter where they live.

There is a historical model for such a system, namely the Ottoman Empire that ruled the Middle East and southeastern Europe from the fifteenth century until it was dismembered after the First World War. Throughout this immense territory, members of numerous Christian churches (Maronite, Coptic, Chaldean, Greek Orthodox, Armenian Orthodox, etc.) lived alongside the adherents of several Islamic sects (Sunni, Shi'ite, Druze, etc.). There were also important Jewish populations in most parts of the empire. Ethno-religious communities were allowed a substantial degree of autonomy, including not only religious freedom but also their own systems of private law, regulating matters such as marriage, family, and inheritance within their separate communities.

It was in some ways an admirable system, ruling a colourful, polyglot population for five centuries—no mean achievement in itself. But I doubt it is a model Canadians want to imitate, for it was in no sense liberal or democratic. There were no elections or other institutions of representative government. The sultan was theoretically an autocrat, but in fact rule was carried out by the imperial bureaucracy. The empire existed to collect taxes, keep internal order, and wage war against the neighbouring Persian, Russian, and Austro-Hungarian empires.

Like all liberal democracies, Canada is based on an entirely different set of political principles, most notably the twin concepts of the rule of law and equality under the law. The legal equality of all citizens is what makes democracy possible. As John Stuart Mill argued cogently in his *Considerations on Representative Government*, people cannot participate peacefully and cooperatively in one political system unless they feel themselves part of a single community: "Free institutions are next to impossible in a country made up of different nationalities."[6] A territorial definition of the polity is essential to the existence of liberal democracy. Political and civil rights must be contingent on residence within a specific territory, not membership in a specific race or ethnic group.

Admittedly, Canada as a liberal democracy is challenged by the linguistic cleavage between English and French as well as the ethnic diversity of our Aboriginal and immigrant populations. But, at least prior to the Charlottetown Accord, the solutions toward which we groped were always liberal democratic ones based on legal equality within defined territorial jurisdictions. The French fact in Canada was recognized by creating the province of Quebec, which, although it happens to have a French majority, is a province similar in principle to all the others. The same is true of the largely Inuit province of Nunavut. It is a territory within which an Inuit majority controls a liberal democratic system of government, not an Inuit ethnic polity.

The Aboriginal self-government provisions of the Charlottetown Accord would have changed this by authorizing an ethnically defined third order of government to sprawl across existing territorial jurisdictions. It was a departure from, not an extension of, our federal system of liberal democracy. It is so incompatible with our system that it probably would not have worked at all. But to the extent that it had any effect, it would have encouraged the segmentation of Native people. Wherever there were appreciable numbers of Indians and Métis in our cities, they would have been encouraged to develop their own schools, welfare agencies, justice systems, elective assemblies, and other paraphernalia of government. Instead of being encouraged to take advantage of the opportunities of Canada's urban society and economy, as so many immigrants from the Third World are now doing, Native people would have been led to withdraw further into a world of imaginary political power and all too real dependence on transfer payments.

Finally, even if they could have been made to work in their own terms, the Aboriginal self-government provisions of the Charlottetown Accord would have set up unacceptable pressures to create segmented arrangements for other groups. In addition to setting up the third order of government across the country, the accord provided for unique Aboriginal participation in national political institutions: Aboriginal senators, possibly with a "double majority" veto over legislation on Aboriginal matters[7]; Aboriginal members of the House of Commons;[8] and Aboriginal nominations to the Supreme Court, as well as a special advisory role for an Aboriginal Council of Elders.[9] It would not have been long before other groups demanded similar treatment: women's organizations, visible minorities, the disabled, gays and lesbians, and so on. Indeed, demands of this type were heard during the referendum on the accord. Reservation of Senate seats for women was a major issue in certain provinces, notably British Columbia; and Joe Clark promised to revisit the situation of the disabled once the accord was passed. Even if Canada's liberal democracy could have survived the distinct society for Quebec and the third order of government for Aboriginals, it could not survive if every identifiable group set out to entrench its political power in the Constitution. It would be the end of equality before the law, and ultimately of liberal democracy itself.

Up to this point, the tone of my essay has been unavoidably negative, because I was asked to argue the negative side in a debate about Native sovereignty. Let me take the opportunity in closing to state my views in a more positive way.

Status Indians in Canada have certainly failed to thrive under the regime of the *Indian Act* and the Department of Indian Affairs. Bureaucratic socialism has been a failure wherever it has been tried, whether in Eastern Europe or North America. In my view, Indian bands should receive full ownership of their reserves, with the right to subdivide, mortgage, sell, and otherwise dispose of their assets, including buildings, lands, and natural resources. This more efficient regime of property rights would accelerate the trend to Aboriginal entrepreneurship that is already evident on some reserves. Politically, reserves should assume the self-government responsibilities of small towns or rural municipalities. What happens afterward should be up to them. This kind of devolution of power is already possible under federal legislation; it has taken place in a few cases, such as the Sechelt band of British Columbia, and is being negotiated by other bands across the country. It does not require an elaborate metaphysics of sovereignty.

However, a large and ever-increasing majority of Native people do not live on reserves and never will, except for occasional visits. For this majority, neither self-government nor sovereignty can have any meaning except to the extent that they, as Canadian citizens, participate in the government of Canada. For them, the political illusion of self-government is a cruel deception, leading them out of, rather than into, the mainstream of Canadian life. Their future depends on fuller participation in the Canadian society, economy, and polity. They are, for all intents and purposes, internal immigrants, and for purposes of public policy, their problems are fundamentally the same as those of other recent immigrants.

It is now thirty years since Pierre Trudeau became prime minister of Canada. One of his government's early projects was the famous White Paper on Indian affairs, which articulated an approach similar to the one stated here, namely to encourage the social, economic, and political integration of Natives into Canadian society. Sadly (as I see it), Native leaders totally rejected the White Paper and set off along the opposite path of emphasizing separate institutions and political power, pursuing the elusive goals of land claims, Aboriginal rights, self-government, and sovereignty. As far as I can tell, thirty years of this political approach have produced hardly any beneficial results. There are more Native politicians and lawyers than there used to be, but economic and social conditions seem to have improved very little. We still read every day about unemployment rates of 90 percent on reserves, of Third World standards of housing and health, of endemic alcoholism, drug addiction, violence, and family breakdown.

What the black economist Thomas Sowell has written of the United States is equally true of Canada:

> Political success is not only relatively unrelated to economic advance, those minorities that have pinned their hopes on political action—the Irish and the Negroes, for example—have made some of the slower economic advances. This is in sharp contrast to the Japanese-Americans, whose political powerlessness may have been a blessing in disguise, by preventing the expenditure of much energy in that direction. Perhaps the minority that has depended most on trying to secure justice through political or legal processes has been the American Indian, whose claims for justice are among the most obvious and most readily documented . . . . In the American context, at least, emphasis on promoting economic advancement has produced far more progress than attempts to redress past wrongs, even when those historic wrongs have been obvious, massive, and indisputable.[10]

More concisely, but in the same vein, the Tsimshian lawyer and businessman Calvin Helin has written, "It is time for indigenous people to stop dwelling on the rancorous injustices of the past . . . we cannot do anything about history. Our actions now, however, can impact the future."[11]

Helin's words point in the direction of a different understanding of sovereignty, as when political philosophers talk about "popular sovereignty" or economists talk about "consumer sovereignty." These usages refer not to statelike systems of organized authority but to people making decisions for themselves, either as groups (popular sovereignty) or as individuals (consumer sovereignty). They are more or less synonymous with "self-determination."[12] As Helin argues, Native people have to take control of their own lives. They have to find and hold jobs, get better education for their children, and run their own communities more openly and efficiently. None of this requires an elaborate apparatus of government and vocabulary of sovereignty; it is more a matter of change at the individual level.

Native people probably don't value my advice, because I'm not a Native person and haven't experienced what they've experienced. So let me close by quoting Calvin Helin again:

> Aboriginal citizens must take ownership of [their] problems and assert control over their own destinies. We must look immediately to opportunities that are available to generate our own sources of wealth and employment that ultimately could lead to the Holy Grail of rediscovered independence and self-reliance. It is time to re-take control of our lives from government departments, bureaucrats, and the Indian Industry. To do this, we have to create our own wealth, develop a focused strategy to educate youth, and control our own purse strings. Reasserting control with a strategic plan for

moving forward should ultimately lead to more basic personal happiness. The object is to ensure that larger numbers of Aboriginal people are leading more enriched, rewarding lives. Wealth (or money), although needed to provide opportunities, in itself is not the goal, but only a means to this greater end. Successfully implemented, this process in turn should pay huge economic and social dividends for Canada as a country.[13]

NOTES

1. Mark O. Dickerson and Thomas Flanagan, *An Introduction to Government and Politics: A Conceptual Approach*, 7th ed. (Toronto: Thomson Nelson, 2006), pp. 30–31.

2. See Menno Boldt and J. Anthony Long, "Tribal Traditions and European-Western Political Ideologies: The Dilemma of Canada's Native Indians," *Canadian Journal of Political Science* 17 (1984), pp. 537–553; Thomas Flanagan, "Indian Sovereignty and Nationhood: A Comment on Boldt and Long," ibid., 18 (1985), pp. 367–374; Boldt and Long, "A Reply to Flanagan's Comments," ibid., 19 (1986), p. 153.

3. Debbie Hum, "Ottawa Has No Right to Impose Its Law on Natives: Mohawk," *The Gazette* (Montreal), March 18, 1993.

4. *Wikipedia*, "Caledonia Land Dispute," available at http://en.wikipedia.org/wiki/Caledonia_land_dispute.

5. Charlottetown Accord, s. 41.

6. John Stuart Mill, *Considerations on Representative Government* (Chicago: Henry Regnery, 1962; first published 1861), p. 309.

7. Charlottetown Accord, s. 9.

8. Ibid., s. 22.

9. Ibid., s. 20.

10. Thomas Sowell, *Race and Economics* (New York: David McKay, 1983), p. 128.

11. Calvin Helin, *Dances with Dependency: Indigenous Success through Self-Reliance* (Vancouver: Orca Spirit Publishing and Communications, 2006), p. 264.

12. Terry L. Anderson, Bruce Benson, and Thomas E. Flanagan, eds., *Self-Determination: The Other Path for Native Americans* (Stanford, CA: Stanford University Press, 2006).

13. Helin, *Dances with Dependency*, p. 39.

POSTSCRIPT

The main purpose of the article by Roger Townshend is to demonstrate that Native claims to sovereignty have a strong historical and moral basis. Moreover, the author argues that there is plenty of room to accommodate broader notions of Native sovereignty that would not lead to the destruction of the Canadian state as Thomas Flanagan suggests. Nevertheless, even if we accept his argument, there still are a number of nagging practical questions that remain. Would all of the more than 600 tribal bands in Canada be given equal sovereign status? Or would sovereignty be granted to some kind of pan-Indian confederation? Would such a body constitute a third level of government as envisaged in the Charlottetown Accord? If sovereignty is recognized, and outstanding land claims resolved, would federal and provincial governments, preoccupied with deficit reduction measures, simply withdraw access to all services currently provided? Would small and dispersed Indian bands be able to fund and staff the social, economic, and governmental programs that self-government would necessitate?

One intriguing response to some of these questions has been put forward by Thomas Courchene and Lisa Powell in a volume entitled *A First Nations Province* (Kingston: Institute of Intergovernmental Affairs, 1992). They suggest that instead of creating a third order of government, a First Nations province could be created that would represent Native aspirations, providing the powers, institutions, and ability to carry out intergovernmental relations in largely the same manner as provinces presently do.

The notion of a third level of government was taken up by the Royal Commission on Aboriginal Peoples. In its final report, the commission recommended that an Aboriginal order of government, which would coexist with the federal and provincial orders of government, be recognized. According to the commissioners, "The governments making up these three orders are sovereign within their own several spheres and hold their powers by virtue of their inherent or constitutional status rather than delegation. They share the sovereign powers of Canada as a whole, powers that represent a pooling of existing sovereignties" (p. 244). Although the commission found that Aboriginal communities may choose from one of three different models of Aboriginal government, it recommended that a House of First Peoples be created as a third chamber of Parliament. The House of First Peoples would have power to veto certain legislation that "directly affect[s] areas of exclusive Aboriginal jurisdiction . . . or where there is a substantial impact of a particular law of Aboriginal peoples" (p. 418). Although Aboriginal responses to the report were positive, government complacency and the ongoing preoccupation with unity issues relating to Quebec have ensured that these recommendations have largely been ignored. Some fear that it will take further Oka crises to put the issue of Native sovereignty back at the top of the public policy agenda.

Not everyone sympathetic to Native concerns feels that these demands should be pressed in terms of claims to sovereign statehood. For example, Menno Boldt and J. Anthony Long point out that sovereignty is really a Western European concept based on notions of territoriality and hierarchical authority that are foreign to traditional Native culture. In their article "Tribal Traditions and European-Western Political Ideologies: The Dilemma of Canada's Native Indians," *Canadian Journal of Political Science* 17, no. 3 (September 1984), pp. 537–555, Boldt and Long argue that reliance on the concept of sovereignty has led many Native leaders to reinterpret their own history in a selective way that actually legitimizes European-Western philosophies and conceptions of authority: "The legal–political struggle for sovereignty could prove to be a Trojan Horse for traditional Indian culture by playing into the hands of the Canadian government's long-standing policy of assimilation" (p. 548).

Although Native issues have been ignored for so long, a number of excellent books on the subject have appeared in recent years. *Pathways to Self-Determination: Canadian Indians and the Canadian State*, edited by Leroy Little Bear, Menno Boldt, and J. Anthony Long (Toronto: University of Toronto Press, 1984) is a useful set of essays (many written by Native leaders) for beginning to explore these issues. *Nation to Nation: Aboriginal Sovereignty and the Future of Canada*, edited by John Bird, Lorraine Laud, and Murray MacAdam (Concord: House of Anansi Press, 2001), contains a series of thirty essays that deal with the issues surrounding sovereignty, land claims policy, and Native/non-Native relations. Also useful are the following volumes: J. Frideres, *Native People in Canada: Contemporary Conflicts*, 3rd ed. (Scarborough: Prentice-Hall, 1988) and B. Morse, *Aboriginal Peoples and the Law: Indian, Métis and the Inuit Rights in Canada* (Don Mills: Oxford, 1984). Another good resource, Tim Schouls's recent book, *Shifting Boundaries: Aboriginal Identity, Pluralist Theory, and the Politics of Self-Government* (Vancouver: University of British Columbia Press, 2003), focuses on the importance of the question of formation and protection of Aboriginal identity to the notion of self-government.

Perhaps the most detailed resource on this issue is the five-volume Report of the Royal Commission on Aboriginal Peoples. Especially useful on the issues of sovereignty and self-government is the volume titled *Restructuring the Relationships* (Ottawa: Report of the Royal Commission on Aboriginal Peoples, Volume 2, 1996). For a critical perspective on the issue of Native sovereignty, see Melvin Smith, *Our Home or Native Land?* (Victoria: Crown Western, 1995).

Two of Canada's noted political scientists have published books on Aboriginal policy from quite different perspectives. Tom Flanagan published *First Nations? Second Thoughts* (Montreal and Kingston: McGill-Queen's University Press, 2000), which sets up to refute what he sees as the primary "myths" surrounding the debate over Aboriginal rights. Alain Cairns, in *Citizens Plus: Aboriginal Peoples and the Canadian State* (Vancouver: University of British Columbia Press, 2000), looks at ways in which the gap between Aboriginal people and non-Aboriginal people can be bridged in a way that respects the distinctive needs of First Nations peoples. While he thinks that Aboriginal nations will not opt for a form of sovereign independence that exceeds their capacity to govern, Cairns encourages Canadians to seek ways to improve the living conditions of Aboriginals and give them greater control over their daily lives while recognizing that a certain degree of integration into modern society, an option he calls "citizens plus," is essential. Cairns concludes, "So the choices that we have to make for territorially based nations are the nature and extent of Aboriginal self-government and how we organize our common life in the areas beyond the reach of self-government" (p. 212). For an assessment of Cairns's argument, see Heidi Libesman, "In Search of a Postcolonial Theory of Normative Integration: Reflections on A.C. Cairns' Theory of Citizens Plus," *Canadian Journal of Political Science* (December 2005).

Will Conservatism and the Conservative Party Fail?

✔ **YES**
NELSON WISEMAN, "A Dead End: Conservatism and the
Conservative Party"

✘ **NO**
FARON ELLIS, "Twenty-First Century Conservatives Can
Continue to Succeed"

In 2003, members of the Progressive Conservative Party and the Canadian Alliance party agreed to combine their forces to create a new national political party. The two representatives of conservatism in Canada would be replaced by one single entity called the Conservative Party of Canada. Not surprisingly, the new party subscribed to beliefs and principles associated with modern conservative thinking. Government would be small; elected officials would be accountable; and individual rights and freedoms would be emphasized. Progressive social policies, such as health care and the environment, would be respected, but the well-being of the country would rest on the efforts of individual Canadians and not on government.

The genesis of the Conservative Party lay in developments that took place in the preceding decade. The Progressive Conservatives historically had been the standard-bearer of conservatism in Canada. But in the late 1980s, the Reform Party rose in an attempt to more accurately represent those with conservative views (and to better serve interests in the western provinces). The two parties tangled in federal elections, each frustrated in the belief that the other had divided the conservative vote. The result was easy victories for the Liberal Party of Canada. Faced with this situation, efforts were made to unite the two parties of conservatism. Initial efforts managed only to alter the makeup of the Reform Party and to give it a new name (the somewhat awkward Canadian Reform Conservative Alliance, shortened to Canadian Alliance). Eventually, the endeavour to unite the right led to serious discussions between the leaders of the two conservative parties and the creation of the Conservative Party of Canada. Canada would now have a single, united party dedicated to conservative principles and ready to govern.

The question was whether Canadians were ready to accept conservatism and its representative. Early indications certainly suggested that Canadians were willing to give the two a chance. In the 2004 federal election, the new Conservative Party won 99 seats and helped force the ruling Liberals into a minority situation. In the 2006 election, the Conservative Party of Stephen Harper won a minority government with 124 seats and, in 2008, another minority government with 143 seats. Then, in 2011, the Conservative Party achieved its goal: a majority government, with 166 seats. The rather quick ascendancy of the new party is impressive, but these gains have been achieved with little increase in the Conservative popular vote. Moreover, certain regions of the country—Quebec, most importantly—remain beyond the reach of Prime Minister Harper and his party. It seems that the election of Conservative governments, whether minority or majority, has not resolved the issue of whether modern conservatism has a future in Canada, but rather has only made it a more interesting question to ponder.

In the minds of some, Canada has never been and for the foreseeable future will never be suited to conservatism and conservative parties. In the past, conservatism was less hostile to government than its modern counterpart and more willing to respect traditions. But it largely lost out to the emerging liberalism and its focus on individualism and progressive policies that challenged past practices. In this environment, the Progressive Conservative Party experienced mostly failure and had to watch the triumphant Liberal Party of Canada become the nation's governing party. Modern conservatism differs from the old conservatism and indeed reflects some of the attributes of classical liberalism (for example, small government and a focus on economic freedoms). However, it seems that the country has moved on and is embracing a liberalism that provides for active government and that has little time for those with qualms about same-sex marriages, easy access to abortion services, and state support for regulated child care. In other words, modern conservatism fits uneasily, if at all, into the Canadian reality. Accordingly, the Conservative Party faces only disappointment.

There are others, however, who feel differently and believe that Canada is ready for a party that advocates limits on government and that reminds people of the importance of traditional institutions such as the family and church. The challenge is to ensure that the party plays to its strengths and resists the temptation to be all things to all people (which is the Liberal way). Already some believe that the party has pursued policies and actions little different from its Liberal predecessor. It must also ensure that extremists in the party—those who wish to use the state to impose moral choices on the citizenry—are unable to wield much power or gain much notice.

In the readings, Nelson Wiseman, a professor of political science at the University of Toronto, argues that modern conservatism and the Conservative Party have little future in Canadian politics. Faron Ellis, a political scientist at Lethbridge College and recently elected alderman on the Lethbridge City Council, makes the case that Canada is fertile ground for modern conservatism and that the Conservative Party can position itself to take advantage of this situation.

✔ **YES**

A Dead End: Conservatism and the Conservative Party

NELSON WISEMAN

This is a tale of two quite different conservative philosophies and two quite dissimilar Conservative parties that share the same label but differ in thought and development. According to our story, both variants of conservatism have failed. The fortunes of both Conservative parties relate to the shortcomings of the conservative ideologies that have infused them. The denouement to this account is—alas for conservatives and Conservatives—the continuing hegemony of liberal-social democratic values in Canada.

To be sure, the Conservative Party has had electoral successes. It racked up the largest parliamentary majorities in Canadian history in 1958 and 1984, tenuously triumphed in 2006, and won an outright majority in 2011. Periods of Conservative success have been relatively brief, however, best seen as temporary interregnums between long periods of Liberal rule. Conservative governments have served as a default option for the electorate when the Liberals have faltered. The conservative impulse, in both its older manifestation and its newer incarnation, is a minoritarian one in Canada. The overarching mainstream ideology—liberalism—has been the principal driver of Canadian politics and political thought. The periodic, transitory victories of the Conservative Party have come as reactive jerks to the Liberals when they appeared arrogant, tired, or disorganized. Chastened by the electorate from time to time, the Liberals once consistently bounced back, more effectively capitalizing on the evolving values and social composition of Canadians than did the Conservatives.

The older Canadian conservative tradition and Conservative Party are those of the nineteenth century. Rooted in British conservatism or Toryism, early Canadian conservatism reacted to American revolutionary liberalism. The conservative creed—carried to Canada by decamped and expelled American Loyalists—expressed itself earlier, in a Gallic manifestation, in French Canada's quasi-feudal structures and practices. The War of 1812 and Britain's imperial reach reinforced conservatism in Canada: for example, the early influence of a high Tory right in the form of Upper Canada's Family Compact and Lower Canada's Chateau Clique. In French Canada—which appeared more like pre-liberal, pre-revolutionary Old France than Europe's liberal, revolutionary New France—the ultramontane Roman Catholic Church came to hold sway a few decades after the Conquest. It deferred to British leadership in matters of state and economy. In exchange for its fealty to the British, the conservative clerical class was left at the commanding heights of French Canada's separate, segregated culture and society. It was a mutually reinforcing division of labour: the economically dominant British—driven by a possessive individualist outlook—tended to industry, finance, and commerce protected by a strong centralized state, while the economically subordinate but proud French Canadians looked inward to their religion for spiritual inspiration to preserve their traditional conservative and rural ways. Canada's founders in 1867 were America's anti-revolutionary liberals—those with a Tory streak buttressed by their British connection—working with French Canadian conservatives.

The new conservatism—and the new Conservative Party—are that of the late twentieth and early twenty-first centuries. Unlike the old conservatism and the old Conservative Party, they are not repelled by America. Proximity and attraction to America's evolving neoconservatism (also known as "neoliberalism") pollinate the new conservatism. Both Canadian liberalism and the new Canadian conservatism have drawn heavily on American thought and models, while the older conservatism and Conservative Party had greater British impetus. A massive influx of nineteenth-century Britons who had experienced the rise and success of the anti-Tory and liberal British Reform Party bolstered Canadian liberalism as Upper Canada's population exploded from 77,000 in 1811 to 952,000 by 1851. British liberalism, streaked by Tory conservatism, was sustained in Canada by the opportunities afforded in an expanding frontier economy where land was free or cheap. Liberalism grew and further eclipsed Toryism because, while Old World social structures such as rigid class divisions and a state-sanctioned Anglican church could be wistfully imitated in Canada, they could not maintain their early hold. They were not native to, nor an organic part of, the North American reality and came to be rejected. Canada's conditions, however, favoured some Old World Tory notions, such as a respected and strong state. It was indispensable to the settlement of the Canadian West and the building of a national economy and culture using, among other instruments, Crown corporations.

Modern conservatism claims to reject Keynesianism, the liberal economic paradigm that took hold after the Second World War. In the Keynesian schema, the state guides macroeconomic supply and demand, that is, society's gross production and consumption. It does so by manipulating the levers of fiscal policy, public sector spending, and taxation. Modern conservatism, in contrast, emphasizes ardent support for free-market practices and laissez-faire. It wishes to shrink the state, privatize state enterprises, deregulate industries, liberalize trade regimes, outsource state functions to profit-motivated contractors, and cut back social entitlements.[1] This new conservative agenda seeks to downsize government and offload its activities. The new conservative focus is on what private enterprise, acting freely, can do to boost the economy, not on what the state can do to manage it. The state's role as a social engineer in the form of affirmative action and other programs for disadvantaged groups is rejected by neoconservatives and ridiculed as setting quotas. On some social issues, such as abortion and gay marriage, however, the new conservatism's partisans are divided. Some fear moral anarchy and are puritanical on matters such as gay marriage, abortion, drug use, pornography, and prostitution. Others adopt libertarian positions—the church of the self—on such issues.

Times change, ideas evolve, political parties reinvent themselves, and new groups of Canadians appear as older ones fade from influence and die off. Canadian society is always in flux but successful institutions, ideologies, and political parties outlive their competitors and shift with the changing temper of the times. The weakness of the old and new federal Conservatives has been, in part, a product of political geography: the key to federal power is to capture the larger cities consistently. There, the Liberals had dominated between the 1960s and 2011. In most provinces, in contrast, the road to provincial power lies in the rural and outlying districts, where Conservatives have been more successful.[2] The key to winning over the ever-changing electorate has been to change with it. Ontario's Progressive Conservatives did that during their unmatched dynasty of forty-two consecutive years in office between the 1940s and 1980s. The party bridged the Old Ontario and the New Ontario; it maintained its Anglo-Saxon rural/small town support and augmented it with those in the growing, more ethnically and ideologically diverse metropolitan centres. The party was by turns—sometimes simultaneously as need be—"progressive" and "conservative," a formula that worked.[3] In contrast, the federal Conservatives have largely acted as followers, not trailblazers, in the political and policy arenas. The opponents of conservatism successfully characterize the old and new Conservative parties, both their older Tory and newer neoconservative thinking, as reactionary and keen to perpetuate an inegalitarian status quo that serves established interests.

THE OLD CONSERVATISM

Classical conservatism or Toryism as articulated by Edmund Burke was receptive to change so long as society's fundamental institutions were preserved. In this view, organic change—where society's classes and groups worked together harmoniously for the beneficial maintenance of the whole system—was natural and welcome. Fundamentals were to prevail over innovations when they clashed. This older strand of conservatism harked back to the wisdom of the ages, and there is a quaint, archaic flavour to it. It warns of the dangers of experimentation and cautions people to do and think as their forebears did. It sees man as born flawed, he and his world as imperfect. Classical conservatism knitted together a number of interconnected and reinforcing principles. In addition to an adherence to tradition, they included the maintenance of social order through strong authority, authority that demanded and deserved deference. Order required protecting the weak as well as the strong and meant a muscular, but not necessarily big, government. Classical conservatism was less optimistic about human nature than classical liberalism or neoconservatism, which place less faith in government's wisdom and planning abilities and more faith in the individual's capacities.

Classical conservatism embraced hierarchical institutions as guarantors of stability. These institutions—such as the Crown, the church, the military, the patriarchal family, and other hierarchies such as corporations and universities—were organized and understood to provide reinforcement and direction for the community's common interests. Such institutions worked as partners, in collaboration; they neither competed with each other nor were internally driven. In this Tory cosmology, political society is a hierarchically structured organic-corporatist-communitarian entity comprised of unequal classes—some more privileged than others—all sanctioned by heredity and tradition and relating to each other cooperatively. It was a compassionate conservatism in that society's privileged were duty-bound to protect and aid the less fortunate out of a sense of noblesse oblige. Classical conservatism's collectivist and elitist elements were considered natural as well as necessary bulwarks against revolutionary chaos, class conflict, and anarchy. The old conservatism thus viewed democratic stirrings and unshackled individual freedoms with suspicions of "mobocracy."

The creation of the modern Canadian state was a conservative triumph over liberalism in that market logic, which dictated Canada's absorption by the American economic behemoth, was resisted on nationalist grounds. Politics trumped the economic allure of continental integration. Nevertheless, the old conservatism or Toryism was always a minoritarian impulse in the political culture; it infused Canadian liberalism but did not displace it as the dominant outlook. The state's Tory institutions were deployed in the interests of liberal acquisitiveness and economic expansion. The old conservatism, for example, underwrote private enterprise at public expense for national economic development and "national purpose" in projects such as the Canadian Pacific Railway.[4]

Joe Clark highlighted the old conservatism's notion of community when he portrayed Canada as a "community of communities." Brian Mulroney preached an aggressive market liberalism and reversed his Conservatives Party's historical protectionist posture vis-à-vis the United States, but he described Canada's universal social programs as a "sacred trust" not to be violated and "a cornerstone of our party's philosophy."[5] Socialists, however, had first championed such programs and the old Conservative Party opposed their implementation by welfare liberals. Perhaps one of the last gasps of the old conservatism came on the eve of the 2003 merger of the Progressive Conservative Party and the Canadian Alliance. Lowell Murray, a Progressive Conservative senator and former Mulroney cabinet minister, wrote that as a Progressive Conservative,

> We believe that government's job is to provide stability and security against the excesses of the market. Democratic politics must define the public interest and ensure it always prevails over more private ambitions. To that extent the forces of technology and globalization need to be tamed. . . . Reform [the new] conservatism which is what the Alliance [party] practises [sic] relies on people's fear of moral and economic decline. . . . It spoils all the good

arguments for the market economy by making a religion of it, pretending there are market criteria and market solutions to all of our social and political problems.[6]

Clark and others in the older Tory mould, such as former Progressive Conservative cabinet minister Flora MacDonald, left the party after the merger of the Progressive Conservative and Canadian Alliance parties, with the claim that the new Conservative Party had left them. MacDonald reportedly then voted for the New Democratic Party (NDP), possibly because it represented more of Toryism's communitarianism than the new Conservative Party's neoconservatism.[7]

THE OLD CONSERVATIVE PARTY

John A. Macdonald's old Conservative Party was undeniably successful; it won five of Canada's first six elections. The party, however, floated on the shaky foundations of a shifting coalition of forces rather than being constructed on solid pillars. Indeed, the very first Conservative government was actually a Liberal–Conservative one, bringing together anti-American Tories and Montreal-based English Canadian financiers and business liberals who sought to build an economic empire via railway construction. This alliance drew on the support of Quebec's conservative *Bleus* and some of Canada West's Reformers who were also tied to railway interests. The old Conservatives' triumphs lay in Macdonald's skill in organizing and dispensing bureaucratized patronage: Conservative constituency associations operated like employment agencies where individual party activists formally applied for government positions and traded on their financial or campaigning contributions. Such behaviour was considered normal and legitimate, based on the idea that "to the victor belongs the spoils."[8] Notwithstanding its brokerage orientation and pork-barrelling—traits shared with the Liberals—the old Conservative Party differed from the Liberals in that it was the carrier of what there was of the old conservatism.

The old Conservative Party's undoing was its failure to continue to broker successfully between the British and French on issues of language and religion. French Catholic Quebec was upset with the execution of Métis leader Louis Riel and the suppression of French language schooling in New Brunswick, Ontario, and especially Manitoba. The party appeared fiercely Protestant and British, and Quebec was lost to the Conservatives as they further distanced itself from the Québécois on issues of international empire, war, and conscription. The Conservatives could thus not muster enough support to win more than four Quebec seats in any of the four elections between 1917 and 1926; they won none in 1921. Six decades later, the story had not changed much. Only two seats in Joe Clark's governing caucus in 1979 were from Quebec and, in 1980, the party won but one. The Conservatives did not select a French Canadian leader (Jean Charest) until the party was in its death throes in the 1990s. John Diefenbaker's Conservative victory in 1958 and Mulroney's landslides in the 1980s had proved to be false indicators of Conservative viability in Quebec. The party had benefited from the fleeting tactical acquiescence of Quebec's old and new nationalists, the Union Nationale and the Parti Québécois, as well as, in Mulroney's case, the provincial Liberals.

Another source of the Conservatives' undoing was, paradoxically, their most notable policy accomplishment: the National Policy of 1879. The construction of a Trans-Canada railway, the settlement of the West, and the imposition of tariffs facilitated the development of central Canada's nascent industrial economy but the tariff, a regionally discriminatory transportation policy, as well as the power of financial institutions associated with the Conservatives of Montreal's St. James Street and Toronto's Bay Street, turned the West against the party. It became a Liberal stronghold and a wellspring for third-party protest (in the form of the Progressives, Social Credit, and the Co-operative Commonwealth Federation [CCF]). R.B. Bennett's Conservatives held power during the Depression but came to be blamed for it. Diefenbaker's Conservatives swept the West in 1958 in part because his populism and background were so different from those, like Ontario's Colonel George Drew, who preceded him as party leader. The party had anointed westerner John Bracken as its leader during the Second World War, but the country was not prepared to switch leaders then or in the war's aftermath. The challenge to the ruling Liberals then was from the left (the CCF) rather than the Conservative right. Bracken's singular contribution to the party was to change the "Conservative" brand to "Progressive Conservative," but the party did not live up to its new billing.

The chronic electoral weakness of the old Conservative Party was evidenced in the thirty elections between 1896 and the party's last outing in 2000: it won nine of them, but in only six did it win a majority of seats. In all three elections that returned Conservative minorities, the party attracted fewer voters than the Liberals. As the "government party," the Liberals held office in parts of all but twenty-five years between 1896 and the old Conservatives' demise in 2003. The old Conservatives served as the natural "opposition party." A telling sign of their vulnerability came in Canada's first multiparty election in 1921: they ran third behind the upstart, loosely organized Progressives, who themselves became a dilapidated annex of the Liberals. In all three elections between 1993 and 2000, the old Conservatives claimed that they were the only "national" alternative to the Liberals but they ran last in a five-party system. The relatively few Conservative victories in the twentieth century were more rebuffs for the perceived shortcomings of Liberal regimes than Conservative mandates. In only four of the twenty-six elections after 1921 have the Conservatives won with wide national support.

Unlike parties of principle like the Progressives, CCF–NDP, Social Credit, the Reform Party, and the Canadian Alliance, the old Conservative Party styled itself, like the Liberal Party, as a brokerage party. Its strategy was to build a tent large enough to hold Canadians from all strata of society. It operated as a cadre party—deferring to its leader and his entourage on major issues of policy. No Conservative convention or policy gathering, for example, debated or endorsed free trade or the GST before their institution by the leader. Gaining a few seats and a higher vote share is deemed a victory by a small party like the NDP, but Conservatives measured their leader by a higher standard: outright victory. The more they found themselves relegated to the opposition benches, the more a mindset of defeat and self-destructive tendencies set in. A "Tory Syndrome" took hold, where a weak election performance led Conservative partisans to attribute failures to their leader, which weakened him and his ability to take the party forward.[9] As a near per-petual opposition party, the old Conservatives projected the image of naysayers with little or no experience in fashioning public policy or responsibility for public administration. More often than not, the party's Members of Parliament (MPs) appeared uncoordinated in their opposition roles, some working at cross-purposes with their leader. When they occasionally did hold office, as in the Meighen, Bennett, Diefenbaker, and Clark years, they offered incoherent and unsynchronized policy direction or struggled with crises beyond their control (for example, the Depres-sion and skyrocketing oil prices in the 1970s).

The Mulroney Conservative victories in the 1980s were the fruit of a tenuous alliance of western Canadian rural and fiscal conservatives on the one hand and Quebec nationalists on the other. There had always been substantial Conservative support in Ontario and the Maritimes—the very creatures of Loyalism—but it had not been sufficient to propel the party to power. Quebec's francophone Conservatives were first and foremost nationalists whose nationalism transcended the liberal-conservative-socialist cleavage of English Canada. Once Quebecker Mulroney left the stage, the party plummeted in the province from sixty-three seats in 1988 to one in 1993 and reverted to its longstanding marginal position.

Socio-demographic change eroded the historic bases of support for the old Conservative Party in English Canada. The Maritimes' constantly shrinking share of the population in the twentieth century made the region count for less and less. Loyalist and early post-Loyalist rural Ontario was transformed into an increasingly urban, multicultural, kaleidoscopic society. The Liberals benefited. The outcome of the four minority elections between 1957 and 1965 reflected that change: southern, metropolitan Ontario's swing seats determined whether Conservatives or Liberals would come out on top as the rest of the country was in a state of electoral stasis with few seats changing hands. Immigrants, soon naturalized as citizens, were more favourably disposed to the Liberals, as was a rising class of young, upwardly mobile, urban professionals. These groups saw Liberal immigration and urban policies as more positive than those of the Con-servatives. Old Tory Toronto, once a Conservative stronghold, became a Liberal bastion. The Conservatives' battles against bilingualism and the maple leaf flag (they fought to retain the Red Ensign with its Union Jack) did not resonate with either Quebeckers or Ontario's newer ethnic minorities. The Liberals reinforced their standing with these groups, and the Conservatives weakened theirs, on issues such as multiculturalism, affirmative action programs, and social policy. The old Conservatives represented the Old Canada, disproportionately those of British ethnic descent, Protestant, and rural/small town. They could not shake that image.

THE NEW CONSERVATISM

The new conservatism is a modern variant of the old liberalism. The new conservatism or neoconservatism assigns priority to the individual over the community, which is defined atomistically as the sum of its self-governing, equally free-willed individuals. Margaret Thatcher captured this sentiment with her observation, "There is no such thing as society." The new conservatism, unlike the old conservatism, is loath to use the state to protect the public good or for broad community interest at the expense of the private freedoms—the negative liberties—of its autonomous individuals. An exception is made for the state's war-making capacity and police functions. The new conservatism depicts society as a one-class citizenry rather than as a society of unequal classes, as both Tories and socialists do. Thus, the neoconservatives of the Reform/Alliance Party, until they came to power as the rechristened Conservatives, favoured an individual-based participatory form of democracy; they embraced the use of referenda and the potential recall of elected representatives and argued that elected representatives must serve as delegates who communicated their electors' unmediated views. The new conservatism claimed not to see politicians, as Burke and the old conservatism did, as trustees elected to exercise their personal judgment of what is best and held to account in elections based on stewardship.

Neoconservatives view the state as a constantly renewed and voluntary arrangement among contemporaries. This jettisons the Tory conceptualization of state and society as an inherited ancient bond that links past, present, and future generations. The new conservatism moves on popular impulse, operating on the principle that society is a compact among equal citizens. Hierarchical and monarchical institutions—like an appointed Senate and the Crown's residual prerogatives, which are exercised by the prime minister—were condemned by neoconservatives as outdated remnants of the old conservatism until the new Conservative Party came to power and exercised those prerogatives. The new conservatism lambastes the old conservatism for offering an unreal, inferior understanding of the existing socioeconomic order and how it should work. Neoconservatives indict the old conservatism as a reactionary vision of the future.

The new conservatives, however, are divided on the moral, as opposed to economic, sphere of human behaviour. Social conservatives abhor traditionally proscribed acts—homosexuality, abortion, suicide, drug use, and so forth—while libertarian conservatives tolerate them so long as such behaviour is freely chosen. Social conservatives, unlike libertarians, believe government must not remain neutral on moral issues and look to government to preserve and promote traditional values and institutions such as the traditional family and to do so in the schools, the law, and the media. They condone teaching religion in schools as part of education's bedrock function. In contrast, libertarians would leave the teaching of religious doctrines to the educational marketplace. It is a comment on its evolution that the old Conservative Party by the 1990s had come to look at abortion and gay rights more favourably than the Reform/Alliance Party's social conservatives who upheld the moral cudgels of an older Canada.

Where the libertarian and social conservative tendencies of the new conservatism merge is on rejection of state intrusion in economic matters, with the exception of state intervention in support of private enterprise. Their common objective goes beyond shrinking the state to reducing its very capacity to act. They would place much of the traditional public policy agenda beyond the reach of government and, consequently, beyond the reach of citizens who may wish to have their government steer a more collectivist course. Wedded to free-market solutions, the new conservatives would limit the instrumentality of government in pursuit of social justice objectives. This dampens the prospect for public embrace of the new conservatism because Canadians have become inured to and expect government action in the liberal reform tradition. For neoconservatives, a preoccupation with individual and corporate rights and unfettering the market economy towers over considerations of social and economic justice. But, "Like nature itself, the market order knows neither justice nor injustice," writes Cy Gonick. "Social obligation, the idea of solidarity between self and community, has no place..." in this logic.[10] Nationalism is a litmus test differentiating the old and new conservatism. Tory conservatism expressed itself in a certain anti-Americanism. Anti–free trade crusader David Orchard carried its banner in his bid for the old Conservative Party leadership in 1998 and 2003. Red Tories and old-style Burkean Tories had been nationalist communitarians who opposed class struggle and promoted a national identity to counter American influence. The Liberals' liberalism, in contrast, had not been philosophically or historically linked to statism or nationalism until Pierre Trudeau led them. The closer the new Conservative Party moves toward contemporary American conservatism, the farther it moves away from the Tory nationalism that had informed the old Conservative Party.

The last Conservative leader who underlined the links between his party and its British Conservative Party roots was Robert Stanfield; he cited both Burke and the pioneering factory legislation of Britain's Conservatives in the nineteenth century as part of Canadian conservatism's legacy. Stanfield justified restraint of the individual in the interests of the community's welfare as a whole. Melded to conservatism's elitism and its sense of noblesse oblige, his Tory sensibility led him to propose protection for the less secure. He became the first major Canadian political leader to endorse a guaranteed annual income in an election campaign.[11] Such a policy and the old Conservative Party's British political pedigree are alien to the new conservatism.

THE NEW CONSERVATIVE PARTY

There is no single genesis for the new Conservative Party: its roots lie in some elements of the populist agrarian revolt of the 1920s, the Social Credit phenomenon of the 1930s, the appearance of the Reform Party in the 1980s, and the demolition of the old Conservative Party in the 1990s. Social Credit, preaching the virtues of monetary reform, wedded it with messianic evangelicalism, its logo a green Christian cross on a white background. Ernest Manning, Alberta's premier for a quarter-century, reflected Social Credit's transmutation from assaulting to making peace with finance capital. He served as Alberta's anti-bank provincial treasurer in the 1930s but became a director of the Canadian Imperial Bank of Commerce in the 1960s when he urged the merger of Conservatives and Social Crediters into a new party that stressed "Social Conservative ideals and principles." He wrote of "the responsibility of governments to give first consideration to human beings as individuals (as persons) rather than to human beings in the aggregate." He deemed the family as the "most fundamental unit of human association," pointed to the public's "spiritual resources," and proclaimed "the Sovereignty of God." The "Social Conservative," wrote Manning, "will speak of a 'society of great individuals,' before he will speak of a 'great society,'" a term popular among welfare liberals and in the American Democratic administration in the 1960s.[12]

Social Credit disappeared but Manning's son Preston and his Reform Party resurrected the division among conservatives in the 1980s. Under Mulroney's old Conservatives, blatant favouritism for Quebec's aerospace industry at Manitoba's expense sparked Reform's creation and the new party smashed the old Conservative base in English Canada. The policy inclinations of Reform's activists, however, limited the party's appeal. A survey of the party's 1992 Assembly—attended by the elder Manning who termed it a "crusade"—showed that 99 percent agreed that government ought to reduce its deficit as much as possible, 96 percent thought the welfare state made people less willing to look after themselves, 98 percent opposed a constitutional veto for Quebec, and 97 percent opposed increased government efforts to further multiculturalism.[13] Reform and its successor, the Canadian Alliance, competed with the old Conservatives for the same minoritarian right-wing vote with failing results for both parties, but especially the old Conservatives, in the three elections between 1993 and 2000. Some policy convergence facilitated the parties' merger; electoral arithmetic compelled it. In 1997, the economic and fiscal planks in the old Conservative and Reform Party platforms were near carbon copies. Where they differed was on the recognition of Quebec's distinctiveness, bilingualism, immigration, and institutional reform. In the 2000 election, Clark's old Conservatives, with their only remaining electoral base in Atlantic Canada, somewhat tempered their market liberalism as they spoke of social safety nets and equalization payments.

The Conservative government's behaviour since 2006 betrays the new conservatism. Although they had denounced the Liberals as spendthrifts, Stephen Harper's Conservatives increased deficits and the national debt to unprecedented levels in an orgy of incontinent spending. The new Conservatives' first two budgets increased program spending by more than 7 percent annually at a time that inflation was running near 2 percent, and their spending continued to exceed inflation even before the recession of 2009. The Conservatives also expanded public sector employment at a higher rate than the Liberals had.[14] "Who would have thought that Harper, the former Reform MP, the noted fiscal hawk, the man who once led the right-wing National Citizens Coalition, would ever be the one who would recklessly plunge Canada into a sea of red ink?" lamented Gerry Nicholls, vice-president of the National Citizens' Coalition, which Harper headed before becoming the Conservative leader.

> It's no wonder Canada's conservative community, those Canadians who actually believe in things like minimal government and balanced budgets and fiscal prudence are currently in a state of shock... Stephen Harper was supposed to be their champion. He was the guy who was going to roll back the state, make government smaller and usher in a new conservative Canada. They expected Harper to be Canada's Ronald Reagan. What they got instead was Bob Rae.[15]

The new Conservatives have failed to instill a libertarian political culture in Canada. In opposition, they criticized the Liberals for keeping too tight a regulatory rein on banks, but as the world's financial system shook in 2008, the Conservatives praised those regulations. They offered huge subsidies to large corporate interests, which they had once condemned, took part ownership of General Motors and Chrysler, back-stopped banks on mortgage insurance, expanded the government's stable of regional development agencies, extended benefits for the unemployed, and, despite their criticisms of government-funded child-care spaces, increased funding for them.[16]

The Conservatives abandoned their putative populism and commitments to openness, accountability, and transparency. They closely manage the dissemination of information and govern in a top-down style more authoritarian and secretive than that of the Liberals whose behaviour on such issues they had castigated. Conservative MPs have acted as pawns of the party leader and not as delegates for their constituents. More than ever, cabinet ministers serve as the prime minister's servile minions, their every utterance vetted before delivery by his office. After condemning the patronage practices of the Liberals and pledging Senate reform, Harper appointed thirty-three unelected partisan Senators in less than five years. The Conservative promise of a public appointments commissioner has gone unfulfilled, and although the Conservatives created, as they had pledged, an ostensibly independent parliamentary budget office, it is leashed and starved for funding and staff.

Conservative policies flip-flopped across a range of issues. After he dismissed climate change and the Kyoto Protocol as a socialist fraud, Harper described global warming as "perhaps the greatest threat to confront the future of humanity today." After he beat the war drums on Canada's role in Afghanistan and vowed not to "cut and run," he asked a former Liberal foreign minister for policy direction and adopted the Liberals' position on military disengagement.[17] After he declared that his government would not sell out its human rights beliefs "to the almighty dollar" in dealing with China, he made improving ties with it a high priority and dispatched four ministers to kowtow there on four separate occasions in the space of four months in 2009.[18] The re-imagined Canada of the new conservatism's populist discourse had challenged the "politics of cultural recognition" with the principle of "universal citizenship"[19] and Harper's Reform Party had denigrated special status for Quebec, bilingualism, multiculturalism, Aboriginal self-government, and existing levels of immigration. He, however, moved a parliamentary motion to recognize the Québécois as a nation, requires all ministers to include French in their speeches, zealously courts ethno-religious communities, and has boosted immigration to record levels, not reduced it.

THE FUTURE: A DEAD END

In the 2006 election, the Conservatives eked out a plurality of seats and formed a minority government, but they only lurched ahead of the Liberals after the RCMP launched an investigation into a leak of the Liberal government's tax policy. Benefiting from the failings of the Liberals—in particular, the "sponsorship" scandal documented in a scathing judicial report—the Conservatives came to office not by virtue of their neoconservative philosophy but in spite of it. They made further gains in 2008 and in 2011, but their victories have been shallow in terms of changing the philosophical and policy inclinations of Canadians.

Despite the advantages of incumbency and their triggering an election in 2008 in violation of the spirit of their fixed-election date law, the Conservatives increased their support by only just over 1 percent from 2006. In 2011, they increased it by a further 2 percent. Their greatest strength lay precisely in those areas where Social Credit, Reform, and the old Conservatives had been strongest, the West. They are weakest where Reform and the old Conservatives since the 1960s had been weakest, the cities and Quebec. This suggests continuity, not dramatic change.

In the 2011 election, the Conservatives captured less than 40 percent of the vote. The four parties critical of neoconservatism and that elected MPs won about 60 percent. The number of Conservative voters in 2011 increased by over 600,000 over 2008, but the number of voters endorsing the social democratic NDP swelled by two million. A poll in the immediate aftermath of the election revealed that Conservative support had not increased—a usual occurrence for a party in the wake of an election victory—while NDP support grew to within three percentage points of the Conservatives.[20] To be sure, polls fluctuate but a Conservative Party that cannot attract more of the electorate will not easily reconfigure Canadians' values. The Conservatives have failed to persuade a majority of Canadians to embrace the neoconservative tonic of limited government. The party's philosophy will continue to fail unless more women, urban residents, and Quebeckers flock to the party's banner. The liberal-social democratic ethos of the other parties will continue to overwhelm neoconservative thinking, especially among women.

A majority election victory for the new Conservative Party is a necessary, but not sufficient, condition for the new conservative philosophy to prevail. As new Canadians settle in the New Canada of cosmopolitan, polyethnic, metropolitan cities, the Conservatives' Old Canada base—rural/small town, Protestant, English Canada—continues to shrivel. The Conservatives have potential for few further gains in English Canada's suburban and the exurban areas. In the 2008 election, they squandered their prospects in Quebec with their funding cuts for culture, their crime and punishment agenda, and their attack on Québécois nationalists as separatists. In 2011, they elected the fewest Quebec MPs of any governing majority party in Canadian history. "Canada is not yet a conservative or Conservative country," wrote Tom Flanagan, the 2004 Conservative national campaign director. Notwithstanding the Conservative victories of 2006 of 2008 or of 2011, "neither the philosophy of conservatism nor the party brand comes close to commanding majority support."[21] Citing Burke, Flanagan urged Harper's government to pursue "moderation," "inclusion," and "incrementalism." This revealed both a lingering touch of the old conservatism and the need to imitate liberal-social democratic ways as the path to electoral success.

Conservatism and the Conservative Party have had an embedded place in Canada's political culture, but the new conservatism of the late twentieth- and early twenty-first centuries appears to have stalled. Perhaps it has been a passing phenomenon. The appeal of the new conservatism is limited so long as Canadians invest in defining themselves by who they are not—Americans—and so long as the new conservatism is driven by similar ideas and demographic forces as those that drive American neoconservatives. The new Conservative Party's prospects only brighten when they behave as the opportunistic Liberals once did.

NOTES

1. Stephen McBride and John Shields, *Dismantling a Nation: The Transition to Corporate Rule in Canada*, 2nd ed. (Halifax: Fernwood, 1997), p. 18; and John Shields and B. Mitchell Evans, *Shrinking the State: Globalization and Public Administration "Reform"* (Halifax: Fernwood, 1998).

2. Timothy L. Thomas, "An Emerging Party Cleavage: Metropolis vs. the Rest," in Hugh G. Thorburn and Alan Whitehorn, eds., *Party Politics in Canada*, 8th ed. (Toronto: Prentice-Hall, 2001), ch. 30.

3. John Wilson, "The Red Tory Province: Reflections on the Character of the Ontario Political Culture," in Donald C. MacDonald, ed., *The Government and Politics of Ontario*, 2nd ed. (Toronto: Van Nostrand Reinhold, 1980).

4. Reg Whitaker, *A Sovereign Idea: Essays on Canada as a Democratic Community* (Montreal: McGill-Queen's University Press, 1992), p. 20.

5. Quoted in Colin Campbell and William Christian, *Parties, Leaders, and Ideologies in Canada* (Toronto: McGraw-Hill Ryerson, 1996), p. 52.

6. Lowell Murray, "Don't Do It, Peter," *The Globe and Mail*, June 23, 2003.

7. Thomas Walkom, "Still Feeling Jilted after Right-Wing Marriage: Many Unhappy with PC-Alliance Union," *The Toronto Star*, November, 12, 2005.

8. Gordon T. Stewart, "Political Patronage under Macdonald and Laurier, 1878–1911," *American Review of Canadian Studies* 10, no. 1 (1980), pp. 3–26.

9. George C. Perlin, *The Tory Syndrome: Leadership Politics in the Progressive Conservative Party* (Montreal: McGill-Queen's University Press, 1980).

10. Cy Gonick, *The Great Economic Debate* (Toronto: James Lorimer, 1987), p. 130.

11. Robert L. Stanfield, "Conservative Principles and Philosophy," in Paul Fox and Graham White, eds., *Politics: Canada*, 8th ed. (Toronto: McGraw-Hill Ryerson, 1995), pp. 307–311; and Rodney S. Haddow, *Poverty Reform in Canada, 1958–1978: State and Class Influence in Policy Making* (Montreal and Kingston: McGill-Queen's University Press, 1993), p. 167.

12. E.A. Manning, *Political Realignment* (Toronto: McClelland and Stewart, 1967), pp. 65–70.

13. Keith Archer and Faron Ellis, "Opinion Structure of Party Activists: The Reform Party of Canada," *Canadian Journal of Political Science* 27, no. 2 (June 1994), Table 5, pp. 295–297.

14. Bill Curry, "Performance Pay for Senior Bureaucrats Up Sharply," *The Globe and Mail*, August, 13, 2010; and Statistics Canada, "Employment and Average Weekly Earnings (including Overtime), Public Administration and All Industries," available at http://www40.statcan.gc.ca/l01/cst01/govt19a-eng.htm. Accessed Sept. 29, 2010.

15. Gerry Nicholls, "Et tu, Stephen?: Fiscal Conservatives Feel Betrayed by the Man They Thought was Their Champion," *The Gazette (Montreal)*, February 4, 2009, available at http://www2.canada.com/montrealgazette/features/viewpoints/story.html?id=60fe5fd6-9f0e-49b3-804d-0b8f0d9788e9. Accessed Sept. 7, 2010.

16. James M. Flaherty, *The 2007 Budget Speech: Aspire to a Stronger, Safer, Better Canada* (Ottawa: Dept. of Finance, March 19, 2007), p. 6.

17. Quoted by Lawrence Martin, "Unlike George, Steve Keeps God to Himself", *The Globe and Mail*, July 5, 2007; and CBC News, "Canada Committed to Afghan Mission, Harper tells troops," March 13, 2006, available at http://www.cbc.ca/world/story/2006/03/13/harper_afghanistan060313.html. Accessed September 24, 2010.

18. CTV News, "Cda. Won't Appease China on Human Rights: Harper," November 15, 2006, available at http://www.ctv.ca/CTVNews/CTVNewsAt11/20061115/china_snub_061114/; and CBC News, "Harper Urged to Talk Human Rights with China," December 1, 2009, available at http://www.cbc.ca/world/story/2009/12/01/harper-china-visit.html. Accessed September 24, 2010.

19. Steve Patten, "The Reform Party's Re-imagining of Canada," *Journal of Canadian Studies* 34, no. 1 (Spring 1999), pp. 27–51.

20. Bruce Cheadle, "Poll Suggests NDP Election Day Support has Solidified," *Winnipeg Free Press*, June 2, 2011, available at http://www.winnipegfreepress.com/canada/breakingnews/123025923.html. Accessed June 2, 2011.

21. Tom Flanagan, *Harper's Team: Behind the Scenes in the Conservative Rise to Power* (Montreal and Kingston: McGill-Queen's University Press, 2007), p. 275.

✗ NO
Twenty-First Century Conservatives Can Continue to Succeed
FARON ELLIS

> In order that our free will may not be extinguished, I judge that it could
> be true that fortune is the arbiter of half our actions, but that she lets the
> other half, or nearly that, be governed by us.

> —Niccolo Machiavelli, *The Prince* (1513) XXV

Included in Machiavelli's message to sixteenth-century princes is advice that contemporary political parties should heed: although they cannot control their entire fate, they can control some of it. By making provisions to help withstand the ravages beset upon them by their opponents, they are better armed to accomplish their primary goals: to guide public policy, voters, and public discourse toward their objectives and away from their opponents'. For conservatives, this includes establishing a set of core principles that, after considerable compromise by all the disparate and divergent interest that makes up the loosely knit Canadian conservative movement, they can agree to champion as the best way to achieve some of their objectives. For the Conservative Party of Canada, the overall task is similar, but complicated by the structural requirement of building those common objectives into an organization capable of fulfilling its primary purpose: to successfully compete for votes in a manner that affords it the opportunity to form a national government and implement policies based on conservative principles. Ideologically, Canadian conservatism has been composed of an often fractious, complex mix of seemingly contradictory ideological streams. Elements of Toryism, business liberalism, nationalism, and populism, among others, have all enjoyed periods of support,[1] making Canadian conservatism, like most ideologies, a very amorphous entity. The Conservative Party of Canada, on the other hand, is a political party, and parties are first and foremost organizations. As organizations operating within a larger institutional context, parties have different demands placed on them than do movements or ideologies. As such, parties are subject to different pressures for accommodating the wide variety of perspectives that underpin their overall electoral constituency. They are also subject to standards of compromise and cooperation that are unique to them as organizations, including deciding what constitutes their core ideology, values, or principles. They must determine how much of each competing sub-ideology will be represented and how far the organization will go in accommodating more peripheral elements. Attempting to accommodate too many peripheral elements often comes at the expense of fulfilling the party's ultimate purpose: successfully competing for votes.

The founding liberal-pluralist political culture in this country dictates that Canadian parties cannot afford to become too ideologically doctrinaire in either their policies or their leadership selection, at least not if their intentions are to form a national government. To a certain extent, this is what three-time Harper campaign manager Tom Flanagan expresses in his "Ten Commandments" of Conservative campaigning.[2] In particular, he advocates *moderation* because "Canada is not yet a conservative or Conservative country."[3] Citing game theory, he reminds Conservatives that if they veer too far to the right of the median voter they will not win elections. Note Flanagan's somewhat hopeful use of the term *yet*. He does not say that Canada will never be a conservative country, only that in 2007, it has not *yet* become one. In order to move the median voter closer to conservatism, Flanagan advocates an *incrementalism* in which conservatives must be satisfied with making progress in small, practical steps. In allowing that "sweeping visions have a place in intellectual discussion," he is unequivocal that they are "toxic in practical politics."[4]

There is considerable truth in Flanagan's analysis. In particular, it is true that practising politicians must effectively mediate competing political demands much more so than do even the most practically minded academics writing from the somewhat detached isolation of academe. Also, minority governments must be particularly cautious given their precarious existence. But it is also important to remember that neither can parties become so amorphous, or unfocused, as to be devoid of any tangible identity onto which voters can grasp and thereby attach their partisan and voting loyalties. In acknowledging that Conservatives cannot be seen as straying too far to the right, they also cannot attempt to extend their support base so broadly as to appear to have no principles at all, a real risk the editors of this book have alerted us to in previous editions, and exactly what *Maclean's* national editor Andrew Coyne accused the Harper Conservatives of doing during their first five years in government.[5] So complete has been the betrayal of conservative principles, argues Coyne, that "conservatism is not just dead but, it appears, forgotten."[6] Others, including *Maclean's* national affairs columnist Paul Wells tends to agree more with Flanagan. In conceding that the Conservatives have not adopted as many traditionally conservative principles as many of its core supporters may have hoped for, Wells argues that during their first five years in government the Conservatives have nonetheless made progress by "chipping away at the foundations of the idea of government the Liberals built over decades."[7]

It will be argued here that although the Harper Conservatives have indeed made progress, for a variety of reasons—their minority government status, the need for incrementalism as opposed to revolution, and the vast conspiracy of enemies, to mention but a few—they have not yet fully defined their core identity. If they choose to do so based on libertarian-conservative principles, by more forcefully championing a limited-state that promotes not only economic liberty, but also moral and social liberty, they will be in an even better position to deflect charges such as those levelled by fellow conservatives like Coyne, as well as those from their more traditional foes. Further, subscribing to a clearly defined core identity need not come at the expense of electoral success. Here, it is important to remember that even when attempting to win a majority of seats in the Canadian House of Commons, a party need not command majority support within the voting electorate. That is, it need not dilute its core principles to the point of confusion and inconsistency in order to appeal to a grand coalition of voters. A minimal winning coalition is not only all that is required, as evidenced by the 2011 election results,[8] but they also tend to be more manageable and stable over the long term. The Liberals demonstrated this thoroughly throughout the last half of the twentieth century and acutely from 1993 to 2000 when they won three consecutive majority governments, never once achieving more than 42 percent of support among the roughly two-thirds of eligible Canadian voters who chose to cast ballots.[9]

There is also considerable truth in Professor Wiseman's arguments, so much so that we can begin by conceding half, or nearly that much, of his position. He is correct in his assertion that conservatives fail when they pursue an Old Canada vision with values rooted in the nineteenth century and that survive primarily in rural Canada. He is also correct in his assertion that conservatism will continue to be at best a default option for voters who tire of corrupt or arrogant Liberal governments if Conservatives continue to be united by no greater principles than their mutual distaste for Liberal regimes. As long as Conservatives refused to embrace the overriding, mainstream, liberal political culture of contemporary Canada, including the primacy of pluralism and individual rights, they were destined to suffer from a schizophrenia that exposed their unreadiness to govern. Denying that liberalism is the foundation of Canadian political culture, and is here to stay, was a prescription for failure, while simply attempting to rebuild previously failed coalitions would have been as irrational as it had been unproductive.

But the continuing hegemony of liberalism in Canada need not necessitate continued Liberal Party hegemony. As Wiseman correctly concedes, the Canadian Liberal Party has shown itself to be at best a liberal–social democratic pretender. To that we can now add that it has been exposed as such and therefore rejected by voters seeking the real thing in the NDP. The Liberals have also become overly statist at a time when many middle-class Canadians are questioning the limits of a purposive state. In their quest to provide continuing rationale for a strong national government, and federal powers more generally, Liberals have been seemingly obsessed with providing Canadian voters with statist responses to most social, economic, and political issues, real or imagined. In the process, the federal Liberals have become so illiberal that they can no longer legitimately claim the mantle of liberty's defenders. These conditions all but necessitated a libertarian-conservative response to Liberal party electoral hegemony.

It is here where Conservatives can continue to succeed. By consistently following a few simple principles, albeit most involving ongoing tough choices, considerable discipline, and tremendous resolve, Conservatives can complete the project of building a mainstream party around a core set of libertarian-conservative principles that will enhance their ability to consistently compete for power in the twenty-first century. This has required a leap of faith for some. But as the evidence and rationale that follows will demonstrate, accommodating Canadian liberalism's new manifestations in a complex, urban, pluralistic polity is not as radical a transformation for Conservatives as it may have first appeared. The libertarian core of both the former Reform and Alliance Parties, as well as the disparate remaining non-Tory elements of the Progressive Conservative Party have several common foundational elements upon which a natural governing party can be built—and to which many mainstream voters can be recruited. Quite clearly, the Harper-led Conservative governments have gravitated toward some of these principles in the short term. As discussed below, their securing of a majority government in the 2011 federal election has some analysts already describing them as Canada's next governing dynasty.[10] While one majority victory does not a dynasty make, they have won three successive elections and made significant gains in areas and among voters once thought to be far out of reach for conservative parties. What remains to be seen is whether or not the Conservative Party of Canada has the vision and discipline to continue building an enduring political institution upon those foundations.

VARIOUS KINDS OF CONSERVATISM

All the forms of conservatism that have emerged in all the federal and provincial party systems over the years can be distilled down to three:

1. Toryism of the nineteenth century—combining a reverence for tradition with support for state maintenance of an ordered and structured society—that in various incarnations sputtered through the twentieth century.

2. Libertarian conservatism in the form of nineteenth-century liberalism—with its emphasis on economic liberty, free markets, capitalism, and a limited state—that reappeared in the late twentieth century as neoconservatism or neoliberalism.

3. Social conservatism of the nineteenth century—with its emphasis on traditional, primarily religious moral values and opposition to advancing liberal pluralism—that manifested itself in the late twentieth century as the religious right.

Innumerable hybrids of one or more elements of each have appeared in the various parties, movements, and factions that have called themselves conservative over the past 150 years.

The most important dimensions of conservatism at the beginning of the twenty-first century revolve around the relative unity of conservatives in support of fiscal conservatism and the need for dismantling late twentieth-century state-sponsored "left-wing" social engineering public policy. There exists, however, a wide gulf between libertarian and social conservatives on moral issues, and each has recently taken up common cause with populists in an effort at improving their fortunes. Each errs in doing so, but for different reasons, which shall be elaborated upon later.

Conservatives should relegate Toryism, with its accompanying statism, to the dustbin of history or to the Liberals and their socialist allies. Social conservatism should be tolerated, in the same manner in which all competing ideas should be tolerated. It should not, however, be adopted as part of the defining identity of the national Conservative Party. Hybrids must also be rejected for practical and strategic reasons; most important among these being the propensity for hybrids to be so amorphous that they provide conservatism's enemies with frequent, numerous opportunities to distort and mischaracterize the Conservative Party. Only by defining a core libertarian-conservative identity will Conservatives find the ideological consistency necessary to maintain a successful, enduring national electoral coalition.

REFLECTIONS ON THE WISEMAN "DOOMED TO FAILURE" THESIS

Many grains of truth are contained in Nelson Wiseman's review of Canadian conservative history. Most students of Canadian politics are introduced early in their undergraduate studies to the Hartz-Horowitz "Tory touch" fragment thesis and to Wiseman's application of the thesis to the study of Canadian prairie political culture.[11] Both continue to serve as exemplary readings when conceptualizing and teaching Canadian political culture, as much for their utility in engendering critical thinking as for their other virtues. The thesis posits that political cultures in new societies are primarily fragments cast off from the European ideological dialectic. Separated from the original dialectic, new societies lose the impetus for change and remain frozen fragments of the prevailing ideology that existed at the time of their founding. Having been founded when liberalism dominated, Canadian and American political cultures are primarily liberal. But because Canada contained a quasi-feudal French element as well as an English Tory element, the Canadian political culture, although primarily liberal, is touched with Toryism, thereby making a synthesis to socialism a possibility. Because a full critique of the thesis is outside of the parameters of this debate, readers are directed to previous rebuttals[12] and the commentary here will be restricted to how this historical thesis impacts on the contemporary debate about the future of conservatism and the Conservative Party of Canada.

Initially, pining for the virtues of a mythical Toryism, while at the same time portraying all libertarian elements of conservatism as inherently vicious, is in keeping with the standard statist attack on the "new right." It is typically the purview of hostile academics and media pundits, but not necessarily that of Canadian voters. It is no coincidence that the death of the Progressive Conservative Party, and by default the "Tory touch" mythology, was bemoaned far more by the former than the latter. After all, without a party vehicle to which the myth can remain attached, the Tory element of the dialectic appears more difficult to substantiate and the Marxist tautological house of cards begins to collapse. In effect, without Toryism, the desired end state of socialism becomes unattainable. Liberalism's triumph leaves Toryism a relic of the past, and socialism a never-to-be-achieved fantasy. But the next generation of Marxist academics need not despair. They will likely find enough anti-American and statist Toryism within the Liberals and NDP to keep the myth alive. The fact that a wide variety of left-wing pundits see so much to mourn in the death of the Progressive Conservative Party should give conservatives cause for celebration. For it was the Tory element of the coalition that failed conservatism in the 1980s and has been at least partially responsible for keeping them from succeeding since. Conservatives should bid a fond farewell to the vanguard of former Progressive Conservative "red Tories" and rejoice at the prospect of extinguishing them and their fellow travellers from their ranks.

Secondly, it is correct to assert that if the new Conservatives were to have remained geographically anchored in the West and rural ridings, they would have likely been destined to perpetual opposition. But as demonstrated by the results from last three federal elections, history need not dictate a predetermined future. Canadian voters are characterized by a number of traits and among these is their well-deserved reputation for vote switching.[13] The persistent shattering, rebuilding, or creating anew of electoral coalitions and partisan alignments is one of the most enduring features of Canadian party systems.[14] Not only do Canadian voters regularly realign their partisan attachments in tectonic shifts that shatter the old order, they also exhibit a high degree of vote switching between non-monumental elections. Wiseman implies this when he states that Toronto used to be a Conservative bastion but is now a Liberal fortress. Or at least it was until the 2011 election when the Conservatives won nine of twenty-one seats within the city, and swept all but one of the GTA's suburban ridings on their way to winning over two-thirds of the provinces' seats. They did so by appealing to large numbers of voters who have tired of bearing an increasingly disproportionate burden for the multiplicity of statist schemes designed to address issues that affect them only marginally, or not at all. Given that the Conservatives offered voters who were suffering most from the economic crisis the least statist economic plan, and although it may be premature to declare Ontario a conservative province, voters there have clearly indicated their willingness to "experiment" with becoming a Conservative province.

Not surprisingly, many who switched to the Conservatives were previous Liberal voters. Evidence abounds suggesting that the Liberal coalition, although consistently the largest, was increasingly the most susceptible to erosion while Conservative voters tend to be much more loyal. For example, while the Conservatives brought 83 percent of their 2004 voters back to them in the 2006 election, the Liberals retained only 53 percent of their 2004 voters. Further, the 2006 pattern was not simply a temporary manifestation of the Liberal's misfortunes. Since 1993, the Liberals consistently retained less than two-thirds of their former voters between elections while the Reform-Alliance-Conservative parties have consistently retained over 80 percent of their voters.[15] This should also give pause to those who believe the Conservative coalition would be most susceptible to fracturing under various hypothetical electoral reform or party competition scenarios.

With that said, if the new Conservatives do not succeed in defining a libertarian-conservative vision for these voters, but instead allow their opponents to define conservatism as inhospitable to the individual and collective ambitions of central Canadian urbanites, Conservatives will not continue to succeed. Opponents will use simplistic but often effective guilt-by-association tactics such as those marshalled against Reform (familial and/or ideological: what former Alberta premiers Aberhart and Manning stood for in the 1930s is equivalent to what Preston Manning stood for in the 1990s);[16] the Canadian Alliance (operational and/or ideological: Stockwell Day is not competent at least partially because he is beholden to the religious right);[17] and the Conservatives (dictatorial and/or conspiratorial: Steven Harper is a control mongering thug[18] who is quite likely under the influence of the vast, U.S.A.-based, religious, right-wing conspiracy).[19] Attempting to equate what Preston Manning advocated in the 1990s to what his father or Aberhart advocated in the 1930s and 1940s stretched credibility too far to be effective.[20] But Day's use of social conservative activists and their organizational muscle in his Alliance leadership campaigns legitimized the "too scary" stigma, adding significantly to his inability to establish a positive public image of his own making.[21] And although Harper's electoral prospects suffered from the "vast right-wing conspiracy" attacks more in the 2004 election[22] than in 2006,[23] 2008,[24] or 2011,[25] the overall political problem remains: until very recently, conservatism's opponents have been more successful at defining conservative parties' identities than have conservatives. The "reactionary agents of their own privilege" case has been repeatedly made, and it has repeatedly stuck. When supported by frequent, often outlandish public comments made primarily but not exclusively by undisciplined Members of Parliament, an image of Reform and the Alliance emerged that often didn't mesh with members' and voters' core values. In both cases, the parties tended to be mischaracterized as much more socially conservative, more pro-American, and more anti-French than were either their memberships or their voting bases.[26]

Professor Wiseman's selective use of the attitudinal data that Archer and I collected at the 1992 Reform Assembly is instructive on these points. He correctly points out that virtually all Reform delegates thought the federal government should seek to reduce its deficit as much as possible—neither a surprising nor unreasonable finding given the soft question (standard at the time) and the fact that the federal government was continuing to borrow between $30 and $40 billion annually on its way to building a half-trillion dollar national government debt. He also quite correctly characterizes Reformers as fiscal conservatives. But little evidence exists to support the characterization of Reform as antiabortion and therefore upholding the "moral cudgels of the Old Canada." Clearly, Reformers held solidly libertarian, not social conservative, positions on the abortion choice issue by a two-to-one margin (61.5 percent agreed abortion choice is a private matter to be decided by a woman, 30.9 percent disagreed, and 7.5 percent were uncertain).[27] Opinion structure among delegates attending the Alliance's only convention in 2002 was also clearly pro-choice and not significantly different from Reform (56.2 percent agreed, 34.8 percent disagreed, and 9 percent were uncertain).[28] Delegates to the 2005 Conservative convention adopted as policy, by a margin of 55 percent to 45 percent, the most libertarian position possible by committing the party to not restricting abortion choice.[29] Post-convention survey results indicate that the majority of Conservative delegates in all provinces except Saskatchewan were pro-choice.[30] During the 2008 election campaign, Harper reinforced the convention delegates' position by clearly stating that his government "will not open the abortion debate and will not allow another opening of the abortion debate." He has consistently repeated that message in every election campaign since and has lived up to that commitment for the first five years in government.

Yet the mischaracterizations continue, are strategic, and aptly demonstrate the challenges faced by Reform and the Alliance. The Conservatives have only begun to address the challenge of positively defining a vision for conservatism before the many entrenched interests—who correctly view conservatism as a threat to their state-sponsored privilege—define conservatism's public image negatively. The fact that their opponents' tactics are as predictable as they are transparent makes that task somewhat easier for Conservatives than it was for either Reform or the Alliance.

Finally, despite his general characterization of libertarian conservatives as atomistic hedonists with no collective consciousness, and the corresponding implication that socialists have a monopoly on what constitutes social justice, Wiseman is correct to state that conservatives tend to be relatively united on economics but divided on moral matters. More problematic is his inclusion of "the role of the state" on his list of "conservatives' common objectives." While it is true that general agreement exists about reducing the state's capacity to excessively engage in socialist economic engineering, the various factions within conservatism are bitterly divided over the state's role in legislating moral issues—a point Wiseman concedes about the moral divisions but not about the state's role in defining or regulating moral decision making.[31]

The problem for libertarian conservatives, and many voters who are intrigued by but have not yet voted for conservative parties, is their suspicion that social conservatives want to simply replace left-wing economic social engineering with right-wing moral engineering. Libertarian conservatives are as opposed to the latter as they are to the former. They share these sentiments with growing legions of Canadian voters who have become either suspicious of or hostile to forty years of statist public policy and the corresponding price tag, but have repeatedly demonstrated that they are more distrustful of right-wing moral engineering than they are of left-wing social engineering. Which brings us to the choice Conservatives face: which type of party and which vision of conservatism are they prepared to champion to Canadian voters over the long-term? The contention here is that a libertarian-conservative vision within the mainstream of Canadian liberalism offers the most effective strategy for continued Conservative success. While this analysis will not presume to prescribe what specific policy measures Conservatives should adopt, it will conclude by offering a few suggestions as to the direction their policy positioning should take as the party continues to define its identity and its electoral constituency. It will also review and evaluate a selection of the initial steps the party has taken toward (or away from) achieving that goal.

In essence, Conservatives need to clearly articulate and begin implementing fiscally conservative, non-statist economic policy. They need to define a libertarian core vision that includes drawing a line in the sand across which social conservatives will not be allowed to drag the party. And most importantly, they must avoid the *populist trap* by setting clear limits on the party's use of populist decision-making mechanisms.

ESTABLISHING LEGITIMATE FISCAL CONSERVATIVE CREDENTIALS

The Harper Conservative governments have at best a mixed record on establishing legitimate fiscal conservative credentials. After inheriting an enviable fiscal situation from the Liberals, the first Harper government appeared to view successes in battling the evils of annual deficits as a victory in the war on socialist fiscal policy and was therefore satisfied with simply using unanticipated surpluses to marginally reduce the national debt. They have not yet presented Canadians with a comprehensive, bold, or clear fiscally conservative economic platform that includes substantial, broadly based middle-class income tax cuts. Spending increases in its first three budgets rivalled that of the previous three Liberal budgets.[32] Despite rhetoric to the contrary, the government did not deliver broad-based income tax cuts. They instead offered up a 2 percent reduction in the GST and a series of selective "boutique" tax cuts in attempting to win over targeted voters. But in order to finance these minor reductions, and the laudable further reductions in business taxes announced in the government's October 2007 *Economic Statement*, Canadians' personal tax burden is increasing and is projected to rise to its highest level in fifteen years by 2012–13.[33] This is far from satisfactory given the prominence fiscal conservatism plays in uniting the various conservative factions.

The Conservative's most noteworthy fiscally conservative pronouncements came in its ill-fated November 2008 economic statement that contained no massive stimulus program similar to what other national governments were planning during the initial stages of the 2008–2009 economic crisis.[34] However, in a post-election fit of strategic hubris, the government attached a clause to the economic statement that would have eliminated per-vote public subsidies to political parties. By the time the government regained its footing after having come close to being defeated and replaced by an unconventional coalition of the combined opposition parties, the full international efforts to forestall an economic collapse were well underway. The Conservatives too became Keynesians, offering up a generous stimulus package that included bailouts for the North American auto sector, support for Canadian banks (although they didn't need it), and massive infrastructure spending, all financed by deficits originally predicted to exceed $30 billion per year for two years and eventually rising above $50 billion.[35] The net result was too much for conservative critics such as Coyne, who declared the death of conservatism in Canada,[36] but was rationalized by others, including Wells. Citing the Conservatives' cancelling of the Liberals' statist child care plans and expensive Aboriginal policies in the Kelowna Accord as evidence, Wells deployed the last arrow in supporting conservatives' quivers: that the situation would have been much worse under a Liberal government and that indeed the Conservatives were making real, albeit modest, policy changes that were incrementally shifting the political culture to the right.[37] A corollary can be added that it would have been unreasonable to expect any Canadian government to willingly pay the political price of standing on the sidelines while the American government bailed out its auto sector and other G20 countries engaged in an orgy of economic stimulus.

Be that as it may, by focusing, (or being forced to focus) on achieving strategic, short-term electoral gain, the Conservatives have not yet provided a comprehensive vision for a limited state that most of its core supporters agree should underpin a conservative economic agenda. Although the Harper governments should be given credit for not being reckless, and thereby partially inoculating themselves against charges of extremism or of harbouring a radical right-wing economic agenda, their fiscal policies have not been nearly bold enough to meet even minimum expectations from most of their core electoral base. Conservatives should rise to the challenge of living up to their rhetoric about Canadians being overtaxed and provide meaningful evidence that they take their sloganeering seriously. If public opinion is not yet fully onside with this agenda, it is incumbent upon Conservatives to convince more voters of the wisdom contained in their vision rather than shirk from it and yield the economic agenda to their competitors. Conservatives should emulate past successes where they have led rather than followed public opinion on conservative economic policy. The battles against deficits and the fights to achieve free trade should serve as reminders of how voters have handsomely rewarded politicians who demonstrate leadership.

Conservatives must also be cautious about being further distracted in their economic policy development by national unity or regionalism issues. Most importantly, they must resist the temptation to adopt "special case" exemptions from the limited-state agenda for the sake of vote buying, traditionally in Quebec or Atlantic Canada but now also in Ontario.[38] The mobilization strategy for all regions of the country should be based on conviction of principle and the consistency and comprehensiveness of the vision rather than opportunistic piecemeal regional graft. Dedication to the rule of constitutional law, including respect for the division of federal powers, is consistent with a libertarian, non-statist approach to economic issues, with an overall agenda of reducing centralized social engineering, and in support of provincial equality and autonomy. Corporate welfare in the form of subsidies to regionally based industries, hugely disproportionate equalization asymmetry, and regionally structured employment insurance programs should be as anathematic to Conservatives as are billion-dollar gun registry bureaucracies and affirmative action agendas.[39]

DEFINE THE CORE LIBERTARIAN IDENTITY

Conservatives should adopt social and moral policies that are consistent with their economic positions. That is, if Conservatives can justify limiting the state from excessively interfering in Canadians' economic lives, they should also be able to justify, with equal conviction, the legitimacy of limiting the state from excessively interfering in Canadians' personal lives. By boldly articulating the moral legitimacy of individual liberty, the rule of law, political freedom, responsive and accountable governing institutions, and free political expression, Conservatives can succeed in defining an identity for themselves that is consistent, principled, and enduring. Social conservatives need to be assured that they are welcome in the coalition,[40] but they also need to be reminded that the planned dismantling of left-wing social engineering will not be accompanied by a corresponding increase in right-wing moral engineering. Ensuring that this libertarian core philosophy is established and clearly communicated is both honourable—in that it will allow social conservatives to make informed decisions about their participation—and necessary to continue attracting moderate voters who are still repelled by the possibility of a social conservative hidden agenda. Social conservatives need to understand that by remaining within the mainstream of the Conservative coalition they are likely to achieve about half of what they want, or nearly that much. But social conservative zealots who refuse to defer to party policy, or who plan to continue championing their moral causes at the expense of the greater electoral good of the party, should be thoroughly, swiftly, and efficiently extinguished from the ranks of the Conservative Party.

Conservatives began making progress toward libertarian principles and away from social conservative principles at their 2005 policy convention.[41] The Harper government quickly followed up with its tactically brilliant and strategically adroit handling of the same-sex marriage issue. Given that opinion among party activists was running three-to-one against same-sex marriage,[42] and Harper had committed to campaign in support of those opinions during his speech at the party's first policy convention, he had little option but to include opposition to the Liberal's same-sex marriage legislation in the 2006 election campaign. But the way in which he approached the issue should be considered a textbook example of how to achieve both short-term tactical electoral advantage and long-term strategic positioning. In announcing on the first day of the 2006 election campaign that his government would hold a free vote on the same-sex marriage issue, Harper achieved the former by defusing the issue early. But even more impressive was the decision to hold a free vote on the issue, virtually guaranteeing that the motion would be defeated, allowing the Conservatives to put the issue behind them. The transparency of the tactical decision was obvious to all but the most zealous social conservatives. To ensure that the motion would not succeed, it was written to include enough seemingly contradictory provisions to allow MPs on either side of the issue vote against it based on one or another of its provisions. When the parliamentary vote was held in December of 2006, Conservative MP support was sufficiently muted that the caucus was correctly accused of "merely going through the motions" of fulfilling an election promise.[43] The Prime Minister then put the issue to rest by declaring that the "decisive result" had determined the issue once and for all, and that he did not anticipate "reopening this question in the future." Harper also poured cold water on any hope of a compensatory motion to strengthen religious freedoms. Ardent social conservatives such as the Canadian Family Action Coalition were predictably outraged, and reacted to the government's "betrayal" of social conservatism with declarations that "their" party had abandoned them. Those reactions enhanced an already successful strategy by further distancing the Conservatives from organized social conservative interests and their overall policy agenda. Further evidence of how far Conservatives have moved on this dimension came during the 2011 election campaign, when several prominent social conservatives publicly bemoaned their exclusion from the Conservative's election agenda and therefore from the campaign issue matrix more generally.[44]

The Conservatives have also made considerable progress in attracting voters from formerly inhospitable enclaves such as new and ethnic Canadians.[45] Libertarian conservatives should follow up on this successful political strategy by making an articulate case for the moral legitimacy of pluralism. Although Canadian conservatives have succeeded in making their opposition to state-sponsored social programs well known, because their opposition extends to programs that are targeted at identifiable groups they have been much less successful at defending themselves against charges that their lack of support for government sponsorship of specific groups equates to hostility toward the groups themselves. It is here where libertarians have failed Canadian conservatism most: by not countering the charges of intolerance with a staunch defence of the diversity that is by definition a necessary component of pluralism.

Liberal pluralism entails a diversification of power and the existence of a plurality of organizations that are both independent and non-inclusive. Central to this is a limited state that leaves individuals free to voluntarily enter into multiple associations with others. But it is yet more. Pluralism entails not only the recognition and articulation of diversity or differentiation: it assumes a particular belief content that contains its own morally authoritative claim on legitimacy. In other words, pluralism is a normative as well as a descriptive concept. Pluralism asserts that not only do differences exist, but also that difference itself is a moral good. Difference rather than likeness, dissent instead of unanimity, and choice above conformity are all fundamental to pluralism. Advocating for the liberty to voluntarily enter into non-inclusive associations without state interference requires the recognition of competing associations with which one may choose not to associate. Libertarians need to further argue that these choices and associations are private and that the state should not be making decisions about which groups are to be publicly sponsored and which are not. But in advocating for private choice, a diversity of competing perspectives is assumed. Libertarians owe it to conservatism to firmly establish that Conservatives are as supportive of diversity and choice in private moral matters as they are supportive of private religious or economic associations. Libertarians must begin to vigorously counter all charges to the contrary from both within and outside of the conservative movement.

For the most part, Prime Minister Harper has taken the lead on this dimension, albeit incrementally and primarily on the international front. Examples include his government's unyielding support for Israel at the expense of its non-liberal democratic neighbours, his hectoring of China over its human rights record, and his lectures to Latin and South American political leaders.[46] Even after his approach was credited with Canada losing its 2010 attempt to reassume a temporary seat on the UN Security Council—the first rejection of a Canadian bid in the organization's history—during a visit to Eastern Europe Harper stuck to his principles and denounced the authoritarian tendencies of the new Ukrainian president. All of this makes a speech he delivered to a Manning Centre for Building Democracy conference in 2009 that much more curious. In addressing fellow conservatives, the Prime Minister attacked libertarians as he attempted to enunciate his vision of conservatism based on the "3-Fs" of freedom, faith, and family. He situated his brand of conservatism somewhere in the moderate middle between big-spending Liberals and near-anarchist (in his view) libertarians. Although clumsily reasoned and delivered, inconsistent with his previous publicly stated principles, and easily refuted by libertarians who until that moment thought they were kindred with the Prime Minister's true philosophical dispositions, the speech did serve to illustrate two important features of the current state of libertarianism within Canadian conservatism. Initially, as well articulated by the *National Post's* Terence Corcoran, the speech signalled that Harper viewed libertarians as a greater threat to his incrementalist approach than are social conservatives.[47] Further, the swift and widespread negative reaction to the speech by many conservatives who do not typically describe themselves as libertarian—but began to do so as a result of this challenge—demonstrates the potential for growth if conservative principles are packaged in libertarian logic and rhetoric. This point was not lost on several erstwhile successors to Harper, including Conservative cabinet minister Maxime Bernier.[48]

AVOID THE POPULIST TRAP

Both social conservatives and libertarians have periodically attached themselves to populism. In doing so, the various elements of conservatism created a populist trap that had the effect of limiting their electoral success. Social conservatives frequently embraced populism in the naive hope that direct democracy mechanisms would somehow help them stem the tide of an increasingly secular, liberal political culture. Libertarians, although philosophically opposed to social conservative moralizing, did not fear the consequences of putting their differences to the test of a populist dispute-resolution mechanism because doing so usually wasn't much of a risk on the policy front. Libertarians know that under most direct democracy scenarios, they will come out winners when the mainstream liberal-pluralist political culture expresses its collective will in favour of rights, autonomy of individuals, freedom of choice, and liberty. A referendum on same-sex marriages today would likely maintain the status quo. A vote on abortion would be a slam-dunk in favour of choice. But in not fearing the outcome of populist decisions, libertarians too often and too easily surrender the moral legitimacy of their principles at the same time as they seemingly abandon their very legitimate concerns about the potential for majority tyranny. By legitimizing the populist dispute-resolution mechanism, libertarians legitimize the majoritarian principles contained in them, and thereby legitimize the potential for the suppression of individual rights, autonomy, choice, and liberty; so long as it is done democratically. Libertarians should stop surrendering to populist expediency and begin a concerted defence of libertarian pluralism.

Populism has also been thought to offer conservatives an escape from having to take firm stances on moral issues so as to not alienate one or the other key elements of the contemporary coalition.[49] And herein lays the populist trap. It is a function of both excessive cleverness and cowardice to not adopt firm positions on divisive policy domains. By substituting populist direct democracy decision-making mechanisms for firm policy stances, conservatives institution-alize unknowns into their platforms and their parties' identities. By definition, direct democracy contains a quality of the unknown, for if a party's policy plat-form dictates the eventual public policy outcome, the direct democracy decision-making exercise is meaningless. Conversely, institutionalizing direct democracy decision making severely restricts the party from taking firm positions on con-troversial issues when needed, most importantly during election campaigns. The latter creates uncertainty in the minds of voters. No one can say for sure what the party stands for because, prior to consulting the people, it does not know itself where it stands. More importantly, the institutionalized uncertainty affords the party's opponents ample opportunity to fill in the unknowns with negatives, especially when supported by the often-extreme utterances of undisciplined party members. It also serves to deny Conservatives the ammunition needed to defend their positions with any certainty, clarity, or conviction. No party can afford to turn over the definition of its own identity to its opponents. New parties with high levels of unknown quantities can afford it the least.

The populist trap plagued Reform in its attempt to expand its base outside of western Canada. It helped turn much of the Alliance's 2000 election campaign into a fountain of comedic material and political ridicule. Harper has so far successfully avoided building a populist trap of his own making—witness the noticeable lack of advocacy for a referendum to resolve the same-sex marriage or abortion issues—but to some extent he has suffered from a residual populist trap hangover from the Reform/Alliance era. It stalled Conservative momentum in the 2004 election and quite possibly was the single biggest issue to forestall their ascension to government at that time. Since then Harper has increasingly adopted a libertarian position when discussing populism. His September 2007 speech to the United Nations Council on Foreign Relations is instructive both for its critical, and at times hostile treatment of populism as well as for its messaging. At one point he all but equates "political populism and authoritarianism." And while the content of the speech was primarily directed toward Latin American nations, he concluded by admonishing the North Americans in the audience that this is not simply a problem for the developing countries: "[T]here is nowhere in the hemisphere that those forces [populism, nationalism, and protectionism] can do more real danger than those forces in the United States itself," and by extension, also in Canada.[50] This speech provides the best example to date of what many conservatives believed to be the real Steven Harper, at least in as much as it is illustrative of his thinking and public pronouncements while he was an opposi-tion MP and while he served as president of the libertarian-conservative National Citizens Coalition.[51]

The Conservative Party would be wise to carefully consider their leader's words and limit their proposed use of referenda to only constitutional or other grand institutional changes. Free parliamentary votes can remain a symbolic aspect of the overall platform, but should not be relied on so frequently that it delegitimizes using the "whip" when important and often divisive matters of core principle need to be acted upon. As the Harper government has demonstrated, its Members of Parliament and other party officials must exercise the discipline necessary to act as a cohesive organization, thereby providing Canadians with the assurances that they are competent enough to continue governing. Doctrinaire populists, and those willing to use populism as an excuse for a lack of discipline, should be told respectfully but firmly that their opinions would be better expressed through advocacy groups than from within a party organization, and their presence within the Conservative party should be extinguished.

As part of this process, Conservatives must judiciously avoid the temptation to enlist help from mercenary interest groups: social conservative, populist, or otherwise. They tend to be the most undisciplined of all associates, will tarnish the party's image, and will abandon it when their most zealous pursuits are not realized. Their potential for short-term electoral help is dwarfed by the detriment they cause to the long-term objectives of establishing a broadly based coalition built upon a libertarian-conservative core. And once associated with their causes, it is difficult for the party to overcome the negative impression that will have been implanted in the minds of many voters. Trying to extricate the negativity by purging itself of these associations at a later date will likely also prove futile. Few elections have been won on the slogan "You can trust us…now that we have turned on our former friends."

CONCLUSION

In the short span of only eight years since the merger of the Canadian Alliance and the Progressive Conservative Parties, Stephen Harper and the Conservatives have fundamentally altered the federal political landscape in Canada. To their credit, they have done so by successfully avoiding the populist trap and resisting the temptation to enlist social conservative mercenaries. Work remains on building the libertarian-conservative identity while even more effort is needed to establish legitimate fiscal conservative credibility. But they have built the most successful and effective political machine in Canadian federal politics on their way to establishing one of the most stable electoral coalitions any Canadian conservative party has cobbled together in generations.[52] They turned marginal gains in voter support into maximum seat gains in the 2011 election and clearly demonstrated that the Conservative Party of Canada has taken another important step toward building the foundations for an enduring and competitive national political party. They won seats in every province and increased their vote in each of them except Quebec on their way to winning their first majority government. They continued to gain support from new Canadians and penetrated deeply into most urban centres outside of Quebec, including Toronto. Indeed, so successful were the Conservatives that even Andrew Coyne was among the plethora of commentators marvelling at their accomplishments,[53] with some venturing to call them the next natural governing party.[54]

Rather than denying the continued progression of liberal pluralism in Canada, Conservatives have succeeded by incrementally embracing it. They have staked out reasonably clear positions in defence of individual liberty while their leader has consistently and articulately promoted the virtues of pluralism. By and large, they have sided with individual choice in opposition to an expanded state presence in the day-to-day lives of Canadians. By more fully eschewing both left-wing social engineering and right-wing moral engineering, by standing in defence of liberty in moral as well as economic affairs, Conservatives can further define a place for conservatism in the mainstream of Canada's liberal-pluralist political culture. If carefully organized and executed with discipline, the Conservative Party of Canada has the potential to end Liberal Party hegemony and establish themselves as legitimate contenders to become Canada's natural governing party for the twenty-first century.

NOTES

1. For a concise introduction to these and other issues involving ideology and parties in Canada, see Faron Ellis and Heather MacIvor, *Parameters of Power: Canada's Political Institutions*, brief edition (Toronto: Nelson, 2008), in particular, chs. 1, 4, and 5.

2. For a list of "Ten Commandments for Conservative Campaigning," see Tom Flanagan, *Harper's Team: Behind the Scenes in the Conservative Rise to Power* (Montreal & Kingston: McGill-Queen's University Press, 2007). Important among Flanagan's "Ten Commandments" are unity, moderation, incrementalism, and policy.

3. Ibid., p. 278.

4. Ibid., p. 282.

5. See Andrew Coyne, "Do Nothing, Say Nothing Politics Rule Ottawa," *Maclean's*, September 16, 2009, available at http://www2.macleans.ca/2009/09/16/do-nothing-say-nothing-politics-rule-ottawa/. Accessed August 14, 2010.

6. Andrew Coyne, "An Empty, Almost Flippant Budget," *Maclean's*, March 4, 2010, available at http://www2.macleans.ca/2010/03/04/the-government-delivers-an-empty-almost-flippant-budget/. Accessed August 14, 2010.

7. Paul Wells, "Harper's Got Us Just Where He Wants Us," *Maclean's*, August 5, 2010, available at http://www2.macleans.ca/2010/08/05/harpers-got-us-just-where-he-wants-us/. Accessed August 14, 2011.

8. See Jon H. Pammett and Christopher Dornan, eds., *The Canadian Federal Election of 2011* (Toronto: Dundurn Press, 2012).

9. In the last half of the twentieth century, only in 1949 (49.2 percent) and 1953 (48.8 percent) did the Liberals approach majority popular vote territory. In most of their other election victories, they garnered less than 45 percent of the popular vote.

10. See Lawrence LeDuc and Jon H. Pammett, *The Evolution of the Harper Dynasty*, in Pammett and Dornan, *The Canadian Election of 2011*.

11. For concise versions of each, see Gad Horowitz, "Conservatism, Liberalism and Socialism in Canada: An Interpretation," pp. 90–106; and Nelson Wiseman, "The Pattern of Prairie Politics," pp. 351–368; both in Hugh G. Thorburn and Alan Whitehorn, eds., *Party Politics in Canada*, 8th ed. (Toronto: Pearson Education Canada, 2001).

12. See Nelson Wiseman, "Canadian Political Culture: Liberalism with a Tory Streak," pp. 56–67; and Janet Ajzenstat and Peter J. Smith, "The 'Tory Touch' Thesis: Bad History, Poor Political Science," pp. 68–75; both in Mark Charlton and Paul Barker, eds., *Crosscurrents: Contemporary Political Issues*, 4th ed. (Scarborough: Thomson Nelson, 2002).

13. See Harold D. Clarke, Jane Jenson, Lawrence Le Duc, and Jon H. Pammett, *Absent Mandate: Interpreting Change in Canadian Elections*, 2nd ed. (Toronto: Gage Educational Publishing Company, 1991).

14. See R.K. Carty, "Three Canadian Party Systems: An Interpretation of the Development of National Politics," in Hugh G. Thorburn and Alan Whitehorn, eds., *Party Politics in Canada*, 8th ed. (Toronto: Prentice Hall Canada, 2001), pp. 16–32; and R.K. Carty, William Cross, and Lisa Young, *Rebuilding Canadian Party Politics* (Vancouver: UBC Press, 2000).

15. For evidence, see Ellis and MacIvor, *Parameters of Power*, ch. 5 and in particular the table entitled "Canada by the Numbers 5.4: Voter Loyalty 1988–2006," p. 198.

16. See Sydney Sharp and Don Braid, *Storming Babylon: Preston Manning and the Rise of the Reform Party* (Toronto: Key Porter, 1992). For a critique of these early analysts, see Tom Flanagan, *Waiting for the Wave: The Reform Party and Preston Manning* (Toronto: Stoddart Publishing Co., 1995).

17. Trevor Harrison, *Requiem for a Lightweight: Stockwell Day and Image Politics* (Montreal: Black Rose Books, 2002).

18. Lawrence Martin, *Harperland: The Politics of Control* (Toronto: Viking Canada, 2010).

19. Marci McDonald, *The Armageddon Factor: the Rise of Christian Nationalism in Canada* (Toronto: Random House Canada, 2010).

20. Faron Ellis and Keith Archer, "Reform at the Crossroads," in Alan Frizzell and Jon H. Pammett, eds., *The Canadian General Election of 1997* (Toronto: Dundurn Press, 1997), pp. 111–133.

21. Faron Ellis, "The More Things Change…The Alliance Campaign," in Jon H. Pammett and Christopher Dornan, *The Canadian General Election of 2000* (Toronto: Dundurn Press, 2001), pp. 59–89.

22. Faron Ellis and Peter Woolstencroft, "New Conservatives, Old Realities: The 2004 Election Campaign," in Jon H. Pammett and Christopher Dornan, eds., *The Canadian General Election of 2004* (Toronto: Dundurn Press, 2004), pp. 66–105.

23. Faron Ellis and Peter Woolstencroft, "'A Change of Government, Not a Change of Country': The Conservatives and the 2006 Election," in Jon H. Pammett and Christopher Dornan, eds., *The Canadian Federal Election of 2006* (Toronto: Dundurn Press, 2006), pp. 58–92.

24. Faron Ellis and Peter Woolstencroft, "Stephen Harper and the Conservatives Campaign on their Record," in Jon H. Pammett and Christopher Dornan, eds., *The Canadian Federal Election of 2008* (Toronto: Dundurn Press, 2009), pp. 16–62.

25. Faron Ellis and Peter Woolstencroft, "The Conservative Campaign: Becoming the New Natural Governing Party" in Pammett and Dornan, *The Canadian Election of 2011*.

26. For an analysis of Reform opinion structure, see Faron Ellis, *The Limits of Participation: Members and Leaders in Canada's Reform Party* (Calgary: University of Calgary Press, 2005). For a comparison of attitudes of party members in Canada with specific analysis of ideological divisions, see William Cross and Lisa Young, "Policy Attitudes of Party Members in Canada: Evidence of Ideological Politics," *Canadian Journal of Political Science* 35, no. 4 (December 2002), pp. 859–880.

27. See Keith Archer and Faron Ellis, "Opinion Structure of Party Activists: The Reform Party of Canada," *Canadian Journal of Political Science* 27, no. 2 (June 1994), pp. 277–308.

28. Faron Ellis, "Canadian Alliance Party Profile: Results of the 2002 Alliance Convention Delegate Study," Citizen Society Research Lab Seminar Series, March 15, 2005, Lethbridge College.

29. See Conservative Party of Canada, "Results of the March 17–19 2005 Founding Policy Convention."

30. Faron Ellis, "Conservative Party Profile: Results of the 2005 Conservative Party Convention Delegate Study," Citizen Society Research Lab Seminar Series, November 9, 2007, Lethbridge College. Overall, 55.5 percent agreed that abortion is a matter of private choice, 38.1 percent disagreed, while 6.4 percent were uncertain.

31. See Cross and Young, "Policy Attitudes of Party Members," for a comparison of differences between Alliance and Progressive Conservative members' attitudes.

32. See Department of Finance Canada, *Budget 2008: Responsible Leadership for Uncertain Times*, available at http://www.budget.gc.ca/2008/home-accueil-eng.html. Accessed August 14, 2010.

33. See Dale Orr, "1: Income Tax Cuts," *National Post*, November, 15, 2007, FP15; and the federal government's October 2007 *Economic Statement* available at www.fin.gc.ca/budtoce/2007/ec07_e.html. Accessed August 14, 2011.

34. Department of Finance Canada, *Economic and Fiscal Statement: Protecting Canada's Future*, November 27, 2008, available at www.fin.gc.ca/ec2008/ec-eng.html. Accessed August 14, 2011.

35. Department of Finance Canada, *Budget 2009: Canada's Economic Action Plan*, available at www.budget.gc.ca/2009/home-accueil-eng.html. Accessed August 14, 2011.

36. Andrew Coyne, "The End of Canadian Conservatism: How Harper Sold Out to Save Himself," *Maclean's*, January 29, 2009 available at http://www2.macleans.ca/2009/01/29/the-right-in-full-retreat/. Accessed August 14, 2011.

37. Paul Wells, "Does Harper Have a Plan?" *Maclean's*, October 4, 2010, available at http://www2.macleans.ca/2010/10/04/does-harper-have-a-plan/. Accessed August 14, 2011.

38. See Federal Economic Development Agency for Southern Ontario at www.feddevontario.gc.ca.

39. As of the end of 2010, the Conservatives had failed in multiple attempts to dismember the national long gun registry but had begun a review of affirmative action policies within the federal bureaucracy. Their 2011 majority victory all but ensures the end of the gun registry.

40. For further thoughts on these matters see Flanagan's "Ten Commandments," (1) Unity, and (3) Inclusion, in *Harper's Team*, pp. 277–281.

41. See Ellis and Woolstencroft, "A Change of Government," pp. 62–65.

42. The formal vote on the issue at the 2005 Montreal convention resulted in 74 percent of delegates voting to uphold the traditional definition of marriage.

43. Janice Tibbetts, "Same-sex Debate's Over, Harper says: MPs Soundly Defeat Motion 175–123," *The Gazette (Montreal)*, December 8, 2006, p. A1.

44. See Ellis and Woolstencroft, "Becoming the New Natural Governing Party."

45. See Stuart Soroka, Fred Cutler, Dietlind Stolle, and Patrick Fournier, "Capturing Change (and Stability) in the 2011 Campaign," *Policy Options* (June 2011), pp. 70–77.

46. See for example, Stephen Harper, "Prime Minister Harper Signals Canada's Renewed Engagement in the Americas" (speech delivered in Santiago Chile, July 17, 2007); or "Prime Minister Harper Concludes Meetings with CARICOM Leaders," (Bridgetown, Barbados, July 19, 2007). Both these and many other of the Prime Minister's speeches are available in multimedia format on the government's web pages at http://pm.gc.ca/.

47. Terence Corcoran, "No Room for Libertarians in Harper Conservatism," *National Post*, April 30, 2009, available at http://network.nationalpost.com/np/blogs/fullcomment/archive/2009/04/30/terence-corcoran-no-room-for-libertarians-in-harper-conservatism.aspx. Accessed August 14, 2011.

48. Don Martin, "True Blue Believer Bernier Squares Off with Jim 'Deficits' Flaherty," *National Post*, October 14, 2010, available at http://fullcomment.nationalpost.com/2010/10/13/don-martin-true-blue-believer-bernier-squares-off-with-jim-deficits-flaherty/. Accessed August 14, 2011.

49. See Ellis, "Limits of Participation," for an analysis of Reform's approach to wrestling with this dilemma.

50. Steven Harper, "PM Addresses the Council on Foreign Relations," New York, September 25, 2007, available at http://pm.gc.ca/eng/media.asp?category=2&pageId=46&id=1830. Accessed August 14, 2011.

51. Harper served first as vice-president (1997) and then as president (1998–2002) of the National Citizens Coalition, an advocacy organization that has as its slogan "More freedom through less government."

52. See Tom Flanagan, "The Emerging Conservative Coalition," *Policy Options* (June 2011), pp. 101–103.

53. See Andrew Coyne, "A New Power Couple: The West is in and Ontario has joined It in an Unprecedented Realignment of Canadian Politics," *Maclean's*, May 16, 2011, pp. 60–63.

54. See Adam Daifallah, "Rescuing Canada's Right: Five Years Later," *Policy Options* (June 2011), pp. 109–112.

POSTSCRIPT

In his article, Nelson Wiseman sees dim prospects for modern conservatism and the Conservative Party in Canadian politics. Though there are many reasons for this expected fate, the main one appears to be that modern conservatism is out of step with the beliefs of most Canadians. The tendency of the Harper government to act in a manner quite similar to its Liberal predecessors is seemingly only one manifestation of this assertion. Yet the claim can be questioned. In Wiseman's view, most Canadians supposedly believe in a government that takes a leading role in shaping society and providing service; but there are signs that Canadians appear less deferential to elected officials and more willing to challenge their actions. Wiseman also points to what many think to be the Achilles heel of the Conservative Party—namely its potential to support reactionary or extreme stances on moral issues. But the party has so far been able to steer well clear of positions that would limit access to abortion services or marginalize gays and lesbians. And as for Wiseman's belief that certain elements of the electoral map—large cities, certain regions of the country—are beyond the grasp of the Conservative Party, it can be argued that Canadians are more than capable of switching their allegiances. For supporting evidence, one need only look at the 2011 federal election. Nothing in Canadian politics is set in stone.

For his part, Faron Ellis is much more positive about the chances of conservatism and the Conservative Party. Indeed, it seems that Conservatives need only be themselves and electoral success will come their way, a belief seemingly proven with the results of the most recent federal election. But, as with Wiseman, there are questions. Ellis himself raises important queries. An important element of conservatism and the Conservative Party is a fiscally responsible state; yet Ellis suggests that the Harper government has fallen well short of this goal. The same might be said of the wish for a more libertarian party, which seems to have been frustrated by the prime minister and his push for electoral success. Perhaps more interesting is the possibility that the Liberal beast has been slain only to be replaced by a new liberal beast—the Conservative Party of Canada.

For an understanding of the new Conservative Party of Canada, one might start with Faron Ellis and Peter Wollstencroft's contribution in Jon H. Pammett and Christopher Dornan, eds., *The Canadian General Election of 2004* (Toronto: Dundurn Group, 2004). This article discusses the origins of the party and contains references to documents necessary for appreciating the position of the Conservative Party. A follow-up to this article is another piece by Ellis and Wollstencroft in Jon Pammett and Christopher Dornan, eds., *The Federal General Election of 2006* (Toronto: Dundurn, 2006). For a more detailed examination of the Conservative Party and its electoral experiences, students should see Tom Flanagan, *Harper's Team: Behind the Scenes in the Conservative Rise to Power*, 2nd ed. (Montreal and Kingston: McGill-Queen's University Press, 2009). This exciting text also includes much on what is central to the debate on the fate of conservatism and the Conservative Party, namely the appropriate strategy for the new Conservative Party.

Flanagan has recently added to his thoughts on strategy in Tom Flanagan, "The Emerging Conservative Coalition," *Policy Options* (June/July 2011).

With this understanding of the party, students might wish to back up and acquire a better picture of the overall party system in Canada, as well as predecessors to the Conservative Party. For these insights, Hugh Thorburn and Alan Whitehorn's *Party Politics in Canada*, 8th ed. (Toronto: Prentice-Hall Canada, 2001), is the place to go. Also useful is James Bickerton and Alain-G. Gagnon, "Political Parties and Electoral Politics," in James Bickerton and Alain-G. Gagnon, eds., *Canadian Politics,* 4th ed. (Peterborough: Broadview Press, 2004). For some deep history on conservative parties in Canadian politics, a good source is Dan Azoulay, *Canadian Political Parties: Historical Readings* (Toronto: Irwin Publishing, 1999).

The debate addresses not only the Conservative Party but also the ideology of conservatism. For information on conservatism and the competing ideologies in Canadian politics, a good place to start is Colin Campbell and William Christian, *Parties, Leaders, and Ideologies in Canada* (Toronto: McGraw-Hill Ryerson, 1996). There are also some useful chapters on this topic: David Bell, "Political Culture in Canada," in Michael Whittington and Glen Williams, eds., *Canadian Politics in the 21st Century*, 7th ed. (Scarborough: Thomson Nelson, 2008); and Neil Nevitte and Mebs Kanji, "New Cleavages, Value Diversity and Democratic Governance," in James Bickerton and Alain-G. Gagnon, eds., *Canadian Politics*, 4th ed. (Peterborough: Broadview Press, 2004). Nelson Wiseman's book, *In Search of Canadian Political Culture* (Vancouver: UBC, 2007), should also be consulted, as should Travis Smith's insightful article on conservative thinking, "Why Canada Needs Conservatives, Though It Tends to Imagine Otherwise," *C2C: Canada's Journal of Ideas* 1, no. 1. Finally, Hugh Segal has written a recent book on the history of conservatism in Canada from pre-Confederation times to the present: Hugh Segal, *The Right Balance: Canada's Conservative Tradition* (Vancouver/Toronto: Douglas & McIntyre, 2010).

A number of books have been written about conservative parties in Canadian politics that preceded the formation of the Conservative Party of Canada. These include Jeffrey Simpson, *The Discipline of Power: The Conservative Interlude and the Liberal Restoration* (Toronto: MacMillan, 1980); George Perlin, *The Tory Syndrome: Leadership Politics in the Progressive Conservative Party* (Montreal and Kingston: McGill-Queen's University Press, 1980); Tom Flanagan, *Waiting for the Wave: The Reform Party and Preston Manning* (Toronto: Stoddart, 1995); Trevor Harrison, *Of Passionate Intensity: Right Wing Populism and the Reform Party of Canada* (Toronto: University of Toronto Press, 1995); and Faron Ellis, *The Limits of Participation: Members and Leaders in Canada's Reform Party* (Calgary: University of Calgary Press, 2005). Books have also been written on Stephen Harper and the Conservative Party of Canada: William Johnson, *Stephen Harper and the Future of Canada* (Toronto: McClelland & Stewart, 2004); Bob Plamondon, *Full Circle: Death and Resurrection in Canadian Conservative Politics* (Toronto: Key Porter, 2006); and Paul Wells, *Right Side Up: The Fall of Paul Martin and the Rise of Stephen Harper's New Conservatism* (Toronto: McClelland & Stewart, 2006).

PART TWO

THE CONSTITUTION AND FEDERALISM

Is the Canadian Charter of Rights and Freedoms Antidemocratic?

Should the Federal Government Play a Leading Role in Health Care?

Robyn Mackenzie/Shutterstock

Is the Canadian Charter of Rights and Freedoms Antidemocratic?

✔ **YES**
ROBERT MARTIN, "The Canadian Charter of Rights and Freedoms Is Antidemocratic and Un-Canadian"

✘ **NO**
PHILIP L. BRYDEN, "The Canadian Charter of Rights and Freedoms Is Antidemocratic and Un-Canadian: An Opposing Point of View"

Do terminally ill patients have the right to a doctor-assisted suicide? Should women have unrestricted access to abortion without fear of criminal penalty? Does freedom of expression include the right to produce and distribute pornography? Are Sunday shopping regulations a violation of freedom of religion? Should people be able to marry same-sex partners? All of these questions raise difficult issues regarding the relationship between individual citizens and their government. In essence, they each pose the same questions: What civil rights does an individual have, and how are they to be protected from the intrusive arm of the state?

In choosing to establish a system of parliamentary government on the "Westminster model," the founders of Canada adopted a British solution to this problem. Parliament would be supreme and would act as the ultimate guarantor of individual rights and freedoms. This solution reflects an implicit trust in both Parliament and the basic democratic values of civil society. It assumes that civil liberties are so deeply ingrained in the national political culture that parliamentarians and citizens alike would never seriously consider using the power of government to infringe upon them. Public opinion and tradition would act as a powerful constraint against any violation of the fundamental civil and political liberties that are considered to be an inherent part of a democratic system. With the establishment of a federal system in Canada, courts were given the task of deciding whether federal and provincial legislatures were acting within their respective jurisdictions, not whether their actions violated civil and political liberties. There was no perceived need to give such rights special judicial protection that put them outside the reach of legislators.

Not everyone was happy with this solution. They pointed to a long history of both provincial and federal governments' trampling of the rights of citizens. In the early part of the twentieth century, British Columbia passed laws denying Asians the right to vote in provincial elections. During the Second World War, the federal government arbitrarily seized the property of Japanese Canadians and placed them in internment camps without due process of law.

These experiences, and others, convinced many Canadians that greater protection of civil rights was needed. The Americans provided an alternative solution: define the rights of citizens in a written constitutional document that is beyond the reach of the legislature. The courts, through the power of judicial review, can then pass judgment on whether the legislation passed by a government infringes on civil liberties. John Diefenbaker began to move Canada in this direction in 1960, when his government passed the Canadian Bill of Rights. But this bill was simply an act of Parliament and applied only to the federal government. As a result, Canadian courts made only limited use of the Bill of Rights.

With the adoption of the Canadian Charter of Rights and Freedoms as part of a larger constitutional package, the government of Pierre Trudeau brought in a new era in 1982. With the entrenchment of the Charter in the Canadian Constitution, not only were Canadians given an explicit definition of their rights, but also the courts were empowered to rule on the constitutionality of government legislation.

There is little doubt that the adoption of the Charter has significantly transformed the operation of the Canadian political system. Since the adoption of the Charter over a quarter of a century ago, the Supreme Court of Canada has been involved in virtually every issue of any great political significance in Canada. As a result, there has been a growing public awareness about the potential "political" role that the Supreme Court now plays in the lives of ordinary Canadians. Canadians now primarily define their needs and complaints in the language of rights. More and more, interest groups and minorities are turning to the courts, rather than the usual political processes, to make their grievances heard. Peter Russell has described the dramatic impact of the Charter on Canadian politics as having "judicialized politics and politicized the judiciary."

Has the impact of the Charter been a positive one? Has the Charter lived up to its promise to enhance Canadian democracy through the protection of civil liberties? Robert Martin, a former law professor at the University of Western Ontario, feels that the impact of the Charter has been largely a negative one. In particular, he argues that the Charter has had an antidemocratic effect on the country and has accelerated the Americanization of Canada. In contrast, Philip Bryden, dean of the Faculty of Law at the University of Alberta, argues that the Charter plays an essential role in protecting and enhancing the quality of Canadian democracy.

✔ **YES**

The Canadian Charter of Rights and Freedoms Is Antidemocratic and Un-Canadian

ROBERT MARTIN

INTRODUCTION

On April 17, 1982, the Canadian Charter of Rights and Freedoms became part of our Constitution. Everyone who has written about the Charter agrees its effect has been to change profoundly both our politics and the way we think. Most of the commentators have applauded these changes. I do not.

I believe the Charter has had decidedly negative effects on Canada. It has contributed to an erosion of our democracy and of our own sense of ourselves. It is time for a serious and critical stocktaking.

Let me be clear that I am not suggesting the Charter itself has actually done any of this. A central problem with the Charter has been its contribution to our growing inability to distinguish between the concrete and the abstract. The Charter is simply words on a piece of paper. What I will be addressing are the uses to which the Charter has been put by human beings. I will look at the antidemocratic effects of the Charter and then turn to an analysis of its un-Canadian character.

THE CHARTER IS ANTIDEMOCRATIC

By their nature, constitutions express a fear of democracy, a horror that the people, if given their head, will quickly become a mindless mob. As a result, constitutions, all constitutions, place enforceable limitations on the powers of the state and, more particularly, on the lawmaking authority of the people's representatives.

Prior to 1982, the Canadian Constitution did contain such limitations. Our central constitutional document, the British North America Act of 1867, divided lawmaking authority between Parliament and the provincial legislatures and, thereby, limited that authority. But these limitations were purely functional. The authority to make laws about education, for example, rested with the provinces. Ottawa could not make laws about education, and if it attempted to do so, the attempt could be struck down by the courts. The courts had no authority to tell the provinces how to exercise their authority over education, to tell them what kind of laws they should make about education.

This is what changed in 1982. The federal division of powers remained, but for the first time, substantive limitations were placed on lawmaking authority.

The judges were given the power to strike down laws that, in their opinion, were inconsistent with the Charter.

It is crucial to understand basic distinctions between legislators and judges. Any Canadian citizen over the age of eighteen is eligible to be elected to Parliament or a provincial legislature. Elected members are directly accountable to their constituents. They must face reelection at least once every five years. By way of contrast, to become a senior judge in Canada, you must be a lawyer, and you must have been one for ten years. You are appointed until age seventy-five through a closed process that a former chief justice of Canada described as "mysterious," and you are made constitutionally independent, directly accountable to no one.

The defining feature of representative democracy in Canada has been that it is up to the elected members of our legislatures to resolve issues of social, economic, and political policy, subject, of course, to the approval or disapproval of the people, which is expressed at periodic elections. This has changed since the adoption of the Charter. Judges can now overturn deliberate policy decisions made by the elected representatives of the people where those decisions do not accord with the way the judges interpret the Charter. This is undemocratic. Some of our commentators call this "counter-majoritarian," but the phrase is pure obfuscation.

We seem to be experiencing great difficulty today in grasping this simple truth about the antidemocratic nature of judicial review of legislation. One explanation for our difficulty is that we have forgotten that liberalism and democracy are not the same thing. Liberalism is about individual rights, about the ability of individuals to do as they please without interference from the state. Liberalism makes protection of the autonomy of the individual more important than the promotion of the welfare of the collectivity. Democracy is, and always has been, about the interests of the collectivity, about majority rule, about power to the people.

There is an inherent and irreconcilable tension between liberalism and democracy. This tension has always been built into our political system, a system that is ordinarily described as liberal democracy.

The Charter is a liberal document. It sets out fundamental notions about the rights of the individual that have always been at the core of liberalism. More to the point, the Charter has led to a shift in emphasis in Canadian liberal democracy. The balance has been tilted in favour of liberalism and away from democracy.

Members of the judiciary, led by the Supreme Court of Canada, have shown little restraint in arrogating to themselves a central policymaking role. In 1984, they conferred upon themselves the distinction "guardian of the Constitution." They haven't looked back.

Our judges have not hesitated to substitute their views of acceptable or desirable social policy for those of our legislators. When the judges have not agreed with the policy decisions of our elected representatives, they have invalidated the legislation that expresses those decisions. But the judges have been prepared to go further. They have shown themselves willing to write legislation, to even go to the point of imposing financial obligations on the state.

The willingness to interfere with the traditional policymaking functions of legislatures has not been restricted to the courts. Administrative tribunals now sit in judgment on the validity of legislation, and boards of inquiry set up under human rights acts rewrite legislation and create new legal responsibilities for individuals.

We have become more and more inclined to seek to resolve the central questions agitating our society in the courtroom, rather than through the political process. The result of this is to surrender to lawyers control of the social agenda and of public discourse.

In a similar vein, the Charter has given a great boost to interest-group politics. Indeed, an active judicial role and interest-group politics seem made for each other.

Interest-group politics is antidemocratic in two respects. It erodes citizenship, the essential precondition to democratic politics. People are induced to define themselves according to their race or sex or sexual preference or some other ascriptive criterion, rather than as citizens. And, in practice, interest-group politics has meant seeking to use the courts as a means of short-circuiting or bypassing democratic processes.

The Charter has thus, in an institutional sense, had an antidemocratic effect. But it has also reinforced ideological currents that are antidemocratic. The most important of these stem from our growing obsession with "rights."

Our fascination with rights has been central to a process through which we seem to have come to prefer the abstract over the concrete. "Rights" appear to be more attractive than real things such as jobs or pensions or physical security or health care. We have been persuaded that if we have "rights" and these "rights" are enshrined in a constitution, then we need not concern ourselves with anything else. It is difficult to describe as "democratic" a public discourse that avoids addressing actual social and economic conditions.

Rights discourse itself encourages antidemocratic tendencies. The inclination of persons to characterize their desires or preferences as "rights" has two unfortunate results. First, there is an inevitable polarization of opposing positions in any debate. And, second, the possibility of further discussion is precluded. If you assert that something is your "right," my only possible response is, "No, it isn't."

Finally, the interest in rights has done much to promote individualistic and, therefore, antisocial ways of thinking. My impression is that many people view their rights as a quiver of jurisprudential arrows, weapons to be used in waging the ceaseless war of each against all.

THE CHARTER IS UN-CANADIAN

It is difficult to imagine any single event or instrument that has played a more substantial role in Americanizing the way Canadians think than has the Charter. The Charter clearly did not begin this process, but it has, since 1982, been central in it.

The basis for my assertion about the Americanizing effects of the Charter is a recognition that, historically and culturally, the Charter is an American document.

This truth is seldom adverted to. As a technical drafting matter, the Charter, it is true, was the creation of Canadian lawyers. But the document's roots lie elsewhere. The idea of enshrining the rights of the individual in a constitution and then protecting those rights through judicial intervention is uniquely American. It may well be a good idea, but no one who had the slightest acquaintance with our history could call it a Canadian idea.

"Life, liberty, and the pursuit of happiness" are not simply words in the Declaration of Independence; they are essential notions defining the American experience. Up until 1982, the central Canadian notions were profoundly different. Our social and constitutional watchwords were "peace, order, and good government."

That has changed. I now teach students who are convinced that we did not have a Constitution, that we were not a proper country until we adopted the Charter. We have worked diligently to abolish our own history and to forget what was once our uniqueness. We are now told that the Charter is a basic element in defining what it means to be Canadian. And many Canadians do appear to believe that we can understand ourselves through our approach to the constitutional protection of rights.

The Charter has promoted our Americanization in other ways besides helping persuade us that we don't have a history. We have, as has already been noted, become more individualistic in our thinking and in our politics over the last decade. Again, it would be foolish to see the Charter as the only cause of this, but it is noteworthy that the first decade of the Charter saw an increase in the concrete indications of social alienation—crime, marital breakdown—as well as in more subtle forms—incivility, hostility, and so on. There was a time when one had a palpable sense, on crossing the border, of entering a different society. This is no longer true.

The Charter has led us to forget our uniqueness as Canadians and to disregard our history. It has had an incalculable effect in Americanizing both the way we think and the way we see ourselves. We have become incomparably more individualistic. Our collective sense of ourselves, and our idea of responsibility for each other and the society we share, has been seriously weakened.

Like Americans, we now believe there must be a legal remedy for every social ill. Like Americans, we put "me" first.

CONCLUSION

Many Canadians have contrived to forget that most of the things that once made Canada a fine country—physical security, health care for all, reasonably honest and competent government, sound education—came about through the political process, not as gifts from beneficent judges.

The fact is that, during the period the Charter has been part of our Constitution, ordinary Canadians have seen a steady erosion of their standard of living.

Unemployment is high and rising. Social services, health care, and pensions are threatened. Not only has the Charter not been of any help in preventing this erosion; it has served to distract our attention from what has been going on.

The great beneficiaries of the Charter have been the lawyers. They are consulted on issues of public policy, they pronounce on the morality or desirability of political and social beliefs and institutions, their advice is sought in a vast array of situations. The number of lawyers grows exponentially as does the cost of retaining their services.

The Charter has, to judge by media commentators, become the basis of our secular religion. And the lawyers are the priests. At some time, Canadians will decide to take control of their agenda back from the lawyers. That is when we will begin to give serious thought to repealing the Charter.

✗ **NO**
The Canadian Charter of Rights and Freedoms Is Antidemocratic and Un-Canadian: An Opposing Point of View
PHILIP L. BRYDEN

Robert Martin's essay launches a two-pronged attack on the Canadian Charter of Rights and Freedoms. The Charter is, according to Professor Martin, both anti-democratic and un-Canadian, and the sooner we Canadians come to our senses and realize that our lawyers have hoodwinked us into believing that the Charter is a good thing, the better off all of us (except maybe the lawyers) will be. My own view is that Professor Martin's essay presents a caricature of both the Charter and modern Canadian democracy, and that when we put the Charter in a more realistic light, we will see that the Charter can, and does, make a valuable contribution to Canada's democratic system of government.

The more powerful of Professor Martin's criticisms is his argument that we should get rid of the Charter because it is antidemocratic. Its attraction is that it contains a germ of truth. Like most half-truths, however, it hides more than it reveals.

In its simplest terms, the argument that the Charter is antidemocratic rests on the superficially plausible idea that if nonelected judges are empowered to over-turn the decisions of elected politicians, the document that gives them this power must be antidemocratic. The usefulness of the argument lies in its reminder to us that the greatest challenge for a court that has the kind of authority granted by our Charter is to interpret the vague but meaningful generalities on which this authority rests—ideas such as freedom of expression, fundamental justice, and equality—in a way that is consistent with our commitment to democratic govern-ment. Where the argument begins to mislead is when its proponents assume that because some judges have had difficulty meeting this challenge in the past, the whole enterprise is doomed to failure.

More specifically, two myths that underpin the notion that the kind of judicial review created by our Charter is inherently antidemocratic need to be exposed. The first myth is that the decisions of our elected legislators and the will of the majority of the electorate are one and the same. Democratic government as it is currently practised in Canada bears little resemblance to the workings of the Athenian polis or a New England town meeting. That observation is neither a disavowal of our current system of representative democracy nor an assertion that the way we presently govern ourselves stands in no need of improvement. It is, however, a reminder that when skeptics examine the record of judicial review using our Charter and point out some court decisions that deserve criticism, we should be evaluating that judicial performance against the reality of parliamentary government in Canada today and not against some romanticized portrait of government of the people, by the people, and for the people.

The second (and ultimately more damaging) myth is that majority rule is, or ought to be, all that modern democratic government is about, and it is in perpetuating the myth that "there is an inherent and irreconcilable tension between liberalism and democracy" that Professor Martin makes his most serious error. My point is not simply that we need a Charter to protect us from the tyranny of the majority, though I think it is dangerously naïve to believe that our fellow citizens are somehow incapable of tyranny. Rather, I want to suggest that democratic government as we should (and to a significant extent have) come to understand it in Canada consists of a complicated web of commitments to each other, only one of which is the commitment to government that in some meaningful way reflects the will of the people.

A belief that important decisions can be taken only after a free and public discussion of the issues, a willingness to abide by a set of rules that govern the way we make authoritative decisions, an acceptance of significant constraints on the use of force—these and many other commitments, some contained in the Charter and others not, are not mere side effects of modern Canadian democracy. They lie at the very heart of democratic government in Canada. And they are part of the reason that the Canadian system of government—notwithstanding all its shortcomings—is respected by people around the world.

This is, I freely acknowledge, a liberal conception of democratic government. Moreover, I recognize that there are other visions of democracy—the kind of Marxist democracy practised by Chairman Mao's Red Guards during the Cultural Revolution, for example—that leave no room for special protection of those who are not able to identify themselves with the will of the majority. For very good reasons, however, Canadians have accepted a liberal notion of democracy, and our commitment to this version of the democratic ideal was firmly in place long before we adopted the Charter.

The real issue is not whether placing some constraints on our legislators is inherently antidemocratic—it isn't. Instead, we ought to ask whether Canadian judges using the Charter can play a useful role in enhancing the quality of our democracy. The answer to this question is not obvious, but I believe that our judges can play such a role, and that by and large our experience during the first few years of the Charter bears this out.

Robert Martin leaves the impression that the Charter has fundamentally undermined the power of our elected representatives to shape the laws that govern our society. If we take a closer look at both the structure of the Charter and the judicial record in interpreting the Charter, however, I find it very difficult to see how that impression can be substantiated.

Because of the types of rights it does (and does not) guarantee, the Charter has little relevance to large and important areas of our political life, notably economic and foreign policy. The judiciary did not bring us free trade with the United States—our political leaders did. And our elected representatives, not our judges, will decide the shape of any new trade pact we may enter into with the United States and Mexico. Our elected representatives decided to commit our troops in the Persian Gulf War, and they, not our courts, will decide what role we play in other trouble spots around the world.

Where the Charter has had some potential to conflict with social policy, our judges have tended to be rather reluctant to accept claims that individual rights should override important governmental interests. Thus, our Supreme Court has decided that provincial Sunday closing laws reasonably limit freedom of religion and that Criminal Code prohibitions on hate speech and obscenity are acceptable constraints on freedom of expression. We may or may not agree with the wisdom of these and other decisions upholding the right of our politicians to pass laws that place reasonable limits on our constitutionally protected rights and freedoms, but this is certainly not the record of a judiciary that is attempting to undermine democratic government in Canada.

This is not to say that Charter litigation is meaningless because the government always wins. Our courts have made important decisions upholding the rights of refugee claimants, of people accused of crimes, of women, gays and lesbians, and many others. Once again, many of these decisions have been controversial, but I believe they have raised our sensitivity to the concerns of people whose interests are not always well represented through our political process. And in so doing, I would argue, they have enhanced the quality of Canadian democracy.

Professor Martin seems to believe that the Charter has undermined our sense of ourselves as a collectivity and contributed to the rise of a political life that is alternatively characterized by narrow interest-group politics or pure selfishness. To the extent that this description of contemporary Canadian politics has an aura of authenticity about it, however, I think it confuses cause and effect. The popularity of the Charter (indeed much of the need for a Charter) arises from the fact that Canadians understand the diversity of their interests and want to incorporate into their democratic system of government a recognition of the vulnerability of some of those interests.

This diversity of interests was not created by the Charter, and getting rid of the Charter is not likely to usher in a return to a mythical golden age of harmony and communitarian spirit. Throughout our history, Canadians have recognized and sought to give legal protection to our diversity on regional, linguistic, religious, and other grounds, and I suspect that only someone from Ontario could imagine characterizing this as an erosion of citizenship.

Again, the problem of the fracturing of our sense of ourselves as a political community that Professor Martin identifies is a real one, and it is a challenge for supporters of the kind of political ideals that the Charter represents to realize their goals in a way that does not irreparably undermine other political values that are important to us. What Professor Martin fails to do, in my view, is make a convincing case that it is not possible for us to meet this challenge or that it is not worthwhile for us to try to do so.

Professor Martin's second criticism of the Charter is that it is un-Canadian, by which he seems to mean that the Charter contributes to the "Americanization" of Canadian political life. It would be foolish to deny the influence of the United States Bill of Rights on both the content of the Charter and the political will that animated its adoption. In my view, however, Professor Martin is wrong in his attempt to characterize the Charter as a species of cuckoo in the Canadian political nest that seeks to supplant domestic institutions and traditions with unsavoury ideas from south of the forty-ninth parallel.

In response to Professor Martin, I would begin with the rather obvious point that even if some of the important ideas embedded in the Charter were imported into Canada from abroad, so is much of the rest of the apparatus of Canadian government. Canada's parliamentary and common law traditions were imported from England; our federalism was imported (albeit in a substantially altered form) from the United States in 1867; and our civil law traditions were imported from France. In each instance we have made these traditions our own, in some instances by performing major surgery on them in the process.

The Charter itself follows in this tradition of domesticating foreign political ideas and structures. For example, a central element of the American Bill of Rights is the protection of the right to private property. The drafters of the Canadian Charter (wisely in my view) decided that our normal political processes were adequate for the protection of the rights of property owners and that judges should not be given this responsibility under the Charter. In addition, the Charter recognizes certain rights of French and English linguistic minorities, expresses a commitment to our multicultural heritage, and contains approaches to equality and other rights that set it off as a document that is quite distinctive from the American Bill of Rights. The Charter's roots may lie in American soil, but the tree that springs up from those roots is distinctively Canadian.

The more subtle but significant point on which Professor Martin and I disagree is that he seems to use the term "Americanization" as a sort of shorthand for most of what he doesn't like in contemporary Canadian political life. No doubt there are plenty of Canadians who prefer the kind of life we had in the 1970s (or the 1950s for that matter) to the kind of life we have today. What is unclear to me, however, is how unemployment, family breakdown, the consequences of massive public-sector debt for our social welfare programs, and the other things that trouble Professor Martin about life in Canada in the twenty-first century can be laid at the door of the Charter.

In fairness, Professor Martin does not ascribe these social ills to the Charter itself, but he says that the Charter has "served to distract our attention from what has been going on." If the Charter has served to distract Canadians from thinking about the problems of high unemployment and threats to the continued viability of our present schemes for delivering social services, universal health care, and pensions, this is certainly news to me. And I dare say it would come as news to those who took part in the 1993 federal election campaign that revolved around these very issues. Professor Martin is probably correct when he states that the Charter is not going to be of much help in addressing these problems, but nobody ever claimed that it would. More important, we shouldn't assume that because the Charter doesn't address these important problems, the issues the Charter does address are somehow insignificant.

The Charter does not represent the sum of Canadian political life, any more than the American Bill of Rights represents the sum of political life in the United States. From a political science standpoint, what the Charter represents is a special way of addressing a limited range of issues that we feel are unlikely to get the kind of attention they deserve in the ordinary process of electoral politics, and a formal commitment to ourselves that the ideals such as freedom, justice, and equality that the Charter enshrines deserve a special place in our democratic political life. I think this was a commitment that it was wise for us to make in 1982, and that Canadians are right to be proud of this new and distinctive feature of our democracy.

POSTSCRIPT

The debate between Robert Martin and Philip Bryden on the Charter of Rights and Freedoms dates back to 1994. Robert Martin has more recently expanded his critique of both the Charter and the role of the Canadian Supreme Court in a strongly written book entitled *Most Dangerous Branch: How the Supreme Court Has Undermined Our Law and Democracy* (Montreal and Kingston: McGill-Queen's University Press, 2004). In this book, Martin writes, "As someone who is committed to the maintenance of constitutional democracy, I cannot avoid seeing the Court as a collection of arrogant and unprincipled poseurs, largely out of control."

But Martin is not the only one to express serious reservations about the impact of the Charter on Canadian political life. One of the most caustic critiques of the Charter has been written by Michael Mandel. In his book *The Charter of Rights and the Legalization of Politics in Canada,* rev. ed. (Toronto: Wall and Thompson, 1994), Mandel argues that the Charter has led to the "legalization of politics in Canada." Because the scope of interpretation of the Charter is very broad, judges make highly political decisions. They are not just interpreting the law according to some technical, objective criteria but are actually making the law, usurping the role traditionally reserved only for elected legislators. Because of the high cost of litigation, the legalization of politics, according to Mandel, leads to a conservative, class-based politics that works against socially disadvantaged groups.

Like Martin, Seymour Lipset, a noted American sociologist, argues that the Charter threatens to erase the cultural differences between Americans and Canadians by transforming Canada into a "rights-centred" political culture. See his *Continental Divide* (New York: Routledge, 1990). Christopher Manfredi argues that part of this Americanizing influence is reflected in the frequency with which Canadian judges cite American precedents when making their decisions.

Because of the growing importance of the Charter to Canadian politics, there has been a steady flow of books on this subject in recent years. In addition to the works cited above, students will find the following helpful: Rainer Knopff and F.L. Morton, *Charter Politics* (Scarborough: Nelson, 1992); Patrick Monahan, *Politics and the Constitution: The Charter, Federalism and the Supreme Court* (Toronto: Carswell, 1987); and David Beatty, *Putting the Charter to Work* (Montreal and Kingston: McGill-Queen's University Press, 1987). A book written by a civil rights activist who supports Philip Bryden's arguments is Alan Borovoy's *When Freedoms Collide: The Case for Our Civil Liberties* (Toronto: Lester & Orpen Dennys, 1988). See also Janet Hiebert, *Charter Conflicts: What Is Parliament's Role?* (Montreal and Kingston: McGill-Queen's University Press, 2002); Christopher Manfredi, *Judicial Power and the Charter, Canada and the Paradox of Liberal Constitutionalism,* 2nd ed. (Toronto: Oxford University Press, 2001); Peter McCormick, *Supreme at Last: The Evolution of the Supreme Court of Canada* (Toronto: Lorimer, 2000); and Rory Leishman, *Against Judicial Activism: The*

Decline of Freedom and Democracy in Canada (Montreal and Kingston: McGill-Queen's University Press, 2005).

If we accept Martin's argument that we should be concerned about the impact of the Charter, what can be done? Martin's closing suggestion that many Canadians may begin thinking about repealing the Charter seems unlikely now that a whole new generation has grown up with the Charter as an accepted fact. Perhaps a more likely development is that Canadians will begin to take a more careful look at the record of individual judges and to demand more say in their appointment. This has led some to argue that Parliament should review the appointment of Supreme Court judges as the Senate does in the United States. However, would such a move be a positive step or lead only to a very politicization and Americanization of the Canadian judicial system?

Should the Federal Government Play a Leading Role in Health Care?

✔ **YES**
ANDREW HEARD AND DANIEL COHN, "The Federal
Government Should Stay Involved: The Case for a Strong
Federal Role in Health Care"

✗ **NO**
PAUL BARKER, "The Case Against a Strong Federal
Role in Health Care"

Federalism is a form of government that divides powers and responsibilities between national and regional governments. The intent behind selecting this type of governing arrangement is to increase the chances that local differences are respected while simultaneously allowing for the achievement of countrywide goals. At first glance, it may seem that the two levels of government would operate independently, each looking after their respective duties. But in reality, they often interact. The lack of clarity in a nation's constitution, the refusal of policies to fit easily into legislative categories, and the sheer competitiveness of governments are some of the factors that lead to a high degree of interdependence in federal states. Given this quality, there is a continuous struggle to sort out the roles of federal and provincial governments. Some areas of policy will, eventually, fall mostly to national governments (e.g., national security) and others to provincial ones (e.g., education). But with some policies, there will be disagreement and confusion over who should assume prominence. In Canada, this last situation prevails in relation to health care.

The Canadian health care system (or medicare) offers comprehensive physician and hospital care to all citizens at no direct cost. It is an impressive policy accomplishment and often ranks as the most important public issue in the minds of Canadians. For this reason alone, it is felt that the federal government should take a leading role in the area of health care—medicare is truly a national program and appreciated as such by all Canadians. Supporters of a strong federal role also point to the need for a single authority to offer direction on reforms to the health care system. Medicare needs to continually change to ensure that Canadians are able to receive effective health care, and some believe that the federal government is best positioned to orchestrate the introduction of necessary reforms. In addition, the Canadian health care system has become an important symbol of Canadian values, a situation that also seems to argue for a strong federal presence.

There is, however, a view that suggests that it is unwise for the federal government to assume a lead role in health care. One reason for this is legal: health care is largely a provincial responsibility. The rule of law, an important element in any constitutional democracy, would be allegedly weakened without the provinces directing medicare. A further argument against a strong federal role is that the health system would perform better with the provinces largely in charge. Medicare is in reality ten provincial plans (plus three territorial ones) knitted together by a commitment to principles contained in a piece of federal legislation called the *Canada Health Act*. Accordingly, the provinces have much more experience with health care and much more expertise as well. More generally, it is felt that the case for a strong federal role in health assumes a notion of leadership that requires some consideration and arguably some reformulation.

There are also some who feel that the two orders of government should share duties when it comes to health care. It might be said that this is the way it has been done in the past. The federal government sets out the broad principles of health care and provides much-needed financial assistance, while the provinces administer the health care plans. A closer look, however, at the history of medicare shows that there has always been a lead player in health care, whether it be the federal government in the initial stages of medicare or the provinces in more recent years. A decade ago, the federal government attempted to reassert itself. Through various health care accords and a national commission, it had sought to play a guiding role in the reform of the Canadian health care system. The election of a Conservative government at the federal level ended this trend—Prime Minister Harper felt that health care belonged to the provinces. But the need to renew a major federal–provincial financing arrangement for health care in 2014 offers the opportunity for a change of mind. The question for this debate is, in a way, whether a shift in federal thinking bodes well for health care in Canada.

In the readings, Andrew Heard and Daniel Cohn, two political scientists with Simon Fraser University and York University respectively, claim that the Canadian health care system requires a strong hand from the federal government. Paul Barker, one of the editors of *Crosscurrents*, makes the case against a strong presence for Ottawa in health care.

✔ **YES**

The Federal Government Should Stay Involved: The Case for a Strong Federal Role in Health Care
ANDREW HEARD AND DANIEL COHN

Health care is one of the most important areas of public policy. Canada's system of provincial-run single-payer universal health insurance plans (popularly known as medicare) enjoys widespread and stable long-term public support.[1] Included in this public judgment is the belief that the maintenance of medicare is a joint responsibility of the federal and provincial governments.[2] Our medicare system has become an important symbol of Canadian identity. Opinion polling conducted in 2005 found that 85 percent of Canadians believed that eliminating public health care would fundamentally change the nature of Canada.[3] The universal and comprehensive medical care that all Canadians are entitled to has long been one of the most visible differences between Canadian and American cultures. Even with the reforms Americans have adopted under President Obama, most Americans will still receive less complete coverage, and families will pay more for it than Canadians. The private-for-profit basis of the U.S. health insurance system has been left largely intact, and the new legislation does nothing to eliminate co-payments, deductibles (i.e., user fees), limits on coverage, nor specify what insurers must cover. In the words of one American health policy scholar, Canadian health care is "remarkable" for the degree to which medical need has supplanted wealth as the principal upon which care is allocated.[4] From its public proposal in 1945 through to today, the federal government has played a lead role in creating and guiding medicare. While provincial premiers have taken turns protesting the federal government's invasion of "exclusive" provincial jurisdiction, a brief analysis shows that the federal government is completely justified in taking a lead role. Far from being an invader, it is simply continuing to protect a system it helped develop decades ago. At its heart, medicare in Canada draws its strength from providing basic medical care for all Canadians, regardless of which province they happen to live in. The federal government has an important role in continuing to shape and protect this national treasure.

Some historical context is vital to understanding the reasons the federal government plays a substantial role in health care, and also why that role is on solid constitutional ground. When the Fathers of Confederation settled on a division of powers between the national and provincial governments, the guiding principle was that the federal government would be responsible for the most important areas of public policy, and the provinces would deal with matters of more "local and private concern." Health care then was still very primitive, with only the most rudimentary care available; indeed, it was well into the twentieth century before contact with a doctor was actually likely to improve one's chances of survival. At the time of Confederation, most hospitals were run by religious orders, with a few others set up by other charitable groups or municipalities. The *Constitution Act, 1867* gave the provinces jurisdiction over charities, hospitals, and insane asylums, while the new federal government gained control over marine hospitals and quarantine. These are the only direct references to health care in the formal constitutional documents. All that the provinces were explicitly granted in 1867 was the right to keep an eye on the churches and municipalities that ran the few small hospitals existing at the time. In addition, the provinces were responsible for licensing physicians as a consequence of their jurisdiction over "property and civil rights"; civil rights in this context meant one's rights in property, and not the idea of civil liberties we think of today.

Canadian society responded to such profound disruptions in the twentieth century as the Great Depression and the Second World War with new ideas about the role of the state to foster the social welfare of its citizens. The original division of powers between the federal and provincial governments in the *Constitution Act, 1867* proved to be unadaptable to the new social and economic realities of the twentieth century. First, the Great Depression showed the necessity of providing people with some insurance against unemployment. The courts ruled that this was a provincial responsibility because of their control of most employment contracts, but the provinces simply did not have the financial resources to implement employment insurance. As a result, the *Constitution Act, 1940* was passed to enable the federal government to take responsibility for this area of public policy. Similarly, the post–Second World War era saw the acceptance of a universal pension scheme and supplemental benefits as a way to care for senior citizens. Again, the provinces had constitutional responsibility but were without the practical ability to provide these benefits. A constitutional amendment was passed in 1951 to allow the federal government to create the Canada Pension Plan, and another in 1964 authorized it to provide Old Age Benefits; these amendments preserved provincial jurisdiction as well, because Quebec preferred to launch its own version of these schemes. Thus, the context of the period in which medicare was first created was an era of increasing federal government responsibility for social welfare programs—with the full agreement of the provincial governments at the time. Far from being a constitutional invader, the federal government was welcomed by many as a white knight.

Without federal policy leadership, it is doubtful that most Canadians would have public health insurance today, as the provinces proved very reluctant as a group to be policy innovators. While Saskatchewan's Co-operative Commonwealth Federation–New Democratic Party governments are popularly given credit for "inventing" medicare, it must be pointed out that Canadians would have had a complete public health insurance plan at the end of the Second World War if the provinces had accepted the proposals that Ottawa put forward in 1945. Instead, they walked out of the post-war reconstruction conference. Rebuffed when it first raised the topic of public health insurance, the federal government offered to subsidize the creation of universal single-payer provincially run hospital and diagnostic services insurance in 1957, as well as insurance for physician bills in 1966, only after support for each measure had reached critical mass in provincial capitals and with voters.[5]

In order to evaluate the merits of the federal government's role in health care policymaking, we must first identify medicare's actual character and scope. Canada's system of provincially run single-payer universal health insurance plans is not a coherent countrywide program, nor does it represent the full extent of public involvement in the financing of health care. Rather, it should be seen as the backbone of a framework within which each province has designed its own system for financing and delivering health care. This framework provides provincial governments with unparalleled autonomy in designing their own health care systems. In a study of health care policymaking in federations, K.G. Banting and S. Corbett found that all of the federal governments that they looked at played some role in structuring health care, and that Canada had the most decentralized health care policymaking process among the countries studied. The high degree of decentralization present in Canada as compared to other countries has also been confirmed by other researchers, including C.H. Tuohy.[6]

In order to qualify for the full value of the transfers that provinces are entitled to under the Canada Health Transfer,[7] they must abide by the five conditions of the *Canada Health Act*. These govern the way that they manage and finance physician, hospital, and diagnostic services:

- Universality: All permanent residents of the province must be eligible to join the plan.

- Comprehensive: All medically necessary services must be insured. In practice, there is no agreed list of services. Rather, it has been left up to each province to determine what is and is not medically necessary (subject to objections from the federal health minister).[8]

- Accessibility: Services must be reasonably available, and there can be no out-of-pocket charges to patients for those services covered by a provincial plan. Initially, only hospital and diagnostic services were covered by this ban on user fees. However, the *Canada Health Act* extended this ban to physician services. This act also specifically gave the federal minister the power to reduce a province's subsidy by one dollar for each dollar of user fees that it allowed.

- Portability: The plan must provide coverage for members travelling outside of their province.

- Public Administration: The plan must be run by an agency responsible to the provincial legislature on a not-for-profit basis.

As noted above, in comparative terms, Canadian provinces have a great deal of autonomy. However, even the five terms noted above are less stringent than they would first appear. The federal government has only rarely found provinces to be so far out of compliance as to warrant penalties in the form of deductions from their transfer payments.[9] The power exercised by successive federal governments to ensure compliance with these terms has been so light it has raised questions from the Auditor General of Canada.[10] In fact, since 1977, provinces have not even been required to spend the money sent to them by Ottawa, or the supporting tax powers that Ottawa has given them (through programs such as the Canada Health Transfer and its predecessors), on the provision of health care. For the financing and delivery of health care goods and services other than physician, hospital, and diagnostic services—important items provided outside of hospitals such as dentistry, optometry, physiotherapy, nursing homes, and elder and home care—even the loose rules of the *Canada Health Act* do not apply.

It has been suggested that Ottawa has periodically used its strong fiscal position when compared with the provinces to exert control over provincial health policy. However, there is little evidence that Ottawa gained any additional leverage over provincial decision making as a result of increases in transfer payments that occurred in 2000, 2003 and 2004. Most notably, the 2004 First Ministers' Health Accord, which committed Ottawa to substantially increase transfer payments for the subsequent ten years, required the provinces to publicly report on how they were using the additional funding granted to them so as to improve health care. These reporting commitments have gone substantially unmet. Not surprisingly, results have been mixed. Those provinces that have adopted coherent plans, including meaningful targets and indicators, have had more success. Nevertheless, the federal funds have continued to flow to all provinces equally. The 2011 Health Council of Canada report on progress on implementing the 2004 accord makes it clear that, despite improvements across a range of areas, several provinces have failed to meet some of the commitments they made in the accord.[11] Therefore, it is a bit difficult to argue that the federal role should be reduced further. Canadian provinces already have more autonomy than sub-national jurisdictions in other major federations, and the rules that constitute the existing minimal federal framework tend to be enforced very moderately and with great discretion.

A federal role is also required because the provinces have proven reluctant to manage health care. When Saskatchewan created its physician insurance plan in the early 1960s, doctors went on strike to protest the loss of professional autonomy that they felt would result. The strike ended with an agreement that set the terms for the subsequent spread of provincial physician insurance plans. Provincial governments would be responsible for overall funding but would leave professional management of care in the hands of physicians, who would work (for the most part) as private entrepreneurs, billing the province on a fee-for-service basis. Those who wanted could "opt-out" and bill their patients directly either for the same fee set by the province or an additional amount. In these cases, the patient would apply to the province for reimbursement at the provincially set rate. As concern moved from building provincial health systems in the 1950s and 1960s to placing them on a more financially sustainable footing in the 1970s and 1980s, the provinces proved unwilling to make the tough choices needed to control health care costs, because it would involve confronting the medical profession and other powerful interest groups.

What started as a concession to ease the concern of a few doctors became a means for the provinces to avoid managing their health care systems and a potential threat to health care accessibility. This was exacerbated in 1977 when Ottawa agreed to grant the provinces more leeway in how they managed their health care systems. Instead of being reimbursed 50 cents on the dollar for providing services Ottawa approved of, provinces received a block grant to spend as they wished. Therefore, if the provinces could not keep costs under control, they, not Ottawa, would be responsible for the extra costs. User fees provided a loophole that would allow provinces to avoid managing their problems or paying the price for their inability to manage them: if the physicians' fee chart was kept artificially low, the patient—not the province—was on the hook for the extra costs. In some provinces, there were substantial problems accessing care without user fees. Most notable in this regard was Ontario, where more than half of all anesthesiologists and more than one-third of obstetricians were extra billing. It was at this point that Ottawa stepped in and banned extra billing with the introduction of the *Canada Health Act.* It is worth pointing out that the decision to ban user fees for physician, hospital, and diagnostic services was seen as so essential that the *Canada Health Act* received unanimous support in the House of Commons on final reading.[12]

This pattern has been repeated on other occasions as well, with the majority of provinces refusing to make the tough decisions necessary to manage their health care systems until Ottawa has taken some determined action that compelled the provinces to face their problems. The most recent example of this is the wave of hospital rationalizations that swept the provinces during the 1990s and the early years of the new millennium. Although some provinces, such as Alberta, acted on their own, most did less than they could have done until confronted with the cuts to transfers implemented by the federal budgets in 1994–95 and 1995–96. Given that the majority of provinces are reluctant to either innovate or manage their health care systems, a minimal federal health policy framework is necessary to ensure provinces maintain the key features of the program, let alone modify it so as to take better account of the reality of modern health care by providing universal access to home care and pharmaceutical coverage. Among its other recommendations, the Romanow Commission on the Future of Canadian Health Care found that new programs to ensure universal access to home care and coverage for illnesses involving catastrophic drug costs to the patient, were needed to both enhance the quality of care Canadians receive and to place health care on a more sustainable basis.[13] As part of the 2004 Health Accord, the provinces agreed to move toward these and other objectives, including reducing wait times for care. However, progress has been slow at best in most provinces, results have been difficult to measure, and there is a growing sense among experts that unless there is greater federal leadership the situation will remain stalled.[14]

It is also worth pointing out that the national consensus exhibited when the *Canada Health Act* was unanimously passed by the House of Commons appears to be holding firm. When Prime Minister Harper's Conservatives came to power, many feared that the five principles embedded in the *Canada Health Act* might be watered down or simply ignored (especially the prohibition on user fees). After all, as leader of the right-of-centre National Citizens Coalition, Prime Minister Harper had urged his home province of Alberta to take complete control over health policy and simply ignore the terms of the *Canada Health Act*.[15] Yet, the Conservatives have been in power since 2006 and no changes to the act have been proposed, and none appear on the horizon. In fact, both the prime minister and his then health minister, Tony Clement, sided with opponents of Alberta's government when it tested the waters on policy changes that would have violated the act.[16] During the 2011 election, the prime minister re-iterated his commitment to the *Canada Health Act* as a tool for managing Canadian health care policy, given the recognized constitutional authority of the provinces.[17] While some critics suggest that the Harper government has not been aggressive enough in enforcing the terms of the act's prohibition on user fees, it is difficult to say if they have been any more lax than the Liberal government that proceeded them.[18] In recognition of Quebec's distinct nature, the Conservative platform also promised a willingness to negotiate a unique arrangement with that province when the 2004 First Ministers' Health Accord expires. Since the election, rumours have begun to circulate that the federal government contemplates reaching separate agreements with each province and territory, rather than negotiating a single nationwide plan. This would cause Ottawa's involvement in health care policymaking to increase, not decrease, as it sorts through the details unique to each province and territory. It would also have the potential to make the provinces more accountable for the commitments that they make in return for federal funding.[19] As with the Mulroney Conservatives, who supported the passage of the *Canada Health Act* while in opposition, and the Diefenbaker Conservatives, who appointed the Royal Commission that recommended that provincial hospital insurance be extended to cover physician bills in the 1960s, today's Tories seem to have concluded that Ottawa has an important role to play in health care policymaking, that reducing this role does not make sense, and that, in fact, a moderate strengthening of the federal role might be in order.

Finally, health care is both an expensive and extensive activity, representing a relatively consistent 10 to 10.5 percent annual share of Canada's gross domestic product. Among the G7 countries, Canada is in the middle of the pack. In today's dollars, health spending is about $192 billion when including both public and private expenses.[20] If health care's share of the gross domestic product were to rise, Canada's international economic competitiveness could be undermined. Because the maintenance of this competitiveness is a major concern and responsibility of the federal government, Ottawa has no choice but to take a hand in health policy and not simply restrict its role to financier of provincial programs. This is especially the case in that medicare provides Canada with a competitive advantage over the United States in many vital industries. This is still the case even after the major reforms to U.S. health care introduced by President Obama. Although a significant improvement over previous U.S. legislation, individual Americans and families will still continue paying more out-of-pocket for care than Canadians do and get less care, most insurance will still be paid for by employers, and the reforms are unlikely to control the growth in costs.[21] Canadian medicare also protects most Canadians from the harsh financial realities of American health care. In 2007, 62 percent of all American personal bankruptcies were due to medical expenses incurred when individuals were seriously ill, despite the fact that 78 percent of these individuals had health insurance.[22] With an appreciation of the actual nature and extent of the federal government's role in health care, one can examine the constitutional grounds for this role. Some provincial leaders trumpet health care as the "exclusive jurisdiction" of the provinces and feel that any federal involvement violates the Constitution. Like many good myths, this view has some real basis in fact. Indeed, the opening words of section 92 of the *Constitution Act, 1867* declare: "In each Province the Legislature may exclusively make Laws in relation to Matters coming within the Classes of Subject next hereinafter enumerated...." This statement is followed by a list of areas of public policy, including charities, asylums, and hospitals. Some believe that this is conclusive evidence that the federal government is treading on provincial toes by daring to legislate on insured medical treatments. However, there are two crucial pieces that must also be fitted into the picture before one can draw proper conclusions on the subject.

First, the whole Constitution is much more than just the literal words found in the documents comprising the formal Constitution of Canada. If those documents were to be taken literally, then the federal government would be fully entitled to exercise its powers of reservation and disallowance to veto any provincial legislation to which it objected. While the constitutional documents list certain areas of public policy as the "exclusive" jurisdiction of one level of government or the other, the modern reality is that just about every area of public policy is affected by the activities of both levels of government. For example, the federal government has "exclusive" jurisdiction to legislate on criminal law, but major changes are almost always discussed first with the provincial governments in an effort to get a consensus of support before amending the Criminal Code. A complex pattern of interaction among all governments is sustained right across the policy spectrum.

Second, modern Canadian federalism depends to an enormous extent upon "fiscal federalism," which has its origins in the formal Constitution but has developed into a much broader and more substantive framework through intergovernmental agreements. These arrangements have allowed the provincial governments to implement important policies that would otherwise have remained only possibilities within the provinces' theoretical jurisdiction. The profound differences in economic activity across this country mean that Canadians would have vastly different provincial public services if the provincial governments relied exclusively on the income generated within their provinces. A belief in the basic equality and worth of Canadians fostered the development of a succession of financial schemes to transfer money from the federal government to the provinces so that Canadians across the country would receive roughly similar benefits. At various times, those federal funds have accounted for up to half of some provincial budgets. Without funding from Ottawa, Canadians living in several provinces would almost certainly still not have comprehensive medical coverage. There is simply no way that the poorer provinces could have afforded to implement the medicare programs that are so appreciated by all Canadians today.

The main federal involvement in medicare is the transfer of money to the provinces, with some conditions attached, rather than legislation aimed purely at regulating insured medical services. The conditions, as discussed above, are aimed at maintaining some common benefits for Canadians across the country. The crux of the debate, then, really revolves around the constitutionality of these conditional grants.

There are two basic grounds for justifying the federal government's ability to set some conditions on the grants given to the provinces. The first is the notion of the "federal spending power." In its essence, this idea suggests that the federal government is free to make gifts to the provinces and to attach some conditions upon the receipt of those gifts. While there is some debate over the extent of the federal spending power, there can be little doubt about its basic constitutionality. In *Reference re Canada Assistance Plan* (1991), the Supreme Court of Canada upheld the basic ability of the national Parliament to create conditional block grants and to alter their terms unilaterally.[23] A key point for the court was that the federal legislation principally sets the terms under which federal money can be transferred and does not attempt a broader regulation of a provincial matter. The *Canada Health Act* would appear to satisfy this approach to the federal spending power. The only real "enforcement" under the act is the withholding of federal funding, and actual enforcement is sporadic and limited.[24] If a provincial government were to violate any one of the five main conditions of the *Canada Health Act*, the federal government *may* withhold funds after consulting with the provincial government; the withholding is discretionary. The only mandatory withholding of funds is provided in the case of a province that permits extra billing; the federal government's contribution for health care is reduced on a dollar-for-dollar basis. The *Canada Health Act* might be constitutionally vulnerable if the provinces could establish that the impact of the federal legislation negated their ability to exercise their policy powers on the matter.[25] However, the provincial governments are ultimately free to pursue their own policies if they are prepared to substitute their own revenue for the money that the federal government would otherwise donate. As a result, the act seems to be consistent with the Supreme Court's view that federal legislation under the spending power must concern conditions of dispensing its own funds and not attempt a broader, independent regulation of provincial matters.

It is important to note, too, that Canadians support the federal government's power to attach conditions to its health care transfers. While 72 percent of Canadians in 2004 believed that the federal government was not paying its fair share of health care, 67 percent believed that new federal spending should come with conditions rather than letting provincial governments administer the funds as they see fit.[26] Admittedly, this poll contradicts the findings in other surveys that have asked more generic questions about whether the provincial governments should be able to spend health care funds according to their own priorities; in most of these polls, respondents favoured provincial autonomy. It is nevertheless revealing that when Canadians were asked to focus specifically on the federal government's role, a strong majority believed that the federal government should direct how new funds are spent. Moreover, a 2011 poll found that Canadians continue to support a strong federal engagement in health care; 73 percent felt that health care should be the federal government's top priority, and 88 percent believed that the federal government should take the initiative in discussions to replace the expiring federal–provincial health accord.[27]

The other possible constitutional justification relies on the courts' interpretation of the opening words of section 91 of the *Constitution Act, 1867* that empower the federal government to "make laws for the Peace, Order, and Good Government of Canada [POGG]." In an enduring contradiction, the courts have declared this statement to mean that the federal government may pass laws that would normally be in provincial jurisdiction, when the plain English reading of this whole clause seems to explicitly preclude federal legislation on matters listed in section 92 as belonging to the provincial legislatures. As bizarre as this may seem, it is nonetheless an important doctrine of the Constitution and has been developed by the courts for well over a century now.

The federal Parliament may, in two general sets of exceptional circumstances, pass laws that would normally be matters for the provinces. The first is in times of emergency, but this does not apply to health care. The other set of circumstances is when there is a matter of "national concern" or "national dimensions" are involved. Both of these could possibly apply to the *Canada Health Act*. Health care is so vital to Canadian society that the most basic tenets of public health insurance need to be set nationally. If some provinces strayed from the agreed programs, the viability of the coast-to-coast coverage of all Canadians could be seriously threatened. Minor provincial variations could be tolerated, but any significant deviation would undermine medicare. In the case of extra billing, some doctors charging small amounts would not threaten public health care, but many doctors charging substantial fees would bring a very different stress to the program. Events in the early 1980s showed how quickly extra billing could spread to defeat the basic premise of public health care. By 1983, 62 percent of anesthetists and 39 percent of obstetricians in Ontario were charging their patients significant amounts for any operations in which they took part.[28] In particular regions of Ontario, every single member of a medical specialty was billing extra, charging fees that could reach as high as $400 for the delivery of a baby. While many doctors waived fees for their poorest patients, such a situation presented other people with an expensive outlay for health care. What was supposed to be a universal program of health care funded from insurance premiums and tax dollars soon threatened to degenerate into a patchwork across the country; in most provinces all insured services remained free, but in others the extra billing meant that Canadians living in those provinces faced significant charges for basic health care and hospital treatment. Had the federal government not intervened in 1984 and had the trend of extra billing continued, the medicare system might not have survived into the twentieth-first century in a form we would recognize.

These circumstances might possibly meet the test laid down by the Supreme Court of Canada in the *Crown Zellerbach* case.[29] In that decision, the court held that federal legislation could be enacted under the POGG power on matters of provincial jurisdiction if provincial inaction or inability would lead to the collapse of a particular regulatory scheme. The corollary of this position could occur if one or more provinces willfully pursued contrary policies that seriously undermined a public policy in which there was a real national interest. The real-world experience of provincial innovation with extra billing indicates that the medicare system might require federal legislation if it is to survive.

In conclusion, it is both desirable and constitutional for the federal government to play a substantial role in health care. Canadians deeply value the comprehensive medicare programs that insure everyone across the country for a comprehensive range of treatments, as well as ensuring that their coverage moves with them across the country. Federal grants have permitted all Canadians to enjoy relatively comparable levels of health care that simply could not have been achieved without the federal government. A 2003 Ekos poll found that, in the public's eyes, the single most important aspect of the Canadian health care system was equal access to health care for all Canadians.[30] While there are still differences in treatment and waiting times from province to province, those differences pale in comparison to what might exist without the lead role taken by the federal government. Provincial autonomy in health care still exists; any province could pursue its own objectives if it is prepared to fund medicare itself. So far, at least, provincial governments have decided to abide by the collective vision of health care that successive federal governments have defended. Even the richest provinces have concluded that it is better to abide by the national policy preferences. It is important to note, too, that provincial autonomy does not necessarily mean advancements in health care. The track records of some provincial governments in experimenting with extra billing in the 1980s and hospital closures in the 1990s and early 2000s demonstrate that provincial innovations can have a very negative impact on health care. Neither does the participation of the federal government stifle policy development. Organ donation and better management of spending on prescription drugs are just two of the many areas where federal, provincial, and territorial governments are working collaboratively to develop better public policy for all Canadians. It is important to note that it is the provinces and territories themselves that wish to see such partnerships. It is not a case of Ottawa trying to muscle in on their turf.[31] Ultimately, the federal–provincial dynamic provides a system of healthy checks and balances that depends upon a national consensus to survive. Medicare is a unique policy area that accommodates differences in provincial political cultures while transcending them. Medicare was created by the leadership shown by the federal government, and that role is needed just as much today.

NOTES

1. M. Mendelsohn, *Canadians' Thoughts on Their Health Care System: Preserving the Canadian Model through Innovation* (Ottawa: Commission on the Future of Health Care in Canada, 2002); and S.N. Soroka, *Canadian Perceptions of the Health Care System: A Report to the Health Council of Canada* (Toronto: The Health Council of Canada, 2007).

2. A. Maioni, "Federalism and Health Care in Canada," in K.G. Banting and S. Corbett, eds., *Health Policy and Federalism: A Comparative Perspective on Multi-Level Governance* (Montreal and Kingston: McGill-Queen's University Press, 2002), p. 177.

3. S.N. Soroka, *Canadian Perceptions of the Health Care System*, p. 23.

4. P.C. Newman, "Remembering Pierre Berton," *Maclean's*, December 13, 2004), 36–38; M.A. Rodwin, "Why We Need Health Care Reform Now," *Journal of Health Politics, Policy and Law* 36 (2011), pp. 597–599; and T.R. Marmor, "Philosophical Premises in the Long-Running Health Care Debate," *Journal of Health Politics, Policy and Law* 36 (2011), pp. 568–569.

5. D. Cohn, "The Canada Health and Social Transfer: Transferring Resources or Moral Authority?" in P.C. Fafard and D.M. Brown, eds., *Canada: The State of the Federation, 1996* (Kingston: Queen's University Institute of Intergovernmental Affairs, 1996), pp. 169–171.

6. K.G. Banting and S. Corbett, "Health Policy and Federalism: An Introduction," in K.G. Banting and S. Corbett, eds., *Health Policy and Federalism: A Comparative Perspective on Multi-Level Governance* (Montreal and Kingston: McGill-Queen's University Press, 2002); and C.H. Tuohy, "Single Payers, Multiple Systems: The Scope and Limits

of Substantial Variation under a Federal Policy Framework," *Journal of Health Politics, Policy and Law* 34 (2009), pp. 458–459.

7. From 1977 to 2005, there were three different federal transfers to the provinces for the nominal support of medicare and to which the terms of the *Canada Health Act* applied after it passed in 1984. From fiscal 1977/78 to 1996/97, there was the Established Program Financing (EPF) transfer, which funded medicare and post-secondary education. In the 1995/96 budget (effective 1996/97), this was merged with the Canada Assistance Plan (CAP), which funded social programs, including the cost of medical and health services for low-income families not covered by medicare (called "extended health" services), to create the Canada Health and Social Transfer (CHST). In the 2004/05 budget, the CHST was split into the Canada Health Transfer and the Canadian Social Transfer.

8. This has led to federal–provincial disputes as to what should be covered. The most persistent case surrounds the unwillingness of some provinces to fund abortion services. See L. Eggerson, "Abortion Services in Canada: A Patchwork Quilt with Many Holes," *Canadian Medical Association Journal* 164 (March 20, 2001), pp. 847–849.

9. K.G. Banting and R. Boadway, "Defining the Sharing Community: The Federal Role in Health Care," in H. Lazar and F. St-Hilaire, eds., *Money, Politics and Health Care: Reconstructing the Federal-Provincial Partnership* (Montreal and Kingston: The Institute for Research on Public Policy and the Institute of Intergovernmental Relations, 2004), pp. 15–16.

10. Auditor General of Canada, *Status Report of the Auditor General of Canada to the House of Commons* (Ottawa: Office of the Auditor General of Canada, September 2002), ch. 3.

11. C. Tuohy, "Single Payers, Multiple Systems," p. 466; and Health Council of Canada, *Progress Report 2011: Health Renewal in Canada* (Toronto: Health Council of Canada, 2011).

12. S. Heiber and R. Deber, "Banning Extra-Billing in Canada: Just What the Doctor Didn't Order," *Canadian Public Policy* 13, no. 1 (1987), pp. 62–74; M. Begin, "Revisiting the Canada Health Act: What Are the Impediments to Change" (speech given to the Institute for Research on Public Policy, Montreal, February 20, 2002); and Joseph Magnet and Sandra Rodgers-Magnet, "Medicare Under Siege," *The Globe and Mail*, December 29, 1983, p. A7.

13. Roy J. Romanow, *Building on Values: The Future of Health Care in Canada*. Final Report of the Commission on the Future of Health Care in Canada (Ottawa: Government of Canada, November 2002).

14. Health Council of Canada, *Progress Report 2011*; P.C. Hebért and M. Stanbrook, "The Federal Government's Abandonment of Health," *Canadian Medical Association Journal* 182 (December 14, 2010), p. E809; K. Seggewiss, "Variations in Home Care Programs Across the Country Demonstrate Need for National Standards and Pan-Canadian Program," *Canadian Medical Association Journal* 180 (June 9, 2009), pp. E90–E92; M. Stanbrook, P.C. Hebért, J. Couts, N. MacDonald, and K. Flegel, "Can Canada get on with National Pharmacare Already?" *Canadian Medical Association Journal* (April 26, 2011), early release available at www.cmaj.ca. doi:10.1503/cmaj.110643.

15. S. Harper, T. Flanagan, T. Morton, R. Knopff, A. Crooks, and K. Boessenkool, "The Alberta Agenda [An open letter to the Hon. Ralph Klein, Premier of Alberta]," *Policy Options* (April 2001), pp. 16–17.

16. D. Walton and B. Curry, "Alberta Backs Off Private Medicare Blueprint," *The Globe and Mail*, April 21, 2006, p. A1.

17. Conservative Party of Canada, *Here for Canada: Stephen Harper's Low Tax Plan for Jobs and Growth* (Ottawa: The Conservative Party of Canada), p. 30.

18. André Picard, "Don't Let Leaders Duck Health Issues this Election," *The Globe and Mail*, March 31, 2011, L1; and Anonymous, "Hypocrisy on Health Care; Don't Like Private Clinics, Mr. Ignatieff, Then Blame Paul Martin," *National Post*, April 21, 2011, p. A12.

19. Conservative Party of Canada, *Here for Canada*, p. 30; and André Picard, "Why this Health Accord will be Different; CMA expects Government to Forge Series of Bilateral Agreements with Provinces, Rather than Strike National Deal," *The Globe and Mail*, May 28, 2011, p. A16.

20. Canadian Institute for Health Information, *National Health Expenditure Trends, 1975-2010* (Ottawa: Canadian Institute for Health Information, October 2010).

21. M. A. Rodwin, "Why We Need Health Care Reform Now," pp. 597–599; J. Oberlander, "Throwing Darts: America's Elusive Search for Health Care Cost Control," *Journal of Health Politics, Policy and Law* 36 (2011), pp. 477–484; and M. K. Gusmano, "Do We Really Want to Control Health Care Spending?" *Journal of Health Politics, Policy and Law* 36 (2011), pp. 495–500.

22. C. Arnst, "Study Links Medical Costs and Personal Bankruptcy," *Bloomberg Businessweek*, June 4, 2009, available at http://www.businessweek.com/bwdaily/dnflash/content/jun2009/db2009064_666715.htm. Accessed July 13, 2011.

23. Reference re *Canada Assistance Plan* [1991] 2 *Supreme Court Reports*, p. 525.

24. Sujit Choudhry, "The Canada Health Act and the Social Union: The Need for Institutions," *Osgoode Hall Law Journal* 38 (2000), p. 39.

25. Dale Gibson, "The Canada Health Act and the Constitution," *Health Law Journal* 4 (1996), p. 1.

26. Soroka, "Canadian Perceptions of Health Care," p. 35.

27. Ipsos Reid, "Canadians Agree Healthcare Should Be the Priority for Both the Provincial (84%) and Federal Governments (73%)," January 25, 2011, available at http://www.ipsos-na.com/news-polls/pressrelease.aspx?id=5111. Accessed July 13, 2011.

28. Magnet and Rodgers-Magnet, "Medicare Under Siege."

29. *R. v. Crown Zellerbach* [1988] 1 *Supreme Court Reports*, p. 401.

30. Ekos Research Associates, "Romanow Tracking Poll (November 2004)," available at http://www.ekos.com/admin/articles/Romanow24Nov2003.pdf. Accessed March 17, 2005.

31. The Canadian Council For Donation And Transplantation, *Enhancing Tissue Banking In Canada: Phase I Sustainability* (Edmonton: The Canadian Council For Donation And Transplantation, 2007), pp. 1–4; and Conference Of Provincial/Territorial Ministers of Health, "News Release: Health Ministers Continue Working on the National Pharmaceuticals Strategy," July 5, 2006, available at http://www.Scics.Gc.Ca/Cinfo06/830882004_E.Html. Accessed November 1, 2007.

✗ NO

The Case Against a Strong Federal Role in Health Care

PAUL BARKER

In the next few years the two senior orders of government in Canada must meet to discuss significant matters relating to health care. This prospect leads to a question that emerges with any important development in health care: what order of government, federal or provincial, should assume the dominant position in ensuring that Canadians receive effective health care services? Doubtless, some hope that neither prevails—the two work hand in hand, but experience suggests otherwise. In the past, the federal government has been central to the introduction of hospital and physician programs, the core elements of the publicly funded health care system in Canada known as medicare. More recently, it has reached agreements with the provinces that require the latter to introduce health care reforms that are consistent with the wishes of the federal government. Some are comfortable with the federal government in this role and believe that a service as important to all Canadians as health care requires a great deal of direction from the centre. Not only will this increase the chances of ensuring that all parts of the country have access to medically required care, but it will also confirm health care as an important symbol of Canadian citizenship and values.

There are others, however, who are uneasy with a strong federal presence in the area of health care. They believe that such a presence may violate the country's Constitution, which authorizes the provinces to handle most aspects of health care. The federal government has authority to act on public health matters and to provide health services to specific groups. But legal responsibility for the major elements of the Canadian health care system—hospital care, physician services, community-based care, and prescription drugs—rests with the provinces. Those who find little favour in a major federal role in health care also believe that the goal of providing high-quality care will be best achieved by allowing the provinces to head the effort at reforming health care services. The sheer experience and expertise of the provinces, garnered through three decades of directly administering their health plans, almost alone makes the case for this argument. A final contention is that a strong federal role in health care assumes an increasingly unworkable notion of leadership. This notion centres on the need to determine a leader who in turn creates the situation required to achieve the ends of leadership. A newer notion, a preferable one, sees leadership arising from a deliberative process that places little emphasis on the leader. With this latter notion, the argument for a strong central government in health care falls away.

LEGAL ARGUMENT

The legal argument against the primacy of the federal government in health care relies on two considerations. One is that such a role may violate the terms of the Constitution. The written Constitution places the great bulk of responsibility for health care with the provinces, yet federal actions in this area take little notice of the division of powers. The other consideration is that a strong federal presence offends the spirit of the Constitution and its treatment of health care. Even if a constitutional challenge to aggressive federal actions in health care were to fail, it could still be argued that a strong federal role takes insufficient heed of the intent of the Constitution to have the provinces carry the brunt of the load in health care.

Provisions in the Canadian Constitution and accompanying judicial review suggest that responsibility for the Canadian health care system lies mostly with the provinces. Section 92(7) of the *Constitution Act, 1867* states that the provinces have legislative responsibility for hospitals, and case law has interpreted other heads of provincial powers as giving the provinces authority over such matters as the regulation of doctors, the training of health professionals, and the operation of social insurance plans. It thus seems fair to conclude that "[w]hen it comes to health, the provinces hold the front lines."[1] However, it would be wrong to argue from this that a federal presence is obviously unconstitutional, for there are powers in the Constitution that give authority to the federal government to act in the area of health. The most important of these is the federal spending power, which allows the federal government to transfer funds to the provinces and place conditions on the use of these funds as long as these conditions fall short of an attempt, in effect, to regulate in an area of provincial jurisdiction. Many believe that federal conditional grants for health—which have formed the basis for Ottawa's involvement in medicare—respect the limits of the federal spending power.[2] They allow the federal government to shape activities in health care without crossing the line by attempting to effectively legislate elements of provincial health plans. The question of the constitutionality of the federal actions hinges in part on the veracity of this claim.

It seems clear that traditional federal conditional grants for health care are safe from any constitutional challenge. These grants simply stipulate that the provinces follow some quite general requirements in return for receiving financial assistance from the federal government. For instance, the provinces should endeavour to ensure that their plans offer a "comprehensive" set of services and are "universal" in the sense that all residents are covered. Similarly, residents must have "reasonable" access to health care services, and efforts ought to be made to make health benefits "portable" and administered on a nonprofit basis. All of these conditions or requirements give the provinces some flexibility in the management of their plans (or stipulate requirements that no government would do otherwise even in the absence of the stipulations). But other aspects of the federal role paint a different picture. The *Canada Health Act*, a piece of federal legislation, outlines the aforementioned general conditions, but it also includes a further condition: namely, the provincial plans prohibit hospital user fees and physician charges at point of service. This prohibition is achieved by reducing federal grants to the provinces equal to the amount of user fees and physician charges levied in the province; a province that levies, for example, $2 million in hospital user fees loses the same amount in federal funding. This condition, unlike the other conditions in the federal legislation, appears to be more precise in its aim and more determined to shape a particular aspect of provincial plans—in other words, there is no room for flexibility, and hence this condition takes on the character of a regulatory activity. Federal–provincial accords also suggest that the federal government has become more specific in its requests. In the accords, the provisions state that new monies must be spent on particular areas (e.g., primary health care, home care), and some even go so far as to require the purchase of particular items relating to health care (diagnostic imagining machines).[3] As with the prohibition on charges and fees, these too appear to be an attempt to regulate health care through the provinces and hence constitute an unconstitutional use of the federal spending power.

A defence against this last claim can be made based on a distinction between compulsory regulation and voluntary regulation.[4] Clearly, a federal law that forces the provinces to do something within the latter's jurisdiction or directly regulates a matter that is a provincial responsibility would be in violation of the Constitution. This is compulsory regulation. But it is argued that the use of the federal spending power in health care does not engage in this type of regulation. Rather, it engages in a voluntary form of regulation—here, the provinces can either accept or reject the health care conditions. Admittedly, a rejection of federal conditions means less or even no federal money, but still the absence of compulsion is apparent. The problem with this line of defence is that there is an element of compulsion. In light of the high cost of health care, the provinces really have no choice: they must gain access to the federal funds and hence must observe the accompanying conditions. It is an offer the provinces are unable to refuse.

The second consideration in the legal argument against a strong federal role is that such a role is inconsistent with the spirit or overall intent of the Constitution. An impressive number of heads of power in section 92 of the *Constitution Act, 1867* place most of the responsibility for health care services with the provinces. These heads include property and civil rights, matters of a local or private nature, and management of hospitals. Accordingly, surveys of constitutional responsibility of health care inevitably conclude that the overall aim of the Constitution is to allow the provinces to take the lead in health care. Some might argue that this is an artifact of circumstance, that the Fathers of Confederation would have allocated powers differently if they had been able to foresee the import of health care to the nation. But the centrality of the provinces is also a product of judicial review, which is of much more recent vintage. And for some legal scholars, it makes sense to place responsibility with the provinces—the drafters of the *British North America Act* were more prescient than we give them credit for[5] (plus experience suggests amendments would have been made if any serious problem prevailed). A primary federal role thus seems out of place, for the relevant law and the accompanying spirit appear determined to give the provinces pride of place in the area of health care. Of course, it is possible that a strong federal role might be ruled consistent with the letter of the law. The federal spending power, for instance, might be invoked to support aggressive federal actions in the area of health care, and there is case law to back up such an interpretation. In this guise, the spending power means that Ottawa "may attach to any grant or loan any conditions it chooses, including conditions it could not directly legislate."[6] But surely this is equivalent to engaging in an end run on the Constitution, an activity that hardly respects its spirit.

Developments in the first part of the new century supply some evidence for revealing how the spirit of the law goes unrecognized. In 2001, the federal government set up a commission to study the future of health care without any provincial participation in its activities. As Richard Simeon says, it seems strange to examine medicare without the inclusion of government entities most identified with health care.[7] Not surprisingly, the report of the commission talks insistently about the need for federal leadership and a strong presence at the centre.[8] In 2003, the federal and provincial governments agreed to an accord stipulating that new federal monies had to be spent on particular areas, and a year later another accord followed the same line of development.[9] As mentioned already, the accords can be seen in violation of the letter of the law. But perhaps the greater injury is to the spirit, because the accords reverse the process that is to be expected: the federal government submits its plans, and the provinces inevitably accept them. The provinces have attempted to introduce their own plans for reform into the proceedings, but these have been summarily rejected. The accords also made provision for a national body—the Health Council of Canada—whose main task is to monitor the implementation of the provisions contained in the accord of 2003. This, too, represents a failure to appreciate the intent of the Constitution, for the council endeavours to track the behaviour of the provinces and report on any shortfalls. More ambitiously, it also seeks to provide some leadership on issues it deems important to the health of Canadians (for example, waiting lists). The council, while well intentioned, fails to respect the fact that it is the provinces that are largely responsible for the maintenance and development of the Canadian health system. Supporters of the council are quick to point out that the council includes members from provincial governments, but the fact is that the federal government initiated the proposal without effusive support from the provinces (and, indeed, Quebec and Alberta refused to accept the body). As with many developments in health care, acceptance of the council was a price that the provinces had to pay in order to get federal funding.

POLICY ARGUMENT

Any federal state seeks to establish arrangements between the two levels of government to produce the best policies and programs possible. The legal division of powers is one such arrangement. But sometimes a state's constitution fails to allocate responsibilities in a way that provides for good public policy, and a disjunction between the legal and desired division of roles emerges. In this situation, a need to supplement or amend the legal structure becomes evident. However, with respect to health care in Canada, no such disjunction exists. As shown, the Canadian Constitution places responsibility squarely with the provinces, and, as will be shown now, this is an allocation that contributes to an effective and equitable health care system in Canada. A strong federal leadership role in health care is thus not only inconsistent with the Constitution but also detracts from the effort to produce good health care programs in Canada.

The policy argument against a strong federal role in health care begins with a consideration of claims made in favour of giving the provinces primacy in formulating and implementing health care programs. In a federal state, the policy role of the national government can be derived from an attempt on the part of central authorities to address the failings of the provinces; such an exercise thus requires first an understanding of the benefits of leaving policy to the provinces.[10] There are at least three reasons for believing that the aim of producing good health care policy will be best met by strong provincial leadership. One reason is that the provinces are better positioned than the federal government to determine the differing health care preferences of individual Canadians across the country. Although all Canadians wish for an effective health care system, they may differ in how this is best achieved. Some may feel that a strong hospital sector is necessary to achieve this end, while others may prefer a more community-based approach. Similarly, the provinces may differ on the appropriate decision-making structures in relation to health care—nearly all provinces have set up regional health authorities, but the membership, structure, and duties of these bodies are not the same across the country.[11] The fear associated with a strong federal role is that the national government will be insensitive to these differing preferences in its attempt to offer a national health care system; a major attraction of federalism is its capacity to reflect the diversity of a nation, yet a too-strong national government can nullify this quality.

A second and related reason is that the provinces are better informed on what it takes to build a workable health care system. The greater expertise stems from the past thirty years of making and carrying out health care programs. During these years, the federal government has participated in making the Canadian health care system a success, but its role has largely been related to providing for conditional grants—not running health care programs. It has been the banker of health care, not the maker. A case might be made that the federal government was not at an informational disadvantage in the early stages of developing this country's health care system. But medicare in Canada has long left this stage of development and now finds itself in a period of renewal, which requires a level of expertise derived from close experience working with health care programs. Such challenges as reorganizing the delivery of primary health care (including the re-defining of responsibilities of health care workers), rationalizing the supply of hospital services, and determining the efficacy of medical procedures are hardly suited for an order of government with little familiarity with the intricacies of health care services. Moreover, the informational requirements also extend to an appreciation of the political dynamics associated with health care reform. It is not enough to know what has to be done: success in health care also depends on knowing how it is to be done. And, again, the provincial governments are better positioned to understand the local politics of health care.

A third and final reason for provincial primacy in health policy is that it increases the chances of policy experimentation. A strong federal role does not necessarily rule out experimentation, but a strong provincial role guarantees a country with ten laboratories in which to test new ideas. The attraction here is that one or two provinces may experiment with a proposed change in health care and not put the entire health care system in harm's way. If the innovation tests well, the other provinces can elect to incorporate it into their health care systems; if it fails, then little damage is done. A famous U.S. Supreme Court justice nicely captures the essence of this third benefit of provincial primacy:

> It is one of the happy incidents of the Federal system that a single coura-geous state [or province] may, if its citizens choose, serve as a laboratory, and try moral, social, and economic experiments without risk to the rest of the country.[12]

At present, there is evidence of the desire of some provinces to experiment. Among these provinces, Alberta is arguably the most ambitious. At times, it has believed that medicare would benefit if the private sector were more greatly involved in health care through the provision of necessary health care services. The province has also believed that various types of direct patient charges might ease the pressure on provincial health care plans. Most experts find little research to support such initiatives, but the latter have not been thoroughly tested in Canada. Most recently, Alberta eliminated regional health authorities—entities to be found in nearly all provinces—and replaced them with one single health care board. Again, Alberta has provided an opportunity to learn. Experimentation can help eliminate the uncertainty about privatization and do so without incurring the possibility of injury to the entire Canadian health care system.

The preceding suggests that substantial policy benefits arise from giving the provinces primacy policy over health care. It is also true, however, that this same arrangement can lead to some costs. Any significant differences in provincial health care programs may dissuade some Canadians from moving from one province to another—for example, to take a new job. This would be an undesirable development, because a smooth-functioning market needs people to use their skills in the most productive way. A province may also make decisions that have unwanted effects on other provinces; for instance, it may refuse to provide full health care coverage to residents visiting from other parts of the country. The aforementioned costs are associated with losses in efficiency, in that provincial decisions on health care may have negative effects on the allocation of scarce resources in the country. But the more important cost might be in relation to equity and the aim of any nation to instill an element of fairness in its provision of public services throughout the country. Provinces acting on their own without central direction may produce a health system that fails to provide all Canadians with a set of roughly comparable health care services. Considerations of fairness suggest that it is appropriate that health care programs—in either their structure or effect—be fairly similar across Canada. Unity considerations also come into play at this point: a country with widely disparate levels of services may produce tensions and animosities between regions that threaten the viability of the country.

All of these possible costs point toward the need for a federal role that reduces the prevalence of the difficulties created by the provinces. But this need not be a strong role. What is required here is what the federal government has done in the past, which is to set out some general conditions that remind the provinces of their commitment to making medically necessary health care accessible to all Canadians. And the emphasis here is on a *gentle* reminder, for the provinces mostly act as one in relation to the broad strokes of health policy (though, as mentioned, differences in details may appear). A perusal of provincial health plans reveals a great deal of similarity in terms of their basic contours, and a review of provincial planning for the future again reveals similar thinking (reform of physician and hospital care, more community-based services, greater emphasis on promotion and prevention). In the past decade, the federal government has felt it necessary at one time or another to become more aggressive in monitoring the provinces and to make available monies only for certain services and programs. But many of these services and programs have been under consideration by the provinces for several years. There is, in other words, no great need for a federal role in health care policy that goes beyond the general conditions contained in the *Canada Health Act*. And even if provincial plans were to diversify more in the future, an argument could still be made for limiting Ottawa's role. Canadians may decide that the benefits of differentiation more than compensate for the loss in comparability. Alberta may begin to charge patients directly, Quebec may pursue more aggressively its use of for-profit imaging clinics, and Ontario may lean heavily on nurse practitioners to solve its perceived shortage of doctors—and Canadians may accept these developments with little notice. The balance between achieving similar health plans and allowing the provinces to go their own way has historically been in favour of the former, but this balance is not set in stone. Indeed, opinion surveys show that Canadians are willing to try new ways of delivering and financing health care.[13]

LEADERSHIP ARGUMENT

Underlying the position that supports a strong role for the federal government in health is a traditional concept of leadership. This concept sees the leader giving direction to followers in order to achieve an end that both leader and follower accept. Sometimes the follower needs a lot of direction, to the point of even playing little or no part in the formulation of the end and the means to achieve it; other times the follower requires only motivation to take the necessary action; and in still others there is a relationship somewhere between the first two possibilities. However, what is common to all the variations or definitions is a clear leader. This is the notion that supporters of a strong central government adopt. In the past years, a different way of looking at leadership has emerged in the scholarly treatment of leadership.[14] It can be identified through definitions of leadership that are without reference to a leader or a reference that breaks from tradition. This new perspective wishes to do a couple of things. One is to sever the link between leader and leadership and the conviction that the latter can only come about with the leader producing leadership. Another related task is to emphasize leadership as an effect of the group in question. It is not something caused by an entity—a leader—but rather the product of a process whereby a group of people, regions, provinces, or other entities try to accomplish some purpose. What we have here is not leaderless leadership, because a formal leader may still be present or someone in the group may emerge to perform this role; but what is missing is the emphasis on a leader and his or her designation at the start of whatever task is at hand. This new concept arises partly from the belief that it more accurately captures the true dynamics of leadership. Perhaps more interesting, it seems more consistent with societies that have higher levels of education and a more richly democratic culture. Put differently, it rejects the heroic-leader model of leadership, the idea that leadership revolves around the presence and need for great men and women.

This new notion is, of course, consistent with the position that the federal role should remain less than large. It means that the leadership for health care in Canada can emerge out of provinces pursuing goals that almost every Canadian appreciates (and other developed nations, too). It means looking to the provinces for innovation—a form of leadership—which can inspire other provinces to do the same. The federal government can also be involved here, but what is rejected is the kind of attitude that causes us to first look to the federal government. What is to be avoided is the Royal Commission or other similar body at the federal level that believes it can rush in and supply a blueprint for health care reform. It also means bringing the provinces and Ottawa together in various forums to talk about health care and to learn from each other, to exploit the "wisdom of crowds."[15] It may even mean spending less time respecting the *Canada Health Act* and more about "rollin' up the sleeves" to solve the problems of medicare. The legislation represents an important symbol of Canada's commitment to a public health care system, but it cannot become a distraction or an obstacle to new thinking.

Close observers of federal–provincial relations may identify this new leadership with a health care arrangement that is not really new, at least for federalism in Canada. In the mid-1990s, the federal government appeared to give up its role in health care (and other areas) because of large deficits and forces of decentralization in the Canadian federation.[16] In this environment, proposals arose that urged the provinces to move ahead on health care and other areas on their own and achieve a social and economic union through inter-provincial coordination. The provinces might create, literally, a new *Canada Health Act* (for example, the *Well-Being Act*)[17] that goes past the old medicare system and erects a framework that focuses not just on physician and hospital care. As one such proposal suggested for health care and other affected social programs, the provinces would put together an "[e]nforceable inter-provincial accord whereby the provinces jointly implement and maintain a framework of principles and standards/equivalences that will guarantee across Canada rights such as mobility and portability."[18] A little later, the provinces established a body called the Council of the Federation, and it, too, had the flavour of going it alone on public policy. Though similar to the new concept of leadership, these proposals venture beyond what we propose here. The new concept seeks not to exclude players, but rather to understand that pinpointing a leader is hardly the most crucial thing to do. In some respects, this new concept of leadership is consistent with a relationship similar to the present one for health care minus the attempts of Ottawa to target funding for areas which it thinks require attention.

At first glance, it may seem incongruous—absurd, in other words—to tie responsibility for a health care system with scholarly work on leadership. The one is earthy and practical, the other theoretical and without any immediate consequence. But sometimes to make an argument a different approach is vital. This essay argues for a less-than-dominant position for the federal government in health using well-known claims about constitutional authority and economic efficiency. Though these claims are with substance, our familiarity with them makes them less than wholly persuasive (and the same goes for claims and arguments on the other side of the debate). Accordingly, what is required is a claim that approaches the issue differently. This is what considerations of leadership try to do for health care. Ultimately, the debate about health care in Canada is about leadership, so the aforementioned absurdity begins to dissipate. And, increasingly, research suggests that in our modern age leadership should not take the form of a single leader, but be the product of a process of deliberation and experimentation. Basically, Ottawa is unable to assume a prominent position because this type of position is inconsistent with what leadership is becoming.

RECENT DEVELOPMENTS

Recent developments suggest a federal government more willing to act in a manner that respects both the legal preeminence and policy expertise of the provinces in health care. On being elected in 2006, the government of Stephen Harper pursued a promise of patient wait-time guarantees by which provinces would set a reasonable wait time for specified procedures and arrange for care elsewhere if this time were exceeded.[19] However, it proceeded cautiously on this matter in light of provincial demands for additional federal funding to finance the guarantees; the tepid embrace of the guarantees also reflected the beliefs of the prime minister, who felt that "the federal government should live up to its financial commitments but should otherwise let the provinces exercise their constitutional jurisdiction [in health care]."[20] Eventually, by April 2007, the federal government and the individual provinces and territories had come to an agreement on patient wait-times guarantee. In exchange for new federal assistance, each of the provinces (and territories) would set out wait-time guarantees for one of the designated priority fields in health care by 2010.[21]

An equally sensible and recent federal approach to health care can also be seen in the reaction of Ottawa to provincial health initiatives. In 2006, the Alberta government announced a new health plan containing some noteworthy proposals. One proposal allowed doctors to practise in both the public and private health care systems; another authorized the purchase of private insurance for medically required care; still another stressed the need to consider reducing the number of services insured under the medicare system.[22] In the past, similar provocations on the part of Alberta had led to a federal government aggressively demanding a withdrawal of the proposals (or actions) and threatening to withhold federal funds on the grounds that the *Canada Health Act* had been violated. However, this time the federal government, as with the guarantees, acted more cautiously. The federal health minister said he would have to look at the proposals carefully and see whether they fit with the aforementioned federal legislation.[23] The prime minister then followed up with a letter to the premier of Alberta, arguing that the province's proposals would generate some unwelcome outcomes.[24] A short time later, the Alberta government withdrew its proposals.

At the same time, the Quebec government announced some new health measures in response to an earlier decision of the Supreme Court of Canada. The court had found the province's prohibition on the purchase of private health insurance to be in violation of the Quebec Charter of Rights, and the fear was that the decision would open up the floodgates in Quebec to the development of a parallel private health care system accessible only to the well-off. The response of the Quebec government was to provide immediate access to private insurance, but only for specified procedures that could be provided only by doctors operating outside the provincial health plan. It also set out a health care guarantee by which patients could secure care in a private facility in cases where wait times in the public system exceeded a certain period of time.[25] The actions of the Quebec government amounted to an attempt "to lift the ban on private insurance without undermining the public health system."[26] Watching these developments in Quebec, the federal government might have been tempted to assume an aggressive stance, one that placed the entire emphasis on the protection of the public health care system and on strict adherence to the *Canada Health Act*. But Ottawa understood that the courts had placed the province in a difficult situation and that the Quebec government had to be accorded some flexibility. Even more recently, Quebec proposed a user fee for medical services, an action that might have precipitated an aggressive federal response. But Ottawa waited patiently for political sense to prevail—and it did. Under public pressure, the provincial government declined to move forward with the proposal.[27]

There have been other relevant developments in the last few years—the increasing presence of private health clinics, for example—but arguably the most important recent development relevant to health care is in the developing stage. In 2014, fiscal arrangements facilitating the transfer of monies to the provinces for health care must be renegotiated (or renewed). Differing viewpoints have already emerged on how Ottawa should approach the negotiations. Some suggest that Ottawa should play fiscal hardball with the provinces and say no to increases comparable to current rates.[28] Others urge the federal government to replace the Byzantine-like health transfers with a straightforward transfer of GST revenues (seemingly with no conditions).[29] Still others insist that Ottawa make the provinces more accountable for their use of federal transfers, something that they have allegedly failed to do with the current agreement. As for the newly elected Harper government, it has already promised to maintain the level of funding under the current arrangement and ensure that the provinces are responsible for their actions (again, more of the same). Also, the Conservative Party platform for the recent election said the government would "respect the fact that health care is an area of provincial jurisdiction" and that it would also "respect limits on the federal spending power."[30] These are sentiments of a government willing to allow the provinces to largely figure out what to do about the health care challenge in Canada.

CONCLUSION

For the most part, the federal role in health care in Canada has been to provide the provinces with financial assistance along with the stipulation that provincial health plans observe some general conditions. This is a role that recognizes the primacy of the provinces in health care. The provinces are allowed to shape their plans with little interference from federal authorities, a situation consistent with the constitutional framework and with the requirements of sound public policy. It also increases the chances that the national government will concern itself with truly national matters and not be distracted by issues that can be handled by the other order of government. Accordingly, a strong federal role in health care upsets traditional arrangements for health care and puts at risk the benefits of these arrangements. At present, some feel that the challenges facing the health care system require federal leadership; Ottawa needs to use its spending power (and financial resources) to force the provinces to make the necessary reforms in their health care plans. But the policy benefits of such action will be negligible—the provinces are better positioned to reform medicare—and it will be contrary to the spirit of the Constitution.

NOTES

1. Andre Braen, "Health and the Distribution of Powers in Canada," in Tom McIntosh, Pierre-Gerlier Forest, and Gregory P. Marchildon, eds., *The Governance of Health Care in Canada*, Romanow Papers, Vol. III, (Toronto: University of Toronto Press, 2003), p. 30.

2. See, for example, Peter Hogg, *Constitutional Law of Canada*, loose-leaf ed. (Toronto: Thomson Carswell, 1997), p. 6.8.

3. Canadian Intergovernmental Conference Secretariat, First Ministers' Meeting Communiqué on Health, September 11, 2000, available at http://www.scics.gc.ca/english/conferences.asp?a=viewdocument&tid=1144. Accessed August 15, 2011; and 2003 First Ministers' Accord on Health Care Renewal, February 5, 2003, available at http://www.hc-sc.gc.ca/hcs-sss/delivery-prestation/fptcollab/2003accord/index-eng.php. Accessed August 15, 2011.

4. Hogg, *Constitutional Law of Canada*, p. 6.8.

5. Braen, "Health and the Distribution of Powers in Canada," p. 42.

6. Peter Hogg, quoted in Keith Banting and Robin Boadway, "Defining the Sharing Community: The Federal Role in Health Care," in Harvey Lazar and France St-Hilaire, eds., *Money, Politics and Health Care: Reconstructing the Federal–Provincial Partnership* (Montreal and Kingston: The Institute for Research on Public Policy and the Institute of Intergovernmental Relations, 2004), p. 6.

7. Richard Simeon, "We've Tied the Commission's Hands," *The Globe and Mail*, April 13, 2001, p. A13.

8. Romanow Commission on the Future of Health Care in Canada, *Building on Values: The Future of Health Care in Canada* (Ottawa: Government of Canada, November 2002), ch. 2.

9. First Ministers' Meeting, A 10 Year Plan to Strengthen Health Care, September 2004, available at http://www.hc-sc.gc.ca/hcs-sss/delivery-prestation/fptcollab/2004-fmm-rpm/index-eng.php. Accessed August 15, 2011.

10. Robin Boadway, "The Folly of Decentralizing the Canadian Federation," *Dalhousie Review* 75, no. 3 (Winter 1996), pp. 333–334.

11. Carolyn Tuohy, *Accidental Logics: The Dynamics of Change in the Health Care Arena in the United States, Great Britain, and Canada* (New York: Oxford University Press, 1999), p. 98.

12. Harvey Rosen et al., *Public Finance in Canada*, 2nd ed. (Toronto: McGraw-Hill Ryerson, 2003), p. 166.

13. Matthew Mendelsohn, *Canadians' Thoughts on Their Health Care System: Preserving the Canadian Model through Innovation* (Saskatoon: Commission on the Future of Health Care in Canada, June 2002), pp. 9–13.

14. For a discussion of this shift, see "Leadership Definition," in Antonio Marturano and Jonathan Gosling, eds. *Leadership: The Key Concepts* (London and New York: Routledge, 2008).

15. James Surowiecki, *The Wisdom of Crowds* (New York: Doubleday, 2004).

16. Paul Barker, "Disentangling the Federation: Social Policy and Fiscal Federalism," in M. Westmacott and H. Mellon, eds., *Challenges in Canadian Federalism* (Toronto: Pearson Education, 1998).

17. Institute of Intergovernmental Relations, *Assessing Access: Towards a New Social Union* (Kingston: Institute of Intergovernmental Relations, Queen's University, 1996), p. 92.

18. Ibid., p. 89.

19. Conservative Party of Canada, *Stand Up for Canada: Federal Election Platform*, 2006, p. 30.

20. Tom Flanagan, *Harper's Team: Behind the Scenes in the Conservative Rise to Power* (Montreal and Kingston: McGill-Queen's University Press, 2007), p. 79. The sentiment is reflected in the Conservative Party's policy of "Open Federalism." According to Young, the basic intent of the policy is "that the central government should intrude less in areas of provincial jurisdiction, and restore a respectful balance between the two orders of government." See Robert Young, "Open Federalism and Canadian Municipalities," in *Open Federalism: Interpretations, Significance* (Kingston: Institute of Intergovernmental Relations, 2006), p. 17.

21. Andrew Mayeda, "Tories Claim Victory on Wait Times," *National Post*, April 5, 2007, p. A4.

22. Government of Alberta, *Health Policy Framework*, February 2006, available at http://www.health.alberta.ca/initiatives/health-policy-2006.html. Accessed August 15, 2011.

23. Gloria Galloway, "'We're Studying It,' Ottawa Says," *The Globe and Mail*, March 1, 2006, p. A4.

24. Brian Laghi, "PM Warns Klein of Gaps in Care, Queue Jumping in Health Plan," *The Globe and Mail*, April 8, 2006, p. A9.

25. Government of Quebec, *Guaranteeing Access: Meeting the Challenges of Equity, Efficiency and Quality*, Consultation Document (Government of Quebec, February 2006), available at http://www.fmrq.qc.ca/formation-medicale/actualitesDetails_ang.cfm?noActualite=58. Accessed August 15, 2011.

26. Rheal Seguin, "Quebec Government Walked Fine Line to Shape Health Plan," *The Globe and Mail*, February 18, 2006, p. A7.

27. Ingrid Peritz, "Quebec Drops Plan for $25 User Fee for Doctors' Visits," *The Globe and Mail*, September 23, 2010, p. A9.

28. Editorial, "Just Say No to 6 Per Cent," *The Globe and Mail*, April 26, 2011, p. A16.

29. Andre Picard, "Why this Health Accord will be Different," *The Globe and Mail*, May 28, 2011, p. A16.

30. Conservative Party of Canada, *Here for Canada: Stephen Harper's Low-Tax Plan for Jobs and Economic Growth* (Ottawa: The Conservative Party of Canada, 2011), p. 30.

POSTSCRIPT

In a calm and measured way, Andrew Heard and Daniel Cohn show why many believe the federal government ought to play an important role in health care in Canada. Ottawa was integral to the introduction of medicare, and it has been essential to pushing reluctant provinces into adopting necessary health care changes. It has also been there when the very survival of medicare seemed at risk. For those who fear that the federal government may be treading all over the Constitution, Heard and Cohn argue convincingly that such fears are unfounded. There are, however, a few spots in which the two authors might be more convincing. They say that the provinces are not up to the task of making necessary reforms, yet one wonders whether the provinces are truly incapacitated. No doubt the two authors would point to a report of the Health Council of Canada that gives less than glowing marks to provincial action on important health initiatives. But the same report records some provincial progress and says nothing about actions that fall outside the purview of the council. The two also state that the provinces are free to reject federal transfers if they dislike the attached conditions but acknowledge that these transfers are essential to the well-being of many provinces. Heard and Cohn are also impressed with the fact that the provinces possess a great deal of autonomy in comparison with sub-national states in other federations. But it fails to follow that this opens the door for a stronger federal presence in Canada. Perhaps the Canadian provinces are just better able to handle health care than their counterparts located elsewhere.

In his effort, Paul Barker is concerned that a strong national role will run roughshod over the spirit of the Constitution, if not the actual provisions and judicial interpretations. He also seems impressed with the ability of the provinces to make sound health policies. All of this is perhaps worthy of consideration, but the arguments are vulnerable. As Barker admits, the legal case against a strong federal role seems to rest largely on the rather shaky ground that somehow the spirit of the Constitution—which is not really defined—is somehow violated. He also thinks a strong provincial role is necessary to preserve different approaches to the delivery and financing of health care but later on says that provincial health plans are largely similar. Do we really need to preserve the possibility of differences when few differences actually appear in provincial plans? Finally, the connection between leadership theory and federal–provincial relations is a bit of a stretch. The one is the product mostly of controlled experiments; the other might also be considered an experiment, but hardly a controlled one.

Students interested in this issue might begin with articles that provide an overview of federalism and health care in Canada: Antonia Maioni, "Health Care," in Herman Bakvis and Grace Skogstad, eds., *Canadian Federalism: Performance, Effectiveness and Legitimacy*, 2nd ed. (Toronto: Oxford University Press, 2007) and Katherine Fierlbeck, *Health Care in Canada: A Citizen's Guide to Policy and Politics* (Toronto: University of Toronto Press, 2011), ch. 2 would work well here. Constitutional authority over health care is a key part of the debate, so one should refer to Peter Hogg, *Constitutional Law of Canada*, student ed. (Toronto: Carswell, 2007), chs. 6 and 3, and Andre Braen, "Health and the Distribution of Powers in Canada," in Tom McIntosh, Pierre-Gerlier Forest, and Gregory P. Marchildon, eds., *The Governance of Health Care in Canada* (Toronto: University of Toronto Press, 2004).

To participate in this debate, students need to understand the policy implications of assigning health to one level of government or another. Robin Boadway and his colleagues have provided a useful framework for addressing this most important issue: Robin Boadway, "Recent Developments in the Economics of Federalism," in Harvey Lazar, ed., *Canada: The State of the Federation 1999/2000* (Montreal and Kingston: McGill-Queen's University Press, 2000), and Keith Banting and Robin Boadway, "Defining the Sharing Community: The Federal Role in Health Care," in Harvey Lazar and France St-Hilaire, eds., *Money, Politics and Health Care: Reconstructing the Federal–Provincial Partnership* (Montreal and Kingston: Institute for Research on Public Policy and the Institute of Intergovernmental Relations, 2004).

For differing views on the actual impact of allocating major responsibility for health care to one level of government or the other, students should consult the following publications: Gregory P. Marchildon, *Three Choices for the Future of Medicare* (Ottawa: Caledon Institute of Social Policy, April 2004); Michael Rachlis, *The Federal Government Can and Should Lead the Renewal of Canada's Health Policy* (Ottawa: Caledon Institute of Social Policy, February 2003); Commission on the Future of Health Care in Canada, *Building on Values: The Future of Health Care in Canada Final Report* (Saskatoon: Commission on the Future of Health Care in Canada, November 2002), ch. 2; various chapters in Tom McIntosh, Pierre-Gerlier Forest, and Gregory P. Marchildon, eds., *The Governance of Health Care in Canada* (Toronto: University of Toronto Press, 2004); Antonia Maioni, "Decentralization in Health Policy: Comments on the ACCESS Proposals (and comments by John Richards)," in Robert Young, ed., *Stretching the Federation: The Art of the State in Canada* (Kingston: Institute of Intergovernmental Relations, 1999); and Thomas J. Courchene, *Redistributing Money and Power: A Guide to the Canada Health and Social Transfer* (Toronto: C.D. Howe Institute, 1995), ch. 5.

Finally, an appreciation of the history of medicare in Canada is required. For this, one should read Malcolm G. Taylor, *Health Insurance and Canadian Public Policy: The Seven Decisions That Created the Canadian Health Insurance System* (Montreal and Kingston: Institute of Public Administration of Canada, 1978). There are more recent histories available, but Taylor's work is magisterial in its telling of the story of medicare. For an up-to-date review of the Canadian health care system, see Gregory Marchildon, *Health Systems in Transition: Canada* (Toronto: University of Toronto Press, 2006).

PART THREE

POLITICAL INSTITUTIONS AND PROCESSES

Is the Prime Minister Too Powerful?

Is a Majority Government More Effective Than a Minority Government?

Should Party Discipline Be Relaxed?

Is a Mixed-Member Proportional Electoral System in Canada's Interest?

Should Women Focus on Small-p Politics?

Robyn Mackenzie/Shutterstock

Is the Prime Minister Too Powerful?

✔ **YES**
HUGH MELLON, "Coming to Terms with Political Realities:
Exploring the Breadth of Prime-Ministerial Power"

✘ **NO**
PAUL BARKER, "Limits on the Power of the Prime Minister"

Students of Canadian politics appreciate that the prime minister is at the centre of political life in Canada. As leader of the national government, the prime minister determines the priorities that set the public agenda. The prime minister is also able to make appointments to important positions, and acts to represent Canada on the world stage. Perhaps the greatest indicator of the power and influence of the first minister is his or her sheer prominence. Canadians might be hard-pressed to name the provincial premiers or the chief justice of the Supreme Court of Canada, but few, if any, would experience the same problem with the prime minister.

There is thus little debate about the significance of the prime minister in Canadian politics. What might be debatable, however, is whether the prime minister dominates to the point that he threatens the healthy functioning of democracy in Canada. There are some who believe, strongly, that such is the case. Canada does not really have parliamentary government, they say, but in fact has what might be called "prime-ministerial" government. According to this perspective, the prime minister encounters few constraints on the exercise of his powers. All the typical powers associated with the prime minister—determining appointments, setting the overall direction of the country, representing Canada's interests in foreign dealings—are exercised with very little opposition. The Latin phrase *primus inter pares* ("first among equals") was once used to describe the prime minister's status: the prime minister was powerful (*primus*), but he faced individuals or challengers who were not merely his subordinates but his equals (*pares*) in some respects. Now, it is argued, the prime minister has no equals—he is *primus*, without any qualification.

Any proposition is only as strong as the supporting evidence. A look at Canadian political life does suggest some backing for the thesis of a prime-ministerial government. The prime minister appears able to pass bills into law with little difficulty. He or she also decides who shall sit in cabinet and who shall hold the senior positions in the judiciary and the public service. The prime minister is front-and-centre in the media's coverage of Canadian politics; indeed, he or she might be considered a celebrity or a superstar. The fact that Canadians look instantly to the prime minister in times of trouble also speaks to his or her primacy. When the great recession of 2008 began, most Canadians turned to the prime minister for guidance on how the country should respond.

The question, however, is whether all this is enough to confirm the prime-ministerial government thesis. The corroborating evidence, to be sure, is impressive, but is it sufficiently impressive to allow us to conclude that Canada is a country with a leader who faces few limits to his or her power? Some answer no. How, for example, can one ignore the influence of provincial premiers? Canadians may find it difficult to name political leaders in the provinces, but there is little doubt that premiers can frustrate prime-ministerial ambitions. Similarly, members of the prime minister's own government, the cabinet ministers, can make matters difficult for the prime minister. One day the prime minister appears invincible, the next day quite vulnerable. Such is the life of any celebrity.

In the readings, Hugh Mellon, a professor at King's University College at the University of Western Ontario, contends that the prime minister has an undue degree of power. Paul Barker, one of the editors of *Crosscurrents*, argues that supporters of the thesis of prime-ministerial government exaggerate the power open to the prime minister.

✔ **YES**

Coming to Terms with Political Realities: Exploring the Breadth of Prime-Ministerial Power

HUGH MELLON

From Confederation in 1867 until 2011, a period of 144 years, only twenty-two individuals have served as Canada's prime minister. In one of the world's longest, consistently democratic political systems, fewer than two dozen individuals have held this position. The small number becomes even more striking when you realize that numerous occupants held the office for only a short time and that only a handful of skilled politicians occupied this esteemed position for significant periods of time. John A. Macdonald served from 1867 until 1873 and then from 1878 until his death in 1891, while Laurier was prime minister from 1896 to 1911. Diefenbaker (1957–1963) won two minority governments plus a huge majority in 1958. Borden (1911–1920), St. Laurent (1948–1957), and Mulroney (1984–1993) each won two national elections while Pierre Trudeau held the post from 1968 to 1979 and then from 1980 to 1984, and Jean Chrétien (1993–2003) won three successive majorities. Stephen Harper (2006 onward) won two minority governments and then triumphed with a majority victory in 2011. Yet even these achievements are humbled by William Lyon Mackenzie King, who endured over two decades as prime minister (1921–1926, 1926–1930, and 1935–1948). In short, these ten individuals held the position for well over 80 percent of the time Canada has existed as a self-governing nation. This is a remarkable statistic, one that should give rise to reflection upon the position of prime minister and the autonomy and authority that accompany it.

Even if we are prepared to accept that these individuals were superior political candidates and/or leaders (admittedly a contentious hypothesis), it is sobering to contemplate the limited number of occupants of this powerful position. What happens when so much power is confined for substantial periods to a limited number of individuals? Can we hold governments accountable when we have so few individuals with firsthand experience? Do prime ministers truly represent a popular mandate, or are they the political beneficiaries of an elite system marked by disciplined parties and declining public participation in voting? Bear in mind that voter turnout in the last four Canadian federal elections has ranged between 58 and 65 percent, and in the 2011 Ontario provincial election, was below 50 percent, hardly evidence of mass public participation. Are there institutional and political limits sufficient to regulate the behaviour and occasional excesses of Canada's prime ministers? Taken together, these questions and concerns lead to fears that prime ministers are able to consolidate an excess of power, a situation fraught with significant potential dangers. The argument to be made here is that the limitations provided by the political system upon their power are woefully inadequate, and that this reality should concern all those interested in the state of Canada's democratic experience.

When preparing this argument, it was fascinating to take a moment to glance at the Government of Canada website devoted to the prime minister. Readers are urged to do the same, for the self-presentation of the office is enlightening. On October 16, 2007, the day of a Throne Speech and the convening of Parliament, the site was replete with assertions that the prime minister was taking dramatic action on major issues. The prime minister, Stephen Harper, was accorded credit for commissioning a panel to report on Canada's participation in the Afghanistan conflict, announcing a crackdown on drug crimes, promoting a "bolstering" of Arctic sovereignty, and sorting out matters relating to the Atlantic Accord with the premier of Nova Scotia. Repeating this informal test when updating this chapter on June 27, 2011, one finds similar indications of prime-ministerial primacy in national life. There is reference to the prime minister unveiling the arrangements for an upcoming royal tour, as well as his observance of the national day of remembrance for victims of terrorism. Clicking upon the prime ministerial prompt brings further evidence of prime-ministerial leadership supplemented by a designated prime-ministerial photo of the day and the awarding of the "Prime Minister's Volunteer Awards." The accompanying visuals accentuate the prime minister's visibility. Browsers are given the impression of a powerful, overarching prime minister who is leading the action on issues across the board. The combined message is one of assertive action and central direction.

This impressionistic approach to the topic is intriguing but not conclusive, so therefore let us move to making the case for the excesses of prime-ministerial power. Those looking to test the extent of this power have different avenues available to them. What will be attempted here is to examine in turn those sources often cited as offering countervailing influences or checks upon that power in order to show their individual and collective weaknesses as sources of restraint. If each of these sources of control are found wanting, then this consolidates the argument of overreaching prime-ministerial ambition and power. Each of the presumed checks is not without some influence, but as a control upon prime-ministerial determination, they have noteworthy limitations, and while they may on occasion serve as a major check, this is likely more the exception; their ongoing strength should not always be assumed. The sources of restraint to be considered are (1) cabinet and the leading members of the prime minister's political party; (2) public opinion and the constitutional requirement of periodic elections; (3) Parliament and its institutionalized opposition and features such as Question Period; (4) the media; and (5) the workings of Canadian federalism. But first a few words upon the role and constitutional authority of the prime minister are in order.

Those wishing to engage in the debate over prime-ministerial power will find a significant and growing literature on the role and authority of the Canadian prime minister. Notable works include Donald J. Savoie's *Power: Where Is It?* and his *Governing from the Centre*,[1] Jeffrey Simpson's *The Friendly Dictatorship*,[2] and the various prime-ministerial memoirs and autobiographies. In fact, as this essay goes to print, there are two new memoirs hot off the press: Brian Mulroney's *Memoirs: 1939-1993*[3] and Jean Chrétien's *My Years as Prime Minister*.[4] Those looking for a biographical treatment, on the other hand, might try Lawrence Martin's two-volume life of Chrétien (with the prime-ministerial portion covered in volume two, *Iron Man: The Defiant Reign of Jean Chrétien*) or his study of the Stephen Harper government, *Harperland: The Politics of Control*.[5] These and other related works merit examination in light of the debate presented here.

PRIME MINISTERS AND THEIR AUTHORITY

Prime ministers govern formally upon the basis of their ability to lead a ministry capable of retaining majority support in the elected House of Commons. This role is the product of British traditions and constitutional conventions, for, as Peter Hogg reminds us, the *British North America Act*, which ushered in Confederation in 1867, makes no formal reference to the position. Hogg states, "[T]here is no mention of the Prime Minister, or of the cabinet, or of the dependence of the cabinet on the support of a majority in the House of Commons: the composition of the actual executive authority and its relationship to the legislative authority were left in the form of unwritten conventions—as in the United Kingdom."[6] From these beginnings has sprung an office possessing wide-ranging and influential political tools. Parliamentary arrangements fuse power while disciplined political parties make control easier. As a result, the prime minister can oversee both executive authority and legislative deliberations. Today the office wields tremendous control, leading Jeffrey Simpson, a senior Ottawa observer, to conclude, "The Canadian prime minister is more powerful within this system than any democratically elected leader in other advanced industrial countries."[7] American separation of powers and the lesser degree of discipline among British political parties offer stronger restraints than those encountered by a Canadian prime minister.

Prime ministers possess an impressive political arsenal. One highly significant tool is the power to make a multitude of senior governmental and public service appointments both at home and abroad. Among the many prime-ministerial appointees are cabinet members, ambassadors, parliamentary secretaries, the Governor General, senators, and Crown corporation executives. Earlier reference was made to Prime Minister Harper's website and the announcement of an advisory panel of elite Canadians to advise on the Canadian involvement in Afghanistan. The website makes clear that this is a prime-ministerial announcement, and there is a link to a visual in which Harper is seen announcing the panel's creation. When you take this power in its totality, its potential is obvious. Those wishing to get ahead will soon realize whose opinion will determine their possibilities. Party workers dreaming of a Senate appointment or cabinet advancement likewise know where their appointment will come from. Also note that there are fewer restraints upon the appointment power than are found in the U.S. congressional system, in which various key appointments need ratification by another branch of government.

The prime minister exercises parliamentary leadership and directs the flow of events, aided by cabinet and the whip's office. In practice, attention and clout gravitate to the prime minister and his or her centrality to Question Period, media coverage, and debate. What is more, remember that the upper house in the bicameral legislative arrangement, the Senate, is appointed by the prime minister. The house, crafted to offer "sober second thought" coupled with regional representation, is composed of prime-ministerial appointees. Opportunities for conflicts of interest are immediately evident.

Prime ministers have in the past also possessed the power to set the dates for elections, which allows them to capitalize upon the movement of polls or to catch the opposition unprepared. This power may be constrained by the movement to fixed elections at the federal level proposed by the Harper government. Whatever the case regarding fixed or flexible election dates, there is an imbalance in resources between a calculating prime minister and those in opposition.

Prime ministers chair cabinet, which may often entail further strategic advantages, such as the authority to alter cabinet membership, the power to set items on or off a particular agenda, and the ability to offer support or roadblocks to particular ministers. Prime ministers have the authority to appoint senior officials and bureaucrats throughout the government. This comes with ongoing authority to monitor their performance should an issue or political pressures warrant it. These powers are important for several reasons. One is the obvious asymmetrical relationship born of having chosen an individual for a post while retaining the ability to elevate or discipline that person over time. A second is the likelihood of a line of communication from the prime minister through the officials allowing the prime minister to bypass a cabinet minister or ministers. In an environment in which knowledge is power, the availability of multiple information sources is a significant asset. A third reason is the use of appointments and job appraisals to solidify the ranks of loyalists and serve the interests of partisanship and the leader. Political office involves the use of teams of advisors and loyalists, and patronage is one of the most often selected lubricants for the inner workings of this dynamic team and coalition building.

Opposition parties often score points over the presumed excesses of prime-ministerial appointments, but the advantages of the appointment power and back-channels of information are considerable. Jean Chrétien, for example, was one more prime minister who had donned the mantle of outraged defender of the public interest while in opposition. Appointments made by the Mulroney government were scrutinized and frequently challenged. Yet, upon election to the prime ministership, the self-same Chrétien found himself less interested in reform. In their study of the first Chrétien government (1993–1997) Greenspon and Wilson-Smith offer this description of the Chrétien attitude:

> He intended to exercise the prerogatives of the office. "It is better that I make the appointments and be accountable for them," others remembered him saying, "than someone else makes them and I be accountable."[8]

Advisors and bureaucratic aides for the prime minister are built into the institutional order. In the carrying out of his or her role as national leader and voice of the country on the international and domestic stages, the prime minister is aided by central agencies and the top levels of staff at the national office of his or her respective political party. Two central agencies, the Prime Minister's Office (PMO) and the Privy Council Office (PCO), are well connected to the prime minister's political or bureaucratic needs for information, contacts, supporting documents, and advice. Meanwhile, the link to his or her political party allows control over campaign planning, national opinion polling, and candidate selection. Leaders attempting to recruit high-profile candidates can often assure them of an easy ride to a desirable riding nomination. Taken together, the prime minister has access to tremendous supports and avenues for influence. This facilitates prime-ministerial direction over important issues such as national unity and federal–provincial relations. Donald Savoie, a long-time student of government and bureaucracy, reports that with regard to this policy field, "briefing material prepared by the PCO for new ministers makes it clear that 'the Prime Minister has direct responsibility for the conduct of federal–provincial relations.'"[9]

By virtue of their position and the practices of modern communications, prime ministers both deliver government messages and oversee the crafting of communications planning. Whether it be through appearances at vital symbolic events (e.g., Remembrance Day commemorations), leaders' election campaign debates, government websites, or media settings such as the year-end fireside chat, prime ministers are at the centre of coverage. Government media strategies often reinforce the centrality of the prime minister. For example, it was Prime Minister Paul Martin himself who appeared in a highly publicized media address in the spring of 2005 to defend the Liberal Party from allegations arising from corruption within government advertising expenditures. When the government of Brian Mulroney announced its intention to "explore" the possibility of Canada–U.S. free trade, media preparation included a personal call from Mulroney to U.S. President Ronald Reagan and a major prime-ministerial address to the House of Commons.[10]

As with the overtures made to the U.S. leadership about free trade, prime ministers are generally the dominant voice of Canada internationally. They attend highly visible gatherings such as meetings of the G7 or G8, the group composed of the leaders of the richest countries. They also publicly identify themselves with major foreign initiatives. Like his predecessors, Stephen Harper has been the primary Canadian figure at senior international events. Take, for example, Harper's visit to Germany in June 2007, where he participated in talks with both the president and the prime minister of France; the Canada–European Union Summit; and the gathering of the G8, which brought Harper into contact with the political leaders of Germany, the U.S., Great Britain, France, Japan, Italy, and Russia, as well as providing him with introductions to significant German business leaders. He was thereby able to present skepticism about the Kyoto Accord as the official national position at a time when support for greater environmental protection was strongly urged among the general Canadian populace.[11]

The breadth of the responsibilities and power available to prime ministers gives them a commanding role in the machinery of government and the broad political landscape. They have a paramount influence over major government appointments; parliamentary debate and questioning; major policy directions in key fields such as federal–provincial relations, foreign policy, and other government priorities; media coverage and campaign strategizing; and the leadership of their political party. Their judgment is supplemented by the advice and support of two major central agencies, pollsters, and leading strategists in their own political party. They chair cabinet meetings and set its composition and agendas. This is tangible power supported by senior civil servants, cabinet colleagues, and media advisors. If we are serious about controlling or at least constraining prime-ministerial power, we need to devote increased attention to this task, for at the moment, the leading candidates for restraining the political executive are limited, sporadic, and occasionally unpredictable in their impact.

CABINET AND THE LEADING MEMBERS OF THE PRIME MINISTER'S POLITICAL PARTY

Stephen Harper became Canada's prime minister upon the election of January 23, 2006; his new cabinet, which included a high-profile defector from the opposition Liberals, was subsequently unveiled in early February with great fanfare. Yet this new team and its specific ministerial assignments were not to remain in place for long. Within little more than a year and a half, this heralded cabinet was altered by two ministerial shuffles. In January 2007, a shuffle affecting such major departments as Environment, the Treasury Board, Justice, and Citizenship and Immigration took place. Later, in August 2007, a second major upheaval occurred, and those responsible for the high-priority fields of Foreign Affairs, Indian Affairs and Northern Development, Industry, Defence, Heritage, and Agriculture were shifted into other roles. Learning a new portfolio, with its attendant responsibilities and multimillion-dollar expenditures, is a Herculean task. Once appointed, the new minister is badgered by the press and client groups seeking audiences and signs of policy direction. Periodic shuffles force new responsibilities on those already endeavouring to master other cabinet assignments and their associated policy challenges and weighty briefing books.

Amid the shuffles, Prime Minister Harper, the cabinet designer, remained firmly in place at the centre. Donald Savoie explains the strength of the prime minister's position this way:

> Ministers...know full well that they sit in Cabinet only because one person wants them to be there—the prime minister. The prime minister may well be reluctant to swing the axe, but no one knows for certain if or when he will do it.[12]

The power to assign positions permits the elevation of favourites, the demotion of discontents, and the stymieing of the plans of ambitious underlings. Although cabinet selections need to reflect important political cleavages such as region, gender, party factions, and language, do not underestimate the clout arising from the authority to design cabinets and to favour the loyal and supportive.

Prime ministers enter the office with the upper hand over fellow party members. Winning a majority is a tonic for party morale—the leader is a champion. Winning a minority is a disappointment but not necessarily a death sentence. Political parties are often patient with leaders who have been reduced to minority status. Pierre Trudeau successfully endured the humiliation of 1972, and Paul Martin was given another chance after the reduced Liberal numbers in 2004. Prime ministers who win only a minority government typically pledge that they have learned a lesson, that the voters have spoken, and that next time their efforts will produce a parliamentary majority. Meanwhile, minority governments are often in a vulnerable position, and efforts are made within the party to mute expressions of disloyalty to the leader. This should not be surprising, since the potential successor to replace the prime minister is likely to be found in cabinet, and thus his or her approval rating is bound up with that of the government he or she serves.

Note, however, that there is no intention here of speaking of a similar relationship between opposition leaders and their internal party rivals. Past experience, as in the relations between Joe Clark and Brian Mulroney (1980–1984) and between John Turner and Jean Chrétien (1984–1990), indicates that without the lubricant of patronage and power, the party leader is far more vulnerable. Hence, the prime minister likely has better job security than the leaders of the opposition parties.

The condition of contemporary Canadian political parties makes them weak as guardians of ongoing accountability. Many of us may have an image rooted in history of mass parties in which there is an integrated organization with a dedicated membership who form a sort of institutional family with memory and well-worn conventions. This may no longer be a suitable vision. Sid Noel offers an insightful reexamination of parties in his essay "Leaders' Entourages, Parties, and Patronage,"[13] which encourages us to reassess what we expect of parties. In the past, parties were major vehicles for fundraising, member attachment, and campaign preparation. Much has changed, though. Federal campaign reforms have provided public funding for parties. (Note, though that current Prime Minister Harper has indicated the likely reduction and/or termination of these funds, it is difficult at this point to speculate on what will ensue.) Campaigns are often leader-driven media efforts organized around a centrally set theme and schedule. Citizen attachment to politics appears to be waning, as turnout at the last two federal elections was only in the high 50s/low 60s percent level, and a sampling of recent provincial elections in Ontario (2011), Newfoundland (2007), and Nova Scotia (2006) offers little evidence of voter enthusiasm. Even the 2007 Quebec election, which featured debate over sovereignty and national unity, had a turnout percentage only in the low 70s. Party efforts to allow the signing up of new members during leadership selection seem to produce only temporary votes for preferred candidates rather than ongoing life-blood. There are ample reasons for concern about the vitality of Canadian parties.

Noel suggests that we instead think about parties as vehicles taken over for periods by ambitious and well-heeled individuals backed by professional entourages personally loyal to them. The party label becomes more of a brand than a historic family that has shared a history together.

> Though actual titles may vary, the inner circle of a typical entourage consists of a chief fundraiser, a chief organizer or campaign director, a communications director (media adviser), one or two senior strategists, a personal aide ("gatekeeper"), a chief media spokesperson or "spinner" (if this role is not filled by the communications director), an opinion pollster, an advertising director, and possibly a spouse.[14]

These and other professionals directly linked to the leader sustain the leader and drive the political party's national presentation. Who then has the status within the party to restrain the prime minister? Those who suggest that cabinet and its particular political party will serve as controls on prime-ministerial influence and decisions have a difficult case to make. Meanwhile, the political party organizational trends delineated by Noel show little sign of abating.

Before exploring the impact of public opinion on elections, it is important to confront head-on the case of the intra-party feud within the Chrétien government involving the challenge from Paul Martin. Some might imagine that the resulting upheaval and change in leadership upends the argument made here. The conventional narrative is that Martin served dutifully as finance minister between 1993 and 2002, helping to fight the deficit and control government finances. Over time, he chafed under the wear and tear of subservience to an individual whom he had challenged in the 1990 Liberal leadership race. Chrétien, for his part, grew tired of Martin's ambition and the machinations of his loyalists. Their overt jockeying for position and strategizing for the future replacement of "yesterday's man" with the political and economic wizard whose cabinet work was yielding annual fiscal surpluses was incessant. Especially galling to Chrétien was a meeting in Toronto's Regal Constellation Hotel in 2000 that was explained by Martin allies as a quiet gathering of Liberals interested in renewal, at which only some of the attendees were operatives in the service of Martin's cause. Intense press coverage and speculation nonetheless ensued. Chrétien responded by staying on and calling an election for late November, which produced a third majority government for the prime minister. Pressure for change continued apace, though, and in 2002 Chrétien finally replaced Martin in cabinet while also acknowledging that the time until his own upcoming departure from office was limited. A leadership vote was subsequently held in late 2003, and Martin won with over 90 percent of the votes.

But what is the lesson of this fandango of bitterness, intrigue, and media headlines? Is it that the cabinet and the prime minister's political party can, in a timely and effective manner, regularly hold a prime minister accountable for his or her performance? No, it is, rather, that a prime minister, even one who distrusts grand gestures and bold initiatives, can survive for years in office aided by a coterie of loyalists and that change is exhausting, long, and debilitating. Lawrence Martin, the noted biographer of Chrétien, put it this way:

> For those who thought of public service as an altruistic or ennobling pursuit, the endless power struggle between Chrétien and his finance minister was distressingly juvenile. Chrétien had made the public interest such a personal game that he chose to let a meeting of opponents in a hotel room become his ostensible reason for staying in power for four more years.[15]

If there is a moral to this story, perhaps it is that the struggle for leadership within a political party is an awkward, time-consuming, and often embarrassing display of ambition and rivalry. This conclusion is reminiscent in various ways of the struggles during the death throes of the Diefenbaker government during its minority period of 1962–1963.[16] Cabinet members' or other senior party figures' questioning of the party leader is a blunt and cumbersome tool for controlling the prime minister's performance for a number of reasons. One of the most important of these is that the prime minister has to continue to govern while sorting out the party struggle. Many may understandably join the prime minister in labelling the challenge(s) unseemly and counterproductive. The second key reason is that challenging a leader requires a credible alternative party figure willing to engage in the face-off. Announcing such an intention automatically sets the contender apart. Having thrown his or her hat into the ring, it is unlikely that this person could ever regain the trust of many party loyalists. The third major weakness of this check on prime-ministerial power is that it can cause paralysis within the governing party rather than improved accountability and attentiveness.

PUBLIC OPINION AND ELECTIONS

Are elections effective vehicles for the enforcement and maintenance of prime-ministerial accountability? At a basic level, an election offers potential for either changing or maintaining a particular government, but there are practical limits to its use. Power does periodically change hands, as in the federal elections of 1993 (Chrétien Liberals unseated Kim Campbell Progressive Conservatives and win a majority) and 2006 (Harper Conservatives won minority over Martin Liberals). What is more, Canadian elections are generally useful for fulfilling certain other political functions. Pammett regards them as being good at recruiting candidates and potential leaders, and offering political "parties opportunities to revive and re-establish their organizations."[17] Yet there is more to the story. Canadian elections don't securely foster citizen interest and belief in the political system. Voter turnout is mired in a string of sub-par levels. In the seven most recent federal elections—1993, 1997, 2000, 2004, 2006, 2008, and 2011—turnout as a percentage of eligible voters was only in the 60s with the exception of 2008 when it dipped into the high 50s (Elections Canada website). If a winning party's share of the votes ranges from the high 30s to the low/mid 40s, a common occurrence, and only roughly 65 percent of those eligible actually vote, this is hardly strong democratic control. Little wonder that Pammett points to those who feel it an advantage that elites are given opportunities to fashion plans without mass scrutiny.[18] Not surprisingly, he also points out the purposeful vagueness of party campaign appeals and the ease with which parties jettison inconvenient pledges. Party election platforms have an uncertain shelf life once a government has been elected—hardly an effective constraint upon government action.

Elections are about the making of a government in the sense that, after an election, the Governor General reviews the results and asks the leaders of the party with the most elected members, or most visible support within the legislature, to form a government. This is a fundamentally important task, but let us not exaggerate its impact on the power and influence of a prime minister in the conduct of his or her office. Elections are sporadic and much can happen between them. In the past, prime ministers possessed the power to set the dates for elections, which could allow them to capitalize upon the movement of polls or to capture the opposition unprepared. There is currently debate within various Canadian jurisdictions about moving to fixed election dates as in the United States. This may help constrain one aspect of prime-ministerial discretion. It remains to be seen whether it will produce increased accountability, though. Fixed dates of four or five years apart, for example, still leave a long period between elections.

Election campaigns rely upon citizen participation and involvement, but as already noted, there is reason to worry on this front, given the low levels of voter turnout and public interest. Coupled with this lack of popular interest is the resulting opportunity for elites and active interest groups to marshal their resources and influence in support of favoured causes. With regard to the free trade election of 1988, for example, Brian Mulroney's *Memoirs* makes clear his recognition of the value of business support as a counter to the anti–free trade campaign of the Liberals and NDP: "The Canadian business community, led by Tom D'Aquino and the Business Council on National Issues, rallied vigorously in support of free trade. During the election campaign, business leaders spoke out bluntly and purchased ads in favour of the trade agreement. Their support was unprecedented and effective."[19] And in the 1988 election, the Mulroney Progressive Conservatives were returned with a sizable parliamentary contingent of 169 of 295 seats and 43 percent of the popular vote. More than half of voters marked ballots for parties officially opposed to the primary agenda item of the sitting prime minister, yet free trade became a reality.

PARLIAMENT

Our examination now turns to the traditional understanding that Parliament serves as a representative forum wherein governments are judged and regularly called to account through vehicles such as the regular Question Period, the rigours of open debate, and the challenge of maintaining confidence among a collection of active and probing legislators. Assumptions of active and probing debate underestimate the disciplined character of Canadian political parties, which almost always stays on script. Question Period and debate are more often about reciting prepared positions and looking for catch phrases suitable for news coverage than about uncovering underlying realities or scrutinizing administrative detail. Votes are overwhelmingly cast upon party lines. Coordinated party strategy is thus more often a defining feature than an active restraint upon prime-ministerial behaviour.

Prime ministers choose cabinets and lead the parliamentary charge, but it should also be acknowledged that their power depends upon the skillful handling of caucus. Leaders must maintain support through those periods when their government's fortunes appear to be waning. Styles vary, but good team building allows a prime minister great leeway. According to Lawrence Martin, "Mulroney was known for his soothing strokes, Trudeau was a study in patience, Mackenzie King was famous for his incisive summations."[20] Their attentiveness paid off, as each enjoyed a career of striking duration and achievement.

Those across the aisle from the ruling party suffer from several key limitations in the parliamentary fray. First of all, the single-member electoral system used at the federal and provincial levels historically militates against opposition parties that do not have a major regional base, such as the Bloc Québécois.[21] Take the just-mentioned 1988 federal election. The Liberals and NDP together obtained over 51 percent of the votes cast but received only 126 of the 295 seats. For an added example, note the 1997 federal election, in which the Jean Chrétien federal Liberals managed 155 of 301 seats with less than 39 percent of the votes cast. More recently, in the 2011 election, Stephen Harper and the Conservatives took 167 of 308 seats with only 39.6 percent of the votes cast. Voter turnout for this election was only about 61 percent.

A second deficiency is the striking imbalance of resources available to a government as compared to the parliamentary opposition. Being in power means having command of the bureaucracy and enjoying the resulting perks. Prime ministers can direct the preparation of briefing material, can strategize about when to release favourable or damaging information, as well as solicit alternative proposals from staff, with the cost being borne out of government revenues. Governments also engage in active public opinion polling, thus offering the prime minister and his or her cabinet up-to-date insights into the public mood. These opportunities are more pronounced in a parliamentary setting where parliamentarians are often relatively inexperienced. In his 1997 book, *Mr. Smith Goes to Ottawa: Life in the House of Commons*, Docherty refers to this situation and laments instances in which government benches featured more veteran talent than their parliamentary rivals or caucus colleagues: "Simply put, it is difficult for both government backbenchers and opposition members to keep cabinet accountable when they lack the experience and parliamentary savvy of members of the executive."[22]

It must be acknowledged that there are features of parliamentary life that serve to highlight government behaviour and raise questions requiring serious responses. A good example of this was the work done by the Auditor General's office to uncover the details of the sponsorship scandal that plagued the Chrétien and Martin governments.[23] Offices such as those of the Auditor General, the Commissioner of Official Languages, and the Privacy Commissioner have significant powers. These control mechanisms play a valuable role, yet their impact is more often than not momentary, and parliamentary skirmishing overshadows their reports replete with analysis and administrative concerns.

The tests of stamina and commitment provided by the daily grind of Question Period and debate are not without importance. Prime ministers must have a diverse skill set and be accomplished performers as well as administrators. Yet, the question at issue here is not whether the job is easy but, rather, whether there are sufficient controls upon prime-ministerial power. Party discipline, public inattention, and the imbalance of cabinet and opposition resources provide reasons to doubt that there are adequate restraints given the public money and critical issues at stake.

MEDIA

There is always room to make the argument that the media, armed with their rights of free expression and opportunities for investigation, are a source of restraint upon prime-ministerial ambition. Certainly stories critical of the government can be aired, but the deeper, more complicated questions are (1) how much of a government's actions are going to be scrutinized; (2) to what degree Canadians are vigilant about following and working to understand news coverage; and (3) whether politicians are becoming more skilled in massaging press coverage and spinning messages favourable to their cause, thereby gaining an advantage over the press. There is reason to speculate that the answers to each of these will lead us to question further the effectiveness of the media's performance as a check on power.

As to the question of breadth of coverage, there is a limit to how much the media, no matter how vigilant, can be aware of. The Canadian government is a multibillion-dollar enterprise with branch offices (embassies, office buildings, and services) spread out nationally and internationally. How much of this can we reasonably expect the media to cover? At what point will budgets, audience ratings, and entertainment pressures outweigh the coverage of all that governments do? Note that what is being argued here is that the media operate under certain kinds of limitations and work to serve an audience that itself has time and attention pressures. Is it realistic to imagine that the media have resources for news coverage sufficient to oversee the full range of prime-ministerial power?

The second fundamental question is about the vigilance of the audience to (1) demand this kind of detailed coverage and (2) to watch and act upon them. If the media are to act as a check on power that can be regularly depended upon, then there is an implied understanding that the citizens will patronize them. Television ratings, bestseller lists, and so forth do not suggest that expanded news coverage is necessarily prevailing. Instead, it may be an option more appealing in civics classes than in the real world of media ratings and commercial broadcasting. Open-line shows airing aggressive comments supplied voluntarily by opinionated members of the general public may be entertaining, but how worried about such opinions is a prime minister in faraway Ottawa and a couple of years away from an election?

The final question under this heading relates to the balance of power between busy journalists covering a multitude of breaking stories and the expanding ranks of media advisers, spin doctors, and pollsters servicing prime ministers. Governments take great care in choreographing public events with desired story lines. Note, for example, the Harper government's institution of a "Message Event Proposal" system that enables "the increasingly powerful Prime Minister's Office to vet requests for public events across the federal government."[24] Political advisers have grown more adroit in defining media strategies and prescribing visuals that charm the eye but perhaps do little more. Election campaigns seem to be caught up in image management. In the words of Paul Nesbitt-Larking in his well-known Canadian media text, "Winning elections seems to depend more and more on the control of image and style."[25] Thus, with the influence of media gurus shaping the presentation strategies of political leaders, there may well be reason to be cautious in judging the impact of the press in its implicit struggle between the investigation into, and acceptance of, prime-ministerial messages.

THE WORKINGS OF CANADIAN FEDERALISM

A further check upon prime-ministerial ambition may be found in the restraint provided by the division of powers and the existence of assertive and sizable provincial governments. Strong executive power at both the federal and provincial levels has produced a political system in which first ministers' meetings and intergovernmental agreements are important sources of policy decisions. Herman Bakvis, for example, asserts that "while power may be highly centralized in the hands of the prime minister, the same holds true for provincial premiers. In other words, prime ministerial power and ambition can be easily checked by strong resistance from some of the larger provinces."[26] Executive federalism and competing federal and provincial agendas are thus offered as sources of meaningful restraint.

While important as an argument, there is still something troubling about offering the closed and secretive world of intergovernmental bargaining as a constraint upon the actions of prime ministers. Instead of providing comfort that interested citizens might be able to monitor their federal leaders' initiatives, this would seem to intensify the concerns that drive the argument provided by this essay. Many governmental access-to-information regulations offer matters of federal–provincial negotiation as an exception. Which Canadians outside of elite circles had access to the high-stakes negotiations that produced the Constitution Act of 1982, the Meech Lake Accord, the Charlottetown Accord? The restraint offered by federal–provincial confrontation is at best a minimal sort. Advocates of this control assume that provinces and their self-interested political agendas offer more than simply the countervailing force of another competing executive or set of executives. Surely this is a limited type of counter force to underlying democratic fears of overall executive dominance.

Federal and provincial governments have a complex political relationship wherein competing claims are voiced and debated. Attention to the division of powers and to provincial reactions may on many occasion serve to limit federal government proposals. Yet, it is also true that despite having limited jurisdiction in various social policy fields such as health and higher education, the federal government has been able to shape events through the power to spend or to withhold spending, or to re-shape patterns of federal–provincial interactions. What recourse was available to Ontario, Alberta, and British Columbia when the Mulroney government limited the growth in their Canada Assistance Plan transfers in the early 1990s? What recourse was available to provinces when the early budgets of the Chrétien government cut back on transfers and added to provincial expenditure burdens? Federalism and strong provincial governments are a restraint, but do not overlook or underestimate the strength of the federal government position.

CONCLUSION

The prime minister has several sources of significant power, and the political system has inadequate safeguards to combat the excesses of this power. Prime ministers have major advantages in inter-party competition. Elections, meanwhile, are sporadic, and parliamentary life is seemingly more defined by party discipline and the divide between ins and outs than by a collective appraisal of detailed policy and budgetary plans. At the same time, the press contributes to improved accountability, but there are noteworthy limitations to its impact.

Governments are huge entities, and only a selection of events can be reported since audience and budgetary pressures constrain coverage. Prime ministers, meanwhile, are supported by a growing circle of advisors, pollsters, and spin doctors that help protect their position. Constraining power is not an easy task. Considering ways to improve the actual track record on this front is an important topic for future debate.

Only a very few Canadians have ever achieved the prime-ministerial pinnacle. Perhaps one of the reasons for the limited number is the imbalance between restraints upon power and the reinforcements of that power. There is a struggle between the exercise of real power by a relatively small number of ambitious and skilled politicians and the efforts of other political actors to keep that power in check—a struggle that warrants vigilance.

NOTES

1. Donald J. Savoie, *Power: Where Is It?* (Montreal and Kingston: McGill-Queen's University Press, 2010) and *Governing from the Centre: The Concentration of Power in Canadian Politics* (Toronto: University of Toronto Press, 1999).

2. Jeffrey Simpson, *The Friendly Dictatorship* (Toronto: McClelland and Stewart, 2001).

3. Brian Mulroney, *Memoirs: 1939–1993* (Toronto: Douglas Gibson Books, 2007).

4. Jean Chrétien, *My Years as Prime Minister* (Toronto: Knopf Canada, 2007).

5. Martin Lawrence, *Iron Man: The Defiant Reign of Jean Chrétien* (Toronto: Penguin, 2003) and *Harperland: The Politics of Control* (Toronto: Viking, 2010).

6. Peter Hogg, *Constitutional Law in Canada*, student ed. (Toronto: Carswell, 2001), p. 1.2.

7. Jeffrey Simpson, *The Friendly Dictatorship*, p. 4.

8. Edward Greenspon and Anthony Wilson-Smith, *Double Vision: The Inside Story of the Liberals in Power* (Toronto: Doubleday Canada, 1996), p. 220.

9. Donald Savoie, "Power at the Apex: Executive Dominance," in James Bickerton and Alain-G. Gagnon, eds., *Canadian Politics*, 4th ed. (Peterborough, ON: Broadview, 2004), p. 146.

10. Mulroney, *Memoirs*, pp. 394–397.

11. CBC News, "Harper Lands in Germany as G8 Summit Approaches," June 4, 2007, available at http://www.cbc.ca/canada/story/2007/06/03/harper-summit.html?ref=rss. Accessed November 9, 2007.

12. Savoie, *Governing from the Centre*, p. 91.

13. Sid Noel, "Leaders' Entourages, Parties and Patronage" in Alain-G. Gagnon and Brian Tanguay, eds., *Canadian Parties in Transition*, 3rd ed. (Peterborough, ON: Broadview, 2007), pp. 197–213.

14. Ibid., p. 206.

15. Lawrence, *Iron Man*, p. 431.

16. Denis Smith, *Tory Rogue: The Life and Legend of John Diefenbaker* (Toronto: Macfarlane Walter & Ross, 1995).

17. Jon H. Pammett, "Elections," in Michael and Glen Williams, eds., *Canadian Politics in the 21st Century*, 7th ed. (Toronto: Nelson, 2008), p. 164.

18. Ibid., p. 165.

19. Mulroney, *Memoirs*, p. 633.

20. Lawrence, *Iron Man*, p. 373.

21. David Docherty, *Legislatures* (Vancouver: UBC Press, 2005), pp. 125–126.

22. David Docherty, *Mr. Smith Goes to Ottawa: Life in the House of Commons* (Vancouver: UBC Press, 1997), p. 9.

23. Office of the Auditor General of Canada, "Chapter 3—The Sponsorship Program," *2003 November Report of the Auditor General of Canada* (Ottawa, 2003), available at http://www.oag-bvg.gc.ca/internet/English/parl_oag_200311_03_e_12925.html. Accessed August 14, 2011.

24. CBC News, "PMO Holds Grip on Message Control: Records," June 7, 2010, available at http://www.cbc.ca/news/politics/story/2010/06/07/pmo-message-event-proposals.html. Accessed August 15, 2011.

25. Paul Nesbitt-Larking, *Politics, Society, and the Media*, 2nd ed. (Peterborough, ON: Broadview, 2007), p. 146.

26. Herman Bakvis, "Prime Minister and Cabinet in Canada. An Autocracy in Need of Reform," *Journal of Canadian Studies* 15, no. 4 (2001), p. 68.

✗ NO

Limits on the Power of the Prime Minister

PAUL BARKER

Many close observers of Canadian politics believe that political power in Canada resides largely with the prime minister and his small group of close advisers. Those who make this argument are careful to admit that the prime minister comes up against some limits, but at the same time they describe Canada as "a kind of monarchy" that is "mandated by democracy."[1] The source of the prime minister's great influence, they say, lies in his access to so many "levers of power."[2] He leads the governing party, controls cabinet and its members, commands the attention of the media, sets the overall direction of the country, and much more. Also important, highly qualified officials located in the central agencies—"superbureaucrats"—help the prime minister control all relevant matters.[3] There are some who reject the notion that government in Canada amounts to "prime-ministerial government."[4] But such sentiments receive little attention. According to a popular text in Canadian politics, "[m]ost observers agree that Cabinet government has been transformed into a system of prime-ministerial government...."[5] And other reputable sources also diligently outline the case that the prime minister's powers of influence dwarf those of others in the political process.[6]

The belief that the prime minister wields a great deal of power has some merit. The nature of parliamentary government is to situate power in the hands of the political executive, so we expect the prime minister to be influential. But to suggest that this forms the basis of a kind of monarchical democracy goes too far. Though many specific criticisms of the thesis of prime-ministerial government may be made, there are basically two problems with it. One is that it fails to note sufficiently that the prime minister faces some formidable players in the political process. The prime minister is simply not that powerful. There are forces both inside and outside government that can challenge the leader of the governing party. The other problem relates to the conception of competition. The theory of prime-ministerial government assumes that competition for power is viable only when it is patently obvious or present. But prime ministers can be challenged simply by the threat of a new competitive force. The prime minister operates in a world of "virtual competition," in which the challenges sometimes appear as only potentialities. The lack of a corporeal presence matters little, because the prime minister acts as if the challenges are real. The key implication here is that there is indeed competition in Canadian politics—more so than suggested by a counting of the observable competitors—and that Canada is not nearly as vulnerable to the effects of concentrated power as suggested by those who see the influence of only the prime minister.

INSIDE GOVERNMENT

The idea of an almost domineering prime minister certainly exaggerates the power the prime minister commands outside the formal structures of government, and it can be argued that it is an exaggeration also of the power commanded inside government. Let us begin with the latter. Donald J. Savoie writes that "[it] is hardly possible to overemphasize the fact that the Canadian prime minister has no outer limits defining his political authority within the government."[7] In fact, one can overemphasize the influence of the prime minister. Outer limits exist, and one has to look only at the relations between prime ministers and their ministers to see this point. Take, for instance, former prime minister Jean Chrétien and his then finance minister, Paul Martin. According to Mr. Chrétien himself, the finance minister had a great deal of leeway in the making of fiscal policy. "I am not going to tell my finance minister what to do," said Mr. Chrétien.[8] And this has been the tradition at the federal level: the finance minister runs the budgetary process. Of course, this is not to say that the prime minister is shut out of this important process—the national leader can never ignore the economic health of the nation. The fact remains, however, that the finance minister is a powerful player in Canadian politics. Even in the heavily prime-ministerial government of Stephen Harper, events suggest that the finance minister sometimes goes his own way—and gets his way.[9]

There are instances of other ministers taking actions that reveal the limits of prime-ministerial power. Allan Rock, a federal Minister of Health in the Chrétien government, wanted to raise the profile of the federal government in the Canadian health care system. The health minister outlined a "new plan for health care"[10] that would indeed give a greater role to Ottawa but also held out the possibility of major disruptions in relations between the federal government and the provinces. Many assumed, though, that the latter would be acceptable because it was thought that the prime minister had given his consent to the initiative. But the prime minister had done no such thing. A minister had announced a major policy initiative with serious implications for federal–provincial relations—without the prime minister's agreement.[11]

In the government of Paul Martin, signs of conflict between the first minister and elected members of his party became clear. Initially, Prime Minister Martin appeared to look favourably on a decision that would see Canada work with the United States to develop a ballistic missile defence system for North America. But dissent in the party helped produce a contrary decision. The prime minister also faced resistance from Liberal Members of Parliament (MPs) who disagreed with his government's support of legislation favouring same-sex marriage. The weakness of Mr. Martin was in part made possible because backbenchers realized that the prime minister was, most of the time, in a minority situation and needed their support. A majority situation might, of course, easily quash these differences. But the fact is that minority governments are part of parliamentary government, and they serve to lessen the power of the first minister.

The experience so far of the governments of Stephen Harper, at first glance, reveals a prime minister more than able to control his ministers. Reports disclose a number of actions that support this perception. Prime Minister Harper prefers a "hub and spoke" management style, which means that Mr. Harper—as the hub—is able to more easily keep track of the ministers, who are the individual spokes.[12] As with all governments, ministers in the Harper government received "mandate" letters outlining their priorities and what was expected of them, but these letters were much more precise and specific than the usual ones.[13] The Prime Minister's Office (PMO), an agency tied tightly to the prime minister, has assumed much more power and used this influence to carefully prescribe and monitor ministerial statements and interactions with the media and other players in the political process. Yet, even with these developments, cabinet members have managed at times to act in ways contrary to the wishes of the first minister. Harper's minister for intergovernmental affairs publicly disassociated himself from the government's important support of Quebec as "a nation within a united Canada." Other ministers have rebelled against the interventions of the PMO and refused to agree to significant government positions on important issues.[14] More generally, it has to be remembered that the precarious position of minority governments sometimes causes the prime minister to assume a much more controlling posture, a position also made necessary in the case of the Harper government by the relative inexperience of the cabinet. With a new majority Conservative government, it will be interesting to see whether controls are relaxed and pave the way for more differences between the prime minister and his ministers.

Ministerial ambition (combined with backbencher support) can sometimes do more than limit prime ministerial power—it can also fatally weaken the head of the government. At the turn of the century, many in the Liberal Party expected Mr. Chrétien to leave office soon and open the way for a leadership race; he had already governed for two full terms, and he was getting older. But the prime minister, upset by attempts within his own party to oust him, surprised many with his actions. He contested a third election in late 2000—and won—and suggested at a minimum that he would complete his third term as leader of the country. The prime minister's actions, especially his speculations on his own future, infuriated both party members and Liberal MPs who wished to see Mr. Martin become prime minister, and they began to call for Mr. Chrétien to step down. For a time, the prime minister resisted, but it was all to no avail. Mr. Martin had made great efforts to gain support of Liberal MPs who failed to make it into cabinet or who were ignored by the prime minister and his advisers in the Prime Minister's Office. The finance minister also had in place an impressive organization dedicated to making him the prime minister. In August 2002, Jean Chrétien announced he would leave office in early 2004, and, by late 2003, he was gone.[15]

For some, the demise of Mr. Chrétien was a product of special circumstances and hardly a sign of inherent prime-ministerial weakness. The former prime minister had been confronted by a minister determined to succeed him and a large group of returning MPs who received nothing from a prime minister unable to give them much. Mr. Chrétien also had no real organization in place to confront his competition—he was too busy running the government and uncertain about continuing beyond his third mandate.[16] All this may be true. But it is also true that a prime minister had been *effectively* pushed aside, an unexpected event in the life of an individual who has many levers of power at his behest. A former senior official in the PMO and respected observer of government gives his read of the demise of Mr. Chrétien:

> …Savoie's 1999 metaphor of an all powerful love-like prime minister casting bolts of electricity into the system would have to be recast in 2003 as Jean Chrétien has been sent into retirement after losing control first of his party, then of his caucus. The events of the past year prove that Canada does not have a dictatorship, friendly or otherwise.[17]

There is another component of the prime-ministerial thesis that weakens under examination. As part of his attempt to ensure his powerful position, the prime minister (with his advisers) aims to keep his ministers out of trouble so that he "can get things done in areas that matter a great deal."[18] But the prime minister fails in this regard; he is not sufficiently powerful to accomplish this purpose. In these situations, ministers are not acting against the prime minister's wishes. Rather, they are merely being ministers, carrying out their mandates, and in so doing they run into difficulties. One has only to look at the Harper government for confirmation of this point. In 2008, the country learned that the federal Minister of Foreign Affairs had left some confidential papers at the house of his girlfriend. It also turned out that the girlfriend had had intimate relations with a figure connected to the Montreal crime world and had been married to a senior member of the Hell's Angels. The minister lost his job. In 2010, Helena Guergis resigned her position in the federal cabinet following allegations that she, among other things, allegedly permitted her office to be used by her husband to carry out private business. A subsequent investigation found no substance to the claims against the minister, but the damage had been done. Also in 2010, the minister of International Cooperation misled the House of Commons on matters relating to her department—in other words, she failed to tell the truth. Unlike in the preceding two cases, the minister survived the fallout from the action, but she had injured the Harper government.[19] There are other instances in the Harper government—and preceding ones—that could be detailed, but these are sufficient to reveal the limits of prime-ministerial power.

On balance, it seems that the prime minister cannot really control his individual ministers. At times, they will pursue agendas that are inconsistent with the prime minister's actions. As Herman Bakvis says, "one can...find examples of ministers carving out their own sphere of influence and taking initiatives."[20] The odd minister may also try to unseat the prime minister—and succeed. At other times, ministers will seek to please the prime minister, but the nature of the job—the power and responsibilities—will land ministers in trouble no matter what the prime minister and his central-agency officials attempt to do. Moreover, it is not just the individual ministers who can constrain the prime minister. The collective ministerial or cabinet decision-making system operates to disperse power. For proponents of the prime-ministerial government thesis, the cabinet system works largely to the advantage of the prime minister. In cabinet, he purportedly sets the agenda, controls the dissemination of information, and makes the final decision (and sometimes he fails to bring his decision to cabinet's attention). But this, too, overstates the case. Most prime ministers realize, sooner or later, that this is a recipe for prime-ministerial overload and that government functions well only when ministers run their own departments. Consequently, the cabinet system reflects the power of ministers. According to one study of the Chrétien years, the prime minister's "preference [was] to keep out of the hair of his ministers except in the most unusual circumstances."[21] The Privy Council Office (PCO), one of the most important advisory bodies to the prime minister, comes to a similar conclusion. "The tone of government may be set by the Prime Minister and the cabinet," reads a PCO document, "but most of the policies of the government flow from the exercise of the individual responsibilities of ministers."[22] Even in the Harper government, where there are hints of a more centralized cabinet system, official reports insist on a collegial cabinet decision-making system relying on the initiatives of individual ministers.[23]

Government consists of more than just the executive branch. There are the legislature and the judiciary. The functioning of these two branches also contests the notion of an imperial prime minister. Admittedly, the legislature provides less of a challenge for the prime minister than the other two branches. Nevertheless, it can provide a test for the prime minister, and indeed the first minister under pressure can take actions to strengthen this part of government. Former prime minister Paul Martin, for instance, made a commitment to a number of changes that would strengthen the legislature.[24] Under his plan, party discipline in the House of Commons would be loosened and parliamentary standing committees would be granted more influence. Private members' bills would receive closer consideration, and the ethics commissioner would report to Parliament (and not to the prime minister). A proposal that has already had some effect allows parliamentary committees some say in the appointment of Supreme Court justices. Not surprisingly, the current prime minister, when in his minority situation, also felt the influence of the House of Commons, so much so that one of his senior advisers charged that the opposition parties had effectively—and unconstitutionally—become the de facto government.[25]

As for the judiciary, the advent of the Charter of Rights and Freedoms has made the courts a much more important player in Canadian politics. Some downplay the impact of the courts' interpretation of the Charter on other political actors, including the prime minister. But others suggest that the courts, with their interpretation of the Charter, have altered the distribution of power in Canada.[26] Even when decisions that may favour the prime minister are rendered, the transfer of power is taking place because it is the courts that are exercising authority, not the government leader. The prime minister also sometimes fails in an attempt to use the courts to the government's advantage. The Martin government referred its same-sex marriage legislation to the Supreme Court of Canada partly in the hope that the court would find the traditional definition of marriage inconsistent with the Charter of Rights and Freedoms. With this ruling, the prime minister could avoid the politically damaging task of acting against those who still believed in the traditional definition. But the highest court refused to address this issue and simply said that the new legislation outlining a new definition of same-sex marriage was acceptable without saying whether the old definition was unacceptable. The prime minister himself would thus have to apply the deathblow to a definition of marriage still supported by a large part of the electorate. The adjudication of non-Charter issues can also reveal the power of the courts. In 1998, the Supreme Court of Canada laid out the rules that would govern the secession of Quebec from Canada. Though the opinion of the court is non-binding, it has effectively determined how this country might come to an end. Arguably, the most important decision affecting Canada was not made by the most important individual in Canadian politics; it was made by others.

OUTSIDE GOVERNMENT

Proponents of prime-ministerial government claim that their theory applies only to developments *within* government. The fact that the provinces or the media may limit the power of the first minister is irrelevant because the theory of prime-ministerial government does not extend outside the halls of government. Yet, these outside forces are sometimes used to demonstrate the power of the prime minister. The media, for instance, allegedly turn the first minister almost into a celebrity, which adds to the influence of the office of the prime minister. Similarly, globalization—another external force—also seemingly plays into the hands of the prime minister because it increasingly requires national leaders to make important decisions. Accordingly, it appears that these outside forces ought to be considered when attempting to assess the power of the prime minister. When this is done, it can be seen that they represent a double-edged sword for the prime minister. The media can place the prime minister in the spotlight and make the leader of the government appear well beyond others in the political process, but the media can also hurt the prime minister in at least two related ways. The media practise what some call "gotcha journalism," which is an attempt to highlight the gaffes and mistakes of political leaders.[27] Mr. Chrétien was often the target of this kind of journalism, and Mr. Martin also experienced at times a rough ride from the media. Prime Minister Harper has endeavoured to anticipate the influence of the media by restricting their access to ministers and forcing reporters to accept an arrangement whereby the PMO can select who shall ask questions at press conferences. These and other actions—which include calling on the RCMP to eject journalists from a hotel in which Conservative MPs were meeting—suggest a prime minister able to get the upper hand on the media.[28] This is a plausible interpretation, but another is that the Harper offensive against the press reveals the power of the media and the sheer desperation governments feel in their interactions with the fourth estate. The media can also use their investigative resources to force an issue onto the political agenda that can hurt the prime minister. The media made much of Mr. Chrétien's attempt to convince a government agency to provide financial assistance to a business concern in the former prime minister's riding. They also played an important role in making the problems with a government sponsorship program into a scandal. As for the current prime minister, he has so far escaped any full-blown media investigations, but his government's policy on Afghanistan has attracted a great deal of media interest, as has his allegedly Caesar-like style of leading.[29]

Globalization is another external force that may limit the power of the prime minister. *Globalization* has many meanings and definitions, but basically it focuses on how worldwide forces, especially economic ones, are eroding national boundaries. At present, the nation-state is the primary organizing principle of world politics; however, globalization works to supplant this principle and insert a new one that emphasizes the clout of *supra*national institutions (political and otherwise). In these circumstances, leaders of nation-states, including the prime minister of Canada, should see their power reduced. And in fact there is evidence of weakened leaders as they accept the dictates of international trade agreements and new tax regimes that demand a common playing field upon which the world's multinational corporations can play.

Proponents of the prime-ministerial government thesis are, however, unconvinced by this kind of analysis. Savoie, for one, says that leaders still maintain great power in a global world because "[t]he designers of the new order in many ways will have to be national politicians and national public services."[30] But this participation of national leaders may be short-lived; they might turn out to be their own gravediggers. Also, those believing in leaders' continued preeminence may be guilty of confusing globalization with "internationalization."[31] The latter refers to the heightened interaction between nation-states, a development that strengthens nation-states and their leaders. But globalization is different; its functioning does not really depend on national leaders getting together and making decisions. Globalization seeks to bypass nation-states because it sees them as an obstacle. It is of interest to note that the original proponent of the prime-ministerial government thesis in the Canadian context now admits that the "power that any Canadian prime minister is able to exercise has been leeching away."[32] According to Denis Smith, the prime minister can hardly stand up to the relentless effects of multinational corporations, free trade agreements, and the worldwide financial markets. In plain terms, globalization greatly curbs the influence of the prime minister.

The provinces represent another force outside the national government that reduces the power of the prime minister. In fact, it may be argued that the provinces are more deserving of attention than other forces outside government because they effectively are *within* government at the national level. As many students of Canadian federalism have argued, there are few policy matters that fail to involve both orders of government.[33] One order thus constitutes an extension of the other and vice versa. Another way to see the possible uniqueness of the provinces in the theory of prime-ministerial government is to compare the parliamentary system with the presidential one. Those who see the prime minister as being too powerful point to the separation of powers in the American political system and how this arrangement limits the president. They then note that the absence of such an arrangement in Canada strengthens the prime minister. But the supporters of the theory of prime-ministerial government fail to finish the story. Government in Canada may not be divided *within* government, but it is divided *between* governments. The operation of the federal principle in Canada (unlike that in the U.S.) gives Canada its own version of the separation of powers. To exclude the provinces in a consideration of the power of the prime minister is to fail to appreciate the full operation of government in Canada. As Richard Simeon and Elaine Willis suggest, the nature of federalism in Canada almost appears as the natural attempt of any democracy to find ways to ensure that power is never too concentrated:

> In Canada, the closest parallel to divided government is found not in relations between executive and legislative but in federalism itself. Much of the imagery surrounding divided government in the United States is replicated in analyses of federal–provincial relations in Canada. Just as an assertive Congress challenges the president, so do assertive provinces challenge Ottawa.[34]

When one does consider the provinces and their impact on the prime minister, the restraining effect of the provinces can be seen quite clearly. The provinces have constitutional authority over important matters, and they represent strong regional interests that can clash with the overall national interest. The sheer size and wealth of some provinces also play a part in relations between the provinces and the prime minister. Recent developments reveal the difficulties the provinces pose for the first minister. Over the past decade, Mr. Chrétien, Mr. Martin, and even a reluctant Mr. Harper (who respects provincial jurisdiction more than his predecessors) have attempted to establish a role for Ottawa in health care. In these efforts, they have admittedly succeeded in attaching some stipulations to the use of additional financial assistance from the federal government. But the fact remains that the provinces still largely control the shaping and formulating of health policy. Even more recently, Prime Minister Harper sought to make adjustments to a federal–provincial fiscal arrangement that makes available federal financial support to less well-off provinces. Some provinces accepted the change, but one province condemned it and urged all of its residents (and Canadians) to vote against Mr. Harper, while another launched a constitutional challenge.

Contemporary events are not the only relevant pieces of evidence when considering federal–provincial relations and the power of the prime minister. The history of federalism, at least since the end of the Second World War, is the history of declining federal power. "The prominent characterizing feature of the evolution of the Canadian federation in the postwar period," write Robin Boadway and Frank Flatters, "is the gradual but persistent decentralization of fiscal responsibilities from the federal government to the provinces (and their municipalities)."[35] Recently, as reflected in its efforts to affect health care, the federal government has sought to reverse this trend, to give the national interest—and the prime minister—greater prominence in important areas of public policy.[36] But the trend seems too strong. The money and power have shifted from the federal government to the provinces. The prime minister leads a government that must contend with the reality that it exists in one of the world's most decentralized federal states. The implication of this for the thesis of prime-ministerial government should be clear: the prime minister may not have a United States Congress to deal with, but he or she does have the provinces.

VIRTUAL COMPETITION

In a well-received book on Canadian politics, Donald J. Savoie writes that prime ministers "have in their hands all the important levers of power." But a few paragraphs later, he also writes that "one of the main preoccupations of the most senior officials in government is to protect the prime minister."[37] The power of the prime minister is evidently combined with a rather precarious hold on office, a state of affairs that seems distinctly odd. Surely a powerful prime minister is free of constant concern for his or her very survival, yet the reality appears otherwise. Even Mr. Chrétien himself admitted his vulnerability: "It's a survival game played under the glare of light. If you don't learn that, you're quickly finished."[38] The prime minister supposedly governs with few checks; nevertheless, he or she participates in a game of survival in which *all* participants risk fatal blows.

Part of the explanation for this puzzling state of affairs has already been provided. There are constraints on the prime minister's power. The prime minister needs to worry about his or her situation because he or she faces challengers. But the near desperate situation of the prime minister suggests that something more is at work. The prime minister does countenance challengers whom all can see—cabinet ministers, the provinces, the media, the opposition. However, the prime minister also contends with threats to his or her position, which amount to competitive forces that are not so evident—a kind of "virtual competition." Normally, we associate competition with entities that are clearly present, but competition can also come in the form of possibilities and potentialities. The result is an individual or organization that possesses a near-monopoly situation but that feels itself to be under siege. In the world of business, this phenomenon is recognized. Powerful companies dominate sectors of the private market, but their chief executive officers admit that they are almost terrified by competition.[39] The traditional conception of competition demands the existence of clear competitors who force the more powerful actors to adjust their behaviour accordingly, but another conception sees competition in ghostly threats with very imaginable and lethal outcomes.

With this latter notion of competition, the anxiety experienced by the prime minister and his advisers becomes more understandable. The prime minister feels himself to be in a game of survival because he *is* in a game of survival: "The press want to get you. The opposition want to get you. Even some of the bureaucrats want to get you."[40] On the surface, these sentiments of Mr. Chrétien seem mere hyperbole—there are challenges to a prime minister's power, but not to this extent. But perhaps the former prime minister knows better, for he appreciates the possibilities of disaster in his environment. Take, for instance, the opposition. Normally the House of Commons attracts little attention in discussions of the prime minister's power; party discipline reduces the legislature to a bit player in Canadian politics. But a misstep in Parliament, perhaps during Question Period, can damage the prime minister. That is why his senior advisers spend so much time preparing him and cabinet members for their session in the House of Commons. Of course, this is not to say that Parliament rivals the prime minister, but it is to say that members of Parliament have the capacity to ruin a prime minister. Much like a company that can be undermined overnight by a new invention, the prime minister can find himself in serious trouble with a careless response to a question or an insensitive appreciation of a parliamentary matter.

Perhaps even more unsettling in politics (and business) are the threats from the truly unforeseen entities. A prime minister can try to defend himself from the dangers posed by the House of Commons and other well-known elements in the political process. More difficult is a defence against something that essentially emerges from nowhere—a new charismatic leader, a past indiscretion coming to light, a debilitating court decision. In such a world, anything does become possible and prime-ministerial vigilance turns into a practical obsession with challenges to the government.

The important consequence of virtual competition is that the Canadian political process is much less susceptible to the evils of concentrated power than commonly thought. Again, experience in the private sector is instructive. There are well-known companies with positions of incredible influence and wealth who do not act like entities with a near monopoly of the market. Under monopoly conditions, the expectation is that prices will rise, quality will decline, and innovation will disappear. However, this fails to transpire with these companies. Instead, prices fall, quality rises, and innovation takes place.[41] With the appropriate adjustments, the same phenomenon can be seen in political life. Under prime-ministerial government, we should experience high costs, bad public policy, insensitive politicians, and few fresh approaches to societal problems. Some may claim that Canada has all of these, but this would be an exaggeration of the true situation. There are a number of indicators of good government in Canada, a reality that clashes with the predictions of prime-ministerial government. Canada has social policies that are admired around the world, it sometimes serves a useful purpose in foreign affairs, and the United Nations annually places Canada either at the top of or near the top of the list of the world's best nations in which to live. These outcomes hardly seem consistent with the evils of concentrated power.

CONCLUSION

There is no argument with the claim that Canada's prime minister has substantial influence and that he is the most powerful player in Canadian politics. The objections arise when the claim extends to the notion that the first minister has no real challengers. The thesis of prime-ministerial government suggests that the distance between the prime minister and the other players in the Canadian political process in terms of power is great. The reality, however, is that the gap is not substantial and that it can be bridged. Both inside and outside government, there are entities that can remind the prime minister that politics is a game of survival for all players. Inside government can be found ambitious cabinet ministers, disgruntled backbenchers, and newly empowered judges; outside government are the media, premiers, provinces, and a world that pays less and less attention to national leaders. To be fair to those who subscribe to the theory of prime-ministerial government, the challenges that emanate from within and from without government are not equally forbidding. The proponents of prime-ministerial government focus on power relations inside government, and one is certainly on more solid ground when trying to argue for the presence of a prime minister without equals inside government than when endeavouring to do the same in relation to matters outside government. But even inside government the prime minister must be on guard. Moreover, there are always the threats inherent in the world of virtual competition. Many survey the Canadian political process and see very little for the prime minister to worry about, but they do not see what the prime minister sees.

Ultimately, the belief in the all-powerful prime minister founders because it is at odds with the reality of Canada. This country has its problems; nevertheless, it is recognized as a functioning democracy with public policies that stand up well against those of other nations. Unless one believes in benevolent dictatorships, good public policy cannot generally be said to coexist with a political system in which much of the political power lies with one person and his advisers.[42] Canada's national leader is powerful, but not to the point where power turns into a corrupting force. Fortunately, the competitive pressures in Canadian politics are simply too great for us to have reached this point.

NOTES

1. Donald J. Savoie, "The King of the Commons," *Time*, May 3, 1999, p. 64.

2. Donald J. Savoie, *Governing from the Centre: The Concentration of Power in Canadian Politics* (Toronto: University of Toronto Press, 1999), p. 72.

3. Colin Campbell and George Szablowski, *The Superbureaucrats* (Toronto: Macmillan, 1979).

4. Keith Archer et al., *Parameters of Power: Canada's Political Institutions*, 3rd ed. (Toronto: ITP Nelson, 2002), p. 241.

5. Rand Dyck, *Canadian Politics: Critical Approaches*, 6th ed. (Scarborough: Thomson Nelson, 2011), p. 554. Bolding has been removed.

6. See, for example, Donald Savoie, "First Ministers, Cabinet, and the Public Service," in John C. Courtney and David E. Smith, eds., *The Oxford Handbook of Canadian Politics* (Toronto: Oxford University Press, 2010).

7. Savoie, *Governing from the Centre*, p. 108.

8. Edward Greenspon and Anthony Wilson-Smith, *Double Vision: The Inside Story of the Liberals in Power* (Toronto: Doubleday Canada, 1996), p. 163.

9. Lawrence Martin, *Harperland: The Politics of Control* (Toronto: Viking Canada, 2010), p. 175; and Paul Wells and John Geddes, "Why You Don't Know about Stephen Harper," *Maclean's*, February 7, 2010, pp. 24–25.

10. Robert Fife and Giles Gherson, "Rock Proposes New National Health Plan," *National Post*, January 27, 2000, pp. A1, A11.

11. Anne McIlroy, "Rock's Grand Plan Was News to the PM," *The Globe and Mail*, March 4, 2000, p. A3.

12. Brian Laghi, "Discipline, Control Mark PM's Management Style," *The Globe and Mail*, April 8, 2006, pp. A1, A4.

13. John Ivison, "With a Fistful of Power," *National Post*, September 1, 2007, p. A6.

14. Ian Brown, "In Harper's Regime, Big Daddy Knows Best," *The Globe and Mail*, May 13, 2006, p. F6; Brian Laghi and Jane Taber, "Offshore Deal a Crucial Test for MacKay," *The Globe and Mail*, June 13, 2007, p. A12. One might also cite the case of

Bill Casey, a Conservative backbencher who failed to support his party's budget and was subsequently ejected from the caucus of the Conservative Party.

15. For more on this, see Susan Delacourt, *Juggernaut: Paul Martin's Campaign for Chrétien's Crown* (Toronto: McClelland and Stewart, 2003).

16. For a picture of the complexity of Chrétien's situation, see Eddie Goldenberg, *The Way It Works: Inside Ottawa* (Toronto: Douglas Gibson Books, 2006), ch. 22; and the former prime minister's memoirs, Jean Chretien, *My Years as Prime Minister* (Toronto: Knopf, 2007), ch. 14.

17. Thomas Axworthy, "Our Public Service Malady: A Diagnosis," *The Globe and Mail*, September 27, 2003, p. D4. (In this article, Axworthy is reviewing a new book by Savoie: *Donald J. Savoie, Breaking the Bargain: Public Servants, Ministers, and Parliament* [Toronto: University of Toronto Press, 2003].)

18. Savoie, *Governing from the Centre*, p. 336.

19. John Geddes, "The Bev Oda Affair and the Tories Scandal-Management Strategy," *Maclean's*, February 28, 2011.

20. Herman Bakvis, "Prime Minister and Cabinet in Canada: An Autocracy in Need of Reform?" *Journal of Canadian Studies* 35, no. 4 (Winter 2001), p. 65.

21. Greenspon and Wilson-Smith, *Double Vision*, p. 35.

22. Privy Council Office, *Responsibility in the Constitution* (Ottawa: Minister of Supply and Services, 1993), p. 62.

23. Government of Canada, *Accountable Government: A Guide for Ministers and Secretaries of State, 2011* (Ottawa: Her Majesty the Queen in Right of Canada, 2011), p. 37.

24. For a discussion of these changes, see Peter Aucoin and Lori Turnbull, "The Democratic Deficit: Paul Martin and Parliamentary Government," *Canadian Public Administration* 46, no. 4 (2003).

25. Tom Flanagan, "Liberal Tactics Amount to Constitutional Back-seat Driving," *The Globe and Mail*, February 20, 2007, p. A19.

26. See the debate between Peter H. Russell and F.L. Morton in Mark Charlton and Paul Barker, eds., *Crosscurrents: Contemporary Political Issues,* 3rd ed. (Scarborough: ITP Nelson, 1998), Issue 14.

27. George Bain, *Gotcha! How the Media Distort the News* (Toronto: Key Porter Books, 1994).

28. Christopher Dornan, "The Cool on the Hill," *The Globe and Mail*, October 20, 2007, p. F3. For an update on Harper government and the media, see Martin, *Harperland*, ch. 7.

29. See, for example, John Ivison, "With a Fistful of Power," p. A6; and Lawrence Martin, "A Prime Minister at the Top of His Imperious Game," *The Globe and Mail*, October 22, 2007, p. A15.

30. Savoie, *Governing from the Centre*, p. 107.

31. See Jan Aart Scholte, "The Globalization of World Politics," in John Baylis and Steve Smith, eds., *The Globalization of World Politics: An Introduction to International Relations* (New York: Oxford University Press, 1997).

32. Denis Smith, "Is the Prime Minister Too Powerful?—Yes" in Mark Charlton and Paul Barker, eds., *Crosscurrents: Contemporary Political Issues,* 2nd ed. (Scarborough: Nelson Canada, 1994), p. 159.

33. See, for example, Richard Simeon, "The Federal–Provincial Decision Making Process," in *Ontario Economic Council, Issues and Alternatives—1977: Intergovernmental Relations* (Toronto: Ontario Economic Council, 1977), p. 26.

34. Richard Simeon and Elaine Willis, "Democracy and Performance: Governance in Canada and the United States," in Keith Banting, George Hoberg, and Richard Simeon, eds., *Degrees of Freedom: Canada and the United States in a Changing World* (Montreal and Kingston: McGill-Queen's University Press, 1997), p. 171.

35. Robin Boadway and Frank Flatters, "Fiscal Federalism: Is the System in Crisis?" in Keith G. Banting, Douglas M. Brown, and Thomas J. Courchene, eds., *The Future of Fiscal Federalism* (Kingston: School of Policy Studies et al., 1994), p. 137.

36. Gerard Boismenu and Peter Graefe, "The New Federal Tool Belt: Attempts to Rebuild Social Policy Leadership," in *Canadian Public Policy* 30, no. 1 (2004), pp. 71–89.

37. Savoie, *Governing from the Centre*, pp. 72–73.

38. Ibid., p. 313.

39. Robert J. Samuelson, "The Gates of Power," *The New Republic*, April 23, 2001, p. 31.

40. Savoie, *Governing from the Centre*, p. 313.

41. Samuelson, "The Gates of Power."

42. One might also believe in a "friendly dictatorship." See Jeffrey Simpson, *The Friendly Dictatorship* (Toronto: McClelland & Stewart, 2001).

POSTSCRIPT

In his article, Mellon employs a useful approach to making his case. He documents the arsenal of powers available to the prime minister—the powers are truly impressive—and then makes short work of any possible obstacles that might block the path of the first minister. Yet, there are a few openings for those who wish to think differently. Take, for example, the case of former prime minister Jean Chrétien. Mellon himself seemingly admits that Chrétien left office in part because the fates were aligned against him—more concretely, his former finance minister, Paul Martin, and much of his party wanted him gone. Surely, this is evidence that weakens claims of an all-powerful prime minister. Mellon might also be guilty of downplaying the capacity of the media to seriously damage any government and its leader. It is true, as Mellon writes, that the press can cover only so much of government; he is also correct when he says that governments spend increasingly more time managing journalists. But the media need not be expansive in its coverage to hurt a prime minister, and, as Barker says, efforts to curtail the press have the quality of desperation and last resort.

In his article, Paul Barker points out additional problems with the thesis of prime-ministerial government. Ministers can challenge the prime minister—without necessarily facing dismissal—and forces outside government aside from the media can reduce the influence of the prime minister. But Barker, too, may be guilty of exaggeration—he may, in other words, underestimate the true power of the prime minister. He is impressed with how ministers are able to challenge the prime minister, but it looks as if he has ignored the fact that most of these challenges end with the prime minister getting his or her way. As for the prime minister failing to keep the ministers out of trouble, this may be seen as amounting to very little. Finally, Barker might better appreciate that the prime minister has assumed increasing control over the years. The depiction of Prime Minister Harper in Lawrence Martin's recent book *Harperland* suggests the unbelievable: namely, a government leader in reach of full control.

To begin an analysis of the power of the prime minister, the interested student first needs to understand the system of parliamentary government and the prime minister's formal role in it. For this, one might consult Peter Aucoin, "Prime Minister and Cabinet," in James Bickerton and Alain-G. Gagnon, eds., *Canadian Politics,* 3rd ed. (Peterborough: Broadview Press, 1999) or Michael Whittington, "The Prime Minister, Cabinet, and the Executive," in Michael Whittington and Glen Williams, eds., *Canadian Politics in the 21st Century,* 6th ed. (Scarborough: Thomson Nelson, 2004). Jeffrey Simpson's book *The Friendly Dictatorship* (Toronto: McClelland & Stewart, 2001) can then be read for an engaging discussion of the thesis of prime-ministerial government. A more recent journalistic account of the power of the prime minister is Lawrence Martin, *Harperland: The Politics of Control* (Toronto: Viking Canada, 2010).

With these readings completed, the student is ready to tackle the work of Donald Savoie, who is most responsible for the focus on prime-ministerial power: Donald J. Savoie, "The Rise of Court Government in Canada," *Canadian Journal of Political Science* 32, no. 4 (December 1999); Donald J. Savoie, *Governing from the Centre: The Concentration of Power in Canadian Politics* (Toronto: University of Toronto Press, 1999); and Donald J. Savoie, *Court Government and the Collapse of Accountability in Canada and the United Kingdom* (Toronto: University of Toronto Press, 2008). For a shorter presentation of Savoie's position, see Donald J. Savoie, "Power at the Apex: Executive Dominance," in James Bickerton and Alain-G. Gagnon, eds., *Canadian Politics*, 4th ed. (Peterborough: Broadview Press, 2004), or Donald J. Savoie, "The Federal Government: Revisiting Court Government in Canada," in Luc Bernier, Keith Brownsey, and Michael Howlett, eds., *Executive Styles in Canada: Cabinet Structures and Leadership Practices in Canadian Government* (Toronto: University of Toronto Press, 2005). Savoie has recently published an update on his views concerning the power of the prime minister: Donald J. Savoie, *Power: Where Is It?* (Montreal & Kingston: McGill-Queen's University Press, 2010), ch. 6. This is a must-read piece.

To appreciate the genesis of this discussion in Canada, one should read Thomas A. Hockin, ed., *Apex of Power: The Prime Minister and Political Leadership in Canada*, 2nd ed. (Scarborough: Prentice-Hall, 1977). The belief that the position of prime minister has become almost too powerful is not limited to those who examine Canadian politics. Other parliamentary democracies may also be operating under prime-ministerial government. For more on this, see Patrick Weller, *First among Equals: Prime Ministers in Westminster Systems* (London: George Allen & Irwin, 1985). Weller has also produced a consideration of cabinet government and the prime minister in Patrick Weller, "Cabinet Government: An Elusive Ideal?" *Public Administration* 81, no. 4 (2003).

Proponents of prime-ministerial power are not without their critics. A critical examination of their position can be found in Herman Bakvis, "Prime Minister and Cabinet in Canada: An Autocracy in Need of Reform?" *Journal of Canadian Studies* 35, no. 4 (Winter 2001). The article addresses directly the analysis of Savoie and others who subscribe to the theory of prime-ministerial government, and he provides as well a useful bibliography on the topic of prime-ministerial power. For an account of the fall of former prime minister Jean Chrétien, one might read Susan Delacourt, *Juggernaut: Paul Martin's Campaign for Chrétien's Crown* (Toronto: McClelland and Stewart, 2003). But on this subject students should also consult the relevant chapters of the memoirs of former prime minister Jean Chretien and his close adviser, Eddie Goldenberg: *Jean Chretien, My Years as Prime Minister* (Toronto: Knopf, 2007), and Eddie Goldenberg, *The Way It Works: Inside Ottawa* (Toronto: McClelland and Stewart, 2006). Prime ministers in other countries also experienced difficult (and limiting) times, including former prime minister Tony Blair of Great Britain. For more on Blair, one might read Jonathan Powell, *The New Machiavelli: How to Wield Power in the Modern World* (London: The Bodley Head, 2010). Powell, who was Blair's chief of staff, pours cold water all over the thesis of prime-ministerial government.

Finally, a study uses experts to compare the power of prime ministers in various countries. The experts have determined that Canada has the most powerful prime ministers. Need anything more be said? See Eoin O'Malley, "The Power of Prime Ministers: Results of an Expert Survey," *International Political Science Review* 28, no. 1 (2007).

Is a Majority Government More Effective Than a Minority Government?

✔ **YES**
ALEX MARLAND, "The Case for a Functioning Majority Government"

✘ **NO**
ANNA ESSELMENT, "The Case for an Effective Minority Government"

A natural experiment has arisen that allows for resolving a crucial issue in parliamentary politics—which is preferable, a majority or minority government? The former type of government is formed by a political party with a number of legislative seats that exceeds 50 percent of the total number. The latter type has no party with a majority of seats. In 2004, 2006, and 2008, Canadians refused to give any of the federal political parties more than half of the seats in the House of Commons. Accordingly, political scientists, interested observers, and anyone else with a passing interest in politics were given a chance to see a minority government in action. But now a political party—the Conservative Party of Canada—has been awarded a majority government, which offers an opportunity to compare minority and majority governments. The fact that the majority follows the minority governments permits us to assume that any differences in the performance of the national government in the next few years—good or bad—can be attributed largely to the change in the type of government (because most other major factors affecting political life will have changed little—hence the notion of a *natural* experiment). The patient ones with an interest in politics will wait until the next election (in four years) to decide which type is preferable. But others, less patient, will want to begin their assessment early. Among this latter group will be political science students who, aside from being inquisitive about any matters political, may know that a question on majority and minority governments is a good candidate for inclusion in a final examination. And the way to begin investigating this issue is to look at the relevant evidence and arguments on both sides.

A number of arguments favour majority governments. The great fear in parliamentary systems—at least for the party in power—is the loss of a legislative vote. In this situation, conventions of parliamentary government require the dominant party to step down. But with a majority in hand (coupled with party discipline), a government can avoid this situation and accomplish, theoretically, many good things. For one, it can make longer term plans, because it is almost guaranteed a four-year term. Planning requires that a government have the time to think about their intentions, something that is often unavailable to minority governments obsessed with their precarious existence. Some retort that this may be fine, but also say that majority governments can afford to ignore any criticism. This possibility may detract from the quality of policy, but supporters of strong majorities in turn claim that majority situations are not necessarily without effective opposition forces. Finally, there are the supposed failings of a minority government that can be avoided with a majority—the game-playing, the short-run policy focus, and above all the constant posturing by the opposition to force an election in the hope that they can become the government.

The other side accepts some of the criticisms of minority governments, but suggests that these shortcomings can be remedied. For instance, the posturing mentioned above takes place largely because the electoral system—the single-member plurality (SMP) system—allows for significant shifts in seats to take place with insignificant shifts in the popular vote. In the SMP system, seats are allocated based on who wins in each of the ridings, so close contests tempt parties to try again in the knowledge that a swing of a small number of voters from one party to another may change the results. But the adoption of a proportional representation system in which the percentage of seats is roughly proportional to the percentage of votes would end this (a shift of a few percentage points in the popular vote, say, 30 percent to 33 percent, would have little effect on seat allocation). More important, say supporters of a minority government, the absence of a majority in the legislature produces significant benefits. One is that government action is not the result of often imperious majorities, but the product of a consensus built on the contributions of all parties. As well, a minority government gives individual Members of Parliament (MPs) a greater role because the government needs them to survive, which is not the case with a majority government supported by party discipline. And perhaps most relevant, minority governments are hardly aberrations or freaks of parliamentary government. Canada has a history of minority governments and so do other parliamentary democracies.

With their contributions, Alex Marland, a professor at Memorial University, and Anna Esselment, a professor at the University of Waterloo, guide us through the arguments for majority and minority governments.

✔ **YES**

The Case for a Functioning Majority Government

ALEX MARLAND

Canada's parliamentary system follows the principle of responsible government. This means that the executive branch, featuring a cabinet of appointed parliamentarians from the party of the prime minister, must be supported by at least half of the elected members of the legislature. So when a single party holds over 50 percent of the seats, there is minimal risk of cabinet being defeated on bills, on budget matters, or on a motion of nonconfidence. The planning stability, efficiency, and smoother operation of the state that results is generally preferable to the opportunism, political games, partisan conflict, and information secrecy that characterizes a government run by a party with less than 50 percent of the seats.

SUPER MAJORITY VERSUS FUNCTIONING MAJORITY

There are at least two types of majority governments. One is seriously problematic. Recent experience suggests that the other type is a better form of government than a minority. Let's dispense with what can be called a "super majority." This is when the support of the governing party has been so exaggerated by the single-member plurality (SMP) electoral system that there are too few opposition members to provide healthy debate or to participate in legislative committees. This sometimes occurs at the provincial level of government. Some extreme examples are the New Brunswick Liberals, led by Frank McKenna, who held all fifty-eight of that province's seats after the 1987 election; the Liberals, led by Gordon Campbell, who won seventy-seven of British Columbia's seventy-nine electoral districts in 2001; and the Progressive Conservatives, led by Danny Williams, who occupied forty-four of forty-eight seats in the Newfoundland and Labrador House of Assembly after the 2007 election.

A super majority should be actively guarded against. It raises serious concerns about flaws in the electoral system; about the fusion of the executive and legislative branches; about the supremacy of the head of government; and about the health of democracy. Political leaders tend to want freedom from limits on their power,[1] which is not always a bad thing, but a super majority results in superficial scrutiny of the political executive and it undermines responsible government. That super majorities are achieved in provinces, where premiers already have far more localized power than the prime minister of Canada could ever aspire to,[2] is distressing. Yet even then the political executive still faces constraints, such as the division of federal and provincial powers, the monitoring role of press galleries, and the dominance of the rule of law. A good government therefore faces enough opposition members that it is held accountable—but not so many opponents that its work grinds to a halt. When one party has more than half the seats, but does not have a super majority, we can refer to it as a "functioning majority." Functioning majorities tend to be fairly common due to the SMP electoral system. A recent example is the 2011 federal election that saw the Conservative Party of Canada, led by Stephen Harper, win 166 of 308 seats (54 percent) in the House of Commons on 39.6 percent of the popular vote. The Conservative government faces scrutiny from the Official Opposition New Democratic Party (103 seats) and the Liberal Party (34 seats). Two other parties, the Bloc Québécois (4 seats) and a lone Green Party MP, also monitor the government.

Recent experience suggests that a functioning majority is more desirable than when no party controls at least half of the seats in the legislature, that is, a minority government. Federal elections in 2004, 2006, and 2008 all produced minorities, the first headed by Liberal Paul Martin and the latter two by Harper. During this period there was so much political bickering, gamesmanship, and partisan threats to bring down the government that any romantic who hoped that a spirit of cooperation would emerge was bitterly disappointed. Former NDP national director Robin Sears described those governments as "childish, high-volume, low-achievement exercises that have driven more and more Canadians to distraction and dismayed them about the state of Canadian politics."[3] Consequently a 2009 public opinion survey found that Canadians wanted a majority government instead of a minority by nearly a 3:1 ratio;[4] another poll pegged the ratio of majority to minority supporters at 4:1.[5] After the negative experiences of the early 2000s, returning to the relative serenity of majority governance in 2011 was a welcome relief.

THE DISADVANTAGES OF A MINORITY GOVERNMENT
Opportunism and Instability

To establish the benefits of a majority government we first need to acknowledge that there are considerable problems with a minority government. Foremost among these is that the governing party is so constantly threatened with losing power that it cannot deliver good government. It weaves from vote to vote in the legislature, the executive has difficulty planning, and to survive it must emphasize short-term political strategies and tactics. Parliament is shut down more often through prorogation (which ends a session and puts the assembly in recess) or dissolution (which ends the assembly and an election must be held to elect new representatives). When this happens, bills and motions "die on the order paper" and the work must be restarted when Parliament is reconvened.

The possibility of a snap election means that political parties behave as though they are in a permanent election campaign. There are rancorous Question Periods and committee meetings. The governing party groups many bills into a single omnibus bill, daring the opposition to defeat major legislation over smaller issues, and behaving as though it has a majority without such a mandate.[6] Members of non-government parties may skip votes to allow a government bill to pass to avoid triggering an election but they still criticize the governing party's decisions. Premiers and interest groups lobby for special treatment, and their threats carry more weight. For instance, between 2004 and 2008, Danny Williams openly exploited the weaknesses of minority prime ministers. He ordered Canadian flags be removed from provincial buildings to pressure Prime Minister Martin to give Newfoundland more money, and then Premier Williams ran an "Anything but Conservative" campaign against Prime Minister Harper when he didn't get his way. Given this ongoing conflict, minority governments tend to last less than two years before another election is required, and such a short duration is evidence of how unworkable they are in practice.

The one time that minority governments are thought to work is when a Liberal government is propped up by a third party.[7] Such deal making involves post-election negotiations between party elites, as opposed to such choices being vetted by voters, or following known conventions.[8] The 1963–1968 Liberal minorities, led by Prime Minister Lester Pearson with the support of the New Democrats, are often cited as a productive period that produced grand programs such as medicare, the Canada Pension Plan (CPP), and interest-free student loans. Supporters of those parties, of progressive government, and of big spending therefore say that minority government is good. Yet this ignores that much of Canada's social welfare framework, including old age pensions, employment insurance (EI), the family allowance, and the equalization program, had been set by Liberal majority governments. With backroom deals it also becomes difficult to sort out which political parties deserve credit and who should be blamed. Politics being what it is, many parties say that they alone are responsible for good ideas, and are eager to point the finger at others for unpopular decisions.

These grand programs are expensive and are a reflection of ministers in a minority prioritizing proposals that may win votes in the next election. This can produce policy that is poorly researched and/or that contributes to overspending. J.S. Hodgson, who has written about the implications for government staff, observed that

> [l]egislation and programs involving payments or benefits to individuals therefore take on special attraction....A minority government is prone to spend, but because of its relative weakness it is much less likely to impose tax increases. It is therefore likely to incur budgetary deficits.[9]

The need for a minority government to spend money to stay alive goes against the Conservative Party's philosophy of cautious government spending. There are three infamous cases in Canadian federal politics of the instability of Conservative minority governments: the King-Byng crisis of 1926, the Clark budget defeat of 1979, and the Harper coalition crisis of 2008. Each illustrates that the Conservative Party's lack of a political dancing partner is a critical shortcoming of minority governance.

The difficulty of the parliamentary system of government prioritizing parties ahead of leaders, even though Canadians prioritize leadership over partisanship,[10] was exemplified in the mid-1920s. The oddity of a party leader "winning" an election and not becoming prime minister occurred in 1925 when the Arthur Meighen-led Conservatives more than doubled their seat count to 115 (46 percent of the 245 House seats at the time). Prime Minister Mackenzie King's Liberals were reduced to 100 MPs, the Progressive Party was reduced to 22 MPs, and other parties and independents held 8 seats. King himself was even defeated as an MP–and yet he stayed on as prime minister of a minority government by negotiating the support of the Progressives (totalling 122 seats, so nearly 50 percent) and by persuading a Liberal MP to resign so that he could win the seat in a by-election. This led to the King-Byng crisis of 1926 when the prime minister, facing a spending scandal, sought an election but Governor General Viscount Byng instead appointed Meighen as prime minister to avoid yet another election. The Conservatives were promptly defeated on a confidence vote in the House of Commons, and King went on to campaign in 1926 against the "chaos" of minority government in favour of a stable majority government, which electors awarded him.

The short-term decision making that characterizes a minority government is best exemplified by the period after the 1979 federal election. Joe Clark's Progressive Conservatives grew to 136 seats (of 282 at the time, so 48 percent) and replaced Pierre Trudeau's Liberal government, which was reduced to 114 MPs. The Progressive Conservatives' first budget tackled high inflation, ballooning spending, and deficit financing in part by seeking to cut programs and increase taxes on gasoline. John Crosbie, the Minister of Finance, explained this as "short term pain for long term gain,"[11] meaning that sometimes governments need to make unpopular decisions in the best interest of its citizens. But because austerity is not possible in a minority situation, the Liberals and NDP voted down the budget, triggering an election just nine months after Clark had been elected. Trudeau was returned with a majority government.

The most blatant example of Canadian political parties' opportunism in a minority government was the coalition crisis. In October 2008, amid global economic turmoil triggered by the collapse of the American housing sector, the Harper Conservatives were reelected with a larger minority of 143 seats (46 percent of 308). Liberal leader Stéphane Dion announced that he would step down as soon as a replacement could be selected. The finance minister tabled an economic update that contained a provision to eliminate some of the party financing that the Conservatives' opponents depended upon.

Six weeks after the election the Liberals (77 MPs), Bloc Québécois (49 MPs), and NDP (37 MPs) announced that they would bring the government down. They said the lack of stimulus spending to strengthen the economy was unacceptable; in private, they were outraged that Harper was trying to cut their government funding. Sensing the fragility of their hold on power, the Tories removed the controversial proposal, but it was too late. The leaders of the three opposition parties signed an agreement whereby Dion would become temporary prime minister of a coalition government that would include a handful of NDP MPs in a Liberal cabinet. The Liberals and NDP together had fewer seats than the Tories, but with the support of the separatist Bloc Québécois, they would control the House of Commons with 163 MPs (53 percent of seats). The minority government was in crisis. The Governor General rushed back to Canada from a trip abroad; Conservative advertising demonized a "separatist coalition"; supporters and opponents organized competing rallies across Canada; Harper and Dion delivered national televised addresses. Public anger, excitement, and confusion reigned.

Neither a coalition nor eliminating the party subsidies had been debated in the election campaign. Governor General Michaëlle Jean allowed cooler heads to prevail when she agreed with Harper's request to prorogue parliament. Within days the Liberal Party installed MP Michael Ignatieff—who was lukewarm to the coalition idea—as its new leader and the next month the Tories introduced a budget with stimulus spending. The Conservatives then prioritized spending in their own MPs' districts,[12] promoted a so-called "economic action plan" with millions in government advertising, and registered record deficits that the opposition decried. The lesson? That in a minority government, especially in situations when strong leadership is needed, we can expect political parties to put their own interests first, to stir public unrest, and to generally behave poorly.

Political Games and Information Secrecy

In a minority situation the opposition keeps the government unbalanced and under relentless attack. A political entertainment industry emerges to keep track of the games on Parliament Hill. The press speculates about the possibility of an election over and over. Pundits analyze strategic manoeuvring and reporters race to reveal the latest partisan tactics. The drama of by-elections to fill seat vacancies is magnified, questionable decisions are amplified into major scandals, and critics become media stars. Opinion polls keep score of which party or leader is "winning" and who is "losing."

In an effort to neutralize attacks the governing party tries to control the availability of information. The Harper minority era (2006–2011) was hypersensitive about going off message—though this was equally a reflection of the trend toward the centralization of the executive branch and of Harper's leadership style. Secrecy and toeing the party line was deemed essential to his government's survival. For example:

- Access-to-information processing was delayed, and documents that were released were redacted (blacked out) to avoid arming the opposition, most notably information about when the government knew that some prisoners in Afghanistan were being abused.

- People holding senior government positions were replaced for speaking out, such as the president of the Canadian Nuclear Safety Commission, or they resigned, including the Chief Statistician of Canada.

- Party communications were disparaging, most notably the Conservative Party's television ads that relentlessly attacked Liberal leaders, branding Dion as "not a leader" and then Ignatieff as an elitist who "didn't come back for you."

Legislative committees are an important check on government power, but in a minority government, they can become the scene of partisan jockeying. Committees are the small groups of MPs from different parties who scrutinize government bills, spending, and topical issues. In a minority situation, the presence of more non-government members does not lead to more effective committee work,[13] and members may be more prone to grandstand. In 2007, Conservative committee chairs followed a guidebook with instructions on "how to favour government agendas, select party-friendly witnesses, coach favourable testimony, set in motion debate-obstructing delays and, if necessary, storm out of meetings to grind parliamentary business to a halt."[14] Such shameful behaviour was defended as necessary amid a fragmented minority Parliament.

It was a lack of transparency that led to a legislative committee finding the Harper minority government in contempt of Parliament. The Standing Committee on Procedure and House Affairs (SCPHA) investigated the Harper administration's refusal to provide a finance committee with the costs of airplane purchases, of hosting international summits, of reducing the corporate tax rate, and of reforms to the justice system. In denying this request, the Conservatives invoked the privilege of "Cabinet confidence," referring to the fact that some high-level government decisions must be kept secret in order to govern. Eventually additional information was released, but in 2011, the Speaker of the House (at the time, a Liberal MP), who oversees legislative proceedings, ruled that this was insufficient and the committee concluded that "the government's failure to produce documents constitutes a contempt of Parliament." The SCPHA's Conservative members dissented by stating that the main report was "simply a piece of partisan gamesmanship."[15] The contempt ruling was the final straw and led to the minority government's defeat on a non-confidence motion. This parliamentary derision was a re-occurring theme during the ensuing election, and Harper countered by repeatedly positioning the solution as a "strong, stable national Conservative majority government."

Short-Term Public Policy and Inefficient Public Administration

Under minority rule the civil service operates on a temporary basis, and public servants become "like a man treading water because he is free neither to swim nor to come ashore."[16] Planning is complicated by the difficulty of implementing a Throne Speech and the annual budget, which end up reflecting a Frankenstein of ad hoc priorities promoted by various opposition parties, special interests, and premiers. Serious decisions are put off until clarity and permanence can be achieved. There is less time to develop good public policy and a need to fast-track program implementation. The heightened centralization of decision making, such as budget planning between the prime minister and the minister of finance, comes at a cost of excluding other members of cabinet and delaying even basic decisions.[17] Public servants are scared of routine actions or inactions that could get them into trouble and time pressures increase the number of decisions that are made based on hunches rather than guided by data.

In a minority era, money for invisible government operations is harder to come by, and people with party connections put more pressure on bureaucrats to make exemptions to administrative policies. Senior policy advisors are more likely to have any controversial proposals rejected and to find that ministers will not follow their recommendations. They may be tempted to save face by advocating only courses of action that are likely to be adopted. David Good of the University of Victoria identifies the negative implications of a minority Parliament on public administration this way:

> . . . the singular focus of minority governments on their short term electoral prospects has significant consequences for the public service. The scope for the public service to adjust previously announced campaign commitments is sharply reduced; budgetary decision-making and public communications is more centralized; expenditure reductions fall more heavily on the public service; pressure for speedy and error-free implementation of policies increases; ministerial demand for longer term policy analysis evaporates; and the risk of political interference in administrative matters increases.[18]

THE ADVANTAGES OF A MAJORITY GOVERNMENT

Stability, Efficiency, and Smoother Operations

One of the most significant advantages of a functioning majority is that government policy can be improved. This is because it can be designed over a four-year cycle rather than on a three-month survival basis. The governing party's campaign platform, its Throne Speech, and the annual budget provide a more truthful indication of the government's direction. Officials close to the prime minister face less pressure to interfere with ministers and their departments. International planning, trade negotiations, and meetings with other country's representatives can be more fertile. The result is a better government that is still held to account in the House of Commons and which has a record that voters can pass judgment on in the next election campaign.

Whereas leaders of minority governments are in constant crisis, a leader who controls a majority of seats in the legislature can choose between running an activist government to effect major change, or can opt to be a steady hand over the country's political affairs. Mackenzie King, often considered to be Canada's most successful prime minister, governed with caution, sought to overcome differences, and infamously said that "it is what we prevent, rather than what we do, that counts most in government."[19] Prime Ministers Wilfrid Laurier, Louis St. Laurent, and Jean Chrétien likewise ran managerial governments, and electors consistently returned them to office with a majority of seats. Other leaders, such as John A. Macdonald, Pierre Trudeau, and Brian Mulroney have been visionaries who used their majorities to profoundly shape Canada. A democracy needs debate and scrutiny, but public policy should not be merely a popularity contest. We depend on leaders to make difficult decisions, especially in unwinnable "dirty hands" scenarios, and to think beyond next week. It was under majority governments that the Canadian Constitution was amended and the Charter of Rights and Freedoms was adopted. Strong leadership has been needed to deal with national security matters, such as handling the Front de libération du Québec (FLQ) terrorism crisis, leading Canada's response to the 9/11 terrorist attacks, and making the subsequent decision not to send Canadian troops to Iraq. Long-term financial initiatives would not have been possible without strong majority governments, such as the North American Free Trade Agreement (NAFTA), the goods and services tax (GST), and the deficit/debt reduction of the 1990s. The Conservatives' 2011 election platform[20] also featured some domestic and international policy pledges that would be difficult in a minority situation but which are viable with a majority government, such as

- long-term fiscal planning, as evidenced by the party's plans to reduce government spending to eliminate the deficit and balance the budget;

- major international negotiations, notably the completion of a free trade agreement between Canada and the European Union and a Canada–India free trade deal;

- creating Canada-wide standards, such as establishing a national securities regulator to replace the thirteen regulators in the provinces and territories who govern investing in the stock market;

- reforming government, including passing legislation to limit the term in office for members of the Senate; and,

- ending the party subsidies that had triggered the coalition crisis in 2008.

With less than half of the seats, the opposition wields little power over the governing party but a hardworking group can nevertheless hold a functioning majority responsible for its actions. There is time to scrutinize, time to research, and time to produce viable alternatives that are less prone to partisanship, populism, or sensationalism. There are plenty of examples of good opposition during majority governments, such as the Liberal "rat pack" that dogged the Mulroney Conservatives in the 1980s, or the Reform Party pressuring the Chrétien Liberals to reduce spending in the 1990s. Ministers were still held to account and pressured to resign. But with the temperature lowered, MPs from different parties can work behind the scenes together with the understanding that the governing party has the final say. Committees still hold hearings to listen to stakeholders' testimony and may recommend amendments to a bill.[21]

Parliamentarians and lawyers have more time to scrutinize draft legislation that, if necessary, can pass through the three reading stages with fewer delays. Freed from daily firefighting, opposition parties have an opportunity to recharge and rebuild through internal discussions about viable policy alternatives, candidate recruitment, and campaign planning. The public at large also benefits from a functioning majority. Businesses and non-governmental organizations can plan based on reasonably predictable monetary policies and commercial regulations.[22] Citizens are able to get answers to their questions faster because civil servants have clear direction.[23] A majority government can increase the recruitment and retention of talented and/or well-meaning candidates. It also provides stability for the hundreds of political staffers in Ottawa and in constituencies, many of whom are young university graduates who face less angst about suddenly losing their job.

ARE CRITICISMS OF A MAJORITY GOVERNMENT FAIR?

There is a fine balance between a government's right to govern and the opposition's right to hold it accountable. Given all this there is a strong case to be made for a functioning majority government, especially for people who believe in government efficiency and for those who recognize that in practice, party politics is a rough game. Nevertheless two criticisms should be addressed.

One of the biggest critiques of majority government is that is unfair. This is because the SMP electoral system creates what scholar Peter Russell calls "false majorities."[24] This is when the governing party wins a majority of the seats even though more than half of voters actually voted for a different party, as was the case with the Harper Conservatives in 2011. Minority government is said to be more fair, and advocates of a proportional representation (PR) system would agree. In theory this makes sense; however, in practice a minority government can be unworkable, especially under a Conservative regime. Moreover the SMP electoral system tends to grossly overstate the support of smaller regional and/or ideological parties, such as the Bloc Québécois, which gain even more clout in a minority situation as opposed to being held in check by a majority government. Changing the electoral system might be desirable, but until then, functioning majorities offer more stability than fragile minorities do.

Another critique is that the head of government has too much power in a majority government. This is a valid concern and is why super majorities must be avoided; but even in functioning majorities there is much talk about the prime minister becoming a "friendly dictator," as Jean Chrétien was described.[25] Such notions are a gross exaggeration and have been debunked by some political scientists.[26] The prime minister's powers are constrained by federalism, by central agencies, by the auditor general, by government reporting and access to information, by televised proceedings, by the press gallery, and possibly by the Senate or Governor General. There are also the premiers, public opinion polls, the courts and, increasingly, citizen activists such as bloggers and online mobilizers. Internationally the prime minister's policy options are limited by global agreements and diplomacy. There is also the ever-present risk of internal party revolt, including from aspiring party leaders. The issue of the prime minister having too much power is mostly related to the rigidity of party discipline in Canada, a problem that exists in both majority and minority parliaments, and yet is also a source of leadership strength.

CONCLUSION

The recent era of minority government was characterized by instability, short-term decisions, and political games. The record shows that leaders with a minority of votes in the legislature become biased toward increasing government spending and avoiding difficult decisions. Supporters of this form of government tend to draw upon evidence from other countries, to complain about the electoral system, and to cite the Pearson era as the glory years.[27] If Canadians need minority governments it is for two reasons: first, as a warning to political parties, leaders, and cabinet ministers that they must not get too comfortable with the levers of power and, second, to remind voters how much they prefer the comparative tranquillity of life under a majority government.

A functioning majority can provide a strong, stable government and a leader who is able to calmly manage government business or who may actively implement reforms. The governing party can make decisions on behalf of an electorate that is less divided and less agitated. It reflects a democratic compromise of selecting a leader in an election every four years and the ability of that leader to balance short-term and long-term decisions for the good of society as a whole. Given the evidence, it seems clear that a majority government is, all things considered, better than a minority government.

NOTES

1. Peter Aucoin, Jennifer Smith, and Geoff Dinsdale, *Responsible Government: Clarifying Essentials, Dispelling Myths and Exploring Change* (Ottawa: Canadian Centre for Management Development, 2004).

2. Graham White, *Cabinets and First Ministers* (Vancouver: UBC Press, 2005).

3. Robin V. Sears, "Minority Government: From Productive to Dysfunctional," *Policy Options* (October 2009), p. 31.

4. Harris Decima, "Canadians Say It's Time for a Majority Government," July 12, 2009, available at http://www.harrisdecima.com/sites/default/files/releases/071309E.pdf. Accessed August 17, 2011.

5. Nik Nanos, "Canadians Don't Want a Fall Election; Majority Preferred but Minority Expected," *Policy Options* (October 2009), pp. 16–20.

6. Anna Esselment, "Market Orientation in a Canadian Minority Government: The Challenges of Product Delivery," in Alex Marland, Thierry Giasson, and Jennifer Lees-Marshment, eds., *Political Marketing in Canada* (Vancouver: UBC Press, forthcoming).

7. C.E.S. Franks, *The Parliament of Canada* (Toronto: University of Toronto Press, 1987), p. 50.

8. Peter H. Russell, *Two Cheers for Minority Government: The Evolution of Canadian Parliamentary Democracy* (Toronto: Emond Montgomery, 2008), p. 95.

9. J.S. Hodgson, "The Impact of Minority Government on the Senior Civil Servant," *Canadian Public Administration* 19, no. 2 (June 1976), p. 234.

10. Elisabeth Gidengil and André Blais, "Are Party Leaders Becoming More Important to Vote Choice in Canada?" in Hans J. Michelmann, Donald C. Story, and Jeffrey S. Steeves, eds., *Political Leadership and Representation in Canada* (Toronto: University of Toronto Press, 2007).

11. Tony L. Hill, *Canadian Politics: Riding by Riding* (Minnesota: Prospect Park Press, 2002), p. 22.

12. Steven Chase, Erin Anderssen. and Bill Curry, "Stimulus Spending Favours Tory Ridings," *The Globe and Mail*, October 21, 2009, available at http://www.theglobe-andmail.com/news/politics/stimulus-program-favours-tory-ridings/article1333239/. Accessed August 17, 2011.

13. David A. Good, "Minority Government: Politics, Planning, and the Public Service" (paper prepared for the "Governing Without a Majority: What Consequences in Westminster Systems?" conference, Université de Montréal, November 12, 2010, p. 9), available at http://www.criteres.umontreal.ca/pdf/D.Good-presentation.pdf. For an opposing view see Paul E.J. Thomas, "Measuring the Effectiveness of a Minority Parliament," *Canadian Parliamentary Review* (Spring 2007), pp. 22–31.

14. Don Martin, "Tories have Book on Political Wrangling," *National Post*, May 17, 2007, available at http://www.canada.com/nationalpost/news/story.html?id=16b42ac1-56a5-429c-a013-d9464dce3de1&tk=0. Accessed August 17, 2011.

15. Government of Canada, Report of the Standing Committee on Procedure and House Affairs, "Question of Privilege Relating to the Failure of the Government to Fully Provide the Documents as Ordered by the House" (Ottawa: House of Commons, 2011), p. 18.

16. Hodgson, "The Impact of Minority Government on the Senior Civil Servant," p. 233.

17. Good, "Minority Government."

18. Good, "Minority Government," p. 1.

19. John C. Courtney, "Prime Ministerial Character: An Examination of Mackenzie King's Political Leadership," *Canadian Journal of Political Science* 9, no. 1 (March 1976), p. 98.

20. Conservative Party of Canada, "Here for Canada: Stephen Harper's Low-Tax Plan for Jobs and Economic Growth," April 2011, available at http://www.conservative.ca/media/ConservativePlatform2011_ENs.pdf. Accessed August 17, 2011.

21. Aucoin, Smith, and Dinsdale, *Responsible Government*, p. 58.

22. Peter Regenstreif, *The Appeal of Majority Government* (Toronto: Longmans, 1965).

23. Hodgson, "The Impact of Minority Government on the Senior Civil Servant."

24. Russell, *Two Cheers for Minority Government*.

25. Jeffrey Simpson, *The Friendly Dictatorship* (Toronto: McClelland & Stewart, 2001).

26. White, *Cabinets and First Ministers*.

27. Eugene Forsey, "The Problem of 'Minority' Government in Canada," *Canadian Journal of Economics and Political Science* 30 (1964), pp. 1–11; and Howard Cody, "Minority Government in Canada: The Stephen Harper Experience," *American Review of Canadian Studies* 38 (2008), pp. 27–42.

✘ NO

The Case for an Effective Minority Government
ANNA ESSELMENT

The Westminster-style parliamentary system can result in numerous types of governments. In Canada, we are most familiar with majority governments. This is where an election results in one party winning over 50 percent of the seats in the House of Commons (at least 155 of 308). As a result, and with new fixed election dates in Canada, the governing party can control the parliamentary agenda with relative ease for the ensuing four years. When this does not occur, the party with the most seats (but not a majority) may be asked to form the government as a minority. A minority government may govern as a single party on an issue-by-issue basis, or with the declared (but informal) support of another smaller party. A more formal coalition could also result, with a larger and smaller party joining forces to govern, or by a collection of smaller parties banding together to hold the confidence of Parliament.

The predominant wisdom in Canada is that minority governments are unstable, ineffective, and temporary, often laden by partisan rancour and the constant threat of an impending election. When we examine minority/coalition governments both abroad and at home, however, we see that minority governments are not by their nature weak; in fact, a minority situation can be quite effective through its tendency to encourage consensus building, to give a role to smaller parties, to increase the power of individual Members of Parliament (MPs), and to strengthen parliamentary institutions such as committees.

MINORITIES AND COALITIONS ARE NOT RARE

In most other countries that use the Westminster model, it is majority governments that are elusive—electoral outcomes elsewhere tend to result in "hung" Parliaments that demand political parties form either a minority government or engage in coalition building to put together a governing entity capable of securing the confidence of the House of Commons.[1] This occurs quite regularly in countries that have some form of proportional representation in their electoral systems, such as Australia, New Zealand, Germany, and Denmark. More recently, the May 2010 general election in the United Kingdom, which, like Canada, follows the single-member plurality (SMP) system of electing representatives, resulted in a Parliament in which no party had won the majority of seats. For a number of days following the election, the three main political parties—Labour, Conservatives, and Liberal Democrats—negotiated which two among them would be capable of putting together a working coalition. Ultimately the Conservative and Liberal Democrat Parties agreed to form a government together.

In Canada, majority governments have tended to be the norm, although we are not unfamiliar with minority governments. To date there have been thirteen minority governments in Canada. Mackenzie King's first minority government lasted almost four years (1921–1925), the traditional tenure for a majority Parliament. The shortest was led by Conservative Arthur Meighan in 1926, which only held government for two and a half months. On average, the duration of minority governments in this country is almost two years.[2] This is a lesser timeframe than the three to four year terms of parliamentary democracies with the most minority governments (Denmark, Norway, Spain, and Sweden), but it suggests that minorities in Canada are not inherently short lived when compared with others around the world.[3]

PRODUCTIVE MINORITIES AND PARLIAMENTARY CONSENSUS BUILDING

Considering that minority governments are not "extreme" cases in the history of Canadian parliaments, we must examine whether or not they can be as effective as majority governments. One measure of effectiveness is the productivity of government. In other words, is a party leading a minority government able to achieve its agenda? Peter Russell has noted that, save for three administrations, minority parliaments in Canada have been quite effective in passing legislation that has benefited Canadians.[4] For good reason, some observers focus primarily on the achievements of Lester Pearson's two minority governments in the 1960s as the best examples. Under his leadership, the Parliament of Canada set up a national medicare program, the Canada and Quebec Pension Plans, the new Canadian flag, Royal Commissions on the Status of Women and on Bilingualism and Biculturalism, and it refused to send troops to Vietnam.[5] However, the so-called "glory years" should not be confined to Pearson's time as Prime Minister. John Diefenbaker's minority government in 1957 was able, among other things, to increase old age pensions, expand unemployment insurance benefits (as it was then called), provide money to help farmers, cut taxes for low-income families and small businesses, and establish a Royal Commission on Energy.[6] Pierre Trudeau's 1972 minority also cut personal income tax, instituted higher pensions and family allowances, and removed the federal sales tax on children's clothing and shoes.[7] In Paul Martin's time as Prime Minister, he laid the foundation for a national child care program (albeit later rescinded by Stephen Harper's minority government), and in Stephen Harper's first minority, Conservatives cut the GST, reshaped the child care agenda, introduced tougher crime legislation, and imposed a new Accountability Act overseeing conduct within government—in total, his government passed 65 of the 125 bills introduced in Parliament.[8] Clearly minority governments can also be productive governments.[9]

Furthermore, many of these achievements were the result of consensus building within Parliament. Unlike under a majority government, there is no guarantee that a proposed piece of legislation will pass through Parliament. The decree of the Prime Minister and a whipped vote of cabinet and caucus members alone cannot ensure successful passage through the Commons because the government does not have enough votes. Consequently, there is a much greater need to consult with other parties about certain items that are important to the governing party's agenda in order to secure agreement for their success. This requires communication, deliberation, negotiation and, ultimately, Parliamentary consensus on bills with one or more opposition parties. Pierre Trudeau was able to work well with David Lewis, the leader of the NDP, on much of the government's agenda from 1972 to 1974.[10] Paul Martin's 2005 budget included many items requested by the NDP in order to garner that party's support. New funding for housing, seniors, and the unemployed were a result of close cooperation between the Liberals and the NDP. Likewise, the 2008 decision to extend Canada's combat role in Afghanistan and the 2010 decision to continue a "military training" effort in that country was a result of a bipartisan effort that included Bob Rae, the Liberal Foreign Affairs critic at the time, heading a special Commons committee to study the issue. Greater cooperation also informed the contents of the 2009 budget where the Conservatives sought to provide a more palatable response to the global economic crisis and agreed to provide economic updates to Parliament.[11] Seeking a consensus lends greater legitimacy to government decision making since it is the result of true *parliamentary* consultation rather than the decision taking of one person (the prime minister) or party. Considering that the popular vote for the governing party in 2004, 2006, and 2008 did not exceed 38 percent,[12] we see that minority parliaments must take into account the positions of other parties and, by extension, the views of many more Canadians.

GREATER ROLE FOR SMALLER PARTIES

Given the SMP electoral system and Canada's inherent regionalism, there have developed a number of smaller parties at the federal level that may win parliamentary seats but which have little hope of winning government (the NDP and Bloc Québécois come readily to mind). Minority governments provide a way for smaller parties to have more influence without requiring them to shed their identities.[13] Majority governments can ignore smaller parties altogether, and a coalition government between a larger and smaller party often entails the junior partner signing on to a governing agenda that tends to favour the policy inclinations of the larger party. This can have the effect both of diluting the identity of the smaller party and possibly alienating its voter base that may resist being enveloped by a stronger party. In contrast, minority parliaments increase the chances of non-governing parties' bills successfully passing into legislation because of multiparty cooperation and support. Furthermore, the ability to select which bills to support on a more ad hoc basis, or for a certain length of time in Parliament, gives smaller parties influence on those particular issues since the governing party is always seeking support and thus is more amenable to changes that will secure agreement. The 1985–87 legislative alliance between the Ontario Liberals and the NDP is a good case in point. The Ontario Progressive Conservatives had only won a minority government after the 1985 election. The Premier, Frank Miller, tried to lead a government but soon resigned once it became known that the Liberals and NDP had forged an accord that would allow the Liberals to govern, as a minority, for two years with NDP support. No NDP members were brought into cabinet, and the NDP remained the third party in the Legislative Assembly. However, many NDP policies were included in the accord and implemented over the ensuing two years.

We see this greater role for smaller parties at the federal level as well. Mackenzie King worked with the Progressives and, as mentioned earlier, Pierre Trudeau's minority relied on the NDP for support. Paul Martin also worked with the NDP, while Stephen Harper was able to obtain support, at different times, from all three opposition parties throughout his two minority administrations. Giving a stronger role and influence to smaller parties, without asking them to abandon long-standing principles or policies, is unique to minority governments. As with consensus decision making, this enhances the representative role of Parliament. Canadians who voted for parties *other* than the one forming government have increased influence over the decisions of government. This is rarely the case in majority governments where the smaller parties are just that: small players, relegated to the opposition benches with few, if any, opportunities to provide meaningful input into government decision making.

GREATER ROLE FOR INDIVIDUAL MPS

The role of the individual Member of Parliament can be enhanced by a minority parliament. A good indication is the number of Private Members' Bills (PMB) passed. A PMB is introduced by MPs who are not cabinet ministers. They can address any matter, but must not involve the raising or spending of public money unless pre-approved by a cabinet member. It is difficult to pass a PMB, since many tabled by opposition members do not often correspond with the government's policy agenda. Only 235 PMBs have been given Royal Assent since 1910, although many more have been introduced into the legislative process.[14] PMBs do have a better chance of success in a minority Parliament because an MP can cooperate with and/or cajole members of other opposition parties (and occasionally government members) to support his or her initiative. During the combined seven years of minority government under Paul Martin and Stephen Harper (2004–2011), twenty-nine PMBs were passed by Parliament. During the eleven years of majority rule under Prime Minister Jean Chrétien (1993–2004), only twenty-seven PMBs were passed by Parliament.[15]

An individual MP's power is augmented in other ways as well. One is simply that every vote truly does count—the government cannot pass its legislative agenda without the support of some members of the opposition benches. In order to avoid an election for which they may be ill-prepared, some opposition parties have a more open policy about whether their members can vote for government-initiated bills. Having to court these votes "requires a government to consult with MPs in advance to ensure their support and possibly to make changes to policies in order to accommodate their specific interests."[16]

Similarly, in order to increase its seat count, individual opposition MPs may be covertly courted by the governing party to cross the floor. MPs may be persuaded with promises of a cabinet post or other attractive positions within government.[17] Two recent examples are former Conservative MP Belinda Stronach, who joined the Liberals in May 2005 and saved the government from losing a vote of non-confidence, and David Emerson, who crossed from the Liberals to the Conservatives after the 2006 election and resumed the cabinet post he had held under the previous Liberal administration. Targeting and inducing individual members to prominent positions within the government occurs less often in a majority situation.

STRENGTHENING COMMITTEES

The House of Commons has a number of committees that serve to assist in the review of proposed legislation. In a majority Parliament most members of committees are from the government caucus. Consequently, members of the opposition parties do not have much influence over the amendment process and, at the end of the committee stage, bills tend to remain in the same form as they arrived. In a minority government, however, opposition MPs have the upper hand in committees. Debate on the bill is thus more meaningful, proposed amendments more successful, and, arguably, the government is truly held to account.[18] One example of this is Bill C-10, introduced by the Harper government in May 2006, which proposed mandatory minimum sentences for firearms offences. The opposition parties were against the high minimums imposed by the bill and the non-government members of the Standing Committee on Justice and Human Rights made significant amendments that removed what they viewed as the harsher elements of the proposed legislation.[19] While Bill C-10 was later incorporated into an omnibus bill entitled "Tackling Violent Crime" that passed in the House in February 2008, the government proceeded in this manner *because* of the power of the Justice committee to influence the content of its individual crime bills. Combining bills into one larger piece of legislation demonstrates that a government frustrated with committees "bogging down" the process can grind committee work to a halt, as Stephen Harper did in 2008.[20] Learning to compromise at the committee stage is a feature of minority government to which all parties must become accustomed.

HOW TO IMPROVE A MINORITY GOVERNMENT

To this point we have seen that minority governments can be very effective. They can improve consensus building in Parliament, they provide a greater role for smaller parties, the role of the individual MP is enhanced, and they can strengthen certain parliamentary institutions such as committees. Many of these character- istics of minority government are what some scholars desire in their calls for the "reform" of Parliament. At the same time, it is clear that there are ways to improve a minority government in Canada and the following section will outline some possible ideas.

First, we can no longer view minorities as exceptions to the majority rule. Minority government outcomes are distinct possibilities in democracies using par- liamentary systems. While the demise of the Bloc Québécois in the 2011 general election may result in a return to majority governments for the next couple of Parliaments, Canadian politics is always surprising and Quebeckers' experiment with the NDP may be fleeting. The party could lose seats to the Liberals or Con- servatives in the next election or, if nationalism swells again at the provincial level, a resurgent Bloc Québécois or similar Quebec-only party may lead to further minority governments at the federal level. This could also occur if westerners become disenchanted with the Conservative Party, and a new regionally based party in B.C. or the Prairies takes root. Furthermore, while Canadians may not yet realize that minority government can also mean stable, effective government, they continue to embrace electoral reform in order to improve representation in Parliament. A recent poll suggested that 58 percent of Canadians are willing to open up the Constitution in order to bring about changes to the single-member plurality system by which the percentage of seats won by each party is roughly equivalent or proportional to its percentage of the vote.[21] As noted in other coun- tries with proportionality built into their electoral systems, minority and coalition governments become the new reality in governance and that expectation by the public can contribute to the stability of minority governments.[22] Should similar changes be made in Canada, we must be prepared to accept the same.

Second, how the media views and reports on politics during a minority govern- ment must evolve. Because the longevity of government is not guaranteed as it is in a majority, the media focuses solely on clashes between parties and leaders and, by extension, the prospect of the government's demise, instead of the issues and instances of parliamentary cooperation and consensus. Horse-race journalism is certainly a prominent feature of political reporting everywhere, but it can paint an inaccurate picture of parliamentary instability. There will be debate in the Commons, there will be tough questions posed to the prime minister and govern- ment of the day, there will be a degree of political posturing among the members, but none of this implies the implosion of the government and the dissolution of Parliament to make way for new elections. Unless on conventional confidence matters or those motions and legislation explicitly declared as such, bills that fail to be passed by the House should not be portrayed by the media as major defeats for the government. A minority government will suffer more legislative hardships in the Commons than a majority government, but this is simply a characteristic of such a Parliament. Arguably, the media's constant preoccupation with the next election likely fuels election fatigue among Canadians that would not exist otherwise if the perception of minority government as a permanent feature of Westminster systems was an accepted axiom.

Third, and as an extension of the first two points, Canadian political culture must shift to be more accepting of minority governments. As argued above, they can be both stable and effective and are not an "aberration" in Westminster systems. If we consider that Canada's electoral system is predisposed to produce majority governments, the appearance of minority parliaments (especially three in a row) must be for a reason. Canadians of late have been wary of handing over a strong mandate to any one party; "Work together!" seems to be our message to our politicians. In fact, it could be argued that Canadians have shifted to embrace minority government and it is our representatives who must be more accepting and adapt to Parliaments that require greater power-sharing practices, not resist it.[23] Tom Flanagan has suggested that this may entail

> fewer 'bolt from the blue' announcements of new government policies, [m]ore quiet meetings among leaders or their delegates, [g]overnment invitations to opposition parties to contribute to drafting legislation, [and] [a]mendments moved in good faith, not just to obstruct.[24]

Embracing such practices is clearly out of the comfort zone for many of our representatives, particularly those who have extensive experience as members in a majority government and who would prefer to fight in numerous elections until such a Parliament is produced. However, as wisely noted by Eugene Forsey:

> [P]oliticians…have no right to inflict on us the conspicuous waste of a series of general elections just because we elect a Parliament that does not suit them. It is our Parliament, not theirs. They are our servants, not our masters.[25]

Successfully shifting political cultural in Parliament and thus improving a minority government will involve not only greater power-sharing practices, but also a lessening of control over messaging and "permanent campaigning" by all parties, but particularly by the party in power. It is no secret that the Office of the Prime Minister (PMO) under Stephen Harper has tight control over government messaging. Only a few ministers are permitted to speak to the media, civil servants must have press releases or announcements "approved" by the PMO, and early in his tenure as prime minister, Harper implemented a "list" system regarding questions from the press gallery so that he could avoid being ambushed by reporters' questions.[26] Many of these tactics are part of the "permanent campaign"[27] practised by many parties in power. It is certainly important to parties in a minority government since the possibility of being thrown back into an election is greater than those enjoying a majority. In the permanent campaign, politicians and their close advisers consult often with trusted pollsters and strategists to ensure that action taken in government is viewed positively by their supporters and potential supporters. Every move is tactical and geared toward ensuring success at the polls during the next election. In other words, the campaign does not end when the votes are counted—it continues in office in order to prepare for the *next* election, whenever that might be. This explains why having control over the "message" is critical and the steps taken to do so (by silencing Members of Parliament, for example) are to ensure that no dilution or detraction from that message occurs. The advent of the permanent campaign is a result, among other things, of the professionalization of elections, the growing and diversified electorate, and access to sophisticated polling information that gives a party a more accurate snapshot of how segments of the public think about certain issues. While the permanent campaign can permeate majority governments as well, it has less of an impact given the almost guaranteed four-year lifespan of the government. If Canadians in general, and politicians in particular, can increasingly view minority governments as part of the political system, the need for control over the message by the PMO may be alleviated and improve the prospects for minority government.

A fifth, but no means final, change to improve minority government would be a clear understanding of the constitutional rules of parliamentary government. Peter Russell has made a compelling case for the codification of our unwritten conventions;[28] this would clarify the role and powers of the Crown that oversee our parliamentary democracy and arm Canadians with the knowledge of how governments are formed and dissolved. This would also go a long way to debunk the "myths" that the prime minister is directly elected, that *only* an election can determine which party will form the government, and that it is a "coup" for smaller parties in a minority Parliament to suggest forming a coalition to hold the confidence of Parliament. The 2008 constitutional crisis (whereby the recently elected Conservative minority government was at risk of losing power to a proposed formal coalition of the Liberal and NDP parties with BQ legislative support) was a crisis only insofar as there was a general lack of understanding by the politicians[29] and the public about the constitutional conventions that guide parliamentary democracy. As Russell notes:

> At the present time, it appears that there is neither agreement among our political leaders on what these conventions are nor understanding by the majority of politically engaged citizens of what they mean...[t]he lack of political consensus on fundamental principles of our constitution poses a serious threat to the stability of our parliamentary democracy. It means that the principle players in our constitutional politics do not agree on the fundamental rules of the game.[30]

New Zealand has pressed forward with just such a task and its Cabinet Manual[31] outlines in detail the roles and responsibilities of different players (including the

Governor-General, Ministers, and Cabinet) and on "situations" such as elections, transitions, and government formation. A similar undertaking here, made publicly accessible, would assist Canadians in their understandings of our political system and clear up what has to be viewed as the murkier waters of a minority Parliament.

IS A MAJORITY GOVERNMENT REALLY THAT GREAT?

While minority governments are often more stable and effective than we may admit, majority governments have a four-year term during which the party in power can get through its policy agenda more easily. The implication is that a majority government is better equipped for long-term policy planning than a minority government. This is not necessarily true; at most, a majority government is better at four-year planning (the time until the next election must be fought). There are obvious exceptions to this argument: Brian Mulroney helped ensure a steady revenue stream with the implementation of the GST and that Canada would be competitive with American markets by passing the North American Free Trade Agreement. But there are similar examples under minority regimes: Lester Pearson's administration, for instance, implemented national medicare and a pension for all Canadians. In short, long-term policy visions cannot be compartmentalized into "majority" or "minority" categories; they are more likely the result of particular leaders and issues.

Second, minority governments have often been accused of raising the level of partisan attacks in the Commons and seizing opportunities to belittle the opposition or government. Let's be clear—parliamentary government is "party" government. Partisanship is a characteristic of our system and unlikely to fade in any Parliament, be it majority or minority. Moreover, political opportunism is not the sole purview of minority governments. One only need be reminded of the 2000 general election, called early by Liberal Prime Minister Jean Chrétien for the primary reason of demoralizing and undermining the newly formed Canadian Alliance party and its leader Stockwell Day. Merely months after Day had been elected as head of the party, and just weeks after entering the House of Commons, Chrétien and the Liberals asked for a dissolution of Parliament and a subsequent election. While newcomer Day was able to increase the number of parliamentary seats in the House, he certainly did not perform as well as his supporters had hoped. Not surprisingly, Chrétien and the Liberals were able to win enough seats for another majority.

Third, while Marland in this volume correctly distinguishes between a super and functioning majority, he dismisses too easily the phenomenon of a "false" majority. A false majority occurs when the governing party wins a majority of parliamentary seats but fails to win more than 50 percent of the popular vote.[32] Of the forty-one Parliaments in Canada's history, fourteen have been "false majorities"; there have been no true majorities (where the majority of seats and over 50 percent of the popular vote coincide) since 1968. In 1997, for example, Jean Chrétien and the Liberal

Party won a majority government with only 39 percent of the popular vote! This means that over 60 percent of citizens who voted in that election selected a party *other* than the Liberals to represent them. Regionalism and the SMP electoral system have certainly led to these types of outcomes—that point is readily conceded. But the larger implications of false majorities on the representative function of Parliament, and the representation needs of Canadians, are ones that must be seriously considered. Despite the apparent "stability" of majority governments, citizens have become increasingly disengaged with the political and electoral process partly because they lack true representation in Parliament.[33] Minority governments enhance the representative function of Parliament and, by extension, the ability of political parties to represent Canadians across the country.

Fourth, where minority parliaments strengthen the influence of smaller parties, increase the power of individual MPs, and render more meaningful the work done in committees, majority governments can have the opposite effect. Opposition parties are unable to influence the government's agenda when the party in power has a majority. There is little need for consensus decision making, negotiation, or cooperation. Private members' bills from the smaller parties have little chance of success. The majority party also controls the committees and thus the ability of opposition members to contribute to the law-making process with amendments to legislation is substantially reduced. In a way, opposition parties are truly relegated to their "opposing" function and have fewer avenues of keeping the government to account.

Finally, a majority government does not alleviate the overarching role of the PMO. While control over the message may be more tightly regulated in a minority government, the power of the Prime Minister's Office and the excesses of majority government are likely to remain. Donald Savoie has effectively detailed the concentration of power in the "centre" of government (the PMO, PCO, Finance Department and Treasury Board)[34] and the suspicion is that Canada's "friendly dictator"—Prime Minister Harper—will reverse "parliamentary government," arguably enjoyed since 2004, back into "prime-ministerial" government:

> When the same handful of political leaders directs government and controls parliament, these trends are particularly unfriendly to the democratic capacity of parliamentary government….Minority government is no cure-all, but it has the great merit of providing a better prospect of resisting these trends and strengthening the democratic capacity of parliamentary government. As Eugene Forsey put it, "A government without a clear majority is likely to stop, look and listen."[35]

CONCLUSION

This side of the debate has argued that minority government is neither rare nor an aberration of the Westminster system of government. It can increase government accountability, parliamentary representation, the role of smaller parties and individual

MPs, and strengthen committees. Minority government can also be quite stable and effective. The challenge for Canadians and their representatives is to accept that minority parliaments may occur more often and to embrace the advantages they bring. While we have now returned to majority rule under Stephen Harper and the Conservatives, the "excesses" of a majority government that could return over the next four years may serve to remind us that minority parliaments aren't so bad after all.

NOTES

1. A 1990 study found that, between 1945 and 1987, only 13 percent of Western European and Commonwealth parliamentary democracies were single-party majority governments. The rest were either minorities or coalition governments. See Karre Strom, *Minority Government and Majority Rule* (Cambridge: Cambridge University Press, 1990), p. 65.

2. This includes Stephen Harper's 2008–2011 minority government. See Peter H. Russell, *Two Cheers for Minority Government* (Toronto: Emond Montgomery, 2008).

3. Ibid.

4. Ibid.

5. Martha Hall Findlay. "The Potential in a Minority Government," *Policy Options* (October 2010), pp. 54–55.

6. Peter C. Newman, *Renegade in Power* (Toronto: McClelland and Stewart, 1973), pp. 64–65.

7. Richard Gwyn, *The Northern Magus* (Toronto: McClelland and Stewart, 1980), pp. 149–150.

8. CBC News, "The 39th Parliament: A Dysfunctional or Productive Session?" September 9, 2008, available at http://cbc.ca/news/canadavotes/issuesanalysis/sheppard-legislativetally.html. Accessed May 17, 2011.

9. See also Paul E.J. Thomas, "Measuring the Effectiveness of a Minority Parliament," *Canadian Parliamentary Review* 30, no. 1 (2007), pp. 22–31.

10. Gwyn, *The Northern Magus*, pp. 149–150.

11. CBC News, "Ignatieff Puts Tories 'On Probation' with Budget Demand," January 28, 2009, available at http://www.cbc.ca/news/canada/story/2009/01/28/ignatieff-decision.html. Accessed June 2, 2011.

12. Elections Canada, *Elections*, available at http://www.elections.ca/content.aspx?section=ele&lang=e. Accessed June 18, 2011.

13. Joaquin Artes and Antonio Bustos, "Electoral Promises and Minority Governments: An Empirical Study," *European Journal of Political Research* 47, no. 3 (2008), pp. 307–333; and Mark Chalmers, "Canada's Dysfunctional Minority Parliament," *Making Minority Government Work* (Institute for Government UK, December 2009), p. 31.

14. Library of Parliament, "Private Members' Public Bills Passed by Parliament: 1910 to Date," available at http://www.parl.gc.ca/Parlinfo/Compilations/HouseOfCommons/legislation/privatememberspublicbills.aspx. Accessed June 21, 2011.

15. Ibid. Paul Martin was prime minister of the Liberal majority government for a few months in 2004.

16. Chalmers, "Canada's Dysfunctional Minority Parliament," p. 32.

17. Ibid.

18. Thomas, "Measuring the Effectiveness of a Minority Parliament," pp. 24–25.

19. Parliament of Canada, "Bill C-10: An Act to Amend the Criminal Code," June 6, 2007, available at http://www.parl.gc.ca/About/Parliament/LegislativeSummaries/bills_ls.as p?lang=E&ls=c10&Parl=39&Ses=1&source=library_prb. Accessed July 5, 2011.

20. Don Martin, "Tories have Book on Political Wrangling," *National Post,* May 17, 2007, available at http://www.nationalpost.com/news/story.html?id=16b42ac1-56a5-429c-a013-d9464dce3de1&tk=0. Accessed July 5, 2011.

21. Canadian Press, "Are Canadians Over Their Constitutional Phobias?" *CBC News Online,* May 27, 2011, available at http://www.cbc.ca/news/politics/story/2011/05/27/pol-constitution-poll.html. Accessed June 21, 2011.

22. Howard Cody, "Minority Government in Canada: The Stephen Harper Experience," *American Review of Canadian Studies* 38, no. 1 (2008), pp. 28–29.

23. Tom Flanagan, "A Canadian Approach to Power-Sharing," *Policy Options* (September 2010), pp. 32–36.

24. Flanagan, "A Canadian Approach to Power-Sharing," p. 36.

25. Eugene Forsey, "The Problem of 'Minority' Government in Canada," *The Canadian Journal of Economics and Political Science* 30, no. 1 (1964), p. 6.

26. Lawrence Martin, *Harperland: The Politics of Control* (Toronto: Viking Canada, 2010).

27. Sidney Blumenthal, *The Permanent Campaign: Inside the World of Elite Political Operatives* (Boston: Beacon Press, 1980).

28. Peter H. Russell, "Learning to Live with Minority Governments," in Peter H. Russell and Lorne Sossin, eds., *Parliamentary Democracy in Crisis* (Toronto: University of Toronto Press, 2009), pp. 136–149.

29. Some may argue a deliberate misguidance of the public on the issue.

30. Russell, "Learning to Live with Minority Governments," p. 148.

31. Cabinet Office, Department of Prime Minister and Cabinet, *Cabinet Manual,* (Wellington: Government of New Zealand, 2008).

32. Russell, *Two Cheers for Minority Government,* pp. 8–9.

33. Elisabeth Gidengil et al., *Citizens* (Vancouver: UBC Press, 2004).

34. Donald J. Savoie, *Governing from the Centre: The Concentration of Power in Canadian Politics* (Toronto: University of Toronto Press, 1999).

35. Russell, *Two Cheers for Minority Government,* pp. 101–102.

POSTSCRIPT

Alex Marland develops a solid case for majority government. This is done partly by showing not so much what is good about legislative majorities but what is bad about legislative minorities. The latter do seem to get in the way of rational planning and do seem prone to spending money foolishly to ensure support for one party or the other. Marland also reveals that majority governments typically escape these failings of minority governments and allow parties in power to act productively and rationally. But on reading Marland's effort one sometimes gets the feeling that he (along with other Canadians) wishes to take the politics out of politics. The shenanigans and game playing some see in a minority government might be viewed by others as an opening up of a political system that too often is closed and unreceptive. Politics, at least the democratic variety, is messy, so anything that adds to this quality should not be rejected out of hand. Marland also appears to think that productive government can only be synonymous with majority government, but some challenge this claim. From some scholarly viewpoints, the Harper minority governments, for example, did more than nothing.

Anna Esselment also presents a convincing case for her side of the debate. She puts to rest the notion that minority governments amount to irregularities in the body politic—they are clearly not. Esselment also gently leads us through the arguments for a minority government and then offers sound suggestions to make this type of government work even better. She then ends with a query about whether majorities are really as wonderful as people claim them to be (and supplies the expected answer). All nicely done, but we do have a query or two for Esselment. She likes the consensus-based process for policymaking in minority governments, but one wonders if this process nullifies the bold initiatives that are more likely to be the brainchild of a single party (or a few within a party) than the result of a group representing the various parties. Esselment is rightly impressed with the more democratic nature of minority governments, but even she realizes that sometimes the politicking can go too far. One of her solutions to this blemish is the reform of the electoral system, but it is not clear that Canadians are ready for such a reform. Polls may say they are indeed ready, but other indicators say differently (voters clobbered a proposal for proportional representation in the 2007 Ontario election). So we are back to a minority government that can sometimes resemble children playing in a sandbox.

To participate in this debate, a student first needs an understanding of parliamentary government. This can be acquired by reading the relevant chapters of a good introduction to Canadian politics—for example, Heather MacIvor, *Parameters of Power: Canada's Political Institutions,* 5th ed. (Toronto: Nelson Education, 2010). A more thorough treatment can be gained in the student edition of Peter Hogg's *Constitutional Law of Canada, 2010* (Toronto: Thomson Carswell, 2010). The next step is to appreciate more directly the place of majority and minority government in the parliamentary system, and for this one should go to Jennifer Smith, "Canada's Minority Parliament," in James Bickerton and Alain-G. Gagnon, eds., *Canadian Politics,* 5th ed. (Toronto: University of Toronto Press, 2009).

Now we are ready to tackle the literature on the merits of majority and minority governments. The best place to start is Peter H. Russell, *Two Cheers for Minority Government: The Evolution of Canadian Parliamentary Democracy* (Toronto: Emond Montgomery, 2008). The title reveals that the author has a decided preference in this debate, but the volume still offers a good analysis of majority and minority governments. Other relevant readings are Howard Cody, "Minority Government in Canada: The Stephen Harper Experience," *American Review of Canadian Studies* 38, no. 1 (2008), and Paul E.J. Thomas, "Measuring the Effectiveness of a Minority Parliament," *Canadian Parliamentary Review* 30, no. 1 (2007). A study with an international flavour is Joaquin Artes and Antonio Bustos, "Electoral Promises and Minority Governments: An Empirical Study," *European Journal of Political Research* 47, no. 3 (2008).

As both articles in this debate note, minority governments can lead to a lot of manoeuvring, some of which can have major implications for the governing of a country. In late 2008, the newly elected minority government of Stephen Harper faced a situation that appeared fatal to its existence, and the prime minister took actions that startled many Canadians. For readings on this relevant event, see Peter H. Russell and Lorne Sossin, eds., *Parliamentary Democracy in Crisis* (Toronto: University of Toronto Press, 2009), and Peter H. Russell et al., eds. *Essential Readings in Canadian Government and Politics* (Toronto: Emond Montgomery, 2010), chs. 21 (Tom Flanagan) and 22 (various authors).

Should Party Discipline Be Relaxed?

✔ **YES**
DAVID KILGOUR, JOHN KIRSNER, AND KENNETH
McCONNELL, "Discipline versus Democracy:
Party Discipline in Canadian Politics"

✘ **NO**
ROBERT J. JACKSON, "The Imperative of Party Discipline in
the Canadian Political System"

David Kilgour, a former Member of Parliament (MP) from Alberta, had a rocky relationship with the Progressive Conservative Party throughout his career. Elected to Parliament in 1979 as a member of the Conservative Party, Kilgour quit the party caucus in April 1987 in protest over the Conservative government's policies for the West and its failure to develop adequate ethical guidelines for elected representatives. Kilgour rejoined the Tory caucus in February 1988 but soon became critical of his party's proposed goods and services tax (GST). On April 10, 1990, he voted against the government's bill authorizing the GST and, as a consequence, was expelled from the caucus of the Progressive Conservative Party. Kilgour subsequently crossed the floor to sit as a member of the Liberal Party. He has since been reelected four times as a Liberal Member of Parliament.

In April 2005, David Kilgour's parliamentary career took yet another twist. Following revelations of the Gomery Commission into misuse of government funds under the sponsorship program in Quebec, Kilgour announced that he could no longer sit in the Liberal caucus in good conscience. Instead, he indicated that he would henceforth sit as an independent in Parliament and would retire from federal politics when the next election was called. Kilgour retired from politics in 2006.

David Kilgour's troubles with his former parties stem from the well-known tradition of party discipline, which requires Members of Parliament to vote according to their party's position. Clearly, the member from Alberta has some difficulty with this tradition, and he is not alone. Polls show that only a small percentage of respondents believe that the first priority should be loyalty to his or her party.

Despite this, political leaders have long felt that the principle of party discipline was vital to the functioning of parliamentary government in Canada. When necessary, as in the case of David Kilgour, party officials have shown that they are willing to take strong measures to enforce party discipline—by withholding support for a candidate at election time, by denying parliamentary appointments, or even by expelling a recalcitrant MP from the party caucus.

The rationale for discipline in political parties is a simple one. Canada has a parliamentary system of government that requires that the party in power maintain the support and confidence of the majority of the members of the legislative branch. Without this support, the government would find it difficult to carry out the mandate on which it is elected and, more important, to remain in power. Party discipline is a means of preventing these occurrences.

For many Canadians, as reflected in the following two readings, the debate over party discipline hinges largely on whether or not Canada should move closer to an American model, where members of Congress are seen as being relatively free to vote according to personal conscience and constituency interest. Kilgour, Kirsner, and McConnell argue that relaxed party discipline would advance the cause of democracy and provide better representation for individual constituents. Robert Jackson counters that the weakening of party discipline would give Canada an American-style system in which special interest groups, not elected officials, would control our legislative representatives. He suggests that recent political developments have demonstrated that the traditional model of party discipline continues to well serve the Canadian political system.

✔ **YES**

Discipline versus Democracy: Party Discipline in Canadian Politics

DAVID KILGOUR, JOHN KIRSNER, AND KENNETH McCONNELL

Parliamentary democracy in Canada is so dominated by political parties that some experts believe the party discipline exerted on most votes in our House of Commons and provincial legislatures is the tightest in the democratic world. Defenders of our model argue that many Canadians prefer it this way because each party's candidates can be presumed at election time to share the party's position on every issue. Others contend our executive democracy, patterned on a system prevailing in Great Britain at least a century and a half ago, requires iron party discipline if our fused legislative and executive branches of government are to function effectively. Another reason, probably the most important, is that our practice makes life easier for leaders of both government and opposition parties.

Unlike the parliamentary systems of nations such as Great Britain and Germany, virtually every vote in Canadian legislatures is considered potentially one of non-confidence in the government. Even a frivolous opposition motion to adjourn for the day, if lost, can be deemed by a cabinet to have been one of non-confidence. The whips of government parties have for decades used the possibility of an early election to persuade their members to vote the party line. The attitude of opposition parties is often so similar that we had several years ago the spectacle of both opposition parties in the House of Commons arguing that a free vote on an abortion resolution would "rip out the heart" of our parliamentary system of government. The constituents of both provincial and federal legislators would be the real winners if party discipline were loosened. Private members from both government and opposition benches could then take positions on government bills and other matters based on assisting constituents instead of their respective party hierarchies.

PARTY DISCIPLINE IN CANADA

W.S. Gilbert put the continuing Canadian political reality succinctly: "I always voted at my party's call, and I never thought of thinking for myself at all." Canadian members of Parliament are essentially passive observers in the formulation and administration of most national policy. Indeed, Sean Moore, editor of the Ottawa lobbyist magazine *The Lobby Digest*, told a committee of MPs in 1993 that they are rarely lobbied by the almost three thousand reported lobbyists then in the capital because "elected officials play a very minor role in governing."

MPs from all parties vote in solid blocs on almost every issue. Government members do so from a fear that a lost vote on a measure will be deemed by their prime minister as a loss of confidence. This stems from the early- to mid-nineteenth-century British responsible government concept that a government falls if it loses the support of a majority in the Commons.

Besides the threat of parliamentary dissolution, private members are also subject to rewards and punishments from party leadership, depending on how they vote. A "loyal" MP who votes the party line will be a candidate for promotion (if in the government party, perhaps to cabinet) or other benefits from the party, such as interesting trips or appointment to an interesting House committee. A "disloyal" MP who votes against the party leadership may be prevented from ascending the political ladder and could ultimately be thrown out of the party caucus. In light of this, "caucus solidarity and my constituents be damned" might be the real oath of office for most honourable members in all political parties.

Reg Stackhouse, a former Tory MP for Scarborough West, in a submission to the Task Force on Reform of the House of Commons in 1985, commented on the discipline imposed on private members of the government party:

> Not only is it demanded that [the member] vote with the government on crucial matters such as the Speech from the Throne or the budget, but also that he vote, speak or remain silent according to the dictate of the government. Even though a government may be at no risk of falling, it requires this all but unconditional commitment, and renders the member a seeming robot, at least imaginatively replaceable by a voting machine.

This is the major defect in Canadian parliamentary democracy: most MPs are essentially brute voters who submit to any demand from their respective party whips. In Canada's current political culture, a prime minister or premier could in practice on all confidence votes cast proxy votes on behalf of all government members. The same practice prevails in the opposition parties because they think themselves obliged to vote in uniform party blocs virtually always. If not, some of our media, seemingly unaware that parliamentary democracy has evolved elsewhere, report that the opposition leaders cannot control their caucuses. This *status quo* has persisted for so long primarily because party leaders and policy mandarins in the executive branch obviously prefer it. A policy adviser in Ottawa reminded a meeting of the Study of Parliament Group that there are about 270,000 federal government employees who work for the executive and perhaps 1,700 who work for Parliament. Measures going into the House of Commons where one party has a majority usually emerge essentially unscathed. Everything follows a highly predictable script: obedient government members praise it; opposition parties rail against it; and plenty of bad measures become law essentially unamended.

The present regional differences and priorities require much better public expression in Parliament, at least if one central institution of our national government is to reflect adequately all parts of a diverse and vast country. Regional voices are frequently suffocated by rigid party discipline and the entrenched habit of the national caucuses to maintain a close eye on what opinion leaders, particularly columnists in Toronto–Ottawa–Montreal, regard as the national interest on any issue. Reforming the role of MPs is not only essential for parliamentary legitimacy in postmodern Canada but vital to "nationalizing Ottawa."

ELIMINATING EXCESSES

A report by the late Eugene Forsey and Graham Eglington (*The Question of Confidence in Responsible Government*) lists a large number of measures defeated in the Westminster Parliament. On most, the cabinet of the day simply carried on, presumably either dropping the failed proposal or seeking majority support for a different measure. For tax bills, the list of such defeats begins in 1834. During 1975, for example, a financial bill of the Harold Wilson cabinet dealing with its value-added tax rate was defeated, but the ministry carried on in office, treating it as other than a confidence vote.

The Forsey–Eglington Report also emphasizes that in earlier years, government MPs in Canada were permitted to vote against cabinet measures. For example, between 1867 and 1872, their study lists fully eighteen pages of cases in which Conservative MPs voted against measures of John A. Macdonald's government. The sky did not fall; Macdonald's government was able to function effectively; government MPs could keep both their self-respect and their membership in the government caucus.

The study also provides interesting data about voting in our House of Commons during other periods: in 1896, fully sixteen Conservative MPs voted with Laurier's Liberals to adjourn a Conservative measure intended to restore Catholic schools in Manitoba; in 1981, sixteen Conservative MPs, including three who later became ministers, voted against the final resolution patriating our Constitution.

The all-party McGrath Report on parliamentary reform came to the conclusion that the role of the individual member must be enhanced. As James McGrath himself said in 1985, "I wanted to put into place a system where being a member of Parliament would be seen to be an end to itself and not a means to an end." On the question of non-confidence, McGrath recommended the following:

- A government should be careful before it designates a vote as one of confidence. It should confine such declarations to measures central to its administration.

- While a defeat on supply is a serious matter, elimination or reduction of an estimate can be accepted.

- In a parliament with a government in command of a majority, the matter of confidence has really been settled by the electorate.
- Government should therefore have the wisdom to permit members to decide many matters in their own personal judgments.

Reg Stackhouse agrees that party discipline must have limits: "Tight party lines need be drawn only when the government's confidence is at stake, that is, when the government decides the fate of a bill is absolutely essential to its objectives."

One way to reduce party discipline in the interest of greater fairness for every province would be to write into our Constitution, as the West Germans did in their Basic Law, that MPs and senators shall "not [be] bound by orders and instructions and shall be subject only to their conscience." Party discipline has certainly diluted this wholesome principle in West Germany, but when combined with another feature of their Constitution—that no chancellor can be defeated in their equivalent of our House of Commons unless a majority of members simultaneously agree on a new person to become chancellor—there now appears to be a more independent role for members of the Bundestag than for Canadian members of Parliament. For example, in the case of the defeat of the minority Clark government in 1979 on its budget, the West German rule would have kept Clark in office unless the Liberals, New Democrats, and Social Credit MPs could have agreed simultaneously on a new prime minister who could hold the confidence of a majority of MPs. A similar rule, if adopted by the House of Commons, would inevitably weaken our party discipline significantly because MPs from all parties could vote on the merits of issues, knowing that defeat would bring down only the measure and not the government.

Another approach would be for each new federal or provincial cabinet to specify at the start of its mandate which matters at the heart of its program will be confidence issues. The Mulroney government, for example, might have spelled out in late 1988 that the Canada–U.S. Free Trade Agreement would be a confidence issue. In those situations, party discipline would be justifiable. Otherwise, its backbenchers would be free to vote for their constituents' interests at all times. This restored independence for legislators would lead to better representation for all regions of Canada and more occupational credibility for Canadian legislators.

A study of the 32nd Legislative Assembly of Ontario (1981–85) indicated that its members voted in uniform party blocs about 95 percent of the time. The same pattern has applied in recent Parliaments in Ottawa. As mentioned above, the Canadian practice suggests that all of the various party leaders could cast a proxy vote on behalf of all their followers without even bothering to have them physically present. It also overlooks that a majority or even a minority government can function effectively without our present stratospheric levels of party solidarity.

THE AMERICAN WAY

In the United States Congress, where admittedly there is a strict separation of powers between the executive and the legislative branches of government, legislation does get passed with far less party loyalty. The constitutional separation of powers and the weakness of party discipline in congressional voting behaviour greatly facilitate effective regional representation in Washington. Unlike the situation in Canada, where a government falls if it loses the support of a majority in the House of Commons on a confidence vote, United States presidents and Congress are elected for fixed terms. Neither resigns if a particular measure is voted down in either the Senate or the House of Representatives.

The practices in our two countries are so different that *The Congressional Quarterly* defines party unity votes there as those in which at least 51 percent of members of one party vote against 51 percent of the other party. Under this definition, itself astonishing to Canadian legislators, the *Quarterly* notes that for the years 1975 to 1982, party unity votes occurred in only 44.2 percent of the 4,417 recorded Senate votes and in only 39.8 percent of those in the House of Representatives. This sample, moreover, includes the years 1977 to 1980, the last period before 1994 when Democrats controlled the White House and both branches of Congress.

Another feature of the congressional system that fosters effective regional input in national policymaking is territorial bloc voting—something quite unknown in Canada's House of Commons. Representatives from the two political parties of the Mountain states, Sun Belt states, New England states, and others vote *en bloc* or work together in committees to advance common interests.

A good example of how effective regional representatives can influence the geographic location of federal government procurement, which affects the geographic distribution of the manufacturing sector, is the Southern congressional influence. It played a major role in the postwar concentration of federal military and space expenditures in the South and in the general economic revival and growth of the Sun Belt. And during 1981–82, the height of the "boll-weevil era," the longtime legislative coalition of Southern Democrats and Republicans was successful more than 85 percent of the time, due to mutual areas of agreement and interest.

The point of this comparison is only to emphasize that, unlike the American Congress, Canadian bloc voting makes bipartisan or tripartisan agreement on anything in our legislatures exceedingly rare. In our current political culture, if a government or opposition MP's loyalty to his or her province clashes with the instruction of the party whip, putting constituents' or regional considerations first in his or her way of voting subjects the MP's prospects for party advancement to considerable risk. Backbench MPs in Canada are thus far less able to represent regional interests effectively than are their counterparts in Washington, where the congressional system provides the freedom for effective regional representation when an issue has clear regional implications. This, of course, is not to suggest that Canada should duplicate the American congressional style of government. Rather, it is to point out that the best solution to ongoing problems of representative democracy in Canada might be to adopt attractive features from various systems, including the American one.

PUTTING CONSTITUENTS FIRST

Canada is a federal state and federalism means that on some issues the will of the popular majority will be frustrated. If the biggest battalions of voters are to prevail over smaller ones under any circumstances, we should drop the charade that we have a federal system of government that respects minorities in times of stress. The notion that the largest group of Canadians, that is, southern Ontarians and metropolitan Quebeckers, must be accommodated always has resulted in varying degrees of discontent outside those areas and accompanying feelings of regional irrelevancy.

In an increasingly interdependent world, many Canadians in our outer eight provinces and the territories want new or altered institutions that will represent the interest of both "inner Canadians" (those who live in the Toronto–Ottawa–Montreal corridor) and "outer Canadians" effectively. Unless we move away from the notion that "the national interest" is merely a code phrase for the interests of the most populous regions in the country, frictions between inner and outer Canada are likely to worsen.

If party discipline in Canada were relaxed, representation for all areas of Canada would be improved. It would be easier for, say, Western or Atlantic MPs to defy their party establishments, if need be, in support of regional issues. Coalitions composed of members of all parties could exist for the purpose of working together on issues of common regional or other concern. The present adversarial attitudes and structures of Parliament or legislatures, in which opposition parties oppose virtually anything a government proposes, might well change in the direction of parties working together for the common good.

Members of Parliament today represent an average of about 100,000 residents per riding. Few government and opposition MPs have any real opportunity to put their constituents first in votes in the House of Commons. Real power is concentrated in the hands of the party leaderships. Canadian democracy itself would benefit if we put our present mind-numbing party discipline where it belongs—in the history books.

✗ **NO**

The Imperative of Party Discipline in the Canadian Political System
ROBERT J. JACKSON

The fact that Canada has been successful as a state leaves some observers perplexed. The Canadian border encases the second-largest geographic land mass in the world under the authority of one Constitution. At the same time, the country is sparsely populated by a narrow ribbon of inhabitants stretched along the forty-ninth parallel. This widely dispersed population is subject to the pull of global economics dominated by its American neighbour to the south. From its genesis, Canada has been a linguistically and culturally heterogeneous society, and is becoming more so with each successive year. Despite the existence of all these centrifugal pressures, what we know today as Canada has existed and thrived for over a century and a quarter.

It is not by historical accident that Canada occupies the position it does today. On the contrary, the fact that Canada exists is the result of deliberate measures taken by Canadian leaders to establish policies and institutions that transcend diversity and bind the country together. Examples include national economic, health, and social policies, a responsible cabinet/parliamentary system of government, and in particular, the establishment of broadly based and national political parties. Institutional structures, such as political parties, can transcend Canadian diversity and provide poles of allegiance against the ever-present centrifugal influences. In order to fulfill this function effectively, the parties themselves must act as cohesive units and strive for party solidarity. Strong parties, based on a broad consensus, are thus vital to the effective functioning of responsible government and the Canadian state. Party solidarity, the apex of which is party discipline, is the guiding principle of the party system in Canada.[1]

Party discipline refers to the ability of the leader in a democratic state to enforce obedience on his or her followers in the legislature and in the party organization. The argument for relaxing party discipline is that MPs should not be "trained sheep" but should, rather, be free to represent the views of their constituents. Members are, after all, elected by their constituents and should be responsible to them. But the issue is not that simple; the Canadian form of government relies on cohesive political parties. In the responsible government model, the party in power is awarded an electoral mandate to enact a legislative program, and its members must support the cabinet and prime minister in order to accomplish this. An MP is not primarily a delegate of his or her constituents. Rather, an MP is elected to serve as a member of a particular party. Within that party, the MP is called upon to deliberate and participate in formulating policies, and then to accept and support the majority decision. The government will not be made more responsive if its members make it more difficult to pass legislation. The prime minister and government must have the means of achieving their objectives.

The Canadian system is premised on the idea that the reason and judgment of politicians are to be respected in the field of policymaking. Parties must be entrusted to deliberate, decide, and then be judged by the electorate. Otherwise, MPs would be elected to deliberate, but constituents, who have not participated in the deliberations, would retain the right to decide. Such a procedure would be ludicrous. MPs do not and should not directly represent their individual constituencies, provinces, or even regions, polling on every issue to see how they should vote. Rather, they are members of a particular party that provides broad perspectives on national issues. They run under the banner of that particular party and seek the privileges offered by it because they are in general agreement with its broad base of national policy directions, directions that can be influenced and adjusted in caucus.

As a British politician pointed out more than a century ago, "Combinations there must be—the only question is, whether they shall be broad parties, based on comprehensive ideas, and guided by men who have a name to stake on the wisdom of their course, or obscure cliques, with some narrow crotchet for a policy, and some paltry yelping shibboleth for a cry." After all, if MPs do not accept the decision arrived at by their executives and party, which groups will they represent? The special pleading of a particular pressure group that has a narrower conception of the national interest?

Party discipline is a feature inherent in the Canadian model of Parliament, and is inextricably linked to the concept of responsible government and the confidence convention. The *Constitution Act, 1867*, established that Canada would have a responsible cabinet/parliamentary system of government. This is the basis of our current system, whereby the cabinet, as selected by the prime minister, is composed of members of the legislature and must keep the confidence of the House of Commons. The system also presupposes an opposition party or parties that are ready and willing to attack the government in an attempt to alter or reject its legislation. The government must therefore enforce party discipline not only to enact its legislative program, but also for the sake of its own self-preservation.

The United States congressional system of government differs from the parliamentary system in several key areas. Rather than fusing the executive and legislative branches of government, the American system is based on the separation of powers. The president and all of his or her cabinet members are prohibited by the Constitution from simultaneously sitting in the executive and legislative branches. The absence of responsible government and the corresponding absence of confidence convention allow the congressional system to function without party discipline.[2]

Calls for the relaxation of party discipline in Canada are not a recent phenomenon. Like the perennial cure for the common cold, the topic of parliamentary reform provides exaggerated hopes for optimists, then later gives way to despair when it fails. As early as 1923, for example, the MP from Calgary, William Irving, introduced a motion in the House of Commons that would have allowed for the relaxation of party discipline by reducing the number of votes considered to be votes of confidence. The motion was defeated, but to this day "reformers" still look to the United States and see the relaxation of party discipline as the panacea for perceived parliamentary inadequacies. Simplistic prescriptions such as the relaxation of party discipline, while seductive, fail to take into account the complexity of the parliamentary system. It is fallacious to assume that certain selected features of the congressional system can be appended to the parliamentary system without seriously affecting the functioning of the entire system.

Imagine a scenario in which party discipline in Canada was significantly relaxed. Issues formerly resolved along party lines, based on consensual lines and accommodation in caucus, would be decided on much narrower grounds. Regionalism and special interests would dominate decision making in the House of Commons, and political parties would cease to serve their function as institutions that bind the country together. The decision-making model now in place, which requires political parties to produce nationally acceptable compromises, would be replaced by an increase in confrontation. MPs liberated from the yoke of party discipline would be saddled by the demands of lobbyists and others representing narrow special interests and regional interests. This scenario is especially disquieting when taken in conjunction with the fact that there are now four parties legitimately competing for seats in the House of Commons, instead of only two or three.

The prospect of minority governments was greatly enhanced following the growth of the western Reform Party and the Bloc Québécois. Since then there has been about as many minority governments as majority governments. In the context of this development, the importance of party discipline increases exponentially. A lack of party discipline during a minority government would result in a chaotic situation where no prime minister could maintain the confidence of the House. Eight of the seventeen elections held since 1957 have resulted in minority governments.

Many of the arguments against party discipline are founded on misconceptions about the practice. The very term "whip," the name given to the party member charged with the task of enforcing party discipline, conjures up images of a menacing disciplinarian imposing the will of the party on recalcitrant MPs. This is not the case, however. While there are instances in which MPs have been coerced or even threatened with sanctions if they do not conform, party discipline is largely self-imposed. Because the majority of MPs enjoy relatively little job security, they do not relish the prospect of facing reelection. Consequently, never in Canadian history has a government been toppled by a breach in party discipline. Furthermore, recent studies indicate that since 1940, no MP from the governing party has ever broken party ranks during a minority government. Nor has any MP ever left the government side with a majority of fewer than nine seats.[3] This indicates that MPs, at least for the sake of their own self-preservation, are willing to tolerate party discipline.

Another misconception is based on the belief that constituents do not want their MPs to toe the party line. This is a somewhat complex issue, owing to the fact that the vote for the executive and legislative representative is fused into the same ballot in parliamentary systems. While it is impossible to determine the exact weight voters give to the individual candidate and the party label, several studies indicate that parties are more important than individual candidates. One report found that shortly after an election, fewer than two-thirds of respondents could correctly give the name of their recently elected MP.[4] More specifically, from 1940 to 1988, thirty-one MPs ran for reelection in the general election following the parliamentary session in which they revolted against their parliamentary caucus and crossed the floor; only twelve of them were successful in the election, and three were forced to run under their former party banner. Only one independent candidate was elected in each of the 2004 and 2006 elections. These figures contrast sharply with the argument that the voters will reward an MP for acting independently and want independents in the House.

The most recent substantive recommendations for reforming party discipline are embodied in the so-called McGrath Report, released in June 1985. The report had three basic conclusions:

1. There should be attitudinal changes.

2. The parties should relax their discipline.

3. There should be organizational reform.

The committee reported, "We believe the country would be better served if members had more freedom to play an active role in the debate on public policy, even if it meant disagreeing with their parties from time to time." The report then called for an "attitudinal change" by backbenchers and asked the prime minister to accept more dissension and defeat of government measures without recourse to the threat or use of dissolution of the House.

Unfortunately, this part of the report is romantic nonsense for the following reasons:

1. Calls for an attitudinal change are unlikely to be effective. The only practicable reform is one that changes the organization around members.

2. There never was a Golden Age of Parliament, as the report implies. In the period before parties, when Canadian MPs were "loose fish," MPs were not free of financial and other social ties that constrained their voting behaviour.

3. The question should not be whether MPs are free to vote against their parties, but rather, whose interests or groups are they adopting when they do so? Free voting does not mean that MPs are free of pressures to conform with other groups' positions.[5] Is it better to have MPs' behaviour determined by widely based cohesive political parties or narrower interest groups?

The facts also belie such utopian assumptions. There has been no relaxation of party discipline in the House of Commons. The urging cries of "reformers" have had no effect. The reality is that MPs are already free to vote as they wish. The point is that they do not choose to exercise their liberty by taking stands against their parties. They will always be subject to constituents, interest groups, and financial pressures: the only question is whether they will follow the dictates of a broadly based party or those of another group with a narrower conception of the national interest. Those who choose wisely stand solidly with their parties, helping to protect the system of government and providing a counterpoint to the centrifugal influences of our geography and society. The increasing number of minority governments strengthens this argument.

NOTES

1. Robert J. Jackson and Doreen Jackson, *Politics in Canada*, 7th ed. (Scarborough: Prentice-Hall, 2008).

2. Robert J. Jackson and Doreen Jackson, *Contemporary Government and Politics: Democracy and Authoritarianism*, 5th ed. (Scarborough: Prentice-Hall, 2007).

3. Paul Conlin, "Floor Crossing in the Canadian House of Commons, 1940–1992" (Carleton University: Unpublished B.A. (Hons.) research paper, 1993).

4. William Irvine, "Does the Candidate Make a Difference? The Macro-politics and Micro-politics of Getting Elected," *Canadian Journal of Political Science* 15, no. 4 (December 1982).

5. Robert J. Jackson, "Executive–Legislative Relations in Canada," in Jackson et al., *Contemporary Canadian Politics* (Scarborough: Prentice-Hall, 1987), pp. 111–125.

POSTSCRIPT

One's stance on the issue of party discipline depends in part on how one interprets the experience of other countries, particularly the United States. David Kilgour likes the freedom that the relaxed party discipline of the American system gives to members of Congress to represent their constituents, especially their regional concerns. But Robert Jackson is skeptical—he fears that an American-style system of lax discipline leaves the door open to the excessive influence of special inter-ests on members' voting decisions.

But is there another model that could be followed? As Kilgour notes, in Great Britain, members of the House of Commons may vote against their party without fear of recrimination on issues that are understood by all not to constitute a vote of confidence. Accordingly, a government may be defeated on a particular bill and still survive. It is suggested that such a practice allows MPs some indepen-dence in the legislature without putting at risk the life of a government.

Those wishing to understand how Britain has dealt with the issue of party dis-cipline should read John Schwarz, "Exploring a New Role in Policymaking: The British House of Commons in the 1970s," *American Political Science Review* 74, no. 1 (March 1980), pp. 23–37. Schwarz examines the changes made to British parliamentary traditions to permit a greater amount of "cross-voting." He argues that these changes have greatly strengthened the role of the House of Commons in the legislative process.

Not everyone is convinced that the British experience can be readily adapted to Canada. C.E.S. Franks, in *The Parliament of Canada* (Toronto: University of Toronto Press, 1987), notes that there are a number of factors that make the British experience unique. Because of the much larger number of members in the British House of Commons, party discipline is much harder to enforce. A large number of safe seats, in which MPs are confident that they will win reelection, makes them less dependent on party patronage for their post-parliamentary livelihood. The cabinet in Britain is much smaller. Long-serving MPs from safe seats, who are not obsessed with promotion to the cabinet, are much less likely to succumb to the brandishing of their leader, as both Margaret Thatcher and John Major have learned to their chagrin. In contrast, there is a much higher turnover among Canadian MPs, who generally do not feel secure enough to challenge a leader they feel is vital to their own chances of reelection.

The applicability of the British experience to Canada is also explored in Peter Dobell, "Some Comments on Party Reform," in Peter Aucoin, ed., *Institutional Reforms for Representative Government* (Toronto: University of Toronto Press, 1985). Dobell is not optimistic about the prospect of Canadian party leaders relin-quishing their strong control over party discipline in the near future. However, he does propose some minor modifications that would give some flexibility to individual MPs. For a more recent study, which also places the Canadian situation in a broader comparative perspective, see Christopher J. Kam, *Party Discipline and Parliamentary Politics* (Cambridge: Cambridge University Press, 2009).

During his tenure in office, Jean Chrétien tended to take a tough stance on party discipline, not infrequently removing backbenchers for committee assignments or threatening to not sign their nomination papers either for voting against the government or even for absenting themselves from votes. Before succeeding Jean Chrétien as prime minister, Paul Martin, in a speech in October 2002, outlined the ways in which he would bring about parliamentary reforms to enhance the voice of MPs, strengthen accountability, and relax party discipline. His announced plan would introduce a system of identifying three types of parliamentary votes. Only a limited number of votes on "fundamental issues" would require full party support. A second level of votes would require members of cabinet to support the government but allow other party members to vote free from party discipline. And the third category of votes would allow all MPs to vote as they wished, without the pressure of party discipline. Martin noted that this would make up the majority of parliamentary votes in the future. For an analysis of Martin's proposals, see Peter Aucoin and Lori Turnbull, "The Democratic Deficit: Paul Martin and Parliamentary Reform," *Canadian Public Administration* 46, no. 4 (Winter 2003), pp. 427–449.

On becoming prime minister, Martin kept his promise and implemented the new way of classifying votes. During his time in office, the majority of bills fell into the second category. Two bills were defeated during Martin's minority government, both relating to government organizational issues relating to the division of foreign affairs from international trade. But since the government did not consider these confidence measures, their defeat did not bring down the government. Martin's government fell on a straightforward nonconfidence motion in November 2005. Despite Martin's professed flexibility, he did expel Carolyn Parish from the caucus when her outspoken criticism of the United States had become an embarrassment to the government, and two other Liberal MPs, including David Kilgour, left the caucus over disagreements with policy.

Since coming to office in 2006, the government of Stephen Harper, facing a minority situation, tended to take a more assertive approach to party discipline, dismissing Garth Turner from the caucus for his criticism of some Conservative policies. And, in March 2007, Harper expelled Nova Scotia MP Bill Casey from the caucus for voting against the government's budget, after Casey argued that the equalization formula that it contained amounted to the gutting of the 2005 Atlantic Accord negotiated between the provinces and the federal government. In addition, two cabinet ministers, Maxime Bernier and Helena Guergis, were both dropped from cabinet for actions that embarrassed the government. In Guergis's case, she was also expelled from the Conservative caucus and subsequently ran against the Conservatives as an independent candidate. Some critics have suggested that Harper's assertive use of party discipline demonstrates an authoritarian streak in his leadership. However, others have suggested that it was an essential element in his success in bringing the old Reform and Progressive Conservative Parties together and eventually winning a majority government after two successive minority governments. In contrast, they suggest that the failure of both Stéphane Dion and Michael Ignatieff to successfully maintain discipline in the Liberal party led to their demise as party leaders.

Is a Mixed-Member Proportional Electoral System in Canada's Interest?

✔ **YES**
JOHN L. HIEMSTRA AND HAROLD J. JANSEN, "Getting What You Vote For"

✘ **NO**
NELSON WISEMAN, "Unintended Consequences of Proportional Representation"

Canadian elections produce curious results. Take the recent federal election. In an article on the election, political scientists at Simon Fraser University noted a few "oddities." The Conservative Party won 20 percent more seats in Ontario even though their popular vote in Ontario grew only five percentage points—39.2 percent to 44.4 percent. In Quebec, nearly one in four of the voters sided with the Bloc Québécois, but only one in twenty of the seats went to the party (four out of seventy-five). The New Democratic Party (NDP) did very well in the election, but it, too, was hit with weird outcomes. Its share of the vote in Manitoba increased over the previous election, yet, it won only half the seats that it did in the previous election. Even more strange, they received a third of the vote in Saskatchewan but no elected members. For this last result, the scientists at Simon Fraser observed, somewhat facetiously, that "[t]he NDP set a record of sorts for 21st century elections." If these oddities were limited to the 2011 election, they would be of little consequence. But these oddities pop up all the time. In some elections, the winning party secures nearly all of the seats with a percentage of the vote that fails to reach 60 percent; in others, the winners do secure all the seats with barely 60 percent of the vote. This propensity to give parties more than they seemingly deserve means the opposite also happens: political parties receive less than they deserve. The NDP performed surprisingly well in the 2011 federal election, winning a little over 30 percent of the seats with about the same percentage of votes, but in the 2004 election it was a different story—they won 16 percent of the vote, but only 6 percent of the seats.

On viewing these outcomes, one might be tempted to conclude that the Canadian electoral process had simply got the math wrong. Surely, the percentage of seats won should roughly reflect the percentage of votes won. But that is not how elections work in Canada. Instead, the electoral system divides the country into constituencies or districts and then declares the one who receives the most votes as the winner in each constituency. With these rules, a party may win many seats by small margins, producing the resulting disjunction between the distribution of seats and votes. In the Canadian electoral system, there is no reward for coming second, third, or any place other than first. Only the candidate with the greatest number of votes gets to sit in legislative assemblies.

Of course, an explanation is not a defence. For some, the single-member plurality (SMP) system, the name commonly given to Canada's election system, is unacceptable. The system plainly distorts the preferences of voters; it gives some parties too many seats and others too few. In a democracy, it might be argued that an electoral system should strive to represent the true wishes of the people. But this fails to occur in Canada. Accordingly, various types of proportional representation (PR) electoral systems have been proposed to establish a greater equality between the percentage of votes and percentage of seats won. One type of PR system has become especially popular: this is the mixed-member proportional (MMP) system. Under MMP, some seats are still selected through the old system—the winner is the candidate with the most votes in the district—but others are selected or appointed from party lists to ensure that in the end the percentage of seats is proportional to the percentage of votes. Basically, the number of seats won through the SMP method are adjusted through the party lists to provide for greater fairness in the electoral system. One of the attractions of MMP is that it soothes the concerns of those who feel that we are moving too fast with electoral reform. MMP manages to mix the old with the new, a seemingly acceptable arrangement.

But many still remain uncomfortable with MMP and PR in general. Some feel this way because they fear that the reforms inevitably lead to weak coalition governments, while others believe that proportional representation produces elected officials without any constituency responsibilities. Arguably, a more important concern is the inability of PR systems to work well with the possibility of the cycling of majorities in government. Research has shown that voting can lead to one majority being easily trumped by another. PR proponents claim that their system will more accurately reflect the will of the people, but the fact is that there is no one majority that registers the wishes of the electorate—there are many. In light of the inherent instability of government actions, it might be preferable to have an electoral system that allows voters to more easily identify elected officials responsible for the offerings of government. If so, MMP and other versions of PR become unattractive because of their tendency to produce multiparty coalitions. Alternatively, the single-member plurality system looks ideal because it usually elects single-party majority governments. In coalition governments, the existence of many policymakers makes it easier to escape responsibility; in majority governments, the presence of only one party enhances efforts directed at ensuring accountability.

In the past few years, three provinces have held referenda on electoral reform. Two asked the citizenry whether MMP should be introduced, and a third held two referendums on the viability of another type of electoral system. The fact that in three of the referendums a majority of the voters rejected change while the fourth failed to meet the required level of support suggests that Canadians find proposed changes to the way we elect politicians wanting. It is unlikely this issue will disappear soon, however, for perceptions of the failings of the single-member system are too widespread. Plus, academic scholars continue to write on the issue and diligent public interest groups such as Fair Vote Canada (www.fairvote.ca) ensure that the issue remains topical.

In the debate, John Hiemstra, Harold Jansen, and Nelson Wiseman wrangle over the merits of introducing a system of MMP in Canada. Hiemstra is a professor of political science at King's University College in Edmonton, while Jansen teaches at the University of Lethbridge. Nelson Wiseman is a professor of political science at the University of Toronto. A point of clarification: as evident from Wiseman's essay, the Canadian system is sometimes called "first past the post."

✔ **YES**

Getting What You Vote For

JOHN L. HIEMSTRA AND HAROLD J. JANSEN

Some critics say Canada should keep the plurality electoral system because it "works." Who in their right mind would oppose something that works? But how can Canadians know whether an electoral system truly works within our larger political system? We argue that Canadians need to identify all of the relevant normative criteria we want our electoral system to achieve, and then empirically test whether the current plurality system, or a new MMP electoral system, best achieves these values. The literature on electoral systems produces the following list of key values: certainly electoral systems must produce *stable* and *effective* governments. But, the results of elections must also be *fair* for all voters. All voters should be *represented* in the one elected political chamber in Canada, the House of Commons, that votes on legislation affecting us all. The power of every vote cast in an election should be *equal* to all others. Electoral systems should enable citizens to hold governments *accountable* for their actions. The electoral system should *justly accommodate* all sectors of the national political community in ways that encourages national unity. In our essay, we argue that the current plurality electoral system does not "work" because it empirically fails to achieve many of these key values in practice. Adopting an MMP system, on the other hand, would truly "work" because it simultaneously embeds all of these important values in the electoral system that produces the political officials who run Canadian politics.

This essay argues that the plurality method for electing Members of Parliament (MPs) to the House of Commons should be replaced with a system of proportional representation (PR). There are many variants of PR in use around the world, but the one we advocate for Canada is a mixed-member proportional (MMP) electoral system. MMP would make every vote count, enhance national unity, give an accurate reflection of the political opinions of Canadians in the House, and strengthen MPs' sense of obligation to the voters. This essay draws on national and provincial examples to make this case, since both levels currently use the plurality electoral system.

A MODEST REFORM

In Canadian federal elections, we use the current single-member plurality electoral system to decide who will be our representatives in the House of Commons. The country is divided into 308 single-member districts, each of which elects one MP to the House. The winner in each district is decided by the plurality formula.

Simply put, the candidate in a riding who wins more votes than the other candidates—even if the total number of votes is less than 50 percent—is the winner and takes the seat as MP in the House of Commons.[1]

Adopting MMP would require only modest reforms to our current system; it could be implemented by a simple act of Parliament and without a constitutional amendment. The number of federal MPs per province is determined by several factors, of which population is the most important. Under the plurality system, the provinces are carved into geographical electoral districts, with one MP elected in each district. Under MMP, this would continue to happen, but only half of the MPs allocated to each province would represent single-member districts as they do now. The other half would be chosen from each party's lists in such a way as to ensure that each party's representation in Parliament matched its share of the popular vote in that province.

In Alberta, for example, under the plurality formula used in the 2011 national election, the Conservative Party won all but one of Alberta's twenty-eight seats, with the other going to the NDP. If Alberta voters got what they individually voted for, the outcome would have been much different: nineteen Conservative seats, five NDP seats, three Liberal seats, and one Green seat. It's hard to disagree that this would be a fair and equitable outcome. But can we practically achieve this outcome? Adopting an MMP electoral system is a modest reform that would virtually guarantee this outcome.

If the election had been held under MMP,[2] fourteen MPs would have been elected in single-member districts. The Conservatives would likely have won thirteen of those seats and the NDP would likely have won the other. The remaining fourteen MPs for Alberta would not represent specific districts but would be chosen from each of the parties' lists in such a way that their overall number in Alberta's Parliament accurately reflected their share of the vote. The Conservatives' 65 percent of the vote would have entitled them to nineteen of the overall twenty-eight Alberta MPs, so six MPs from the Conservative list would have been added to the thirteen MPs elected in single-member districts, bringing their total to nineteen. The NDP's share of the vote would have entitled them to five seats; they would receive four list seats to add to the one elected under the plurality system. None of the other parties would have won any seats in single-member districts, but their share of the overall vote would have entitled them to some list seats—the Liberals would have been awarded three, and the Green Party, one seat. In this way, MMP would ensure each party earned the number of seats to which it was entitled.[3]

Although the MMP way of calculating the number of seats each party would receive is more complicated than under the plurality system, casting a vote in a federal election under MMP would be straightforward. Voters would vote twice: once for the candidate they want to represent their particular district in the House of Commons and a second vote for the party list they prefer. The local candidate they support may even be from a different party. Voters in countries around the world seem to have no trouble using MMP, so there is little reason to expect Canadians would either.

There are many variations in how MMP systems have been implemented throughout the world. But the increased popularity of MMP reflects an emerging consensus that MMP systems offer the "best of both worlds."[4] Voters continue to have an individual MP who is "theirs" and can deal with local problems they are having with government, which is a distinct advantage of the plurality system. At the same time, however, voters benefit from having their political ideas reflected accurately in our national deliberative chamber, the House of Commons. Clearly, this is the major advantage of proportional representation; an MMP system would ensure that voters consistently get what they actually voted for.

MAKING EVERY VOTE COUNT

As a democratic state, all Canadians should have a say in composing the House of Commons, since it deliberates on and approves the laws that govern us all. Sadly, Canada's plurality electoral system repeatedly fails to deliver just and equitable representation when it allows the "winner to take all."

An electoral system is unjust when it fails to give each vote its due. And what are voters due? The answer is clearly "representation." Surely all Canadian voters have a right to be represented in the one and only chamber that is elected. Our plurality electoral system is frequently unjust. In the 2011 federal election, for example, more than 60 percent of voters supported parties other than the Conservative Party, yet they were represented in the House of Commons by less than half of the members of Parliament. In 2011, fully 49.6 percent of voters cast votes for candidates who did not get elected. Thus, they ended up being represented by MPs they did not vote for and a party they did not support. The plurality system effectively disenfranchised nearly half of the voters in the 2011 election.[5]

The injustice done by the plurality electoral formula is illustrated even better by the results of two provincial elections. In the 2001 British Columbia provincial election, Gordon Campbell's Liberal Party won 97 percent of the seats (seventy-seven out of seventy-nine) with only 58 percent of the vote. That left the 21 percent of voters who supported the NDP with only two seats, and the 21 percent who supported other parties with none. In the 2007 provincial election, Prince Edward Island's Liberals won almost 53 percent of the vote, but took 85 percent of the seats. An even more dramatic case of injustice happened in the 1987 New Brunswick election where the plurality system gave every seat to one party. Frank McKenna's Liberal Party won 100 percent of the seats with 60 percent of the popular vote. This left the other 40 percent of the voters unrepresented by the parties they supported. Besides misrepresenting the views of voters, the single-member plurality system in these cases returned very small oppositions, making it difficult for legislatures to hold the government accountable, the traditional function of oppositions in our British-style parliamentary system. These are not isolated cases, either. In the words of one of Canada's leading scholars of political parties and elections, lopsided provincial election results are the "dirty little secret" of provincial politics.[6]

The other serious defect in the plurality electoral system is its inequity; that is, it often makes your vote count for less than others. For example, in the 2011 federal election, 518,736 voters in Manitoba and Saskatchewan voted Conservative and elected twenty-four MPs. In Quebec, the plurality system rewarded the 627,650 people who voted Conservative with only seven MPs. It took more than 100,000 votes to elect a Conservative MP in Quebec, while in the Prairies, it took just over 20,000 votes to do so. An even more extreme inequity occurred in the 2000 federal election, when 1,051,209 voters in Ontario supported the Canadian Alliance party, but the plurality system gave it only two seats in that province. In British Columbia, on the other hand, the plurality system rewarded the 797,518 Canadian Alliance voters with twenty-seven seats. In other words, it took fewer than 30,000 B.C. Alliance voters to elect an MP, while in Ontario, it took over half a million to do so.

Plurality is a "winner takes all" system that almost always over-rewards the winning party. In contrast, MMP is widely recognized as more just and equitable in that it accurately translates the percentage of the vote each party wins into a proportionate percentage of seats in the House of Commons. MMP would greatly reduce the injustice and inequity experienced by voters under the plurality system. In short, MMP would give you what you vote for, which is reason enough to adopt it in Canada.

MMP AND GOVERNMENT EFFECTIVENESS

Proportional representation systems such as MMP are almost always acknowledged as the fairest electoral systems.[7] Yet some still reject any kind of PR for Canada because they fear it would make the government ineffective. They argue that the plurality method produces stable and effective majority governments out of minority electoral returns, while MMP would produce unstable and ineffective minority governments. While stability and effectiveness are important values, Canadians should not have to choose between these values and justice and equity when designing an electoral system. Fortunately, the experiences of other countries show that PR electoral systems can do both, offering both improved representation and effective government. It is easy to selectively present a specific example of a country where either a proportional or plurality electoral system has worked well or not well. The most valuable evidence, however, comes from studies that systematically incorporate the experience of multiple countries. Arend Lijphart, a noted expert on electoral systems, did just this in a comparative study of established democracies and found that countries using PR maintain public order and manage the economy as well as countries that use majoritarian electoral systems, such as plurality.[8]

Besides this comparative evidence, we can look at Canada's experience with minority governments. Canada has had effective government since well before Confederation. Yet there does not seem to be any connection between this effectiveness and the plurality electoral system's ability to produce majority governments. In fact, the plurality system produced eight minority governments from the seventeen elections since 1962, which is not exactly a stellar record.[9] In spite of these minority governments, Canada's governments have generally been effective. In his seminal study of Canada's Parliament, C.E.S. Franks concludes that "there is no evidence that minority parliaments are less efficient than majorities."[10]

It is true that minority governments have tended to fall more quickly than majority governments in Canada. It is critical to understand that this is due less to the inherent instability of minority governments than to the perverse incentive the plurality system gives to some parties to seek an early collapse of minority governments. Large parties know that a small shift in the vote toward their party will often be magnified into a large increase in seats and thus a majority government for them. The Conservative government proved this in 2011, when they went from a minority government to a majority. Although the Conservative share of seats in the House of Commons jumped 8 percent, going from 46 percent in 2008 to 54 percent in 2011, their share of the vote increased only by about 2 percent, from 37.7 percent to 39.6 percent.

If Canada adopted MMP, minority and coalition governments would undoubtedly be even more common than has been the case historically. But we have already seen that the frequent minority governments under the plurality system do not render the government ineffective. Nor is it the case that coalition governments are automatically weak or unstable. In PR systems such as MMP, political parties normally win a steady percentage of the vote in each election. Since forcing an election under MMP would likely not dramatically alter party strengths in Parliament, this electoral system strongly encourages parties to work for just policy compromises within Parliament. Thus, coalition governments under MMP would be able to "get things done" for Canada. The big improvement that coalitions under an MMP system deliver is that they get things done while involving a majority of the MPs who truly represent more than a majority of Canadians. PR gets rid of artificial majority governments that make decisions on important issues such as health care reform or climate change with the support of less than half of the voters.

Critics also suggest that PR causes unstable governments by promoting too many small parties. Under plurality, however, Canada has already produced many small parties, a contradiction of "Duverger's law," which asserts that a plurality electoral system tends to produce a two-party system. This diversity of smaller parties should not be denied, however, since it reflects the real political views of Canadians. Even so, in most provinces except Ontario and Quebec, the province-wide lists required by MMP would elect relatively few MPs. To earn a seat in the

House of Commons from these party lists, a party would still require a significant proportion of the vote. Thus the system would still discourage splinter parties.

In sum, Canada has remained stable even though the plurality system has produced repeated minority governments and has encouraged destabilizing regional parties. The reason for this is Canada's strong, democratic, and tolerant political culture. Adopting MMP would not suddenly change this. Nor would MMP transform Canada into an unstable regime such as pre–Second World War Weimar Germany.[11] Canada's strong, democratic political culture has kept and will continue to keep our system stable. Canada with MMP would more likely resemble modern Germany, which has used MMP for over five decades and remains eminently stable and unified.[12]

MMP CAN INCREASE NATIONAL UNITY

Some critics also argue that MMP would weaken national unity. They charge that it would magnify divisions between regions and between English and French cultures. They claim that, although the plurality electoral system has treated this diversity unfairly, at least this system has kept our country stable and united. The facts show, however, that quirks in plurality actually serve to worsen these divisions in Canada.

One way the plurality system undermines national unity is by "rewarding" small, regionally concentrated parties. Canadian history is full of examples of small, regional parties that have won substantial representation in Parliament. Parties such as the Progressives, Social Credit, the Creditistes, and the Reform Party have flourished under a plurality electoral system by being able to translate a relatively small number of votes into a relatively large share of the seats. Particularly troublesome is the tendency of plurality to reward regionally concentrated parties that, in some cases, have promoted separatism or a sectional view of Canada. The plurality system has multiplied their negative impact by rewarding them with far more seats than their electoral support warrants. In the 2008 federal election, for example, the separatist Bloc Québécois (BQ) won 65 percent of the seats in Quebec with the support of only 38 percent of Quebec voters. This also occurred in Quebec provincial elections, where the plurality system has allowed the separatist Parti Québécois to form four majority governments even though the party has never won a majority of the votes. In 1998, the PQ won a majority government (76 out of 125 seats) with 42.9 percent of the vote, but the provincial Liberal Party won the support of more Quebec voters, with 43.6 percent of the vote.

Another way the plurality electoral system weakens national unity is by robbing seats from small, nationally oriented parties with supporters dispersed across the country. For example, the NDP is a national party with a social democratic vision for the whole country, with some support in all regions of the country. Yet, under the plurality system, it always receives fewer seats in the House of

Commons than its support would justify. In the 2006 federal election, for example, the NDP earned only twenty-nine seats (9.4 percent) in the House of Commons, even though the party earned 17.5 percent of the vote across the country. Even more shocking is that a million more Canadians voted for the NDP than supported the BQ, but the NDP won twenty-two fewer seats. Under MMP in the 2006 election, the NDP would have won fifty-five seats (from every province in Canada except P.E.I.), a fair reflection of its national support. Unfortunately, the plurality system hurts small parties with support dispersed across the regions, even when they try to appeal to all Canadians, wherever they might live.

The plurality system also weakens national unity by over-rewarding large parties in regions where they have strong support while under-rewarding them where their support is weak. Thus, Canada often lacks truly national parties in the House. When large parties win the majority of the seats in one region and few in another region, the party caucus discussions will tend to be dominated by the larger group, thereby perpetuating and worsening divisions in Canada. In the 1980 federal election, for example, the Liberal Party formed the government but did not win a single seat in British Columbia, Alberta, or Saskatchewan, although it won over 20 percent of the vote in these provinces. Meanwhile, it won seventy-four of seventy-five seats, or 99 percent of the seats, in Quebec with 68 percent of the popular vote. In 2011, more people voted for the Conservative Party in Quebec than in Manitoba and Saskatchewan combined, but the plurality system's distortions gave the Conservatives twenty-four seats in Manitoba and Saskatchewan, but only seven in Quebec. While the Conservatives are undoubtedly strongest in the West, the electoral system does not reflect the depth of their support in Quebec and Eastern Canada. One of the biggest stories on election night was the New Democratic Party's historic breakthrough in Quebec, but this breakthrough was partly a product of the electoral system. Although the NDP took 43 percent of the vote there, the plurality system translated this into over three-quarters of the seats in Quebec. Put another way, only about 36 percent of all the votes cast for the NDP in 2011 were cast in Quebec, but Quebec MPs make up 57 percent of the NDP's parliamentary caucus. This flaw leads voters to develop a regionally skewed perception of the parties' support, in this case overestimating the NDP's support in Quebec, and underestimating the Conservatives' appeal in the same province. It also handicaps the governing and opposition parties' ability to include regional viewpoints in their caucus discussions. In fact, plurality gives parties an incentive to favour regions where they might receive large electoral payoffs, while ignoring other regions.

The weaknesses of the plurality system, Alan Cairns concludes, make Canada's electoral system "divisive and detrimental to national unity."[13] MMP is a better way to handle Canada's regional divisions, since it gives seats to national parties in direct proportion to the percentage of popular votes they win in the election. Since every vote counts in MMP, parties have a strong incentive to take a national viewpoint on issues and to search for votes in all regions. While MMP allows voters to develop and support regional parties, it does not unfairly reward those parties. It also encourages the growth of parties that will integrate the regions of Canada.[14]

THE PLURALITY SYSTEM PRODUCES FALSE MAJORITY GOVERNMENTS

Another claim for the plurality electoral system is that it allows voters to select a government at the same time as they elect their representatives. Indeed, forming a cabinet is largely routine in Canada's parliamentary system, where the party winning the most seats usually forms the government. But it is an illusion to suggest that voters purposefully or automatically select a government. In fact, the majority of Canadians have not been involved in selecting most of Canada's governments. Since the Second World War, only two of our national governments have been formed by a party that won a majority of the popular vote in an election (1958 and 1984).[15] Over time, the plurality system is producing governments with a majority of seats but resting on the support of an increasingly small proportion of the electorate.[16]

In practice, the plurality system routinely allows a minority of voters to select the majority of the seats, and thus determine the government. This problem with plurality is closely related to Canada's multiparty system. In the 1997 federal election, when five major parties contested the election, the plurality system translated the Liberals' 38.5 percent of the vote into a majority government. These results were not an anomaly; such distortions occur repeatedly in federal and provincial elections. The fact that there are four parties in Parliament isn't an accident; it reflects the diversity of political visions in Canada's political culture. This reality must be reflected in our foremost representative and debating legislative chamber.

The plurality electoral system also allows a small shift in the vote to determine who will form the next government. In the 1979 election, Joe Clark's Conservatives were supported by 36 percent of Canadians and took 48 percent of the seats to form a minority government. The Liberals gathered 40 percent of the vote and took only 40 percent of the seats. Nine months later, in the 1980 election, the Liberals increased their share of the vote by only 4 percent but now won a clear majority government with 52 percent of the seats. And in the following election of 1984, a shift of 17 percent of the vote to the Mulroney-led Tories allowed the Progressive Conservatives to increase their seats by 38 percent, from 37 percent to 75 percent of the seats. Defenders of the plurality electoral system often cite this property of the plurality system as a desirable feature. They argue that the sensitivity of the plurality system to small shifts in the popular vote allow voters to defeat governments. Is it really fair and appropriate to give the power to determine who will or will not form a government to a tiny minority of voters?

Furthermore, this mechanism works very inconsistently under plurality. While a shift in the popular vote may cause a change of government, just as often, it does not. The actual seat totals depend on a number of factors, including the regional distribution of the vote, the number of political parties, and the division of the vote between these parties. The relationship between seats and votes under the plurality system is not a smooth line on a graph; it is far more random than that. Should governments be determined by chance factors?

Two sequential provincial elections in British Columbia pointedly illustrate this type of chancy outcome in the formation of governments under plurality. The NDP failed to form the government in 1986 when its 42.6 percent of the vote translated into 31.9 percent of the seats. In the 1991 election, however, NDP popular support dropped to 41 percent of the vote, yet it took 68 percent of the seats and formed the new government. Sometimes, in fact, plurality allows a party to win more seats and form the government with fewer votes than the main opposition party. In the 1979 federal election, for example, the Conservatives formed a minority government when they won 36 percent of the vote and 136 seats, while the Liberals won 40 percent of the vote and only 114 seats. This "wrong winner" phenomenon is even more common in provincial elections, most recently in the 2006 New Brunswick election, when the Liberals won a majority government despite the fact that more voters supported the Progressive Conservative Party. Had then PC Premier Bernard Lord followed the recommendation of his Commission on Legislative Democracy and implemented an MMP system, he might still have been premier.

Selecting a government through the plurality electoral system has the further side effect of producing an unfair public perception of the parties' strengths. A month after the 1988 federal election, nobody remembered that the Tories won 57 percent of the seats with only 43 percent of the vote. The public is constantly reminded of the percentage of seats a party won, but not the percentage of the vote it won. A month after the 2011 election, everyone referred to the "Harper majority government," forgetting he received only 39.6 percent of Canadian votes.

The plurality system is often associated with a two-party political system. The diversity and complexity of Canadian society, however, has meant that Canada has developed many political parties. It is a mistake to think that we can solve the problems created by the plurality system by wishing the country had a two-party system rather than reforming the electoral system itself to reflect the reality of Canadian society. We must accept that Canadians have deeply held political views and choose different parties to express these views. An electoral system should not artificially constrict these views. Political parties ought to play the critical role of providing an integrated set of principles around which they harmonize the many diverse and sometimes conflicting policies into a coherent platform. This would give voters a real choice. The truly democratic response to these voter differences is to amend our electoral system so that it responds to the diversity of beliefs and actions of Canadians, and not to force the current system to produce the number of parties critics want. The real challenge is to allow the deeply held political views of Canadians to be properly, safely, and fairly expressed and accommodated in politics. People with different ethnic, religious, or ideological views often arrive at, or endorse, a particular policy for their own distinct reasons. An MMP system will give no viewpoint a hegemonic grip on the system; rather it will force all parties to discuss their real differences as a means of arriving at mutually acceptable policies. The end result is that governments elected by proportional representation tend to reflect the preferred policies of citizens much better than do those elected by the plurality system.[17]

Since MMP would make the House of Commons accurately reflect the opinions and views of Canadians, it would be better to shift the duty of forming governments away from "chance" and to our MPs. This would give the majority of voters a stronger say in the creation of government. It would place the task of forming governments in the hands of our MPs who currently hold the power of dissolving governments. This conforms with and develops Canada's parliamentary theory.

THE PLURALITY SYSTEM WEAKENS REPRESENTATIVE DEMOCRACY

Indeed, MMP would give voters a greater say over all aspects of their MPs' actions, since it obliges MPs to represent their supporting voters. What we see in Canada today is that the plurality electoral system is weakening representative democracy. Representative democracy was created in response to the historically increasing number of citizens entitled to be involved in politics but who lacked the time or energy to study political issues and devise fitting solutions. Most Canadians expect their representatives to engage actively in policymaking for them. Even so, plurality fails to give representatives a clear mandate from the voters and fails to enable voters to hold MPs responsible for their actions. Instead, the plurality system is increasingly encouraging Canadians to weaken or even bypass representative democracy. The weakening of the relationship between voters and representatives occurs because plurality requires politicians and parties to compromise too early in the process. Before an election, politicians are forced to develop lowest common denominator policies that will appeal to a plurality of voters in each riding. For example, some voters believe the state should strongly intervene to protect the environment, while others believe market forces will correct environmental problems. In response to this spectrum of opinions, most political parties develop a compromised platform that homogenizes the environmental views of Canadians. While this is done to attract the wide range of voters necessary to win a plurality of votes in a single district, it tends to homogenize the resulting MPs' views, and thus undermines wide-ranging debate about environmental policy in the House of Commons.

Early compromises on policy produce pragmatic, look-alike parties. Election campaigns increasingly focus on party leaders and image, and downplay principles, policy platforms, and the teams of politicians behind the leaders. Pragmatic parties make principled discussion rare in the House of Commons and foreclose the opportunity for accommodation between principled party platforms. Consequently, voters seldom know what their MPs and parties stand for and find it difficult to hold them accountable. At the same time, MPs do not receive clear mandates from voters. In these and other respects, plurality weakens the relationship between voters and representatives.

Increasingly, voters are turning away from these indistinct parties. Many are abandoning the electoral process altogether, as Canada's decreasing levels of voter turnout indicate.[18] Some are turning to interest groups for better representation. Political parties are responding to this challenge to their representative role by merely becoming brokers for interest groups. Other voters are pushing reforms such as recall, referenda, and initiative, which bypass representative democracy.[19] Thus, the dynamic set in motion by plurality actually encourages voters to bypass their representatives, a process that is undermining the very essence of our representative democratic system.

IMPROVING THE QUALITY OF REPRESENTATION

In opposition to plurality, an MMP electoral system would strengthen Canada's political system by encouraging a new dynamic. MMP encourages strong political parties, but would also encourage them to define how they are distinct from the others in order to attract votes. To compete effectively, parties would need to develop clearer principles and to define their policy platforms. This would allow political parties to become vehicles for voters to give mandates to MPs and also to hold them accountable between elections. MPs would clearly feel more obliged to act in accordance with the principles and policies that they agreed to with supporters. This would include serving the individual voters according to these principles, if the parties want to maintain electoral support. MPs with a sense of obligation to voters would be a clear advance over the current plurality system that limits voters to rubber-stamping or jettisoning representatives at election time.

One common criticism of MMP systems is that they create "two classes" of MPs, namely, those elected in single-member districts and party list MPs. The argument is that those MPs who represent single-member districts have different responsibilities than those who are elected from party lists. The evidence from Germany, the country with the longest experience with MMP, suggests that such concerns are misplaced. The German experience has been that party list MPs do get involved in constituency work, often focusing on single-member districts where their party lost. There is also little evidence in the German case to suggest that party list MPs are more likely to be cabinet ministers than MPs elected by plurality.[20]

Again, PR has been superior to the plurality electoral system in bringing minority parties into legislatures. Although we can point to specific exceptions in both proportional and plurality electoral systems, the overall evidence from other countries shows that PR improves the quality of representation in various ways. It has also increased the parliamentary representation of women, ethnic groups, and cultural minorities.[21] Significantly, PR has done so without extensive affirmative action programs. PR has also allowed parties to improve the overall quality of individual MPs on their lists. PR also allows citizens to be free to join the political party of their choice and to decide whether their party's MPs will be "trustees" who will independently deliberate on issues; "delegates" who mechanically reflect their views; "mirrors" that reflect their gender, age, ethnic, or other characteristics; or defenders of their party's interests and positions.[22] If "party bosses" dominate under MMP, it will be the fault of those who create parties that tolerate them and of the voters who support them. When this has proven to be a significant problem, many countries have developed systems that allow voters to change the order of the names on the list, thus removing some of the control party officials have over who gets elected.

MMP allows parties and governments to be as good or as flawed as the people they represent. It leaves the public free to decide which groups or principles or approaches it wants represented by creating parties to reflect these concerns. MMP ultimately leaves the voters to decide which parties they want to be represented by in the House of Commons. For example, if 7 percent of Canadians support the Green Party's approach to environmental issues, MMP will give it 7 percent of the seats, no more and no less.

CONCLUSION

Democratic principles are the foundation upon which political life in Canada rests. The plurality and MMP electoral systems are structures through which Canadians can exercise their democratic choices. But structures are not neutral. They reflect values that the people in a society want the system to advance and thus encourage citizens to act in a certain way. The dominant value of our current plurality system is stability—which it is supposed to achieve by translating a minority of votes into a majority government. In spite of the plurality electoral system, however, Canada has frequently produced minority governments. The plurality system also produces electoral outcomes that aggravate and intensify Canada's regional divisions. Too many outcomes of the plurality electoral system have been chancy, unfair, and inequitable. Also, plurality has encouraged the growth of pragmatic and brokerage parties that weaken the incentives of MPs to represent their voters. In spite of these problems, Canada remains a stable, democratic political system.

Since Canada is stable in spite of the plurality system, it has ample room to add the values of justice, equity, and representativeness to stability by adopting an MMP electoral system. MMP makes every vote count and produces results that are proportionate to what voters desire. MMP would also best serve Canada's distinctive needs. It would increase Canada's stability by improving regional representation in major parties, while reducing the unjustified strength of small, divisive parties that happen to have regionally concentrated support.

The biggest asset of MMP, however, is that it enhances representative democracy by encouraging MPs and parties to develop a clearer profile on principles and policies. Voters will have a better idea of the mandate they are giving to MPs and thus be able to hold MPs accountable for their principles, policies, and political actions. An MMP electoral system should be adopted in Canada since it is the fairest and most effective way to fix Canada's real democratic deficit.

NOTES

1. Only 40 percent of MPs elected in 2006 won their seats with a majority of the vote in their constituencies. In fact, one MP won a seat with the support of fewer than a third of the voters in his constituency. This is not unusual: in 2004, only 44 percent of MPs won their seats with a majority of the vote.

2. We are assuming that half of the seats would be allocated in single-member districts, and the other half would be allocated from party lists for the entire province. We are also assuming that voters would support the same party with their list vote as they supported in single-member districts.

3. See David M. Farrell, *Electoral Systems: A Comparative Introduction* (New York: Palgrave, 2001), pp. 97–111, for more details on how MMP works in Germany. See the Law Commission of Canada, *Voting Counts: Electoral Reform in Canada* (Ottawa: Law Commission of Canada, 2004), pp. 83–125, for a detailed discussion on how MMP might be implemented in Canada.

4. Matthew Soberg Shugart, "'Extreme' Electoral Systems and the Appeal of the Mixed-Member Alternative," in Matthew Soberg Shugart and Martin P. Wattenberg, eds., *Mixed-Member Electoral Systems: The Best of Both Worlds* (Oxford: Oxford University Press, 2001), pp. 25–51.

5. This is not an unusual result; in 2004, a majority of Canadian voters (50.2 percent) voted for a candidate in their riding who did not win.

6. R. Ken Carty, "Doing Democracy Differently: Has Electoral Reform Finally Arrived?" (speech delivered at the Timlin Lecture, March 1, 2004, University of Saskatchewan).

7. Andrew Reynolds and Ben Reilly, *The International IDEA Handbook of Electoral System Design* (Stockholm: International Institute for Democracy and Electoral Assistance, 1997), p. 62.

8. Arend Lijphart, "Democracies: Forms, Performance, and Constitutional Engineering," *European Journal of Political Research* 25 (1994), pp. 1–17; see also Arend Lijphart, *Patterns of Democracy: Government Forms and Performance in Thirty-Six Countries* (New Haven: Yale University Press, 1999), chs. 15 and 16.

9. The plurality system not only fails to produce regular majority governments but frequently fails to produce the strong oppositions needed to effectively run a parliamentary system. See Alan C. Cairns, "The Electoral System and Party System in Canada, 1921–1965," *Canadian Journal of Political Science* 1 (1968), pp. 55–80.

10. C.E.S. Franks, *The Parliament of Canada* (Toronto: University of Toronto Press, 1987), p. 50.

11. Enid Lakeman reports that if Weimar Germany had used plurality, the Nazis would likely have won all the seats; cited in Michael Lind, "A Radical Plan to Change American Politics," *The Atlantic Monthly* 270, no. 2 (August 1992), pp. 73–83.

12. In a review of the research on this question, Louis Massicotte, "Changing the Canadian Electoral System," *Choices* 7, no. 1 (February 2001), p. 21, states that claims of PR undermining democracy have been "discredited." Massicotte's study is updated in Paul Howe, Richard Johnston, and Andre Blais, eds., *Strengthening Canadian Democracy* (Montreal IRPP, 2005).

13. Cairns, "The Electoral System and Party System in Canada," p. 92.

14. Harold J. Jansen and Alan Siaroff, "Regionalism and Party Systems: Evaluating Proposals to Reform Canada's Electoral System," in Henry Milner, ed., *Steps toward Making Every Vote Count* (Peterborough: Broadview, 2004), pp. 43–64, conclude that MMP would be among the best choices to prevent exacerbating regional conflicts.

15. Richard Katz, "Electoral Reform Is Not as Simple as It Appears," in Henry Milner, ed., *Making Every Vote Count* (Peterborough: Broadview, 1999), p. 101, points out that if rejected ballots are included in the vote totals for the 1984 election, then even the Mulroney government did not have the support of a majority of voters, leaving only one government that had the support of a majority of the electorate.

16. Richard Johnston, "Canadian Elections at the Millennium," *Choices* 6, no. 6 (September 2000). Updated version of article can be found in Howe, Johnston, and Blais eds., *Strengthening Canadian Democracy.*

17. G. Bingham Powell, Jr., *Elections as Instruments of Democracy: Majoritarian and Proportional Visions* (New Haven: Yale University Press, 2000), ch. 9.

18. Although there are certainly multiple causes for voter turnout levels, most comparative analyses find that proportional representation systems are associated with higher turnout. See Pippa Norris, *Electoral Engineering: Voting Rules and Political Behaviour* (Cambridge: Cambridge University Press, 2004), ch. 7.

19. See Nick Loenen, *Citizenship and Democracy: A Case for Proportional Representation* (Toronto: Dundurn, 1997), ch. 5, for a comparison of PR with these other reforms.

20. Louis Massicotte, *Á la recherche d'un mode de scrutin mixte compensatoire.* Document de travail, Québec, Secrétariat à la réforme des institutions démocratiques, Décembre 2004, ch. 8. Available online at http://www.institutions-democratiques. gouv.qc.ca/publications/mode_scrutin_rapport.pdf. Accessed August 20, 2011.

21. Norris, *Electoral Engineering,* ch. 8, demonstrates that PR enhances the representation of women. The effect for ethnic minorities is more complex. The plurality system represents minorities well if they are geographically concentrated, but has a harder time when minorities are dispersed. See Norris, *Electoral Engineering,* ch. 9.

22. Several conflicting definitions of representation confuse this debate; see Hanna Fenichel Pitkin, *The Concept of Representation* (Los Angeles: University of California Press, 1967).

✘ NO
Unintended Consequences of Proportional Representation
NELSON WISEMAN

One can only be a skeptical agonistic in predicting the consequences of adopting proportional representation. Once implemented, however, it will difficult to undo. The Burkean dictum, "If it is not necessary to change, it is necessary not to change," is the philosophic conservative argument against embracing proportional representation (PR). In this view, opposition to PR is based on the wisdom of historical experience. Some defenders of the status quo consider the devil they know preferable to the one they do not. Cynics intone that PR will not change much. Power, they claim, will be even more concentrated in the hands of party leaders and their entourage of apparatchiks because the commonly proposed variant of PR for Canada, mixed-member proportional (MMP), will likely leave the designation of the candidates elected by PR to party elites.

Stable countries seldom make radical institutional changes. They do not jump on bandwagons that cater willy-nilly to their era's temperament. Canada's fundamental political principles have been shaped without the use of PR. This means that its potential adoption ought to be considered thoughtfully and cautiously. PR may have deleterious implications for the operation of other elements of Canada's institutional infrastructure. PR proponents generally ignore or gloss over them.

SIGNIFICANCE OF ELECTORAL SYSTEMS

The success or failure of polities has relatively little to do with their electoral systems. Canada, in comparative perspective, has not fared poorly with its current first-past-the-post (FPTP), or single-member plurality (SMP), electoral system. Canada belongs to an elite group of states, making up only 13 percent of the world's population, categorized as "full democracies."[1] Some states that sport PR are flawed or flailing democracies. Some are authoritarian. They suffer a "democratic deficit"—the appealing but trite term often pinned on Canada's political condition.

Canada's policy outputs and quality of life are the envy of many in states with PR. Immigrants are not deterred from coming to Canada because of its allegedly democratically deficient electoral system. Canadians, in turn, are not drawn to relocate to states such as Latvia, Bolivia, and Iraq because their PR systems are irresistible democratic beacons. People in those states "know" less about what they are going to get in government policy and performance with their PR electoral systems than Canadians do with FPTP.

Political scientists are in the vanguard of PR's boosters. They consider themselves experts in institutional design. Most political scientists who weighed in on the Meech Lake and Charlottetown Accords favoured those debacles too.[2] The Accords, products of a hyperventilated constitutional reform industry, depleted the capital of the politicians who sponsored them and proved disintegrative for the polity. This has not, however, chastened many of the same political scientists from pursuing a re-engineered electoral system via PR. Historians have been less sanguine about both mega-constitutional tampering and sweeping reforms of the electoral system. They have a better appreciation of the established institutions that have served Canadians well.

FPTP ought not to be judged solely by how precisely votes are converted into party seats. This is too narrow a gauge. What must also be weighed are geography, sociology, and history. Certainly, many states with PR have fared well. They have stable governments, progressive public policies, and honest public administration. PR's partisans are quick to cite states such as Germany and New Zealand. Other states with PR, however, have done poorly.

The United Kingdom and the United States are vibrant democracies. They informed the adoption of Canada's FPTP system. India went from being a British colony, like Canada, to becoming the world's largest democracy, and managed to do so with FPTP. FPTP is a very old institution, but that is an insufficient rationale for its dispatch. Marriage, the family, monarchy, and the church are old institutions too, yet they are not dismissed as outmoded. More vital to a state's welfare than its electoral system are its political cultural underpinnings. This refers to the health and vigour of its civil society, the independence and probity of the judiciary, media freedoms, transparency and accountability in public administration, informed dialogue and debate in the formulation of public policies, and the unfettered competition of political ideas. On these scores, any democratic audit of Canada must regard its electoral system as a sidebar. The term "democracy" is too readily bandied about in debates about the electoral system. Democracy has a kaleidoscopic quality that includes but profoundly transcends its electoral rules.

There are complex ramifications to any change in an electoral system. Change does not occur in an institutional vacuum. With PR, Canadians will still have their parliamentary system, their federal–provincial fandangos, and their beloved Charter of Rights. Canadians may be unhappy with their parliamentarians, but they want to keep their parliamentary system. That system arose in the context of two loosely knit parties, government and a "loyal" opposition ready to take the reins of office if the government faltered. Canadian parliamentary practice evolved with new parties being accommodated within the FPTP system. Party discipline has increased dramatically and many lament this, but PR will reinforce and not reverse it. PR elections, if international experience is any guide, will also lead to the further proliferation of parliamentary parties.[3] This will likely accentuate popular frustration with Parliament.

Most Canadians are unaware that alternatives to the single-member plurality system are not alien to Canada's history. Public appetite for electoral reform was greater a century ago than it is today. In the 1920s, when the Progressives were in full flight as the second-largest federal party, they agitated for PR. Parliament debated its merits and rejected it in a free vote.[4] As the Progressives and their causes quickly lost altitude, nothing came of the PR idea federally. Manitoba and Alberta adopted new electoral regimes that produced more proportionality but that did not render them more democratic in terms of converting public opinion into public policy.

Manitoba used the Hare system of PR—with its single transferable ballot—between the early 1920s and late 1950s to elect MLAs in Winnipeg, which formed one large multi-member constituency.[5] In Manitoba's rural single-member ridings, the alternative or transferable ballot was used. In both cases, voters marked their ballots preferentially (1, 2, 3, and so on if they wished). The victor in rural ridings was declared only after securing 50 percent of the first and subsequently transferred ballots, while Winnipeg candidates required a vote total determined by a formula that divided the number of votes cast by the number of seats. Most of the elections led to coalition governments, but the Co-operative Commonwealth Federation leader who joined one of them came to call it a "fool arrangement,"[6] a nightmare for his party. Most provinces have had multi-member constituencies at some time in their histories, and some adopted a religious denominational basis of representation. These were sometimes legally mandated (as in Newfoundland) and other times (as in Prince Edward Island and New Brunswick) they were governed by customs— unwritten but well understood rules. British Columbia used the alternative vote in the 1950s. It also used dual-member constituencies that only disappeared in 1991.

Proponents of PR argue that the appearance of more parliamentary parties may be neutral because PR eliminates strategic voting. Voters can opt for their preferred party rather than feeling they ought to plump for the lesser of evils, which is what many do under FPTP when they calculate that their party has little chance of success in their riding. A proliferation of parties, however, may also have drawbacks. It may lead to governmental deadlock or produce a government whose agenda results in voters not getting what they thought they had voted for. PR will also further weaken an MP's discretion. Those elected on party lists, as in the MMP system, will be beholden to their party and not to riding constituents since they will not be representing any constituency beyond their party.

DISAPPOINTMENTS OF PR

PR proponents often talk of it as a tonic for citizen alienation, cynicism, low voter turnout, and overbearing, unresponsive government. Claims that link the electoral system to pathologies of citizen disengagement—low voter turnout and low levels of citizen efficacy and trust in government—are dubious. Governments produced by PR are not necessarily more sensitive and responsive to public opinion or more adaptable to changing circumstances and public needs than are governments produced by FPTP. Notwithstanding their MMP system, German political analysts are no less preoccupied with *verdrossenheit*, or voter disillusionment, than their Canadian peers. In the past few decades, voter turnout has decreased across the Western industrialized world.[7] Canada is no exception. In New Zealand, which had a voter turnout of 89 percent using FPTP in 1984, voter turnout in the first election with MMP in 1996 declined to "probably the lowest voting turnout of any twentieth-century" election in the country's history.[8]

There are better indicators of a citizenry's contentment with its electoral system than voter turnout. Like about thirty other states, Italy uses PR, and it had compulsory voting from 1945 to 1993.[9] The efficaciousness of its electoral system therefore could not be measured by voter turnout. Other indicators, however, pointed to the Italian public's discontent with PR. In 1991, Italians voted in a referendum to modify their electoral system so that 75 percent of MPs would be elected by FPTP. They wanted more of what PR proponents allege is the undemocratic, unfair FPTP system. Their referendum victory did not bear fruit, though, as politicians finessed it and, in Italy's 2006 election, eighteen parties elected MPs. Seven parties won thirty or more seats each. In a 2007 reprise of public discontent with PR, more than 800,000 Italians signed a petition to try to force another referendum that would reduce the number of smaller parties by greater use of FPTP. They wanted "to move Italy away from decades of political instability."[10]

Paradoxically, low voter turnout may signify satisfaction or justifiable apathy with the state of political affairs. It may reflect the public's sense that it does not much matter who gets elected, that the ship of state is stable or that its trajectory is impervious to change and that the quality of one's life and material well-being are secure or unaffected by whomever holds government's reins. High voter turnout may reflect societal angst, as it did in Quebec's emotionally charged and divisive sovereignty referendum in 1995. It was an astronomical 94 percent, but families, coworkers, and others with long-standing cordial relations found the passions unleashed by the referendum tore asunder their amicable bonds. That is one reason why there has been little appetite for another referendum.

Expecting that PR would produce a more consensual, accountable, and transparent politics, New Zealanders voted in favour of an MMP system in a referendum. They saw PR as a way of holding politicians to their promises. They realized that there would be more proportionality in their parliament's composition, but they did not appreciate the critical importance of the party vote, rather than the constituency vote, in determining the government's ultimate complexion. After New Zealand's first MMP election, party leaders disappeared behind closed doors for eight weeks, hammered out party alignments, and horse-traded cabinet portfolios. The small New Zealand First party, which had campaigned on getting rid of the National Party government and its fiscally conservative policies, turned around and threw its lot in with it. This is not what those voting for the upstart party expected. Public opinion judged the new style of politics reprehensible. In the aftermath of the first MMP election, politicians—who had been cool to PR—embraced it while the public turned against it. Polls showed that voters would have overwhelmingly rejected MMP in another referendum.[11] New Zealanders' hopes for a less adversarial, more cooperative politics were dashed. They expected that the denial of a majority for any one party would be positive, but they found to their chagrin that coalition cabinets behaved like the old single-party majority ones did. The same is likely to happen in Canada.

One rationale for PR is that it will make Parliament more of a social mirror of society. Proponents foresee more women and minorities placed high on the party lists used in the MMP system so that parliamentary faces will be more diverse. That did occur in New Zealand where women's representation rose from 21 to 29 percent. There is no guarantee, however, that it will happen: Israel's 2006 election returned only 17 women (or 14 percent) to its Knesset, a lower percentage than that in Canada's 2006 election (21 percent) and Ontario's 2007 election (27 percent). Furthermore, the rationale for greater representation of politically disadvantaged groups overlooks where power actually resides in a parliamentary system—with the cabinet and not with the more representative party caucuses. Again, the New Zealand case is instructive: more women than ever appeared in Parliament after the first MMP election, but fewer women, only one, appeared in a cabinet of twenty, a "power reversal" for New Zealand's female MPs.[12] In contrast, women constituted 21 percent of Canada's 1997 post-election cabinet.

There is something troubling about engineering group representation by using PR. It is divisive of a common citizenship. The notion that only a woman, an Aboriginal, or a member of a visible minority can represent members of those groups is pernicious because it categorizes citizens in ways that may not be their primary or preferred political identification. It tells men or non-Aboriginals, for example, that a woman or an Aboriginal may be an unworthy representative of their interests. This view of representation detracts from a cardinal democratic principle: respect for an individual's unmediated choice of who ought to represent him or her. It tells individuals that their gender or the colour of their skin or their Aboriginal status is more important than who they want to represent them.

The Latvian and Belgian experiences are also instructive for Canadians pondering the alleged virtues of MMP. Latvia's population is less than the City of Toronto's, and its size is roughly comparable to the Greater Toronto Area. Latvia's president until recently was a Cold War émigré to Canada. A distinguished graduate of the University of Toronto and McGill University, she served as vice president of the Science Council of Canada and was admitted as an Officer of the National Order of Quebec. Immensely popular in her native land, Vaira Vīķe-Freiberga was drafted to become its president in the post-Soviet era and was twice elected to the post. During her tenure, she wistfully recalled the simplicity of Canada's electoral system and compared it to the daunting challenge she faced in trying to get the leaders of Latvia's eleven parties in the Saeima (Parliament) to construct a stable government.[13] Latvia's experience is a reminder of the potential proliferation of parties and its consequences even in small states. In Belgium, negotiations over forming a government were still ongoing nearly a year after the country's 2010 election.

The proposed MMP system that Ontarians rejected in 2007 by a margin of 63 percent to 37 percent set a bar of 3 percent for a party to gain representation. In Israel's 2006 election, with the bar set at 2 percent, thirty-one parties competed, and twelve won seats. Compare Canada to small states such as Latvia and Israel. When one considers Canada's vastness, its regional and cultural fault lines, and the uneven distribution of its natural resource endowments and economic wealth, the chances are heightened for more parties and for more regionally and culturally divisive ones. In small states, regional parties are not a concern. In Canada— as the Progressives in the 1920s and the Reform Party and the Bloc Québécois in the 1990s demonstrated—an appetite for regional parties exists and they have, by definition, voraciously narrow agendas. These are not broad-based national parties representing a cross-section of socioeconomic interests and groups.

A virtue of FPTP is that it encourages "big tent" or brokerage parties. A party hoping to gain power must strive to incorporate, accommodate, cater to, and express the interests of a medley of groups and regions. Such parties—a mélange of people from different regions and strata of society—fulfill a nationally integrative role. They endeavour to be the representational social mirrors that many MMP proponents eagerly demand of the electoral system. Perversely, MMP could contribute to ghettoizing and dividing groups in the cause of representing them. Senior citizens, for example, concerned that their issues are overlooked, would have an incentive to withdraw from a large inclusive party such as the Liberals, Conservatives, or the New Democratic Party (NDP) and could be encouraged to form, for example, their own Pensioners Party. This occurred in Israel. and when the 2006 election dust settled, the Pensioners Party played a major role in the cabinet's construction and in the discussion of the issue of war and peace, something about which its election platform said nothing. Similarly, Aboriginals, women, or religious minorities may be dissuaded from participation in parties that are broad-based nationally and programmatically. MMP encourages them to hive themselves off and use a new party, constructed on the limited identities of its supporters, to extract concessions for narrow self-serving interests with less pressure to compromise than exists under the present system. The creation of a Toronto Party, insistent on full-blown provincial status for the city, would not contribute to national or provincial unity. If successful, it would be devastating for Ontario's hinterlands; they are dependent on fiscal transfers for social programs and infrastructure made possible by their being part of a larger, wealthier provincial state.

In constructing coalition governments in a multiparty context, the smallest party to the coalition may exert disproportionate influence in determining the fate and policy thrust of the government. Conversely, a party that consistently wins a significant plurality of votes in elections could be kept from participating in government indefinitely. Small single-issue parties could consistently wield more power than the largest, but sidelined, party. Another possibility is a grand coalition of the two largest parties, as occurred in Germany after its 2005 election. Whatever configuration of parties forms the government, it will not be what voters voted for or thought they were going to get. Proportionality in the legislature will likely not translate into proportional influence in government. Coalition governments constructed under MMP—such as one where the largest party teams up with a fourth-place finisher—will give that small party disproportionate influence compared to the second- and third-largest parties.

A threshold of 5 percent of votes as a condition for parliamentary representation, as in New Zealand and Germany, may be thought of as an effective rampart against regional and other culturally divisive parties. The representational bar in Canada, however, whatever the percentage threshold, will be set provincially rather than for the country as a whole.[14] That is, if a party wins 30 percent of Albertans' votes, it will get 30 percent (or at least nine) of the province's current twenty-eight seats in parliament. The three most westerly and resource-rich provinces could throw up a Western Rights Party even more potent than the Reform Party. A British Columbia First Party dedicated to pursuing nothing but B.C.'s interests is conceivable. Such parties will not contribute to national unity and coherent national policymaking. Some in the East will be sure to make a case for an Atlantic Party. Although the four Atlantic provinces account for only 10 percent of the seats in the House of Commons, just a few seats—ten or eleven, which is a third of the Atlantic seats—could propel such a narrowly focused party into a king-maker role in a fragmented Parliament. Imagine a proliferation of provincial and other parties—the Family Coalition Party, the Marijuana Party, the Libertarian Party, the Party of People with Disabilities, and so forth—and consider their influence in the making and breaking of coalition governments. With MMP providing incentives for the formation of such parties, the effect on Canadian unity of the current somewhat unbalanced regional caucuses will appear piddling in comparison.

PUSH FOR PR

Proponents agitate for PR even as public opinion appears disconnected from the issue. In the past decade, five provinces and Parliament have toyed with electoral reform. Prince Edward Island's voters, like Ontario's, when given a chance to weigh in on MMP, turned it down decisively (64 percent said no) in a 2005 referendum. When one considers that turnouts in FPTP elections in P.E.I. have consistently been over 80 percent, public detachment from the electoral reform issue is revealed in the turnout for the referendum: a paltry 35 percent. In Ontario, a poll conducted before its 2007 referendum found that only 28 percent were familiar with the MMP proposal, and the Conservative leader reported that, in all his travelling around the province, only three people raised the issue.[15] In the Ontario referendum, 138,000 fewer valid votes were cast than in the FPTP election that took place concurrently.[16]

Like the constitutional reform misadventures of earlier days, the pursuit of PR is an elite pleasure industry of political scientists, political junkies, and smaller parties such as the Greens and the NDP who have an interest in it. The Ontario referendum won majority backing in only 5 of the province's 107 constituencies, and 4 of those were won by the NDP. Paradoxically, the NDP, which has never secured a percentage of federal parliamentary seats commensurate with its share of the popular vote, may ultimately be a casualty of the MMP system it seeks. Its self-styled coalition of unionists, feminists, environmentalists, gays and lesbians, people of colour, and others may well fracture.

A majority of British Columbia's voters, 57 percent, opted for the single transferable vote (STV) in their 2005 referendum on electoral reform, but that proved insufficient because the B.C. government had set a bar of 60 percent approval for its adoption. One reason support for electoral system change was greater in B.C. in 2005 than in Ontario was that the quirkiness of the FPTP system had been displayed in three consecutive B.C. elections. In 1991, the NDP won power even while its popularity dipped below levels it had attained when it lost in the 1970s and 1980s. Then, in 1996, the NDP was reelected to another majority although the Liberals won more votes. In 2001, when the Liberals swept to power on an impressive 57 percent of the vote, they won a lopsided seventy-seven (or 97 percent) of the seventy-nine seats.

In Ontario's 2003 election, in contrast, the Liberals formed a government with a healthy but more modest majority after capturing a decisive 46.5 percent of the vote. The Ontario result was historically consistent with past results, and the election of a Liberal majority government was not publicly perceived as "stolen," which is admittedly a potentially unseemly upshot of FPTP. Ontario produced a mix of governments—three parties won majority governments over the course of three elections in the span of eight years between 1987 and 1995. While no party captured a majority of the votes, the results in each election reflected a popular consensus for change in favour of the party that prevailed. In B.C., the appetite for electoral reform dampened dramatically after the FPTP system proved less capricious in the 2005 provincial election; the Liberals, with 46 percent of the vote won forty-six seats, and the NDP, with 42 percent, won thirty-three seats. Consequently, in a second referendum on STV in 2009, fewer than 39 percent of B.C. voters opted for changing the electoral system, a sharp contrast to the majority that had supported the idea just four years earlier.

The three provincial governments conducting the referenda did not tell voters that they would set a 60 percent bar when they originally promised a referendum. We may only speculate on why they set it so high. Most politicians, particularly those from the large parties, prefer the status quo. FPTP holds out a better prospect for them to wield majority power. In Manitoba, Saskatchewan, and Nova Scotia, where the NDP is a major party, it has not pursued PR, in contrast to the federal and Ontario NDP, which are minor parties. Politicians from large parties tend not to publicize their preference for FPTP because that could alienate some voters. Nevertheless, they may promise a referendum on the issue because they perceive that the public will appreciate the idea that its will counts, and the public may reward the party that gives it a direct voice in the matter. That is what happened in New Zealand. To capitalize on this belief, in both the B.C. and Ontario cases, the referenda were held by the governing party at the same time as the general election. In Ontario, the Conservatives declared that they were opposed to MMP only on the eve of the referendum, after public opinion surveys made it clear that it would fail.[17]

Both the B.C. and Ontario governments encouraged those favouring PR by opening the issue, but the governments themselves would not speak in favour of it and insisted that they were neutral. Both provinces used a Citizens' Assembly (CA) to consider and propose, if the Assembly so decided, an alternative electoral system. The Citizens' Assemblies were exercises in deliberative democracy, a supplement to representative democracy. Political scientists and others expert in electoral systems educated the Citizens' Assemblies in the various forms and outcomes of PR and FPTP systems. Then, the CA members, meeting on weekends, opted for PR over the FPTP status quo. In Ontario's case, they chose the MMP form of PR by a vote of ninety-four to eight. The ultimate upshot, the referendum's results, demonstrated that the Assembly's members were whistling in the wind: barely more than a third of their fellow citizens embraced their proposal at the ballot box.

The Citizens' Assemblies' members did not reflect their citizen peers' views. Nor was the CA as representative of the public as the government claimed. Unlike a legal jury, randomly selected with service mandatory, only citizens interested in serving on the Assembly could be chosen. In B.C. and Ontario, the CAs were constructed to reflect gender balance. With each constituency permitted one representative, this meant that no men were eligible to represent half of the constituencies and no women the other half. Notwithstanding the gender balance, the Ontario Assembly was not a representative demographic mirror of the public. One Assembly member observed that a third of the members were retirees. Also unrepresentative of their communities were those who appeared at the twenty-nine meetings in seventeen cities. "In some cases the public were homogeneous—e.g., a large group from an old age home."[18] Public interest was also low; attendance ranged from seven in Dryden to about two hundred in Toronto, a city of well over two million.

The CAs' recommendations in both B.C. and Ontario to jettison FPTP were predictable. Those making oral and written submissions to Ontario's CA were not representative of Ontarians' public opinion. Self-selected, they were overwhelmingly in favour of PR with 692 of the 986 submissions offering "pro" comments and only 78 (or 8 percent) tendering "con" comments. A repeated theme in the submissions was that PR would produce a more demographically representative legislature. Women and visible minorities' underrepresentation in political institutions was depicted as systemic discrimination. It is noteworthy, then, that of all the comments submitted to the CA, only 21 percent were by women, a lower percentage than the percentage of women in Ontario's legislature. This suggested that women were less interested than men in the Assembly's work but the Assembly, given its gender composition, could not be accused of systemic discrimination.

CONFRONTING THE OTHER SIDE

John Hiemstra and Harold Jansen offer a number of rationales for discarding FPTP and adopting PR. They project positive scenarios with MMP. They note that one of the main arguments for FPTP is that it offers good prospects for stable government because a plurality of votes for a party usually translates into a majority of seats. As they accurately observe, Canada has nonetheless frequently had minority governments. Indeed, an oddity of the Jean Chrétien years was that—with five parties elected to produce a pizza parliament in 1993, 1997, and 2000—a majority government emerged at all. The 2004, 2006, and 2008 elections, with only four parliamentary parties, yielded the more logical outcome—a minority government. If the current four parliamentary parties survive, and even if new ones do not appear, FPTP majority governments composed exclusively of members from a single party are less likely in the future.

Canada's minority as well as majority governments have provided relative political stability by international standards. The greatest threats to Canadian unity, paradoxically, have come during periods of majority government, as during the Meech Lake imbroglio, the Charlottetown Accord, and Quebec's sovereignty referendums and when all the parties (except for the Bloc Québécois) sided with the government.

Hiemstra and Jansen contend that FPTP aggravates and intensifies regional divisions because it produces regionally lopsided caucuses. Certainly, the success of the Chrétien Liberals in capturing 98 of Ontario's 99 seats in 1993 and then 101 and 100 of the province's 103 seats in the 1997 and 2000 elections respectively demonstrated lopsidedness. The Liberals won those contests with bare majorities of between 51 and 53 percent of Ontarians' votes. The dramatic overrepresentation of Liberals in Ontario was twinned with their substantial underrepresentation in the West. Conversely, the Reform/Alliance Party with the support of between 24 and 26 percent of Ontario's voters in that same trio of elections did not win more than 2 seats in 2000 and was shut out in 1997. Such outcomes are unusual, produced by what proved to be but a temporary fissure on the political right with Reform/Alliance and the Progressives Conservatives competing for the same pool of voters to the Liberals' benefit. The 2004, 2006, and 2008 elections produced more typical and less severe distortions after the right reunited. In Ontario in 2006, the Liberals won 52 percent of the seats with 40 percent of the votes, the Conservatives won 39 percent of the seats with 35 percent of the votes, and the NDP won 12 percent of the seats with their 19 percent of votes.

Neither the lopsided results of the elections in the 1990s nor the more balanced results of more recent elections affected national unity. It is the premiers and the provinces, rather than the federal caucuses that vote along predictable party lines, that are the pivotal players in national unity debates. The impact on national unity of the mathematical asymmetry between seats and votes produced by FPTP pales in comparison to the impact on unity that would happen if unabashedly selfish regional parties were to emerge and take root. MMP would likely unleash them.

Hiemstra and Jansen blithely and naively assume that, with MMP, the existing parties would continue to secure levels of popular support across the country similar to those of the past. What would change positively, from their perspective, is that the existing party caucuses would more accurately reflect those parties' differing levels of regional support. This, however, would almost certainly not occur because the existing party system would most likely fracture, given the incentive MMP provides for regional and narrow single-issue parties. Such parties would likely fracture one or more of the established broadly based parties. By definition, single-issue parties lack an overarching policy agenda and a "big tent" mentality that strives to incorporate people from different backgrounds, interests, and regions. Canada's diversities and social heterogeneity would fuel these new parties. Such parties would not foster what Canadians share in common. They would highlight non-ideological divisions among Canadians rather than economic class divisions, such as the gaps between the rich and poor wherever they live in Canada. Broadly based parties and platforms will compete with and give way to narrow special-interest parties. A virtue of the existing system is that it encourages parties to broker, within themselves, Canada's regional and social diversities.

CONCLUSION

FPTP has served Canada well in comparative perspective. To replace it with MMP would contribute to endangering national unity. MMP could produce governments with policies tailored to single-interest parties that capture very low percentages of the vote. Their handfuls of seats could disproportionately determine the government's complexion and direction. The MMP solution to the shortcomings of FPTP may prove worse than the problem. Adopting MMP is akin to buying a pig in a poke.

NOTES

1. Laza Kekic, "The Economist Intelligence Unit's Index of Democracy," 2007, pp. 3 and 6, available at http://www.economist.com/media/pdf/DEMOCRACY_INDEX_2007_v3.pdf. Accessed August 20, 2011.

2. Alan C. Cairns, "Political Science, Ethnicity and the Canadian Constitution," in David P. Shugarman and Reg Whitaker, eds., *Federalism and Political Community: Essays in Honour of Donald Smiley* (Peterborough: Broadview, 1989), p. 117.

3. André Blais and Ken Carty, "The Psychological Impact of Electoral Laws: Measuring Duverger's Elusive Factor," *British Journal of Political Science* 21 (1991), pp. 79–93.

4. Denis Pilon, "Explaining Voting System Reform in Canada, 1874 to 1960," *Journal of Canadian Studies* 40, no. 3 (Fall 2006), p. 147.

5. *Revised Statutes of Manitoba, 1940*, I, ch. 57. For analysis of the results, see Nelson Wiseman and K.W. Taylor, "Ethnic vs. Class Voting: The Case of Winnipeg, 1945," *Canadian Journal of Political Science* 7, no. 2 (June 1974), pp. 314–328.

6. *Winnipeg Free Press*, Sept. 17, 1949.

7. S. Pharr, R. Putman, and R. Dalton, "Trouble in the Advanced Democracies." *Journal of Democracy* 11, no. 2 (2000), pp. 5–25.

8. Jack Vowles, "Offsetting the PR Effect? Party Mobilization and Turnout Decline in New Zealand, 1996–99," *Party Politics* 8, no. 5 (2002), p. 587.

9. International Institute for Democracy and Electoral Assistance (Stockholm, Sweden) http://www.idea.int/vt/compulsory_voting.cfm. Accessed August 20. 2011.

10. "Italian Election Petition Earns 800,000 Signatures," *The Globe and Mail*, July 25, 2007.

11. Thérèse Arsenau, "Ideas," CBC radio program, February 9, 1998.

12. Thérèse Arsenau, "Electing Representative Legislatures: Lessons from New Zealand," in Henry Milner, ed., *Making Every Vote Count: Reassessing Canada's Electoral System* (Peterborough: Broadview, 1999), p. 140.

13. Interview with Joe Schlesinger, "Foreign Assignment," CBC-TV program, February 21, 2004.

14. *Constitution Act, 1985 (Representation)*, Statutes of Canada, 1986, c. 8, Part I.

15. Robert Benzie, "Reform's on the Ballot: Now If They Only Cared," *The Toronto Star*, September 1, 2007.

16. Elections Ontario, available at http://www3.elections.on.ca/internetapp/realtimereferendum.aspx?lang=en-ca&gf73=0&contestid=2&channel_id={923146e7-4d81-42a8-99f0-e61f5ab50387}&lang=en, and http://www3.elections.on.ca/internetapp/realtimehome.aspx?lang=en&channel_id={923146e7-4d81-42a8-99f0-e61f5ab50387}&lang=en. Accessed October 21, 2007.

17. Robert Benzie, "Reject MMP, Conservatives Tell Voters," *The Toronto Star*, October 9, 2007.

18. Citizens Assembly Blog, "Update on the Consultation Phase of the Ontario Citizens' Assembly," March 3, 2007.

POSTSCRIPT

The two articles present some good arguments, but they also leave some questions unanswered. John Hiemstra and Harold Jansen nicely reveal the benefits of a mixed-member proportional (MMP) system, but one wonders whether they understate the possible costs of such a system. Coalition governments, an inevitable result of MMP in Canada, may produce policies whose coherence is lacking. The benefit of single-member plurality (SMP) is that a single voice typically determines policy, but the multiple voices in MMP may produce government outputs that endeavour to satisfy the demands of the varied parties in government. Hiemstra and Jansen are little worried with the prospect of two types of MPs under MMP. However, it seems possible that those unattached to a constituency may find themselves a little lost, especially in light of the fact that constituency work makes up the bulk of the activity of most elected representatives. The two authors also applaud MMP because of its ability to ensure appropriate representation in government. But again one wonders. The presence of coalition governments will produce power arrangements in government that fail to reflect the distribution of the vote in the legislature. A minor party, with little of the popular vote, may team up with a more powerful party to secure its aims in exchange for support. In other words, there is no guarantee that the distribution of the popular vote will be recorded in the actions of government. MMP addresses concerns of representation in the legislative branch, but may have little effect on the distribution of support in the most powerful branch in parliamentary government—namely the executive branch.

Wiseman makes a number of good points, the most important of these arguably being the failure of some to realize that a rough equating of the quality of democracy with a nation's electoral system is foolish. But it is also true that Wiseman's effort is not invulnerable to criticism. Canada may indeed be more attractive than other countries with PR, but this does not mean that Canada should eschew any serious consideration of electoral reform—successful nations can always become more successful. Wiseman is critical of the attempt of MMP to make formal political life more representative of society, but the fact that women, for instance, typically represent about one-fifth of elected representatives can be unsettling. Finally, Wiseman may also be charged with failing to assuage or ease feelings that the existing electoral system in Canada is simply unfair. There may indeed be problems with MMP—nothing is ever perfect—but at least it seeks to ensure that the parties and their supporters get what they deserve.

Students wishing to pursue the subject of electoral reform might begin with Heather MacIvor's short overview of electoral reform in Heather MacIvor, "A Brief Introduction to Electoral Reform," in Henry Milner, ed., *Making Every Vote Count: Reassessing Canada's Electoral System* (Peterborough: Broadview

Press, 1999). Another useful introduction to elections and electoral reforms is John Courtney, *Elections* (Vancouver: UBC Press, 2004), ch. 6. The next task is to dive into the detailed analyses of the first-past-the-post system and its main competitors. Here, students might start with J. Paul Johnston and Harvey E. Pasis, eds., *Representation and Electoral Systems: Canadian Perspectives* (Scarborough: Prentice-Hall, 1990). This text contains many of the classic articles on electoral reform in Canada, including the seminal article by Alan C. Cairns and the response to his article by J.A.A. Lovink. Other examinations of electoral reform (such as MMP) include Henry Milner, ed., *Making Every Vote Count: Reassessing Canada's Electoral System* (Peterborough: Broadview Press, 1999); Henry Milner, "The Case for Proportional Representation," in Hugh Thorburn and Alan Whitehorn, eds., *Party Politics in Canada*, 8th ed. (Scarborough: Prentice-Hall, 2001); Louis Massicotte, *Changing the Canadian Electoral System* (Montreal: Institute for Research on Public Policy, February 2001); and the entire July–August 2001 issue of *Policy Options*. A rigorous analysis of electoral reform and MMP can also be found in Law Commission of Canada, *Voting Counts: Electoral Reform in Canada* (Ottawa: Law Reform Commission, 2004). For those who wish to see how the electoral system has shaped the history of elections in Canada, the book to consult is Lawrence Leduc et al., eds. *Dynasties and Interludes: Past and Present in Canadian Electoral Politics* (Toronto: Dundurn Press, 2010)

The issue of electoral reform is not merely a matter of concern for academics. Provincial governments in Canada have been looking long and hard at this issue, and some have held referendums on the matter. For more on developments in the provinces, students should see Harold J. Jansen, "Making the Impossible Possible: Electoral Reform and Canada's Provinces," in Thomas M.J. Bateman and Rick Myers, eds., *Braving the New World: Readings in Contemporary Politics*, 4th ed. (Scarborough: Nelson, 2008). As for reports on the referendums, the following are relevant: Laura B. Stephenson and Brian Tanguay, *Ontario Referendum on Proportional Representation: Why Citizens Said No* (Montreal: IRPP, 2009), and Mark E. Warren and Hilary Pearse, *Designing Deliberative Democracy: the British Columbia Citizens' Assembly* (New York: Cambridge University Press, 2008).

The experience of other countries with the plurality system and proportional representation is relevant to the discussion of electoral reform in Canada. On this topic, the following might be consulted: Michael Dummett, *Principles of Electoral Reform* (Oxford: Oxford University Press, 1997), Matthew Soberg Shugart and Martin P. Wattenberg, ed., *Mixed-Member Electoral Systems: The Best of Both Worlds?* (Oxford: Oxford University Press, 2001), and Andre Blais, *To Keep or to Change First Past the Post? The Politics of Electoral Reform* (New York: Oxford University Press, 2008). Also, special attention may be given to Arend Lijphart,

"Democracies: Forms, Performance, and Constitutional Engineering," *European Journal of Political Research* 25 (1994), pp. 1–17. What makes this article so central to the debate is that it denies that one must concede a decline in the effectiveness of government in order to introduce PR. For more on Lijphart's work, students might want to consult Arend Lijphart, *Patterns of Democracy: Government Forms and Performance in Thirty-Six Countries* (New Haven and London: Yale University Press, 1999), chs. 15–16.

Should Women Focus on Small-p Politics?

✔ **YES**
JACQUETTA NEWMAN, "Small-p Politics: Women Working
Outside Formal Political Structures"

✘ **NO**
JACQUETTA NEWMAN, "Say It Five Times Fast: The Pitfalls
of Small-p Politics and a Plea for Large-P Politics"

One of the more salient issues for women in Canadian political life is their failure to achieve greater representation in formal political structures. Women typically constitute only about one-fifth of the members of legislative assemblies, and the percentages are not much better in other institutional parts of government. A great deal of work and thinking has been directed toward fixing this problem. Women have been urged to participate more actively in political parties and to consider more aggressively occupations that increase the chances of gaining entrance into government. Feminist groups have also supported the candidacies of women and provided political muscle to parties that champion the cause of more equal representation in politics. Even political leaders, normally absorbed with electoral victory, have intervened to secure more women for a career in political life.

All of these efforts and more assume that entrance into the world of "large-P politics"—a term to describe the formal structures and processes of government—generates substantial benefits for women. Policies directed at women will become more effective, the value of equality in society will be strengthened, and the manner of doing politics itself may change for the better. Few, if any, question the focus on large-P politics because the benefits of this type of politics is seemingly so apparent. However, there is some concern that the energies of those pressing for these ends may be misdirected. History reveals that important advances for women have not necessarily been achieved through activities in the world of formal politics; rather, it has been the efforts of women in charities, community groups, advocacy groups, and other informal structures that have paved the way for women. These bodies form the world of "small-p politics," and it is this world that has been central to successes in securing greater equality in politics and elsewhere. Accordingly, it is argued that women should rethink their strategy of political activity and pay more attention to those institutions that have worked so well in the past.

Integral to small-p politics and its successes is the notion of "social capital," which refers to the trust and networking abilities people build up by associating with each other through the informal processes and structures of society. Women meet in their neighbourhoods, for example, when looking after young children, and in so doing become aware of their common needs and subsequently enter into discussions about how to meet these needs. Volunteer organizations or community groups also become settings in which women can talk about important issues and make plans for action. Out of these and other types of interactions emerges the social capital that enables the world of small-p politics to become a powerful and influential actor. Just because some societal structures and processes fail to receive the publicity and attention of formal politics, this hardly means they are insignificant.

The claim for small-p political activity is attractive, partly because it suggests that political power can reside in our everyday activities. Women only have to be themselves, to live their normal lives, in order to secure political gains. Yet, there is the uneasy feeling that this seems almost too good to be true. Surely some of the activities associated with small-p politics can actually get in the way of political activity. Looking after children may indeed lead to collective action but can just as easily produce exhausted mothers wishing only for refuge in their homes. Researchers also suggest that the type of social capital produced by women can for one reason or another be difficult to translate into political advancement. Interestingly, men also create social capital, and theirs is seemingly more transferable into political capital. More generally, leaders of women's movements and organizations may cringe at the idea of giving up the fight in the arena of large-P politics. They sense that to make gains in formal politics one has to be in formal politics. To not be involved in political parties and legislative assemblies is to engage in pure folly.

In the readings, Jacquetta Newman, co-author of *Women, Politics, and Public Policy* and a professor of political science at King's University College at the University of Western Ontario, makes the case for and against shifting the focus of women's political activity toward small-p politics and away from large-P politics.

✔ **YES**

Small-p Politics: Women Working Outside Formal Political Structures
JACQUETTA NEWMAN

In democracies there is a tendency to assess a group's political power and influence by measuring its success in attaining positions within the structures of political representation as members of elected government and, more generally, as participants in national and regional assemblies. Our understanding of democratic citizenship is often predicated on the notion of representation and the formal rights to vote and participate in electoral politics, which, as Young and Everitt point out, reflects the centrality to democratic governance of the "representative institutions that achieve their mandates through popular election."[1] Not surprisingly then, the struggle for suffrage in the early twentieth century by the first wave of the women's movement and their achievement of formal political rights for women is a significant benchmark in the struggle for women's equality.

However, two features should be noted here. First, since 1918 and 1929, recognition of women's political citizenship has had only limited success in Canada. Nearly a century later, Canadian women still have not achieved equal representation in Canadian institutions of democratic governance. As of the May 2011 federal election, women make up only 24.7 percent of the Canadian House of Commons—76 women in a 308-member house—ranking fortieth in the world.[2] In the provincial legislatures, supposedly closer to the politicians' homes and more likely to appeal to those who prefer not to have to travel constantly to and from the national capital, the average for women's representation as of February 2010 was 23.9 percent of the seats, from a high in Manitoba of 31.6 percent to a low of 5.3 percent in the Nunavut Territory and 12.7 percent in New Brunswick.[3] Looking at national elections since 1968, we can see that women, who make up half of the population, have found it difficult to break out of the low 20 percent region in terms of their representation in the House. Women interested in political representation have a better chance to enter Parliament as an appointed senator than as an elected MP. Women make up 35 percent of the Canadian Senate.

Second, the political action of women to push for the vote and achieve formal political rights did not occur within the representative and electoral structures, but found its power and expression in communities of women that formed within civil society, outside the formal structures of politics. The example of the first wave of the women's movement illustrates that politics can occur informally in community networks that focus on the day-to-day problems faced by people and can also have influence on public policy. To get the full story regarding women's political activism in Canada, we have to turn our attention from the formal structures of legislatures and political parties to the political work women undertake through and in civil society. It is the intention of this article to address this world of small-p politics.

In *Habits of the Heart*, Bellah et al. make a distinction between three conceptions of politics: (1) the politics of consensual community, (2) the pluralist politics of interest competition, and (3) the politics of nation. The first conception, which Bellah referred to as the politics of community, concerns the activity of putting into effect "the moral consensus of the community, reached through free face-to-face discussion, where, "citizenship is virtually coextensive with getting involved with one's neighbours for the good of the community."[4] It is an activity that participants do not see "as politics at all."[5] The second conception refers to the world of party and electoral politics, "the complicated, professional yet highly personal, business of adversarial struggles, alliance building, and interest bargaining.... For most people, it lacks the immediacy of everyday involvement.... Supporting candidates by voting is the typical expression of this understanding for most people, keeping politics at arm's length."[6] Finally, the third conception, the politics of nation, refers to the high affairs of state that transcend local everyday concerns. It is the first conception of community politics that represents small-p politics; the second and third forms, associated with the structures of the state and the formalized activities of parties, elections, and legislatures, represent the large-P politics that is conventionally defined as politics proper. Birte Siim makes a similar distinction between "'small democracies' of everyday life and the 'big democracy' of political parties and organized government."[7]

Consequently, when we refer to small-p politics, we are envisioning the political nature of local, grassroots-focused (although it may be termed "thinking globally, acting locally"), face-to-face, and day-to-day activities that are often framed in terms of things that have to get done for the good of the community. As such, it comprises charity work, volunteerism, and work with non-governmental and/ or social movement activities. It is a useful distinction because it forces us to broaden our understanding of politics and helps us to explain how the activities of women over the last century have had a far greater impact on Canadian politics and society than their numbers in legislative assemblies reflect. It also opens up the possibility that politics can occur outside the formal structures of the state and that activities within civil society influence, sometimes profoundly, both the state and society.

Simply conceived, civil society is composed of voluntary civic and social organizations that are distinct from the institutions of the state, family, and the economy. This includes organizations such as charities, non-governmental organizations, community groups, women's organizations, faith-based organizations, professional associations, unions, self-help groups, social movements and social movement organizations, business associations, coalitions, and advocacy groups, which as the list suggests come in many forms and with varying levels of formal organization and power.[8] While in the past the activities undertaken in civil society were considered unconnected to the political sphere, or "pre-political," recent work in political science and sociology has come to take more seriously the connection between community life and political life.

This has definitely been evidenced in the popularity of the term *social capital* and the proliferation of studies regarding the requirement of social capital for healthy democracy. The most popular definition of social capital is that of Robert Putnam:

> By analogy with notions of physical capital and human capital—tools and training that enhance individual productivity—"social capital" refers to features of social organization such as networks, norms, and social trust that facilitate coordination and cooperation for mutual benefit....In the first place, networks of civic engagement foster sturdy norms of generalized reciprocity and encourage the emergence of social trust. Such networks facilitate coordination and communication, amplify reputations, and thus allow dilemmas of collective action to be resolved.[9]

In his work on Italy and the United States, Putnam examines how membership in community organizations enhances democratic participation and decision making and how, in the U.S., decline in group membership has consequences for democratic engagement. Social capital has significance for political activity because the experiences, skills, networks, and "capital" developed through these networks of trust and reciprocity bring people into political engagement: "[P]atterns of formal and informal sociability build up relations of trust and reciprocity. The resultant social capital enhances individuals' capacity to join together in collective action to resolve common problems (or ensure that governments address such problems)—it capitalizes political engagement."[10] Other authors conceive social capital more broadly or narrowly[11] with more or less attention to the issue of politicization and conflict. Consequently, there are debates as to what social capital actually entails, and accusations are made that the term suffers from "definitional diversity" and "over-versatility." As Edwards and Foley complain, "the concept seems to take on the property of a gas expanding or contracting to fit the analytical space afforded by each historical or sociopolitical setting."[12] However, for our purposes, we identify the common thread that runs through the various conceptions of social capital: that experience and participation in social networks facilitate the building of values of trust and reciprocity, which provide resources and training to enhance political engagement, participation, and influence.

Why does the idea of social capital have significance for women's politics? The simple answer is that social capital approaches appear to fit well with the social and political activities undertaken by women. Putnam argued that one of the reasons for the decline of social capital in the U.S. is the move of women into paid employment during the 1970s, which gave them less time to commit to social involvement. For Putnam, this indicates that much traditional social capital was built and supported by women,[13] although in later work he qualifies this argument, attributing the decline to factors such as increased physical mobility, changing demographics, and the technological transformation of leisure. However, apart from this suggestion of Putnam's, "social capital studies in political science have tended to focus upon male-dominated activities. They have selected men's social capital–related activities, while often neglecting entire spheres of relevant activity where women's efforts are concentrated."[14] It is only recently that feminist scholars have undertaken to examine social capital and its relevance to women's politics.[15]

As Lowndes argues, "empirically, the concept seems attractive for the attention it directs toward the intersection between community life and politics, and toward informal as well as formal domains of political activity."[16] It fits well because women's activities are assumed to be more involved in community volunteer work and concerned with looking after the local needs of family and neighbours. Social capital addresses the dichotomy between the public and private that feminists argue is at the heart of patriarchy, where *the public* refers to the arena where public decisions are made, the public interest and good are determined, and public policy is decided—the world of large-P politics—and *the private* is removed from formal politics and embedded in the nurturing and domestic duties of the home, that is, small-p politics. This division of society into public and private spheres is nonsense, and social capital helps illustrate this. It is "important in the reconsideration of the role that women play within our political system as social capital focuses attention on the implications of the private sphere and private relationships for public life."[17] It is the so-called private sphere where many relationships of reciprocity and trust are built and the skills and capacity for political engagement are developed.

This is borne out historically; as suggested earlier, one of the notable features of the first wave of feminism was that the campaign for suffrage found its power and expression in the community groups and clubs that brought women together to undertake good works, some associated with churches and others more secular. For example, in Canada, the Canadian branch of the Women's Christian Temperance Union (WCTU) at the turn of the century campaigned to change drinking habits, but it was also concerned with the promotion of family moral values through religious evangelism, voluntary social activism, and education programs. Like the Women's Institutes for farming women, it was significant because it provided "a forum for middle-class women to become active participants in their own communities long before they were accorded the perquisites of full citizenship through the right to vote."[18] Women's associations, clubs, and groups functioned to bring together and create networks of women barred from public political and economic work. They also provided space for women to work for social reform, which sometimes resulted in policy changes, particularly in the regula- tion of alcohol and prostitution. Clearly they asserted that women had a role in determining the public good. This impulse brought women into formal politics because, as their campaigns for social reform expanded, they found that more political leverage was required to achieve action from national and provincial legislatures. An obvious way to create political pressure was the vote.[19]

Arneil, Sapiro, Clemens, and Skocpol[20] tell similar stories regarding the first wave of the women's movement in the U.S. At the turn of the century, women's clubs and charitable organizations channelled social concerns and desire for social reform in a way that blurred any distinction between social and political activity.

> Fraternalism created the singular option of political organization for women under the rubric of women's clubs.... What is striking is how these groups sought to change public policy almost from the beginning. The three major women's groups formed at the end of the nineteenth century were the Women's Christian Temperance Union in 1874, the General Federation of Women's Clubs in 1890, and National Congress of Mothers (later the PTA) in 1897. These women's associations, if seen through a gendered lens, were not simply about building communities and social trust but forums within which women could channel their misgivings about the way politics was being run, particularly in the area of social policy.[21]

These authors also point out that there is an inevitability to the formation of these groups, as they were one of the few ways that women denied formal political power could influence and access political change. As Sapiro argues, "social cap- ital may be an especially potent resource for people who lack political standing or human or financial capital either to compensate for this deficit or to leverage an increase in standing."[22] As a result, we need to recognize these groups as political, not just social, actors. Their social networks and activism do not just "lead to" politics but expand its definition.

This ethos is carried through into the second wave of the women's movement. For the second wave, formal access to rights was clearly not enough to guarantee women's equality, as women's subordination appeared to be maintained in all spheres of their lives: in political institutions, the workplace, schools, churches, clubs, and the family. For example, the practice of consciousness-raising, a hall- mark of second wave feminism that brought small groups of women together to share their experiences of men, work, sex and sexuality, and so on, does not immediately strike one as political. However, in fostering a sense of shared experience, anger, and ultimately empowerment, women came to understand that their personal grievances were political. As Adamson, Briskin, and McPhail argue, consciousness-raising was "instrumental in actually mobilizing [women] as active participants in their own struggle for liberation."[23] Women's anger was transformed into political action, and women were brought to formal organizations through these informal groups. Throughout the second-wave period, women established women-centred services—rape crisis centres, health centres, abortion and contraceptive services, safe houses for battered and homeless women, centres for single mothers, magazines, journals, art galleries, cultural centres, and publishing companies. These grassroots efforts came to illustrate the second wave's feminist character of "women doing it for themselves." As Roberta Hamilton points out, these endeavours influenced the way that mainstream structures thought about and dealt with women.[24] All of these activities were connected to public policy—by making transparent the services women required, providing models for service provision, and in some cases becoming the structures through which policy was applied by state funding.

Current studies of social capital by feminist scholars examine the broadened definition of politics and its consequence for women as political actors. Of particular interest is the role of child and elder care in political activity and engagement. As Herd and Harrington Meyer ask,

A woman spending hours at her mother-in-law's bedside is a dutiful daughter-in-law, while a stranger or neighbor sitting beside the same bed is a hospice volunteer. Hospice and respite care providers often provide the care work that some families do not have the time, money, or other resources to provide. How can we argue that a hospice volunteer caring for a neighbor is engaged in a civic activity, while a woman caring for her elderly aunt is not?[25]

Is there a distinction between the two, and if so, what is the distinction? Herd and Harrington Meyer argue that of course such care is a form of civic engagement, "as voluntary or as altruistic as other forms of civic engagement."[26] While there is a great deal of pressure for women to perform such work, they "can and do walk away from it—they decide not to care." This work intrinsically involves the development of networks of reciprocity and trust between not just family members but neighbours and friends: "A mother picks up her neighbor's children, along with her own, from school or sports practices, knowing that in exchange she can count on her neighbor to oversee both of their children playing in the driveway a couple of afternoons per week. A neighbor takes out an older woman's garbage every Thursday morning so that her daughter does not have to make a special trip."[27] Examining the case of child care, Lowndes concurs: "We know that school runs, child care swaps and baby-sitting circles all involve relationships of reciprocity and mutuality. Child care networks clearly fit with common definitions of social capital forming activities: 'regular contact with others beyond the sphere of the family or the market...the kind of face-to-face relations of relative equality associated with participation in common endeavours.'"[28]

Feminist scholars and activists have discussed and campaigned vehemently on issues regarding the position of women's caring roles in our society, demanding recognition of the value of this unpaid work: "[C]are is work and that care work should be both a right and an obligation of social citizenship."[29] It is private and unpaid and consequently is seen as unproductive, both economically and societally. The study of care work and social capital encourages us to consider that this work not only has value economically but also is intrinsically valuable for democracy and democratic engagement.

In turn, social care work brings women into politics. As Herd and Harrington Meyer report, caring is an oft-cited reason for women's involvement in environmental movements: "[g]ood moms want good air and good water."[30] They go on to list a series of studies where networks based on family care were translated into political campaigns. As Lowndes points out, "shared concerns" developed through the informal relationships around child care "serve to mobilize self-help and campaigning activity, which in turn 'spill over' into the formal political arena as activists' competence grows."[31] It appears fairly clear cut, for example, that a group of mothers chatting while watching their children play road hockey in the neighbourhood gets involved with the municipal government to work on plans for traffic dampening, or a woman caring for an elderly parent becomes involved in efforts to have funding increased for in-home nursing visits. Put this way, the avenues for translating social action into political action appear almost limitless.

The emphasis on small-p politics, or the politics of social capital, has become even more significant as the Canadian state (along with other Western industrial countries) has devolved its social welfare responsibilities to the level of community and voluntary organizations.[32] Consequently, voluntary organizations have become much more active and influential in the policymaking process. As Rachel Laforest identifies, the federal government in Canada has come to recognize "the voluntary sector as an important pillar of Canadian society along with the private and public sectors....More than ever before, voluntary organizations are implicated in the process of governance and the voluntary sector has emerged as an important actor and partner in both policy-making and service delivery."[33] This has the advantage of bringing to light the work undertaken in local communities by women. However, it also has disadvantages, because much of this social work falls to women, who often remain unrecognized and unpaid and now find themselves facing three work shifts: paid employment, family work, and community work. In addition, this volunteer–state partnership can work against political involvement. While Laforest identifies that "forms of political representation are evolving as voluntary sector organizations gain influence in the policy process" and "new opportunities for engagement in policy are transforming the terms of access to policy-making," she also points out that this has changed the "structure of the voluntary sector, its identity, and its pattern of relationship.... [It] signaled to voluntary organizations that advocacy was no longer an appropriate strategy for making one's claims to the state. Increasingly, volunteer organizations engage in political advocacy and campaigning at the risk of losing funding and their claims to legitimacy within policy networks."[34] Therefore, while social capital is developed, its convertibility into political capital may be seriously limited.

This gives us some indications that, as we shall see in the other side of this debate, we cannot be too sanguine about the social capital concept as a "magic bullet" for finding forms of women's political power. However, notwithstanding concerns about the possible limitations of small-p politics, the argument of this essay is that this form of political activity has great potential for women and their participation in politics. Social capital offers a great deal to the study of women's politics primarily because it encourages us to cast our definitional net more widely to include ostensibly social activities as intrinsically political. It allows us to link informal community-based activity with broadly political phenomena, which helps us make visible significant forms of political power. In addition, gender approaches help us to develop a better understanding of social capital and small-p politics. For example, we need to know, as Lowndes asks, "how in different contexts, do relationships of trust and mutual reciprocity 'capitalize' political engagement? Here the social capital debate has much to learn from the existing literature on women's unorthodox routes to political engagement and from feminist perspectives on citizenship."[35]

We also need to more fully examine the complex links between civil society action and public policy.[36] We have to keep in mind that it is difficult to establish clear causality between civil society action and progressive political results for women without factoring in the role of women in formal political structures, the willingness of formal structures to work with women outside the structures, the party composition and associated ideological disposition of government, and the general views on the issue in larger society. As discussed above, more attention needs to be paid to the nature of voluntary work, and because much of this work takes place unattached to organizational and membership structures, methods have to be found to ensure that it is included along with more formal work. Significantly, greater attention needs to be paid to how these social activities are translated into political resources and how social relationships are drawn upon for and in political engagement. One way to approach these concerns is to expand studies of social capital from statistical studies of values, voting behaviour, and organizational membership (but this is not to say this is unimportant) to qualitative case studies, ethnographic studies of informal volunteer networks, and individual life histories. This will help illustrate more fully the mechanisms of social capital development and use.

If politics is the process by which we organize ourselves into collective communities, the conceptions of social capital have the potential to further not only our understandings of women's politics and small-p politics, but all politics in general.

NOTES

1. Lisa Young and Joanne Everitt, *Advocacy Groups* (Vancouver: UBC Press, 2004), p. 22.

2. "Inter-Parliamentary Union," available at http://www.ipu.org/wmn-e/world.htm. Accessed September 8, 2011.

3. Equal Voice, "How Many Women are Elected to Provincial Legislatures?" *Fundamental Facts,* available at http://www.equalvoice.ca/facts.cfm. (Scroll down and click on "Provincial Politics".) Accessed September 8, 2011.

4. Robert Bellah et al., *Habits of the Heart: Individualism and Commitment in American Life* (Berkeley, CA: University of California Press, 1985), p. 200.

5. This is an interesting feature given the literature examining women volunteers where the term *politics* is rejected by participants as a description of their actions. As Vivien Lowndes stated in "It's Not What You've Got, But What You Do With It: Women, Social Capital, and Political Participation," in Elisabeth Gidengil and Brenda O'Neill, eds., *Gender and Social Capital* (New York: Routledge, 2006), "female activists often do not identify themselves as being 'active in the community' because they regard their activities (such as after-school clubs or tenants' groups) as an extension of their domestic caring roles" (p. 224). See also Amy Blackstone, "It's Just about Being Fair: Activism and Politics of Volunteering in the Breast Cancer Movement," *Gender and Society* 18, no. 3 (2004), pp. 350–368, for an interesting discussion of attitudes toward politics, feminism, and activism in the Koman Breast Cancer Foundation, which organizes the "Run for the Cure" in the U.S., and Nina Eliasoph, *Avoiding Politics: How Americans Produce Apathy in Everyday Life* (Cambridge, UK: Cambridge University Press, 1998), for a more general discussion.

6. Bellah et al., *Habits of the Heart,* p. 200.

7. Birte Siim, "Engendering Democracy: Social Citizenship and Political Participation for Women in Scandanavia," in *Social Politics* 1 (1994), pp. 286–305.

8. Centre for Civil Society, London School of Economics, "What Is Civil Society?", March 1, 2004, available at http://www.lse.ac.uk/collections/CCS/what_is_civil_society.htm. Accessed October 29, 2007.

9. Robert Putnam, "Bowling Alone: America's Declining Social Capital," *Journal of Democracy* 6, no. 1 (1995), p. 67.

10. Lowndes, "It's Not What You've Got," p. 213.

11. Pierre Bourdieu and James Coleman, along with Putnam, are most often recognized as having published the seminal work on social capital. For good reviews and critiques of the literature, see Stephen Baron, John Field, and Tom Schuller, *Social Capital: Critical Perspectives* (Oxford, UK: Oxford University Press, 2000); Michael W. Foley and Bob Edwards, "The Paradox of Civil Society," *Journal of Democracy* 7, no. 3, pp. 38–52; and Bob Edwards, Michael W. Foley, and Mario Diani, *Beyond Tocqueville: Civil Society and the Social Capital Debate in Comparative Perspective* (Hanover: Tufts University/University Press of New England, 2001).

12. Foley and Edwards, "The Paradox of Civil Society," p. 42.

13. Putnam, "Bowling Alone," pp. 65–78.

14. Lowndes, "It's Not What You've Got," p. 223.

15. See, for example, Barbara Arneil, "Just Communities: Social Capital, Gender, and Culture," in Elisabeth Gidengil and Brenda O'Neill, eds., *Gender and Social Capital* (New York: Routledge, 2006), pp. 15–43; Barbara Arneil, *Diverse Communities: The Problem with Social Capital* (Cambridge, UK: Cambridge University Press, 2006); Elisabeth Gidengil and Brenda O'Neill, "Removing Rose Colored Glasses: Examining Theories of Social Capital through a Gendered Lens," in Elisabeth Gidengil and Brenda O'Neill, eds., *Gender and Social Capital* (New York: Routledge, 2006), pp. 1–14; Pamela Herd and Madonna Harrington Meyer, "Care Work: Invisible Civic Engagement," *Gender and Society* 16, no. 5 (October 2002), pp. 665–688; Vivien Lowndes, "Women and Social Capital: A Comment on Hall's 'Social Capital in Britain,'" *British Journal of Political Science* 30 (2000), pp. 533–540; Lowndes, "It's Not What You've Got" (above); and Theda Skocpol and Morris P. Fiorina, *Civic Engagement in American Democracy* (Washington, DC: Brooking Institution, 1999).

16. Lowndes, "It's Not What You've Got," p. 215.

17. Joanna Everitt, "Gender Role Orientations and the Conversion of Social Capital into Political Engagement," in Elisabeth Gidengil and Brenda O'Neill, eds., *Gender and Social Capital* (New York: Routledge, 2006), p. 276.

18. Nancy Sheehan, "The WCTU and Education Strategies on the Canadian Prairie," *History of Education Quarterly* 24, no. 1 (1984), pp. 103, 107.

19. Jacquetta Newman and Linda White, *Women, Politics, and Public Policy: The Political Struggles of Canadian Women* (Don Mills, ON: Oxford University Press, 2006), p. 69.

20. Arneil, "Just Communities"; Arneil, *Diverse Communities*; Virginia Sapiro, "Gender, Social Capital, and Politics," in Elisabeth Gidengil and Brenda O'Neill, eds., *Gender and Social Capital* (New York: Routledge, 2006), pp. 15-44.; Elizabeth S. Clemens, "Organizational Repertoires and Institutional Change: Women's Groups and Transformation of American Politics, 1890-1920," in Theda Skocpol and Morris P. Fiorina, eds., *Civic Engagement in American Democracy* (Washington, DC: Brooking Institution, 1999), pp. 81–110; and Theda Skocpol, *Protecting Soldiers and Mothers: The Politics of Social Provision in the United States 1870s to 1920s* (Cambridge: Harvard University Press, 1992).

21. Arneil, "Just Communities," p. 20.

22. Sapiro, "Gender, Social Capital, and Politics," p. 172.

23. Nancy Adamson, Linda Briskin, and Margaret McPhail, *Feminist Organizing for Change: The Contemporary Women's Movement in Canada* (Don Mills, ON: Oxford University Press, 1988).

24. Roberta Hamilton, *Gendering the Vertical Mosaic: Feminist Perspectives on Canadian Society* (Toronto: Copp Clark, Ltd., 1996), pp. 57–60.

25. Herd and Harrington Meyer, "Care Work," p. 674.

26. Ibid., p. 675.

27. Ibid.

28. Lowndes, "It's Not What You've Got," pp. 223–224. (An endnote number (50) has been removed from the quotation.)

29. Herd and Harrington Meyer, "Care Work," p. 666.

30. Ibid., p. 673.

31. Lowndes, "Women and Social Capital," p. 537.

32. See Rachel Laforest, "Governance and the Voluntary Sector: Rethinking the Contours of Advocacy," *International Journal of Canadian Studies* 30 (2004), pp. 185–203; and Janine Brodie, *Politics on the Margins: Restructuring and the Canadian Women's Movement* (Halifax: Fernwood Publishing, 1995).

33. Laforest, "Governance and the Voluntary Sector," p. 187.

34. Ibid., pp. 186, 193.

35. Lowndes, "Women and Social Capital," p. 536.

36. For example, see Cheryl Collier, "Do Strong Women's Movements Get Results? Measuring the Impact of the Child Care and Anti-Violence Movement in Ontario 1970–2000" (paper presented to the annual meeting of the Canadian Political Science Association, London, Ontario, June 2–4, 2005); and Cheryl Collier, "How Party Matters: A Comparative Assessment of the Openness of Left- and Right-Wing Governments to Women's Issues in Ontario and British Columbia" (paper presented to the annual meeting of the Canadian Political Science Association, Saskatoon, Saskatchewan, May 30–June 1, 2007).

✗ NO

Say It Five Times Fast: The Pitfalls of Small-p Politics and a Plea for Large-P Politics
JACQUETTA NEWMAN

Men alone cannot make just laws for men and women, just as any class of people cannot legislate justly for another class. To deny women the right of lawmaking is to deny the principle of democracy. The workingman knows what he wants better than the capitalist can tell him,—the wearer of the shoe knows where it pinches.... The women's point of view has been ignored in the making of our laws, and that is why we have such gross injustice in laws relating to women. Do you think if women had been consulted in framing the laws that a woman's virtue would be held at the same value as a tree or shrub growing in a public park or garden, and valued at five dollars? Yet in our laws of Manitoba today it is so regarded. The abduction of a young girl is punishable by five years' imprisonment but the stealing of a cow is punished by a fourteen year sentence. Property has ever been held dearer than flesh and blood when the flesh and blood are woman's. In March of last year a drunken man turned out into the storm his wife and two children, one an infant, who later died from this exposure. The evidence showed that the poor woman's life had been a perpetual hell of abuse and mortal fear,—the man was given six months, afterwards commuted to two. In Brandon, last September, a farm laborer stole fifteen dollars and a blue silk handkerchief from a companion, and he was sent down for one year with hard labor....

But the day is breaking, and the darkness is fleeing away. Four million women in the United States now enjoy full parliamentary franchise. Women vote in New Zealand, Australia, Iceland, Finland, Norway and China, and have some measure of franchise in many other countries.[1]

—Nellie McClung

The above words were part of a speech made in 1914 by Canadian suffragette Nellie McClung. For the suffragettes, the focus was on formal political rights like the right to vote, because they understood that the way to significantly affect public policy was through electoral influence and ultimately the right to run for and hold elected office. McClung said as much in the same 1914 speech:

For centuries [women] have been acting the good Samaritan by their phi-
lanthropies, their private and public charities, their homes for the friend-
less, for orphan children, free kindergartens, day nurseries; they have been
picking up the robbed, wounded and beaten. Now they are wondering if
they cannot do something to clear up the road. Investigation is now taking
the place of Resignation.... This is the meaning of the woman's movement,
and we need not apologize for it.[2]

Charitable work was not enough, for while it would alleviate suffering in the short
term, it could not solve the causes of suffering. This required a form of social and
political reform that was the preview of the provincial and national legislatures.
For Nellie McClung and the first-wave feminists, the formal structures of large-P
politics mattered, and they still do.

SMALL-p POLITICS IS NOT THE "MAGIC BULLET" TO THE PROBLEM OF WOMEN'S POLITICAL POWER

While a focus on small-p politics illustrates the intrinsically political nature of social
activities often undertaken by women and sheds light on the division of society into
public and private spheres, it also raises a significant question: if women are such
successful social capitalists, why is this not reflected in their political capital? Given
the understood propensity for women to engage in the volunteerism associated with
community care, it seems surprising that women still continue to be largely absent
from formal political activity. One reason is the "luxury of time." Approaches to
social capital need to recognize that, along with enhancing political engagement,
care work can interfere with civic activity. Herd and Harrington Meyer point to the
burden of being both a social and political actor:

[W]e suggest that participation in these traditional forms of civic engagement interferes with the provision of care work such as cleaning, cooking
and bathing. After all someone has to take care of the children while mothers
attend protests and rallies. In fact there is evidence that some women use
their activism to escape domestic responsibilities.[3]

In acknowledging that child care, cleaning, cooking, and bathing are active forms
of participatory citizenship with far-reaching civil benefits, "we recognize not
only that they have civic and political value, but that women's inaction is not
due to a lack of or decline in their moral values, but rather because of the gender
dynamics of care work."[4] Often volunteer community care and social work is not
social capital but just unpaid and unrecognized work that just needs to get done.
If the individual does not have the time or energy to convert work into a form of
social capital, work is just that—work.

The social capital developed by men and women may not translate into the same sort of political capital. In her reservations regarding the concept of social capital, Vivien Lowndes points out that because men and women undertake different types of activities, there are significant differences in the types of social capital developed.[5] In a study of social capital in Great Britain in the 1990s, Lowndes found important differences in the involvement of women compared to men:

> More than twice as many men as women undertook voluntary work related to sports and recreation (29 per cent compared with 13 per cent). Women, by contrast, were more active in voluntary work in the fields of health, education and social services. As for the specific roles undertaken, men were more likely to occupy committee posts, while women dominated in visiting and befriending activities.[6]

This corresponds to research that sees women as more strongly connected to neighbourhood networks than men, having more robust patterns of social exchange, and having more ready access to social support. However, it also illustrates that social capital itself is gendered and, as Lowndes argues, the social capital developed by men may be better suited to "getting ahead" in politics while that developed by women is better for "getting along" in everyday life.[7]

Social capital may get women into politics, but it may also hold them back. We know that women are most active in what could be called the "lower," or more informal, reaches of politics. The more formal the political process becomes, the less likely women are to be active. It seems that women often cross the boundary between community activity and political action in pursuit of particular issues or causes. Having got there, however, they are less likely than men to progress up the political ladder or to move into more formal political arenas.

To crudely follow the economistic analogy at the centre of social capital studies, in making the conversion of social capital to political capital, women find that because their social capital is different, it is of less value. Virginia Sapiro picks up this point when she discusses the fungibility (the ability to exchange or replace a good with one of comparable worth) of social capital.[8]

Not all organizational or interpersonal ties create social capital that is useful for the same purposes, regardless of who is involved. If women's clubs and organizations are generally considered irrelevant to politics, or are not directly interconnected enough with the networks in which political leaders are embedded, there is relatively less politically relevant social capital to be gained from these organizations. If the types of relationships that serve as resources for local political leadership are found among the people who hold elite professional and business positions, and these are male-dominated fields, or among the members of particular clubs and organizations, and these are restricted to men, women's social capital will have little value in politics. Viewed from this perspective, social capital does not really dissolve the division between the public and private. In fact, it perpetuates the division, because women develop private social capital while men develop public social capital.

Ultimately, when we review the reservations voiced by Herd and Harrington Meyer, Sapiro, and Lowndes, the old model of the public man and private woman reappears.

> The argument here is a familiar one in the political, business, and artistic spheres: as the saying goes, behind every great man, there is a great woman.... Women's social capital provides many male politicians with practical support (freeing them from domestic and neighbourhood responsibilities) and also with political support, in the sense of community-based information, knowledge and contacts.[9]

The social capital developed by women actually operates as a resource for men but not for women—in other words, women produce social capital while men spend it. The informal small-p politics of consensual community may actually be a disadvantage for women.

Finally, we need to look hard at the assumption that women undertake the lion's share of voluntary community activism. In Young and Everitt's discussion of advocacy groups, the finding was that "the gender differences among interest group activists are not statistically significant."[10] When we look at formal categorized voluntary participation, the distinction between women and men disappears. For example, a recent report from Statistics Canada on charitable donations claimed by Canadian taxpayers showed that of the 5,752,630 charitable donors in 2006, 44 percent were women while men accounted for 56 percent.[11] The National Survey on Giving and Volunteer Participation (NSGVP), undertaken by Statistics Canada as part of the government's Voluntary Sector Initiative, also found little difference in the participation of women and men as volunteers and donors. The 2004 Canadian Survey of Giving, Volunteering and Participating (Statistics Canada, 2004) reports that 11.8 million Canadians, or 45 percent of the population, volunteered their time to charities and other nonprofit organizations.[12] The most common activities were organizing, supervising, or coordinating activities or events and fundraising, followed by serving as unpaid members of committees or boards and engaging in teaching, educating, or mentoring, which were undertaken in sports and recreation, social services, education and research, and religious organizations.[13] When volunteerism was broken down by sex for rates of volunteerism and hours, the difference was not great, nor was there a great difference between top volunteers (defined as individuals giving 180 hours or more annually).

TABLE 10.1

VOLUNTEER RATES AND DISTRIBUTION OF VOLUNTEER HOURS BY PERSONAL CHARACTERISTICS

Sex	Volunteer rate %	Average annual hours	Median volunteer hours	Population distribution	% of volunteer hours
Male	44	168	60	49	48
Female	47	168	64	51	52

Adapted from Statistics Canada publication, Highlights from 2004 Canada Survey of Giving Volunteering and Participating, Catalogue 71-542-X1E, 2004, p. 34, http://www.statcan.gc.ca/pub/71-542-x/71-542-x2006001-eng.pdf

TABLE 10.2

% OF POPULATION WHO ARE TOP VOLUNTEERS AND % OF VOLUNTEER HOURS

Sex	% of volunteers who are top volunteers	top volunteers as a % of total population	% of total annual volunteer hours
Male	11	5	37
Female	12	6	40

Adapted from Statistics Canada publication, Highlights from 2004 Canada Survey of Giving Volunteering and Participating, Catalogue 71-542-X1E, 2004, p. 36, http://www.statcan.gc.ca/pub/71-542-x/71-542-x2006001-eng.pdf

The NSGVP presents itself as being a "barometer of voluntary and civic action," and the 2004 survey does note that volunteerism does take place outside state-defined "charitable organizations" and traditional community groups.

Many Canadians also help others directly on their own without working through a charitable or voluntary organization.... [T]he most commonly reported activities were providing help at an individual's home such as cooking, cleaning, gardening, maintenance, painting, shoveling snow or repairs (reported by 60%), providing health related or personal care, such as emotional support, counseling, providing advice, visiting the elderly, and unpaid babysitting (50%), and helping by shopping, driving someone to the store or to other appointments (46%).[14]

This clearly speaks to the informal civic engagement identified as primarily the purview of women, but it is not as clear if this volunteerism is included in the numbers given above for rates of volunteerism and hours. If it does, then we must seriously research or reconsider our assumptions of the work undertaken by women. We may have put too much stock in the focus on small-p politics as a way for women to build political power and influence. As the above statistics indicate, women may not hold a special or dominant place in the networks of small-p politics. Men would appear to be equally involved, and when we combine this observation with the previous argument regarding the importance of the "type of social capital" developed, it would appear that men are equally involved in the types of small-p politics that are best for developing political advantage. The focus on women's social capital may have exaggerated the amount and nature of the work undertaken. As a result, we must be very careful in accepting that small-p politics is a magic bullet for women building political power and influence.

There is a need for much further research on the activities of women in our society and more detailed examination of small-p politics and its relationship to the large-P politics of the state. As the "yes" article admits, the links between small-p politics and public policy are very complex, and the role of women in formal political structures, the willingness of formal structures to work with women outside the structures, and the party composition and associated ideological disposition of governments are very significant factors. In short, large-P politics matters, and it matters a lot.

IT IS CRITICAL THAT WOMEN CONTINUE TO ENGAGE IN LARGE-P POLITICS

If the goal is to influence public policy for the good of women, then it is important for women activists to be involved in forums where public policy is decided. As Alexa McDonough, former leader of the Nova Scotia and federal NDP and member of Parliament, states, "[T]hat is where the power lies; that is where decisions are made."[15] Since governments are powerful decision-making bodies, it is important to be where the action is. Therefore, large-P politics and engagement in electoral and legislative politics are critical. This position is reflected in the tendency for the literature on women in politics to focus on the lack of women representatives in political parties and parliaments. The understanding is that the more women are involved in large-P politics and the more success they have in getting elected as representatives, the more power and influence they will have in getting women's concerns onto the political agenda.[16]

Granted, there is no guarantee that women members will act or speak on behalf of other women. The electoral system is based on the conception that the member is representative of a territorial constituency, not a social constituency, and even if it were the case, not all women share the same interests. It is the debate between descriptive or mirror representation—that is, representation based on the proportion to population (women constitute 51 percent of Canadian society; therefore, they should have 51 percent of the seats in the legislature)—and substantive representation, where the ideas put forward by both women and men representatives are in line with the needs and interests of women. However, while it is debatable that complete substantive representation results from closer approximations of descriptive representation,[17] either way, substantive or descriptive, requires a continued engagement in the formal structures of large-P politics. As Bashevkin points out, "although considerable debate has focused on how to define a meaningful presence or 'critical mass' of women in politics, this procedural perspective suggests numbers of women can matter for the climate as well as the content of group debate."[18]

Lisa Young speaks to the risks of focusing on small-p politics and rejecting engagement in large-P politics: "[A]s autonomous political action has gradually supplanted efforts to engage with political parties ... Canadian political parties have become less responsive to the policy concerns of the women's movement and have focused less attention on including women in political elites."[19] Without pressure from women engaging with the political parties, parties have not seen it necessary to respond to women's issues and demands. This is unfortunate, because when we look at examples of governments that have included larger numbers of women or that have been ideologically disposed to listen to women's concerns, the public policy environment has been much more amenable to women.

In 1990, the New Democratic Party of Ontario under Bob Rae won the provincial election, taking 38 percent of the popular vote and 74 of the 130 seats in the province. Significantly, women made up 26 percent of the party's elected members compared to 13 percent for the Liberal opposition, and 15 percent of the Progressive Conservative MPPs. The number of women in the NDP caucus, combined with Rae's stated commitments to women's issues and the women's movement, resulted in a record number of women appointed to the NDP cabinet. Eleven women sat in the twenty-five-member cabinet, a whopping 44 percent, including a number of avowed feminists such as Marion Boyd (Minister of Education 1990, Women's Issues, Community and Social Services 1991, and Attorney General 1993), Evelyn Gigantes (Health 1990 and Housing 1991), and Frances Lankin (Government Services 1990, Health 1992, Economic Development and Trade 1993). In British Columbia, the election of the New Democratic Party in 1991 also saw a significant rise in the number of women in the government caucus and cabinet. British Columbia NDP leader Mike Harcourt "appointed seven women to his cabinet (27 per cent)—at that point the highest percentage of women ever appointed to a BC cabinet—many of them feminists."[20]

TABLE 10.3
WOMEN IN THE ONTARIO LEGISLATURE AND CABINET

Election year	Progressive Conservatives caucus %	NDP caucus %	Liberals caucus %	Government party	Cabinet numbers Women/Total	Cabinet %
1981	6*	5	3	PC	2/28	7
1985	6	12	6*	Lib	2/23	9
1987	6	16	17*	Lib	4/26	15
1990	15	26*	13	NDP	11/25	44
1995	13*	24	13	PC	4/20	20
1999	15*	44	20	PC	5/25	20

* Years when 100% of women elected were promoted to cabinet.

From Cheryl N. Collier, "How Party Matters: A Comparative Assessment of the Openness of Left- and Right-Wing Governments to Women's Issues in Ontario and British Columbia 1980–2002." Paper presented at the annual meeting of the Canadian Political Science Association, University of Saskatchewan, Saskatoon, May 30–June 7, 2007. Used with permission.

TABLE 10.4
WOMEN IN THE BRITISH COLUMBIA LEGISLATURE AND CABINET

Election year	Social Credit caucus %	NDP caucus %	Liberals caucus %	Government party	Cabinet numbers Women/Total	Cabinet %
1979	6	15	n/a	SC	1/19	5
1983	6	18	n/a	SC	1/19	5
1986	8	23	n/a	SC	2/19	10.5
1991	0	31	18	NDP	7/19	37
1996	n/a	31	24	NDP	5/15	33
2001	n/a	100	22	Lib	8/28	28.5

From Cheryl N. Collier, "How Party Matters: A Comparative Assessment of the Openness of Left- and Right-Wing Governments to Women's Issues in Ontario and British Columbia 1980–2002." Paper presented at the annual meeting of the Canadian Political Science Association, University of Saskatchewan, Saskatoon, May 30–June 7, 2007. Used with permission.

As Cheryl Collier and Lesley Byrne relate in their examinations of the success of women MMPs and the women's movement during this time (Collier for Ontario and B.C., Byrne for Ontario), the numbers of women in government and particularly high-profile cabinet positions did have an impact on women's policy. By comparing Ontario policy regarding child care and violence against women from 1980 to 2002, Collier found that "seven positive policy responses (the most by any government in Ontario) and only one mixed response"[21] occurred when the Rae NDP government held power between 1990 and 1995. Byrne, in her work interviewing women cabinet members and MPPs in Ontario during the Rae years, observes

> Clearly, one of the most important tests of substantive representation is the extent to which women cabinet ministers affected feminist public policy. While their impact was less profound than many Ontario women's groups had hoped and expected, the Rae government did enact important milestones in this area. They included a job creation program with specified child care provisions, increases to the provincial minimum wage, extended parental leave provisions, protection for home workers, employment equity legislation that required employers to ensure their workforces reflected the diversity of the larger community, pay equity laws that raised the pay of more than a million women, enhanced funding for violence against women (in areas of prevention, treatment and education) and child care initiatives, the legalization of midwifery and full public health insurance coverage for clinic abortions.[22]

This was, according to the cabinet ministers interviewed by Byrne, the result of the women in cabinet working together on behalf of women's concerns and voting as a block. Similarly, the Harcourt era in British Columbia represented a high point for women's issues: "Harcourt created the Ministry of Women's Equality (MWE) that considerably improved policy for women. According to Gawthrop, from 1991–93, 'the NDP managed to achieve more for women's equality in two years than the Socred did in the previous fifteen.'"[23] On issues of child care and violence against women, Harcourt's NDP government recorded thirteen positive policy responses, the most of any single government in British Columbia.[24]

These studies and others[25] indicate that party ideology is a key element in a government's openness to women's issues, with centre and left-of-centre parties more responsive to women's claims and more amenable to women's participation. They also indicate that having numbers of women in formal politics affects the policies for women. "Parties in power generally are most likely to view women's movement claims as legitimate if they share the same ideological goals and feminists form one of their key constituencies."[26] However, this is not without some qualifications. Both Byrne and Collier point out that while links between the government and the women's movement were more open during the periods of NDP governments, those links were not as open as movement activists and feminist cabinet ministers would have wanted. According to Byrne, in Ontario, "many of the [women's organizations] believed the government had not accomplished enough particularly during the final two years of its mandates when the overwhelming focus was on fiscal restraint rather than social justice issues. Several ministers I interviewed referred to this slowing of progressive policy change as a disappointing part of their cabinet experience that they would not want to repeat."[27] Similarly, in B.C. as the economic climate changed and the commitment to women's issues declined, activists and party insiders interviewed by Collier noted that the rhetoric of fiscal conservatism became more prevalent in the NDP in 1994, threatening women's policy issues. "Over time, Harcourt found it difficult to 'walk the tightrope' between appeasing the core constituencies of the NDP and allaying the fears of business groups that were uncomfortable with a social democratic government."[28] With a change in provincial NDP leadership to Glen Clark, women's issues were less visible in the 1996 election, and while the number of women in cabinet remained stable, only one woman was appointed to a high-profile portfolio.[29]

These qualifications return us to the debate over whether women's political power and influence is best derived from descriptive/mirror representation or substantive representation, but the numbers still appear to matter. It is clearly not a question of either–or; the situation is a complex mix of numbers of women, party ideology, feminist consciousness, political opportunity, and women's movement strength and the strategies it adopts. Nonetheless, it is undeniable that formal political structures, large-P politics, and the willingness and ability of women to engage in them are a critical part of this complex puzzle. "If a party comes to power with feminist principles, and the leader appoints significant numbers of women to cabinet, then we conclude that regime can exert a major impact on public policy."[30]

WHAT DOES IT MEAN TO BE A CITIZEN IN A DEMOCRACY?

Finally, we must view any debate between committing to small-p politics and large-P politics from the perspective of what citizenship entails in our democratic system. As Young and Everitt point out, "at the heart of modern democracy lie representative institutions that gain their mandates through popular election. The location of popular sovereignty in these institutions is the hallmark of modern democracy."[31] Our notions of citizenship are bound up in our understanding of the formal structures of democracy and large-P politics being the centre of political power. Citizenship itself refers to one's membership in a political community and its accompanying rights, particularly access to participate in the political and legal institutions that design and determine that power and how it is used.

Democratic self-government means that people should be able to make decisions about their community and about themselves, by themselves. As Nellie

McClung pointed out in the speech opening this article, "men alone cannot make just laws for men and women, just as any class of people cannot legislate justly for another class." Arscott and Trimble pick up this sentiment, arguing that while it might be true that men are quite capable of representing women's interests, they "cannot claim power for women and they cannot hold power in women's stead."[32] It is not good enough for only men to make policy for women, as it is not good enough for only white women to make policy for women of colour, as it is not good enough for only able-bodied persons to make policy for disabled persons, and so on. Democracy requires some level of participation in voting, in political parties, in elected office and so on, from all the various groups and interests in a society for a community to be considered self-governing.

By removing oneself from the world of large-P politics, one runs the risk of losing one's place and legitimacy in the community's negotiation or discourse of how power should be distributed and wielded. It undermines the conception of democratic citizenship. "From the perspective of democratic representation women's presence as public actors confirms, while their absence disconfirms, the legitimacy of democratic practices."[33] Therefore, while we should not throw the proverbial baby out with the bathwater and reject small-p politics outright, we must recognize the perils inherent in women taking an either–or approach in how they deal with politics. And to that end, we certainly cannot reject engagement in large-P politics.

NOTES

1. Candace Savage, *Our Nell: A Scrapbook Biography of Nellie L. McClung* (Halifax: Goodread Biographies, James Lorimer, 1979), pp. 83–84.

2. Ibid., p. 82.

3. Pamela Herd and Madonna Harrington Meyer, "Care Work: Invisible Civic Engagement," *Gender and Society* 16, no. 5 (October 2002), pp. 669–670.

4. Ibid., p. 671.

5. Vivien Lowndes, "Women and Social Capital: A Comment on Hall's 'Social Capital in Britain,'" *British Journal of Political Science* 30 (2000), pp. 533–540, and Vivien Lowndes, "It's Not What You've Got, But What You Do With It: Women, Social Capital, and Political Participation," in Elisabeth Gidengil and Brenda O'Neill (eds.), *Gender and Social Capital* (New York: Routledge, 2006), pp. 213–240.

6. Lowndes, "Women and Social Capital," p. 534.

7. Lowndes, "It's Not What You've Got," p. 228.

8. Virginia Sapiro, "Gender, Social Capital, and Politics," in Elisabeth Gidengil and Brenda O'Neill, eds., *Gender and Social Capital* (New York: Routledge, 2006), p. 175.

9. Lowndes, "It's Not What You've Got," pp. 230–231.

10. Lisa Young and Joanne Everitt, *Advocacy Groups* (Vancouver: UBC Press, 2004), p. 30.

11. This may be partially explained by the fact that for couples, donations would be applied against the larger income for tax purposes and for the most part that is the male wage-earner. See Dawn Walton, Paul Waldie, and Tavia Grant, "More Donations, Fewer Donors," *The Globe and Mail,* November 2, 2007, p. A1.

12. Statistics Canada, *Highlights from the 2004 Canadian Survey of Giving, Volunteering and Participating* (Ottawa: Minister of Industry, June 2006), catalogue no. 71-542-XIE, p. 33.

13. Ibid., p. 12.

14. Ibid., p. 12.

15. Meredith Ralston, *Why Women Run* (Montreal: National Film Board, 1999).

16. For example, see Joni Lovenduski and Pippa Norris, eds., *Gender and Party Politics* (London: Sage Publications, 1993); Jane Arscott and Linda Trimble, eds., *In the Presence of Women: Representation in Canadian Governments* (Toronto: Harcourt Brace, 1997); Jill Vickers, "Towards a Feminist Understanding of Representation," in Jane Arscott and Linda Trimble, eds., *In the Presence of Women: Representation in Canadian Governments* (Toronto: Harcourt Brace, 1997), pp. 20–46; Manon Tremblay and Linda Trimble, eds., *Women and Electoral Politics in Canada* (Don Mills: Oxford University Press Canada, 2003); Jacquetta Newman and Linda White, *Women, Politics, and Public Policy: The Political Struggles of Canadian Women* (Don Mills, ON: Oxford University Press, 2006), p. 69; Marian Sawer, Manon Tremblay, and Linda Trimble, eds., *Representing Women in Parliament: A Comparative Study* (New York: Routledge, 2006); Sylvia Bashevkin, ed., *Are Doors Opening Wider? Studies of Women's Political Engagement in Canada* (Vancouver: UBC Press, forthcoming).

17. See Lesley Hyland Byrne, "Feminists in Power: Women Cabinet Ministers in the New Democratic Party (NDP) Government of Ontario 1990–1995," *Policy Studies Journal* 5, no. 4 (1997), pp. 601–612; Virginia Sapiro, "When Are Interests Interesting? The Problem of Political Representation of Women," *The American Political Science Review* 75, no. 3 (1981), pp. 701–21; Vickers, "Towards a Feminist Understanding of Representation"; Sawer, Tremblay, and Trimble, *Representing Women in Parliament;* and Bashevkin, *Are Doors Opening Wider?*

18. Sylvia Bashevkin, "Introduction," in Bashevkin, ed., *Are Doors Opening Wider? Studies of Women's Political Engagement in Canada* (Vancouver: UBC Press, forthcoming).

19. Lisa Young, "Can Feminists Transform Party Politics? The Canadian Experience," in Manon Tremblay and Linda Trimble, eds., *Women and Electoral Politics in Canada* (Don Mills, ON: Oxford University Press, 2003), p. 77.

20. Cheryl N. Collier, "How Party Matters: A Comparative Assessment of the Openness of Left- and Right-Wing Governments to Women's Issues in Ontario and British Columbia 1980–2002.," Paper presented at the annual meeting of the Canadian Political Science Association, University of Saskatchewan, Saskatoon, May 30–June1, 2007, p. 15. Used with permission and thanks.

21. Ibid., p. 19.

22. Byrne, "Feminists in Power," and Lesley Hyland Byrne, "Can Changing Nomination Rules Change Public Policy? The Ontario Experience, 1990–1995," in Bashevkin, ed., *Are Doors Opening Wider? Studies of Women's Political Engagement in Canada* (Vancouver: UBC Press, forthcoming).

23. Cited in Collier, "How Party Matters."

24. Ibid., p. 21.

25. See Arscott and Trimble, *In the Presence of Women;* Collier, "How Party Matters"; and Sawer, Tremblay, and Trimble, *Representing Women in Parliament.*

26. Cheryl N. Collier, "Do Strong Women's Movements Get Results? Measuring the Impact of Child Care and Anti-Violence Movements in Ontario 1970–2000," Paper presented at the annual meeting of the Canadian Political Science Association, London, Ontario, June 2–4, 2005, p. 3.

27. Byrne, "Can Changing Nomination Rules Change Public Policy?"

28. Collier, "How Party Matters," p. 15.

29. Ibid., p. 15.

30. Byrne, "Can Changing Nomination Rules Change Public Policy?"

31. Young and Everitt, *Advocacy Groups,* p. 22.

32. Arscott and Trimble, *In the Presence of Women,* p. 4.

33. Bashevkin, "Introduction."

POSTSCRIPT

In her first article, Newman makes the convincing case that the activities of everyday life have the potential to enhance the participation of women in political life and to achieve policy outcomes essential to the equality of the sexes. In a way, this argument is an extension of the feminist belief that the attempt to separate the public and private dimensions of society is ill-advised and may actually be harmful. When women congregate to watch their children play hockey or run into each other at school events, they are developing the networks—the social capital—that can be used to achieve larger political ends. For Newman, women need not look only at formal political structures for advancement. It may be enough to examine more carefully the promise inherent in the routines of their daily lives.

Accordingly, the case for small-p politics is strong, yet it is not totally convincing. At times, it seems too good to be true, and usually phenomena that evoke this quality are indeed too good to be true. It is nice to think that mothers watching a game of road hockey can create better traffic conditions or that a daughter providing comfort to an elderly mother may be transformed into a reformer of long-term care, but one has to wonder whether this is realistic. As well, it seems where social capital may be capitalized is in the formation of powerful women's interest groups, which may be seen more properly as an element of large-P politics. Finally, the opportunity cost of the small-p politics seems high because it means the neglect of the effort to achieve greater women's representation in the offices of government. It is true that success for women lately in large-P politics has been disappointing, but it seems rather premature to give up on this endeavour. Patience is a virtue.

In her second article, Newman furthers the argument against a reliance on small-p politics. Sometimes caring for children or looking after sick ones is exactly what it appears to be: hard work. Such activities have little or nothing to do with politics, and to argue otherwise is to engage in a cruel hoax. It is also true, as Newman claims, that participation in formal politics can precipitate major changes in public policy, something that will likely elude most activities in the world of small-p politics. However, it may be that the Newman of large-P politics slights the insights of the Newman of small-p politics. In the second piece, Newman quotes a former New Democratic Party leader who claims that it is in the formal political institutions "where the power lies" and "decisions are made." Now, it is certainly the case that formal decisions are arrived at in the legislature, but this outcome is not necessarily—and often is not—a result of power within this same body. Rather, power, as Newman reveals in her first effort, can arise out of the activities of women in the vast array of activities found outside of formal politics. Also, the Newman of large-P politics bases her case partly on the claim that the social capital of small-p politics has provided little. But surely we have seen some important advances in the latter world that have contributed to the greater well-being of women.

This debate arises largely out of the disappointments with the representation of women in formal political institutions and processes. For an examination of this situation in Canada, students should read the following: Linda Trimble and Jane Arscott, *Still Counting: Women in Politics across Canada* (Peterborough: Broadview Press, 2003); Jacquetta Newman and Linda A. White, *Women, Politics, and Public Policy: The Political Struggles of Canadian Women* (Toronto: Oxford University Press, 2006); Manon Tremblay and Linda Trimble, eds., *Women and Electoral Politics in Canada* (Toronto: Oxford University Press, 2003); Sylvia Bashevkin, ed., *Opening Doors Wider: Women's Political Engagement in Canada* (Vancouver, Toronto: UBC Press, 2009); Sylvia Bashevkin, *Women, Power, Politics: The Hidden Story of Canada's Unfinished Democracy* (Toronto: Oxford University Press, 2009); and Brenda O'Neill and Lisa Young, "Women in Canadian Politics," in John C. Courtney and David E. Smith, eds., *The Oxford Handbook of Canadian Politics* (Toronto: Oxford University Press, 2010). Some additional readings might be consulted to acquire an appreciation of women and political representation in the United States and elsewhere: Jennifer L. Lawless and Richard L. Fox, *It Takes a Candidate: Why Women Don't Run for Office* (New York: Cambridge University Press, 2005); and Marian Sawer, Manon Tremblay, and Linda Trimble, eds., *Representing Women in Parliament: A Comparative Study* (New York: Routledge, 2006).

As for sources on the world of small-p politics and social capital, students might start with Robert Putnam, *Bowling Alone: The Collapse and Revival of American Community* (New York: Simon & Schuster, 2000), the text that gave widespread currency to a particular conception of social capital. The next task is to consider readings on social capital and women in politics, and for this the interested reader should examine the various contributions in Brenda O'Neill and Elisabeth Gidengil, eds., *Gender and Social Capital* (New York: Routledge, 2006). Additional readings include those listed in the references found at the end of the two Newman papers.

PART FOUR

Do Drinking and Driving Laws
Discriminate Against Young Drivers?

Should Religious Beliefs Be Excluded
from Consideration of Public Policy?

Should Representation in Parliament
Mirror Canada's Social Diversity?

Are the Media Politically Biased?

Robyn Mackenzie/Shutterstock

Do Drinking and Driving Laws Discriminate Against Young Drivers?

✔ **YES**

KEVIN WIENER, "Zero Tolerance for Discrimination:
A Constitutional Critique of Ontario's *Road Safety Act* (2009)"

✗ **NO**

DAVID OLEVSON, "BAC to Zero: Defending the
Constitutionality of Ontario's *Road Safety Act* (2009)"

On August 1, 2010, the Ontario government brought into play a new law that requires a blood alcohol concentration (BAC) level of zero for young drivers less than twenty-two years of age—in other words, no alcohol for young people who drive in Ontario. The province already required a zero BAC level for all novice drivers, who are those in either of the two stages of the provincial graduated licensing program (G1 and G2). The new law expanded the existing law to include all young drivers aged twenty-one or younger. A driver who violates the new law faces an immediate twenty-four-hour licence suspension, and a thirty-day suspension if convicted of the offence, and possible fines amounting to $500. Some harsh realities, said the government, explained the need for the new law. Young people tend to be more involved in drinking and driving collisions than other age groups. More directly, 235 young men and women under the age of twenty-two had been killed in drinking and driving accidents in the ten-year period before 2006. Prominent public-interest groups such as Mothers Against Drunk Driving supported the government action, saying that the new provision would lead to fewer deaths on the road and turn young people into safer and more responsible drivers.

A few days after the implementation of the law, newspaper stories in *The Toronto Star* and *The Globe and Mail* revealed that not all professed support for the new drinking and driving initiative. Kevin Wiener, a university student, charged that the law centred, unfairly, on young people. In legal terms, this meant the law violated the Constitution because it added up to a discriminatory act based on age. A wiser thing to do, said Wiener, was to follow Manitoba, which had a BAC policy for *all* drivers with three years or less of driving experience. If the problem related to inexperienced drivers—and Wiener believed it did—then Ontario had picked on the young. A fifty-year-old person with three years of driving, one could argue, was no further ahead than someone twenty-one years of age with the same amount of driving experience. The Ontario minister responsible for transportation responded that a number of acceptable policies were based on age—voting, drinking, renewal of driving licences (seniors), and so on—and these were deemed acceptable because they were supported by good reasons. The same held, said the minister, for the new BAC law. "We know that at the age of 22 the statistics start to change, so 19, 20, and 21 are really peak years for drinking and driving," said Kathleen Wynne, the Minister of Transportation. For the minister, it was age and not experience that largely explained the driving records of young people. Mr. Wiener disagreed and indicated his intention to pursue a constitutional case against the Ontario government on the grounds that the zero-BAC law violated the equality-of-rights section of the Canadian Charter of Rights and Freedoms.

The question for this debate is whether Mr. Wiener could win his case. Success requires that two steps be taken. The first is to demonstrate that equality rights have been violated. The courts have translated s. 15 of the Charter of Rights and Freedoms such that no discrimination can occur based on a number of personal grounds listed in the section (colour, religion, ethnic origin, age, and so on) or considered analogous or similar to those listed. The Supreme Court of Canada has developed a legal test to determine whether rights have been violated, and in various cases has adjusted the test in one way or another. A very recent case (*Withler v. AG Canada,* in 2011) suggests that the test can be reduced to two considerations: whether the case in question involves one of the listed or analogous grounds and whether the offending legislation perpetuates a prejudice or is premised on a faulty stereotype. Mr. Wiener and like-minded people would have no trouble with the first part of the test—clearly the action makes a distinction by limiting it to young people. It is the second part that might present a challenge. The facts do seem to support the stereotype: young people tend to drive a little recklessly and have little drinking experience. Yet, it is relevant to note that other provinces have tried a different tack, namely to focus not on age but rather on level of experience. Moreover, some data indicate that age has not much to do with the driving behaviour of young people and that level of experience is the determining factor.

The second step is only relevant if the first step uncovers a discriminatory act. If there is no such action, then the case is over and the government wins. But a positive verdict on whether equality rights have been violated means that the second step is pertinent. At this point, the government can argue that the violation amounts to a reasonable limit on a person's rights and freedoms. The test for a reasonable limit is somewhat complicated (and succinctly outlined in each of the two essays), but it is based on whether the offending legislation is logical, restricts the right as little as reasonably possible, and produces a benefit that outweighs any costs associated with the violated right. In the case at hand, one might say that the government would succeed with its claim that the zero-BAC law amounts to a reasonable limit; after all, preventing death is a very clear benefit. But at the same time, one might contest the logic of the law—the aim of the legislation to save lives is not really served well by focusing solely on the young. Plus, we might note the intangible costs of the government's growing willingness to regulate the lives of individual citizens, even to the point of determining what one drinks at the dinner table.

So far we have dealt in law, statistics, and rights—abstractions, in other words—but there remains the reality of drunk driving and young people. In July of 2008, three young men in the Muskoka region of Ontario lost their lives in a single car accident. The driver of the car, twenty years old, was under the influence of alcohol. The father of one of the young men launched a public campaign to toughen the drunk-driving laws in Ontario, and his efforts helped precipitate the introduction of the new zero-BAC measure in Ontario.

Kevin Wiener, a student at the Ivey School of Business at the University of Western Ontario, argues that the new zero-BAC law violates the equality rights of residents of Ontario. David Olevson, a student of law at Queen's University, makes the contrary case.

✔ YES
Zero Tolerance for Discrimination: A Constitutional Critique of Ontario's *Road Safety Act* (2009)
KEVIN WIENER

The issue of balancing the protection of the public with the rights of individuals is something grappled with by governments of all liberal democratic nations. We all value the core principles of liberty and equality, but it is difficult to hold to abstract principles when human lives are at stake. While airport security in Israel includes the use of racial profiling, Canada has decided that the equality of individuals forbids such a practice, even if it lessens our security. Yet freedom of speech is not considered a valid protection for hateful expression in Canada, giving us a less absolutist approach than the United States.

Striking a balance between safety and rights on any given issue is a difficult task, and reasonable people often disagree on how it should be done. Indeed, deciding when security, or another important legislative objective, outweighs individual rights has been a part of nearly every constitutional decision made by the Supreme Court of Canada since the Canadian Charter of Rights and Freedoms first came into force. Section 1 of the Charter holds that rights can be subject to such restrictions as can be reasonably justified in a free and democratic society. How the courts and legislatures deal with this balance is something that impacts all Canadians, yet few outside of the legal profession often give the matter much thought.

This is especially true for young Canadians, yet on August 1, 2010, youth across Ontario discovered that in the interests of public safety they would be subject to age discrimination. On that day, the Ontario government brought into force provisions of Bill 126, entitled the *Road Safety Act* (2009), that made it a condition of every licensed driver under the age of twenty-two that they maintain a zero blood alcohol content (BAC) whenever behind the wheel.[1] Such a provision had only previously existed for novice drivers with a G1 or G2 class licence, but would now be applied to every young driver, regardless of licence class. A driver found in violation of this law would have their licence administratively suspended by the police for twenty-four hours, and upon conviction be subject to a thirty-day suspension.[2]

The week the new legislation came into force, I filed an application in the Superior Court of Ontario asking that the law be found in violation of the Canadian Charter of Rights and Freedoms, and therefore declared to be of no force or effect. Though the courts have not yet ruled in the matter, the precedent will likely be important. The Quebec National Assembly has passed, though not brought into force, similar legislation[3] and other provinces could follow suit. This essay will make the case against the Ontario law. It will first argue the political case against the law by demonstrating that it is experience, rather than age, that is the primary determinant of collision risk for those drivers affected by the legislation. It will then make the legal case, showing how the age discrimination violates s. 15(1) of the Charter and cannot be saved by s. 1. Throughout, it will refute some of the arguments used by proponents of the legislation, showing how those arguments are often based on faulty assumptions or skewed data.

POLITICAL CASE

The primary issue regarding this legislation is whether it is correctly targeting the cause of many of these impaired driving accidents. Those in favour of this legislation point to studies showing that young drivers are involved in impaired driving collisions far more often than their proportion of the driving population. Deeper analysis shows that young drivers are more likely to get into a collision at every level of intoxication than older drivers, though the effect is far less pronounced in females than it is in males. While this correlation undoubtedly exists, it is important to realize the extraordinarily strong correlation between age and driving experience. While not every inexperienced driver is young, all young drivers are inexperienced. This means that these studies are actually showing the combined impact of age and experience on collision rates.

Failing to control for confounded variables such as age and experience can allow society to draw extremely distorted conclusions from data. For example, a study looking to compare the test scores of students of different races might show very different results than a similar study that made sure to control for the family income of those students. Similarly, lawmakers in Ontario passed Bill 126 on the conclusion that age is the determinant of impaired driving risk without examining how much of that risk is actually due to age, rather than the driving experience of the driver. In other words, if we control for experience, we may find that collision rates fail to differ much by age; a twenty-one-year-old driver with four years of experience may have no more collisions than a forty-one-year-old driver with the same amount of experience. Since, however, there are many more inexperienced twenty-one-year-olds drivers than forty-one-year old drivers, aggregating the data would give a false impression that youth, rather than inexperience, causes a higher collision risk.

Yet we need not be ignorant on this matter; there is data from Ontario itself showing the impact of driving experience on collision risk in drivers of different ages. While the study does not include intoxication, it is nonetheless a useful proxy considering how large a proportion of total collisions involve intoxicated drivers. The study is very revealing; when drivers are separated based on how long they have been licensed, the effects of age on collision risk are shown to be much more complex than on the surface, especially for drivers between the ages of eighteen and thirty-four, and for those with more than two years of driving experience. As Figure 1 shows, there is little variation in crash risk among drivers with between two and three years of experience, and nineteen-year-old drivers with from three to four years of experience are actually less likely to crash than those from twenty-five to thirty-four years of age. While the study does show some age-based variation, this variation is mainly concentrated in drivers with less than two years of experience. Yet in Ontario, one cannot get a G-class licence without almost two years of driving experience. The age and experience levels targeted by Bill 126–drivers from nineteen to twenty-one years of age with at least two years of driving experience–do not represent any kind of outlier when it comes to crash risk. These results suggest that the reason drivers from nineteen to twenty-one years of age are overrepresented in alcohol-related collisions has more to do with the average experience level of that age group than anything inherent in the age group itself. Because nineteen to twenty-one-year-old drivers have, on average, less experience than older drivers, they appear to have a higher crash risk. But drivers in that age group with more than two years of experience do not differ significantly in collision risk than older drivers with the same level of experience.

And experience is how some other jurisdictions have chosen to deal with this issue. In Manitoba, for example, one must maintain zero BAC regardless of licence

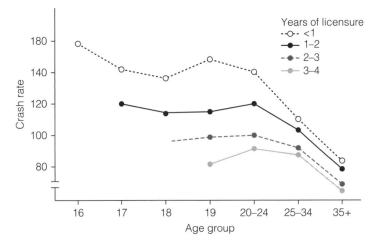

FIGURE 1

MALE DRIVER CRASH RATES PER LICENSED DRIVER DURING ONE TO FOUR YEARS OF LICENSURE BY DRIVER AGE, ONTARIO[4]

Anne T. McCartt, Daniel R. Mayhew, Keli A. Braitman, Susan A. Ferguson, and Herbert M. Simpson (2009): *Effects of Age and Experience on Young Driver Crashes: Review of Recent Literature,* Traffic Injury Prevention, 10:3, 209–219. Data from Mayhew D.R., Simpson H.M., Pak A. (2004). *Age and Experience in Young Driver Crashes.* Reprinted by permission of the publisher (Taylor & Francis Group, http://www.informaworld.com). Permission granted by Copyright Clearance Center Inc.

class for the first three years of holding a full licence.[5] While this has the effect of necessarily applying to every driver under the age of twenty-one, it applies equally to other new drivers. Considering that drivers in Ontario get their first licence at a wider range of ages than in other juristictions,[6] discriminating on experience rather than age would, if anything, be an even more effective way of protecting people from impaired drivers. Though Ontario's law is well intentioned, it is both less effective than Manitoba's model and unnecessarily discriminates against young adults.

LEGAL CASE

Blaming young adults for the accident risk of all inexperienced drivers is not merely unreasonable policy, but it is also an unconstitutional violation of the rights of young drivers. While driving is hardly a right, and driving with alcohol in one's bloodstream is certainly not a right, all Canadians have the right to be treated equally as individuals free from discrimination based on factors such as race, religion, or age. Section 15 of the Canadian Charter of Rights and Freedoms guarantees this right. The fact that driving is a privilege and the law is designed to save lives does not inherently allow for the use of discrimination. Murder is not a right, but surely a law that made murder illegal only for members of one religion would be a case of unconstitutional discrimination. This is because s. 15 is not about all people having the same access to benefits, but about recognizing the inherent value of every individual as a human being and member of Canadian society.

This principle was recognized by the Supreme Court of Canada in *Law v. Canada (Minister of Employment and Immigration)*,[7] Canada's seminal court case on s. 15 rights. The court established a two-part test for whether a law contravenes s. 15. First, it must make a legislative distinction based on grounds enumerated in the Charter, or an analogous ground. Second it must impose a burden or withhold a benefit to the group on the basis of stereotypes that harms the dignity of that group. While the direct impact of that withheld benefit or new burden can be an important part of s. 15 analysis, what is more important is the effect of promoting or perpetuating the negative stereotype. In *Law* (para. 64), the court ruled that

> …any demonstration by a claimant that a legislative provision or other state action has the effect of perpetuating or promoting the view that the individual is less capable, or less worthy of recognition or value as a human being or as a member of Canadian society (whether or not it involves a demonstration that the provision or other state action corroborates or exacerbates an existing prejudicial stereotype), will suffice to establish an infringement of s. 15(1).[8]

Analysis, then, is not so much based on whether there is any "right" to drive with a BAC above zero, but about whether the legislation perpetuates or promotes the view that young adults are less capable or valuable members of society than adults over the age of twenty-one.

Those in favour of this legislation agree that it provides differential treatment on the basis of the Charter-enumerated ground of age. However, they argue that such a distinction is not discriminatory, but merely takes note of the inherent differences of young adults when it comes to driving and alcohol. The court does allow for legislation to take into account differences in a way that respects human dignity. For example, in *Law* itself, the court ruled that it was not discriminatory for pension benefits to be withheld for surviving spouses under the age of thirty-five, since the rules merely took into account that younger adults are less in need of long-term financial security since they inherently have more working years left in their life.[9] The question, then, is whether treating drivers under the age of twenty-two differently than those who are older merely (1) takes into account different abilities or (2) perpetuates harmful stereotypes about young adults.

Those who believe the former point to those studies demonstrating the higher crash risk of young drivers. But as this essay has already demonstrated, those statistics are misleading. The primary factor behind the higher crash risk of youth is that the average young driver has less experience than the average older driver. Under the legislation, however, a twenty-one-year old driver with five years of experience must maintain a zero BAC, while a driver five years older with only two years of experience need not. And it is not as though young drivers are less able to handle the impairment caused by alcohol than older drivers. A study of the effects of cellular phones on the reaction time of drivers showed that a younger driver using a cellular phone had the same reaction time as an older driver without one.[10] While cellular-phone use is not directly comparable to alcohol, it does suggest that, when it comes to reflexes and reactions, young drivers are not impeded by their age.

So if the law does not target experience, and there is no evidence that alcohol causes more impairment for young adults than for older ones, then a reasonable person would be left with the conclusion that young people have worse judgment and less maturity than older adults. This is the harmful stereotype that is at the core of the legislation. While not always overtly stated, it forms the core of government arguments that young people are of a different class, either because they cannot control their alcohol intake or they do not sufficiently appreciate risks to be trusted behind the wheel after having had a glass of wine. The former approach is a sort of "pre-crime," assuming that unless youth are prohibited from drinking any alcohol, they will likely drink too much without realizing it and drive drunk. Such a claim presumes, without any evidence, that twenty-year-old individuals do not have sufficient development and maturity to understand the difference between a drink with dinner and drunk driving, yet presumes that such development and maturity exists in older adults. This has the effect of infantilizing those under twenty-two years of age, and not treating them as full adults.

Similar logic is behind the latter approach, which focuses on the risk posed by driving with any BAC rather than the risk of young drivers unwittingly drinking too much. The core of this argument is that youth don't have sufficient understanding of risk to drive with a BAC between 0 and 0.05. To state that adults are inherently reckless and immature because of their age is the very definition of perpetuating a harmful stereotype through legislation. Voting, jury duty, and military service are all tasks requiring maturity and good judgment, and all are undertaken by adults younger than twenty-two years of age. To promote the view that a certain class of adults has less maturity and poorer judgment than other adults calls into question that judgment and maturity in all situations, and reduces the ability of young adults to participate as valued members of Canadian society. The Ontario Human Rights Code prohibits a landlord to discriminate against tenants based on the belief that young adults will act recklessly toward the rental property,[11] yet the Ontario Legislature uses the same logic to assume that young adults will act recklessly with their lives. Young adults do not have a right to drive with a BAC above zero, but they do have a right not to have their maturity and very status as adults called into question. By promoting the view that young adults are less capable members of society because of their age, Bill 126 is in clear violation of s. 15(1) of the Charter.

Such a violation might still be justified under s. 1, and the courts have set out a four-part test to do so. An otherwise unconstitutional law can still be upheld if it pursues a sufficiently pressing and substantial objective, is rationally connected to that objective, impairs the right as little as is required to achieve the objective, and has benefits proportional to the infringement of Charter rights.[12] Should a law fail any part of this test, it cannot be justified under s. 1.

The objective of the zero-tolerance provisions of Bill 126 is to protect people who would otherwise be injured or killed by impaired driving. It would not make sense to limit the objective to protecting young drivers as a method of claiming that any other provision would not protect that group; there is no logical reason why only young drivers are inherently more worthy of protection so as to justify automatic differential treatment. Further, there is no evidence that the government passed the legislation to protect just that group. The objective of the legislation should be seen as part of a broader effort to reduce dangerous collisions that affect drivers, passengers, and pedestrians of all ages from impaired driving. That protecting these lives is a sufficiently pressing and substantial objective to warrant the breach of Charter rights is something that can be conceded to the Legislature.

The next test is whether the law is rationally connected to this objective. While having less impaired drivers on the road is obviously connected to road safety, this is not the test that must be met. In *Benner v. Canada (Secretary of State)*,[13] children born to a Canadian father could acquire citizenship automatically, while those born of a Canadian mother required a background check and oath. The court ruled that it did not matter whether having a background check and oath was rationally connected to the objective of only admitting secure Canadians committed to Canada, but whether the legislative distinction between those born to Canadian mothers or fathers was rationally connected to the objective.[14] Similarly, the question here is not whether a zero-BAC law is rationally connected to road safety, but whether discriminating against adults younger than twenty-two is. After correcting for experience, there does not seem to be such a rational connection. Young people do not have worse reflexes, nor is there anything else inherent to young adulthood that justifies subjecting only that group to an additional requirement. In the absence of any evidence tying young adulthood to risk besides experience, the legislation does not pass this aspect of the s. 1 test.

But suppose for the sake of argument that young people having less driving experience is enough of a relationship to pass the rational connection test. This leaves the issue of minimal impairment. Age discrimination has been justified before on the grounds that a somewhat arbitrary age line must necessarily be created in the absence of any alternative. In *Fitzgerald v. Alberta (2002),*[15] the Alberta Court of Queen's Bench, in a case subsequently held up by the Alberta Court of Appeal, ruled that the voting age was a violation of s. 15, but that the violation was justified under s. 1. The court ruled that in the absence of any better way to evaluate the maturity of a prospective voter, age was a reasonable litmus test. It further ruled that any age picked would have to be arbitrary to an extent, and that eighteen was no less reasonable an age than sixteen or seventeen.

Such precedence would seem to hold up in this case as well. The main difference between the zero tolerance law and the voting age, though, is that there is a reasonable alternative to the law that does not infringe Charter rights. As previously mentioned, the province of Manitoba prohibits any BAC above zero for the first three years of having a full licence.[16] Insofar as the Ontario legislation is effectively using age as a proxy for experience, an experience-based measure such as Manitoba's would, if anything, be more rationally connected to the objective while avoiding any discrimination on enumerated grounds. It may seem self-contradictory that expanding the scope of a law would be more constitutional, especially when such a law would still have the same effect on young drivers. But the purpose of s. 15 must be taken into account. The law violates s. 15 not because it denies young adults the ability to drive with an above-zero BAC, but because it promotes harmful stereotypes about the lack of maturity and poor judgment of young adults. A law based on driving experience would have no such effect. A twenty-year-old driver would still be forced to maintain a BAC of zero, but only because he or she had too little driving experience, and not because he or she is presumed to be immature or reckless. Because there is a reasonable alternative that would still protect Ontarians from impaired drivers without harming the dignity of adults under the age of twenty-two, the law cannot be saved by s. 1. With such a clear and reasonable alternative, it is not necessary to engage the fourth step of the Oakes test.

CONCLUSION

Impaired driving is a dangerous activity at any level of BAC, and far too many lives have been ended far too soon because of it. Regardless of whether this law is eventually upheld or struck down by the courts, drivers of all ages should always avoid drinking any alcohol before driving. The wisdom of mandating zero BAC for inexperienced, or even all, drivers is not something this essay will answer, but surely the intent of trying to reduce impaired driving fatalities should be lauded, even in this imperfect form. Nonetheless, as a society we should ensure that even the most well-intentioned laws abide by our core principles of liberty and equality. Hopefully, in the future this law will be replaced by one that protects Ontarians from impaired drivers while giving young adults the respect and dignity they deserve.

NOTES

1. Bill 126, *Road Safety Act*, 1st Sess, 39th Leg, Ontario, 2009 (assented to 23 April 2009).

2. *Highway Traffic Act*, R.S.O. 1990, c. H.8, s. 44.1 (3–4).

3. Bill 71, *An Act to amend the Highway Safety Code and other legislative provisions (modified title)*, 1st Sess, 39th Leg, Quebec, 2009 (assented to 10 December 2010).

4. Anne T. McCartt, Daniel R. Mayhew, Keli A. Braitman, Susan A. Ferguson, and Herbert M. Simpson, "Effects of Age and Experience on Young Driver Crashes: Review of Recent Literature," *Traffic Injury Prevention* 10, no. 3 (2009), pp. 209–219. Data from Daniel R. Mayhew, Herbert M. Simpson, and Anita Pak, "Age and Experience in Young Driver Crashes," (unpublished manuscript, Traffic Injury Research Foundation, Ottawa, Ontario, 2004).

5. *Highway Traffic Act*, C.C.S.M. c. H60, s. 26.3.

6. McCartt et al., "Effects of Age and Experience on Young Driver Crashes: Review of Recent Literature."

7. [1999] 1 SCR 497, 170 DLR (4th) 1.

8. Ibid.

9. Ibid.

10. D.L. Strayer, D.L. and F.A. Drews, "Effects of Cell Phone Conversations on Younger and Older Drivers," *Proceedings of the Human Factors and Ergonomics Society 47th Annual Meeting* (Santa Monica, CA: HFES), pp. 1860–1864.

11. R.S.O. 1990, c. H.19, s. 2 (1).

12. *R v. Oakes*, [1986] 1 SCR 103, 26 DLR (4th) 200.

13. [1997] 1 SCR 358.

14. Ibid.

15. 2002 ABQB 1086.

16. *Highway Traffic Act*, C.C.S.M. c. H60, s. 26.3.

✗ NO

BAC to Zero: Defending the Constitutionality of Ontario's *Road Safety Act* (2009)

DAVID OLEVSON

On November 18, 2008, Bill 126 was introduced into the Ontario Legislative Assembly for first reading.[1] The most controversial provision of the proposed law was one that made it illegal for a driver under the age of twenty-two to have a blood alcohol concentration (BAC) level above 0 percent. This provision (referred to as 0 BAC to 21) effectively prevents any driver under the age of twenty-two from consuming any alcohol in the course of, or prior to, operation of a motor vehicle. A contravention of this condition results in a fine not exceeding $500 and an immediate licence suspension of thirty days for a first time offender.[2] In support of the bill, The Centre for Addiction and Mental Health in Toronto introduced evidence proving motor vehicle injuries are the leading cause of death among people from sixteen to twenty-one years of age.[3] Further, alcohol was shown to be responsible for an estimated 40 percent of those fatalities.[4] Overall in Canada, it was submitted, impaired driving has a rate of causing criminal death twice that of all forms of homicide combined.[5] In April of 2009, Bill 126, titled the *Road Safety Act* (2009), was given Royal Assent and passed into law as the amended section 44.1 of Ontario's *Highway Traffic Act* (1990).[6] Since its implementation, critics of this law have contended that it is in violation of section 15 of the Canadian Charter of Rights and Freedoms, which protects the right to equality.

In today's society it is taken for granted that driving is a privilege, not a right. Section 31(a) of the *Highway Traffic Act* (HTA) clearly states: "the *privilege* of driving on a highway is granted to, and retained by, only those persons who demonstrate that they are likely to drive safely."[7] Driving is not a constitutional right; it is a licensed activity that is subject to a number of conditions and requirements.[8] Free speech is a right, freedom of association is a right, but driving is not. However, as per s. 15 of the Charter, freedom from discrimination is also an inherent right. It is illegal for government to discriminate against segments of the population based on the enumerated Charter grounds, or those analogous to them. Nevertheless, every right enshrined in the Charter can be limited for the purpose of protecting the interests of Canadian society at large. These limits of our constitutionally guaranteed freedoms are implemented in accordance with s. 1 of the Charter:

> The Canadian Charter of Rights and Freedoms guarantees the rights and freedoms set out in it subject only to such reasonable limits prescribed by law as can be demonstrably justified in a free and democratic society.[9]

The wording of s. 1 proposes a two-stage process for judicial review of legislation challenged on the basis of Charter infringement. First, it must be determined that the challenged law infringes a protected right. If such a finding is established. then the second stage of analysis is engaged: the court must determine whether the limit of the right is reasonably justifiable in a free and democratic society.[10] Both of these steps are essential to the process of judicial review. As such, each prong of the test must be analyzed separately and made out in full before the next step can be undertaken. Such an analysis will be administered below to determine the constitutional merits of s. 44.1 of the HTA; it will show that the legislation would survive a constitutional challenge.

SECTION 15

Equality rights are entrenched in the Charter under s. 15, which states that "[e]very individual is equal before and under the law and has the right to the equal protection and equal benefit of the law without discrimination and, in particular, without discrimination based on race, national or ethnic origin, colour, religion, sex, age or mental or physical disability."[11] The purpose of this section is to prevent government from making distinctions that are discriminatory and adversely affect members covered by the listed grounds and those analogous to them.[12]

The current test for assessing an alleged violation of s. 15 of the Charter was established in *Withler v. Canada (AG)*.[13] The judgment in this Supreme Court of Canada case reformatted previous jurisprudence to create a two-step test for a s. 15 claim. First, the plaintiff must establish that the law creates a distinction based on an enumerated or analogous ground; in other words, that the legislation discriminates on either one of the grounds listed in s. 15 or on grounds similar to those listed. With regards to s. 44.1 of the HTA, age is an enumerated ground. The second step of a s. 15 analysis as per the decision in *Withler* is to determine whether the distinction is discriminatory by perpetuating prejudice or by having as its base a stereotype that does not correspond with the claimant groups' actual characteristics.[14] Put differently, in order for a law to be deemed discriminatory, its underlying purpose must be based on a stereotype or other false presumption. To assist with this analysis, several contextual factors were established in *Law v. Canada (Minister of Employment and Immigration)*.[15] These factors are not necessarily the only ones to be considered, but can assist with determining whether the second branch of the *Withler* test has been fulfilled.

A contextual factor that may be relevant when considering s. 44.1 of the HTA is the "nature of the interests affected." This factor seeks to determine the extent to which the claimants' rights are being impeded or restricted. With the law in question, the severity of the impugned provision does not seem to be overly intrusive. The affected group (namely drivers below twenty-two years old) are still able to drive; the only restriction is that they maintain a zero-BAC level. Further, the consequences are localized (limited to a small age group) and cease to apply to any specific individual within a few years (once the drivers reach twenty-two years of age). Another relevant inquiry is that of the "correspondence factor." This factor seeks to determine if the differential treatment corresponds to the actual circumstances of the offended group, which is to say, whether the law accurately captures real features of the targeted entity. Substantial evidence exists (and will be discussed later) emphasizing that not only is impaired driving the single largest cause of death for youths, but also that at twenty-three deaths per billion kilometres driven, the rate of death for drivers from sixteen to twenty-four years of age is almost three times higher than any other segment of the population.[16] When coupled with the fact that approximately 40 percent of youth drivers involved in fatal accidents test positive for alcohol, this becomes an actual and serious issue, not merely a stereotype.[17] Overall, an examination of the scientific data suggests that it is possible to uphold s. 44.1 of the *Highway Traffic Act* on the grounds that it does not violate s. 15 of the Charter because it does not operate on stereotypes or discriminatory biases. However, in the event that these arguments are not compelling, the second branch of a claim of Charter infringement will be analyzed, namely a s. 1 analysis.

SECTION 1

Once a breach of a right protected by the Charter has been established, the law can still be upheld by s. 1. The role of s. 1, which transfers the burden of proof to the party seeking to limit the right (usually the government), is to determine whether the discrimination is justifiable (in a free and democratic society), in which case the infringement of a Charter right would be permitted.[18]

The test that established the criteria necessary to ascertain that a limit is reasonable and demonstrably justified in a free and democratic society was established in *R. v. Oakes*.[19] The four principles that must be satisfied are as follows:

1. The law must pursue an objective that is sufficiently pressing and substantial to justify limiting a Charter right.

2. The law must be rationally connected to the objective.

3. The law must impair the right as little as is required.

4. There must be proportionality between the benefits achieved by the law and the limiting of the Charter rights of the claimant.[20]

Step 1: Sufficiently Important Objective

The objective of s. 44.1 of the HTA is to protect youth from impaired driving causing death. More than 40 percent of driving fatalities among those from sixteen to nineteen years old and 50 percent of driving fatalities among those from twenty to twenty-five years old are reported to be alcohol-related.[21] Moreover, those numbers are underrepresentative because they do not consider victims in other cars or pedestrians that may have been injured or killed as a result of impaired driving.[22] In *Irwin Toy v. Quebec* the Supreme Court held that a Quebec law prohibiting the targeting of children by advertisers was a sufficiently important objective to pass this stage of the *Oakes* test.[23] Due to this low threshold, the protection of youths against fatalities caused by impaired driving should be considered an objective sufficient to satisfy this stage of the s. 1 analysis. Moreover, the Supreme Court has been reluctant to challenge government at this first step in deference to the belief that it is unwise in most instances for the courts to challenge the overall aim or wisdom of a legislative action.

Step 2: Rational Connection

The Supreme Court has held that "the requirement of rational connection calls for an assessment of how well the legislative garment has been tailored to suit its purpose."[24] For example, a law that bans all types of pornographic materials for the purpose of reducing serious criminal activity may fail at this step because the linkage between the means and ends of the legislation—the ban leading to less crime—may be unclear and hence not fully rational. With regard to the issue of impaired driving by a specific cohort of the population, there is a clear and rational connection to a prohibition that restricts alcohol consumption by that specific demographic.[25] As with the first step, the courts have only on a few occasions found fault with legislation at this step.

Step 3: Minimal Impairment Test

Although the term "minimal impairment" may connote that the infringement of the Charter right must be slight and insignificant, such is not the case. Instead, it has been interpreted as offering much deference to Parliament. As long as the option selected is one of a possibility of options that is necessary to accomplish the desired purpose of the law, then it will be allowed to stand.[26] Therefore, it is necessary to determine what is required to achieving the desired objective. There are a few solutions to the issue of youth-impaired driving causing death. The United States has chosen to raise the legal drinking age to twenty-one, thereby decreasing the occurrence of impaired driving by youth simply by restricting access to alcohol.[27] Since the implementation of this policy, American states have reported reduced fatality rates of between 9 percent and 24 percent. If similar results are achieved with the implementation of Ontario's law, between 377 and 1,006 drivers twenty years of age or below will be saved from death and injury annually.[28] Unfortunately, increasing the legal drinking age in Canada does not seem plausible politically. Also, increasing the legal drinking age in an effort to reduce alcohol-related motor vehicle deaths would not minimally impair the portion of the population being affected. Not all youths under the age of twenty-two drive and even fewer drive while intoxicated; in other words, an American-style law is too sweeping because it affects those who are unrelated to the problem of drinking and driving among young people. Therefore, a law such as s. 44.1 of the HTA, which only restricts the consumption of alcohol by those youths that are actively operating a motor vehicle, serves the intended purpose of reducing the occurrence of impaired driving causing fatalities among youth while limiting their rights as minimally as is reasonably possible.

Step 4: Proportionality Test

As previously discussed, the amount of intrusion onto the rights of youths is proportional to the benefit being sought by the implementation of s. 44.1 of the HTA. The goal of saving the lives of Canadian youths and preventing the negative impact it has on family members and others that are affected is truly a goal that will benefit all Canadians. The deleterious effects caused by limiting impaired driving cannot be said to outweigh the benefits achieved by saving lives. Critics claim, as will be discussed later, that it would be more proportional, and less intrusive, if the law applied to all novice drivers for a set number of years from the time they receive their driver's licence. However, it is not the responsibility of the court to determine what is the most proportional, but only if the law at issue has a level of proportionality sufficient to justify its intrusion into an alleged violation of a constitutional document. Alternatively, the arguments that will be made with regard to the critic's suggestion will be shown to be flawed in manners that simply cannot be overlooked. As such, s. 44.1 of the HTA, if found to be in violation of s. 15 of the Charter, can be saved by s. 1 as a reasonable and justifiable limit on the right to freedom of discrimination based on age.

CRITICS' ARGUMENTS

Critics of s. 44.1 of the HTA base their position on a variety of assumptions. One of the major critiques is the seemingly arbitrary (as they would have you believe) age of twenty-one that is the benchmark of the 0 BAC to 21 law. The major contention raised by critics is that the law should apply equally to all novice drivers and not just those under a certain age; accordingly, all new drivers would have to wait six years before getting behind the wheel with any alcohol in their system. Although there is an inherent contradiction in an argument that suggests that a law should be repealed completely because it is not stringent enough, there are also a few major considerations that are being overlooked. Critics of this law suggest that inexperienced drivers are such regardless of age, which is true, and therefore should be forced to abstain from alcohol for a legally defined period of time until such a point that they are able to drive in an "experienced" manner. The fallacy of this argument is that it fails to take into account other relevant factors surrounding the institution of young adulthood and of driving that contributes to the occurrence of impaired driving causing death, factors that simply are not present with older novice drivers.

The largest factor of concern is strictly a matter of age. Most of the provinces and territories in Canada have adopted a graduated licensing program that requires the completion of multiple tests and stages before one becomes a fully certified driver. Explicit in these schemes is the condition that drivers without a full licence cannot consume alcohol, *regardless of age*. However, if a youth gets a driver's licence at the first legal opportunity, they complete the graduating licensing program and thus lift the BAC restrictions when they are approximately eighteen or nineteen years old. This directly corresponds to the legal drinking age in Canada's provinces and territories.[29] Therefore, by virtue of their age, youth are inexperienced drinkers and have not yet acquired a tolerance to even small doses of alcohol (unlike older newly licensed drivers).[30] An additional factor that contributes to this issue is the sheer quantity of alcohol consumed by youths when they are first legally able to. Approximately 70 percent of current drinkers from fifteen to twenty-four years of age reported binge drinking (at least five drinks on one occasion) once in the last year, and almost 50 percent of those drinkers reported binge drinking at least twelve times in the past twelve months.[31] The rate of alcohol consumption was most significant amongst those from eighteen to nineteen years old, wherein 42.5 percent said their usual consumption pattern was to drink in excess of five beverages.[32] This age directly corresponds to the completion of the graduates licensing program in most provinces and territories. As can be predicted, drivers within that demographic are largely overrepresented in alcohol-related fatalities and injuries.[33] In fact, Canadian youth from eighteen to nineteen years of age account for 70 percent of all fatally injured teen drivers, substantially greater than their portion of the demographic.[34] Overall, the sheer inexperience that youth have with alcohol, and the amount consumed by youths, should be reason enough to uphold the prohibition of drinking any alcohol before driving. Yet even so, these are not the only reasons to do so.

There are a few distinguishing factors that increase the crash risk for youth, even without the presence of alcohol. First, it is clear that youth are inexperienced drivers and thus pose a greater crash risk. Beginner drivers are less able to detect hazards or potential threats, and this is evident in the sharp declines of rates of crashes that begin within the first months of obtaining a licence (this is the reason for the graduated licensing system that most provinces employ, and everyone must go through it, regardless of age).[35] However, youth drivers are also more likely to speed, follow too closely, or not allow enough time for themselves to merge with traffic. Recent studies show that, not only do youth have the highest rates of self-reported speeding, but they are also most likely to take risks "just for the fun of it."[36] Driver's from sixteen to twenty-four years of age experience approximately twenty-eight deaths per billion kilometres driven, compared to only two for drivers from forty-five to fifty-four years of age.[37] As such, studies have indicated that a sober male driver aged from sixteen to twenty is 5.8 times more likely to be killed in a single-vehicle crash than a male over the age of twenty-five.[38] Hence, the risks to youth drivers derived solely from their inexperience already present an abnormally high risk to themselves and other drivers. To allow alcohol consumption for this demographic would be to create a cocktail of trouble that is begging for disaster. And the statistics reinforce that assertion. When combining the inexperience of youth drivers and the impairment caused by alcohol, the results are dire. Young drivers have a far greater risk of having a fatal car accident at all BAC levels relative to older drivers. In fact, the risk of fatal injury more than doubles for every 0.02 percent increase in BAC levels for youth drivers.[39] In 2003, youth accounted for only 13.7 percent of the population, but were responsible for 32.1 percent of alcohol-related traffic fatalities.[40] Overall, the assertion by critics of s. 44.1 of the HTA that age is not a relevant proxy for experience fails to consider all the factors necessary to make that determination, which, when considered, suggest otherwise.

CONCLUSION

In conclusion, critics have suggested that the *Road Safety Act* (2009) infringes upon the Canadian Charter of Rights and Freedoms. They deem driving to be a right, and not the privilege that it is, and thus any conditions imposed on any licensed drivers have been framed as a severe violation of the rights of Canadians. However, an analysis of the act, implemented as s. 44.1 of the HTA, proves that not only can its provisions withstand a s. 15 Charter challenge, but they can also be upheld on the basis of s. 1 of the Charter as a reasonable and justifiable limit on youths' equality rights. It must be remembered that equality does not mean that everyone must be treated equally; people's differences must be respected. In *Canadian Foundation for Children, Youth and the Law v. Canada* it was decided that parents are allowed to spank children, wherein it would be considered assault if imposed on anyone else.[41] As such, it is clear that children and youth must be treated differently to respect their abilities and mindsets and, above all, to protect their safety. In 2009, MADD Canada gave Ontario a grade of "A−" for its initiatives to limit the occurrence of impaired driving. This was the highest mark issued to any province, and a drastic improvement over the "C+" issued to it in 2000.[42] Overall, the subtle acceptance that Canadians have toward drunk drivers must be overturned. As was quoted by an unknown source, with regards to impaired youth drivers, "The speedway ends at the cemetery."

NOTES

1. Bill 126, *Road Safety Act*, 1st Sess, 39th Leg, Ontario, 2009 (first reading 29 November 2008).

2. *Highway Traffic Act*, RSO 1990, c. H.8, s. 44.1 (3–4).

3. Centre for Addiction and Mental Health, *Written Submission to The Standing Committee on General Government on Bill 126, Road Safety Act, 2008* (Toronto: Centre for Addiction and Mental Health, 2009).

4. E. Chamberlain and R. Solomon, *The Case for a Provincial 0.00% BAC Limit for All Drivers Under the Age of 21* (Rep. MADD Canada, 2001).

5. Supra note 2.

6. Bill 126, *Road Safety Act*, 1st Sess, 39th Leg, Ontario, 2009 (assented to 23 April 2009).

7. Ibid., s. 31(a).

8. *Galaske v. O'Donnell*, [1994] 1 SCR 670, 89 BCLR (2d) 273.

9. *Canadian Charter of Rights and Freedoms*, s. 1, Part I of the *Constitution Act, 1982*, being Schedule B to the *Canada Act 1982* (U.K.), 1982, c.11.

10. Patrick Macklem et al., *Canadian Constitutional Law*, 4th ed. (Toronto: Emond Montgomery Publications, 2010), p. 826.

11. *Canadian Charter of Rights and Freedoms*, s. 15, Part I of the *Constitution Act, 1982*, being Schedule B to the *Canada Act 1982* (U.K.), 1982, c.11.

12. *R v. Kapp*, 2008 SCC 41 at para. 15, [2008] 2 SCR 483.

13. *Withler v. Canada (Attorney General)*, 2011 SCC 12, 15 BCLR (5th) 1.

14. Ibid.

15. [1999] 1 SCR 497, 170 DLR (4th) 1.

16. P. Emery, D. Mayhew, and H. Simpson, *Youth and Road Crashes: Magnitude, Characteristics and Trends* (Ottawa: Traffic Injury Research Foundation, 2008), p. 15.

17. Traffic Injury Research Foundation (TIRF), *The Alcohol-Crash Problem in Canada: 2006* (Ottawa: TIRF, 2009), p. 36.

18. Supra note 16, p. 1169.

19. [1986] 1 SCR 103, 26 DLR (4th) 200.

20. Supra note 16, p. 842.

21. D. Mayhew, S. Brown, and H. Simpson, *The Alcohol-Crash Problem in Canada: 2003* (Ottawa: Traffic Injury Research Foundation, 2005), p. 15. (Note that the *Alcohol-Crash Problem* is numbered incorrectly: there are two page 13s and two page 14s, which contain different material.)

22. Supra note 2.

23. [1989] 1 SCR 927, 58 DLR (4th) 577.

24. *R v. Edwards Books and Art*, [1986] 2 SCR 713, 35 DLR (4th) 1.

25. For an example of a case where the rational connection test was failed see *Benner v. Canada*, [1997] 1 SCR 358.

26. Ibid., p. 860.

27. E. Chamberlain and R. Solomon, "Zero Blood Alcohol Concentration Limits for Drivers under 21: Lessons from Canada," *Injury Prevention* 14, no. 2 (2008), pp. 123–128.

28. Supra note 2.

29. E. Chamberlain and R. Solomon, *The Case for a Provincial 0.00% BAC Limit for All Drivers Under the Age of 21* (Rep. MADD Canada, 2001).

30. Ibid.

31. R. Solomon, J. Organ, L. Gwyer, M. Abdoullaeva, and S. Chiodo, *Alcohol, Trauma and Impaired Driving*, 4th ed. (London, ON: MADD Canada, CAMH, CCSA-CCLAT, 2009).

32. Ibid., p. 23.

33. Chamberlain and Solomon, "Zero Blood Alcohol Concentration Limits for Drivers under 21."

34. Chamberlain and Solomon, *The Case for a Provincial 0.00% BAC Limit.*

35. E. Chamberlain and R. Solomon, *Youth and Impaired Driving in Canada: Opportunities for Progress* (London, ON: MADD Canada, 2006).

36. Ibid., pp. 12–13.

37. Supra note 34.

38. Ibid.

39. Ibid.

40. Supra note 38.

41. [2004] 1 SCR 76.

42. R. Solomon, E. Chamberlain, J. Organ, L. Gwyer, and M. Abdoullaeva, *Rating the Provinces and Territories: The 2009 Report Card* (London, ON: MADD Canada, 2009).

POSTSCRIPT

Kevin Wiener, with his paper, accomplishes what many might think to be impossible: to cast doubt on the wisdom and legality of the zero-BAC law. There is in the general population a belief that young people are indeed drivers with questionable skills and with insufficient experience when it comes to coping with alcohol. Accordingly, the new law makes perfect sense. But Wiener suggests a closer look at some relevant data that points toward the notion that the level of driving experience—and not age—is the key factor in explaining traffic collisions. So Ontario should follow Manitoba and apply the zero-BAC stipulation to all drivers with only three years of experience *regardless of age*. Yet, one still wonders. There are data that appear to support the conventional wisdom—young drivers do differ from others. To some extent the case comes down to a tussle between competing findings on drinking and driving or a willingness to make hard and fast conclusions based on the research. Also, one might agree with Wiener that level of experience in part explains collision rates among young drivers, but also observe that age too brings something to the explanation. The question then becomes whether the impact of age is sufficient to have a zero BAC only for young drivers. Finally, we might push aside the inconclusive research and urge the courts to side with the government's claim that drinking and driving is a problem among young drivers.

As with Wiener, David Olevson supplies us with a closely argued essay that makes a good case for his position. The law escapes any claims of discrimination, he writes, because its assumptions about young drivers are basically sound and so there is no negative stereotype there. The same holds for a s. 1 defence—it easily parries beliefs that the law fails to meet the test for a reasonable limitation. However, we can return to the concern mentioned in the preceding paragraph, namely that we may be too eager in accepting typical beliefs about young people and driving. Olevson points to research that reveals young drivers to be more reckless than older drivers, but one wonders whether the studies are comparing apples with oranges—drivers of differing years of driving experience. Get a forty-year-old individual with four years of driving experience and he or she might just be as reckless as the twenty-year-old driver with the same amount of experience. More generally, when examining young drivers, researchers admit that "[i]t is difficult to sort out the relative contribution of inexperience and age factors to their individual crashes. For example, following too closely and crashing can reflect risk taking or merely inexperience with car placement" (see Williams' article, cited below). Lastly, as with the commentary on Wiener's essay, we might move away from the research—as it fails to resolve the matter—and go with some basic considerations. Here, it might be important to note that the people who are the focus of the zero-BAC law can also be the people who fight wars, sit on juries, and vote elected representatives into office.

This debate is about a legal issue, so we need to begin with the relevant literature on equality rights and the Charter of Rights and Freedoms. Peter Hogg's student edition of *Constitutional Law of Canada* (Toronto: Carswell, 2010) is always a safe place to start for any issue relating to Canadian constitutional law. The text includes a discussion of the Charter and the case law associated with s. 15 (including precedents relating to age). Sharpe and Roach's book on the Charter is also useful: Robert J. Sharpe and Kent Sharpe, *The Charter of Rights and Freedoms* (Toronto: Irwin, 2009). A recent decision of the Supreme Court of Canada is also important to read, largely because it offers a reformulation (and simplification, one might say) of the test for discrimination: *Withler v. Canada (Attorney General)*, 2011 SCC 12. An added bonus is that the case deals with the issue of age discrimination.

As for the law at issue, the Government of Ontario website includes a number of entries dealing with the zero-BAC law, available at news.ontario.ca/mto/en/2010/07/keeping-drivers-safe.html. Shortly after the introduction of the law, Kevin Wiener and the Ontario Minister of Transportation together appeared on the CBC Radio show "The Current" to defend their positions. This is worth accessing at http://www.cbc.ca/thecurrent/2010/08/august-11-2010.html. Finally, the resolution of this debate centres on issues that require resolution through research. For example, there is the major issue of whether age or experience best explains collisions and other traffic incidents. The following three articles provide a start to an investigation of this and other related issues: E. Chamberlain and R. Solomon, "Zero Blood Alcohol Concentration Limits for Drivers under 21: Lessons from Canada," *Injury Prevention* 14, no. 2 (2008), pp. 123–128; Anne T. McCartt et al., "Effects of Age and Experience on Young Driver Crashes: Review of the Recent Literature," *Traffic Injury Prevention* 10, no. 3, pp. 209–219; and A.F. Williams, "Young Driver Risk Factors: Successful and Unsuccessful Approaches for Dealing with Them and an Agenda for the Future," *Injury Prevention* 12 (Suppl 1), pp. i4–i8.

Should Religious Beliefs Be Excluded from Consideration of Public Policy?

✔ **YES**
JUSTICE MARY SAUNDERS, "Opinion in *Chamberlain v. Surrey School District #36*"

✘ **NO**
IAIN T. BENSON, "Living Together with Disagreement: Pluralism, the Secular, and the Fair Treatment of Beliefs in Canada Today"

What role, if any, should religious beliefs play in the making of public policy? While this issue has often been contested in the United States, it has generated less debate in Canada. However, this has begun to change in recent years. During the 2000 federal election, the political opponents of Stockwell Day tried to focus attention on his religious beliefs, suggesting not too subtly to voters that such beliefs could make him dangerous if his party won the election. In the run-up to the 2005 federal election, a *Globe and Mail* article entitled "Christian Activists Capturing Tory Races" noted that the fact that a number of well-known evangelical Christians had won Conservative nominations raised concerns about a "hidden agenda" and the fear that, if elected, they would try to "hijack" the party's policy agenda. In the 2007 Ontario election, when Conservative leader John Tory suggested that public funding should be extended to all faith-based schools, opponents of the measure focused particularly on the detrimental impact that religion frequently has on public life. In Quebec, the government convened a special commission, under the co-direction of the eminent political philosopher Charles Taylor, to examine what constitutes a "reasonable accommodation" of religious beliefs and practices in a modern, secular, multicultural society. And, in 2010, Marci MacDonald published an alarmist book under the title *The Armageddon Factor: The Rise of Christian Nationalism in Canada* (Random House), warning Canadians of what she sees as the growing influence of American-style religious conservatism on Canadian politics.

From these examples, it is clear that the relationship between religious beliefs and public policy continues to be a contentious issue in Canadian politics. This issue has probably received some of its most intense scrutiny in the courtrooms of the province of British Columbia. Bringing much public attention to this issue was the debate surrounding the selection of approved books for primary school children in provincial public schools. In British Columbia, the provincial *School Act* grants school boards responsibility for approving the educational resource materials that teachers use in classrooms. In 1995, the Ministry of Education implemented a new Personal Planning curriculum for kindergarten to grade 7, which included a "family life" component.

In 1996, the Surrey school board passed a resolution that apparently prohibited the use of educational materials that were not on a prescribed list. The Gay and Lesbian Educators of B.C. (GALE)—an organization that advocates for change in the school system to create a positive environment for homosexual and bisexual persons—had developed a list of books that portray homosexual relationships positively. A teacher in the Surrey school district requested that three books from the GALE list be approved for use in teaching kindergarten and grade 1 students in the Surrey school district. The books were reviewed three times by various levels of the school district administrative staff. All agreed that the books dealt with sensitive material and were likely to cause parental concern over the presentation of same-sex parenting to kindergarten and grade 1 children. The superintendent of schools for the school district declared that the three books were unnecessary for achieving the objectives of the school curriculum. Since use of the books would be controversial among the parents in the community, it was decided that the final verdict should come from the school board, which was elected by that community.

On April 24, 1997, the Surrey school board formally considered the request for approval of the three books. The meeting was widely attended and garnered considerable media coverage. Several submissions were received, including ones from GALE and from the B.C. Civil Liberties Association. At the end of the presentation, the school board, by a vote of 4–2, passed a resolution declining to approve the books. Following this result, the teacher involved applied to the B.C. Supreme Court for a ruling that the school board resolution be declared invalid and that an order be issued requiring the school board to pass a resolution approving the books in question.

In the subsequent court case, Justice Mary Saunders of the B.C. Supreme Court determined that indeed the school board's resolution should be quashed. In explaining her decision, Justice Saunders pointed out that section 76 of the *British Columbia School Act* required that all schools be run on "strictly secular and non-sectarian principles." This she took to mean that not only should schools not show denominational bias, they should also be "independent of religious considerations." In other words, all religious motivations and reasons should be excluded from policy decisions. Interestingly, in a dispute between the parties over evidence, the justice allowed the petitioner's lawyers to introduce information regarding speeches given by the chair of the school board prior to taking that office because they gave some insight into the "state of mind" of the board chair in making her decision. The justice seemed to be saying that even if no explicitly religiously based arguments were used, any evidence that decisions taken might be rooted in religious principles could disqualify them from the public arena. Further, while the B.C. *School Act* states that schools should inculcate the "highest morality" in children, the school board is precluded from making any decisions "based in a significant way on religious considerations." Saunders argued that the principles on which this "highest morality" should be based are to be found in the Charter of Rights and Freedoms.

Justice Saunders's finding was appealed by the Surrey school board to the B.C. Court of Appeal. The ruling of the Court of Appeal reversed the previous decision. The justice noted that the school board's decision to refuse approval of the three books did not violate the *School Act* and was fully consistent with the Charter. In making this decision, the Court of Appeal noted that "a religiously informed conscience should not be accorded any privilege, but neither should it be placed under a disability." The Court of Appeal particularly rejected the suggestion by Justice Saunders that moral decisions influenced by religion are excluded under the *School Act*. To accept such a position, the court ruled, "would negate the right of all citizens to participate democratically in the education of their children in a truly free society" and would make "religious unbelief a condition of participation in the setting of the moral agenda" in schools. Thus, Saunders's narrow interpretation of what it means to be secular was not upheld by the Court of Appeal or the Supreme Court of Canada that upheld it unanimously on this point. In a subsequent appeal to the Supreme Court of Canada, all nine justices upheld the B.C. Court of Appeal's ruling regarding the meaning of secular.

This case goes to the heart of some critical questions. Is it permissible for public officials to make decisions that are motivated in part by religious belief? Does the Charter of Rights and Freedoms require that moral beliefs that originate from religious belief be excluded from public debate? Does "secular" essentially mean "non-religious"? What role, if any, should religious convictions play in the public square? How can religious convictions be balanced with the need to respect diversity and tolerance within society? In the first reading below, we have an excerpt from Justice Mary Saunders in the Surrey schoolbook case, in which she addresses some of these issues. In response, law professor and constitutional lawyer Iain Benson provides a critique of the notions of the secular and pluralism that underlie Justice Saunder's decision.

✔ **YES**

Opinion in *Chamberlain v. Surrey School District #36*
JUSTICE MARY SAUNDERS

[…]

THE BOOKS RESOLUTION

[…]

[75] I turn then to the question of whether the School Board, by its Books resolution, acted contrary to s. 76. This is really a question of whether it acted contrary to s. 76(1), whether by its decision it failed to conduct the schools on strictly secular and non-sectarian principles. This is both a question of interpretation of s. 76(1) and a question of fact.

[76] There is no question that the resolution is non-sectarian. The issue is whether it infringes the requirement that the schools "be conducted on strictly secular…principles."

[77] The petitioners contend that the School Board made its decision on a religious basis, running afoul of s. 76(1). The School Board contends that it acted in the best interests of the children, with consideration for the parents' rights to teach their children their religious and moral values and beliefs regarding homosexual conduct.

[78] The words "conducted on strictly secular…principles" have been part of the requirements of public schools for a very long time, but, to the court's knowledge, have not been judicially considered prior to this case. In the education setting, the term secular excludes religion or religious belief. Combining the word "secular" with the words "strictly" and "principles," and considering the history of schools in British Columbia as being beyond overt church or religious intervention or influence, I conclude that the words "conducted on strictly secular…principles" precludes a decision significantly influenced by religious considerations. This interpretation is consistent with the increasingly pluralistic nature of modern British Columbia and accords with the obligation to give statutory provisions a fair, large and liberal interpretation: *Interpretation Act,* R.S.B.C. 1996, c. 238, s. 8.

[79] The School Board submits that the section does not require it to place into the classroom books which are morally contentious. It says that the books in issue here, presenting families with same-sex parents as normal and same-sex parents

as not "bad," are morally contentious, may tend to confuse children and may interfere with parental education on religious and moral matters.

[80] These submissions must be viewed in light of all the language in s. 76. Section 76(1) directs a School Board, administrators and teachers to refrain from religious based education or management motivated by religious considerations. At the same time s. 76(2) directs the moral education of children to a high plain by language requiring inculcation of the highest morality. Section 76 has the effect of distinguishing religious influence from issues of morality, precluding the first while requiring the second.

[81] The issue underlying this case illustrates this difference. Affidavits placed before the court by the School Board depose that some religions or churches with adherents in the community hold that homosexual activity is wrong. Yet in considering the highest morality as those words are used in the *School Act,* it is appropriate to consider the values embodied in the *Charter of Rights and Freedoms* and import them into the moral standard that must be applied: *Hills v. A.G. (Canada),* [1988] 1 S.C.R. 512, at 518. Recent cases under s. 15 of the *Charter of Rights and Freedoms* state that s. 15 protects equality rights for those of a homosexual orientation: *Egan v. Canada,* [1995] 2 S.C.R. 513; *Vriend v. Alberta,* [1998], 1 S.C.R. 493.

[82] The School Board says that s. 15 of the Charter protects persons, not conduct, and thus that it protects homosexual persons, not homosexual conduct. On this reasoning, the School Board says that it sought to balance tolerance for homosexual persons with the views of some parents that homosexual conduct is not acceptable. This position is not consistent with the observations at p. 595 in *Egan v. Canada* by Mr. Justice Cory that:

> …individuals, because of their uniqueness, are bound to vary in these personal characteristics which may be manifested by their sexual preferences whether heterosexual or homosexual. So long as those preferences do not infringe any laws, they should be tolerated.

The protection of the *Charter* is not intended to be hollow. Where a defining characteristic of a person is his or her conduct and the conduct is not unlawful, s. 15 of the *Charter* protects equality rights for that person complete with his or her conduct. I conclude that s. 76 does not protect a decision based on religious views as to homosexual conduct.

[83] I conclude, therefore, that s. 76(2) requires a school board to adhere to a high moral line which is consistent with the *Charter of Rights and Freedoms,* at the same time that s. 76(1) of the *School Act* precludes a school board from making a decision based in a significant way on religious considerations.

[84] On this reading of s. 76 of the *School Act,* the question is whether the Books resolution was based in a significant way on religious considerations. This is a question of fact.

[85] The primary evidence on the basis of the School Board's decision is from the lone trustee who provided evidence and from the Superintendent of Schools.

[86] The deponent trustee, one of the four trustees who voted in favour of the motion, deposed that prior to the April 24, 1997 School Board meeting she had received hundreds of calls from members of the Surrey community, the vast majority of whom supported the April 10, 1997 GALE resolution. She deposed that in reaching her decision on April 24, 1997 she considered as relevant to the motion the questions of age appropriateness of the books' subject matter, their necessity to teach the curriculum and whether they dealt with the subject matter in a way that reflects the needs and values of the Surrey community including parents. She deposed that another trustee who voted in favour of the motion expressed concern that the books would initiate discussion on a sensitive issue. A third trustee in support of the motion expressed concern that if the Board approved the books kindergarten and grade one students in the School District would be exposed to the issues (same-sex parents) raised by them, and stated that he considered the books to be age inappropriate because they would create confusion and conflict.

[87] In cross-examination on her affidavit, the trustee testified that she did not consider that the books by themselves would have an adverse effect on children. She spoke of the lack of community consensus on introducing the books into the classroom, and said that the lack of consensus was a factor in not approving the books. She agreed that the focus of discussion centred on the fact that the books raised issues of a sensitive nature, and weight was given to the concerns of parents. She confirmed her view that teaching on the subject of same-sex relationships should allow a child to validate beliefs that the relationship would be morally wrong from their religious viewpoint.

[88] In his affidavit, the Superintendent of Schools acknowledged his anticipation that approval of the three books as educational resource material would be a very controversial decision among parents. On cross-examination he testified that he felt parents would feel the decision was "values sensitive" for them. He stated that he had questions concerning the age appropriateness of the concepts in the books, but it is clear from the record that he did not recommend that the books not be approved.

[89] In its submissions the School Board referred to affidavits from parents and members of the community in support of its argument on s. (2) of the *Charter* that it had protected the parents' and children's freedom of religion by passing

the Books resolution. This affidavit evidence from parents included the following statements:

(i) "If the Three Books were used in either of our sons' classes, our children would be confused at the challenge to their own faith and family values";

(ii) "...I am opposed to the introduction of the Three Books into Kindergarten and Grade One classrooms for the following reasons:

(a) the Three Books portray same-sex couples...in a manner contrary to my personal religious beliefs";

(iii) "The Three Books would introduce to children in Kindergarten and Grade One a particular worldview or brand of morality. The morality or worldview is directly in conflict with deeply held family and religious values";

(iv) "We believe, and would like to teach our children that according to our religious views, the homosexual lifestyle is wrong";

(v) "This is a matter of significant religious importance to me and the views expressed by the Three Books conflict with my religious views and those of my family";

(vi) "My concern is that I and my wife be able to teach our children according to our religious beliefs without having the school teach them something, at an early age, which runs counter to what we believe";

(vii) "I am opposed in accordance with my religious beliefs to my children being taught a redefinition of the traditional family";

(viii) "We are opposed to the introduction of the Three Books...for the following reasons:

(a) Surrey Schools should not negate our right as parents to teach our children...in accordance with our family and religious views;

(b) it is our strongly held religious belief that homosexual behaviour, including same-sex couples, is contrary to the teaching of the Bible";

(ix) "I wish to teach my children according to my own religious beliefs and oppose lessons at school which contradict what I am attempting to teach my children";

(x) "The Three Books raise issues with respect to homosexuality and same-sex couples that are morally contentious. If used in Kindergarten and Grade One classrooms in Surrey they would create conflict between many families in the District who have religious or moral beliefs opposed to the views presented in the Three Books, and the teacher or school";

[...]

[92] In addition, the School Board filed affidavits from several religious leaders. These affidavits were countered by the petitioners with affidavits from other persons formally associated with churches. The affidavits from religious leaders filed by the School Board in support of its position include the following statements:

(i) from the Steering Committee of the Surrey Evangelical Churches: "Our Churches are extremely concerned that the Three Books present same-sex couples and introduce the issue of homosexuality in a positive light, contrary to the Biblical teachings and doctrine which form the basis of our beliefs";

(ii) from a pastor of a church: "The Three Books would introduce to children at the Kindergarten and Grade One levels a unique board [sic] of morality or worldview. This morality or worldview is directly in conflict with the morality and worldview of most members of the Evangelical Free Church";

(iii) from a priest of a Roman Catholic Church: "I am of the view that the Three Books create an irreconcilable conflict between the views stated in the Three Books regarding the topic of homosexuality, and the doctrine of the Church.

"...I am opposed to the introduction of issues relating to homosexuality and same-sex couples, which issues [sic] necessarily bring into conflict religious and moral views on the subject";

(iv) from a Muslim who is on the Surrey/Delta Management Committee of the B.C. Muslim Association: "The Three Books present homosexuality and homosexual conduct as acceptable and morally equal to heterosexuality. This contradicts the teachings of the Qur'an and the beliefs of Muslims";

(v) from a leader of the Guru Nanak Sikh Gurdwara Society: "In the Sikh faith, homosexuality is considered a moral and social sin which we are instructed to resist.

"I have read the books....This message directly conflicts with the religious teachings of the Sikh faith";

(vi) from a leader of the Verdic Hindhu Society: "...This message [from the books] directly conflicts with the teachings of the Hindhu faith. The Three Books display a lifestyle which we, as Hindhus, believe is immoral...."

[93] On review of all the evidence in this case on the basis of the School Board's decision, I conclude that when the School Board passed the Books resolution, some of the trustees who voted in favour of the resolution were motivated to a

significant degree by concern that parents and others in the School District would consider the books incompatible or inconsistent with their religious views on the subject of same-sex relationships.

[94] In addition to the respondent's affidavit evidence and its submissions in court to the effect that it did consider, and was entitled to consider, the views of parents that use of the books in the classroom would be contrary to their sincerely held religious and moral views, there is evidence that at least one trustee who voted for the motion (who did not provide an affidavit), has campaigned for several years to promote a greater role for religion in governance of the community, including on the issue of homosexuality. The evidence on the views and activities of this trustee, in the absence of an affidavit in explanation, reasonably supports the conclusion that this trustee's decision was significantly influenced by personal religious considerations on the issue of homosexuality.

[95] I conclude that by giving significant weight to personal or parental concern that the books would conflict with religious views, the Board made a decision significantly influenced by religious considerations, contrary to the requirement in s. 76(1) that schools be "conducted on strictly secular...principles."

[...]

V. CONCLUSION

[106] This decision is based upon a very old provision of the *School Act* enjoining religion or overt religious influence in the conduct of the schools. Many other issues were raised by the petitioners under the principles of administrative law. The petitioners also relied upon the *Charter of Rights and Freedoms,* s. 2(a) freedom of religion, s. 2(b) freedom of expression and s. 15 equality rights. In doing so the petitioners and the respondent cited many cases expressing great principles of law, including *Roncarelli v. Duplessis* (1959), 16 D.L.R. 689, [1959] S.C.R. 121 and those cases dealing with race and science in the schools. Given my conclusion on s. 76 of the *School Act,* and for the reasons of Mr. Justice Hollinrake in *Russow v. B.C.* (A.G.), *supra,* I do not address those issues.

[107] I conclude that the Books resolution is contrary to s. 76(1) of the *School Act,* and is therefore *ultra vires.*

[108] The Books resolution is hereby quashed. [...]

✗ NO
Living Together with Disagreement: Pluralism, the Secular, and the Fair Treatment of Beliefs in Canada Today
IAIN T. BENSON

PLURALISM AND THE SECULAR

This essay will examine two key terms in relation to our culture today: "pluralism" and the "secular." It will argue that both terms are generally insufficiently defined in popular contemporary usages, often frustrating rather than furthering the very principles they should represent. After examining these, I will turn to the fair treatment of beliefs in Canada today on the basis of what we have seen in relation to the discussion of pluralism and the secular. First, however, it is useful to note that religious beliefs (linked with "conscience" in section 2(a) of the Canadian Charter of Rights and Freedoms) have public dimensions. That is why our notion of the nature of the public sphere and its relation to beliefs is so critical.

THE PUBLIC NATURE OF THE RIGHTS OF "CONSCIENCE AND RELIGION"

It will be recalled that in the first decision of the Supreme Court of Canada dealing with the definition of Freedom of Conscience and Religion in section 2(a) of the Charter, then Chief Justice Dickson stated:

> The essence of the concept of freedom of religion is the right to entertain such religious beliefs as a person chooses, *the right to declare religious beliefs openly and without fear of hindrance or reprisal, and the right to manifest religious belief by worship and practice or by teaching and dissemination.*[1]

Note that the words employed are active, public words—"declare," "manifest," "practice," "teaching," "dissemination." We would do well to remember those words and their public dimensions at a time when many of the challengers wish to avoid a sharing of the public realm by a privatization of those rights that have a genuinely public dimension. In recent years, some would choose to limit religion by declaring it to be a private right only—something for home or church. Or else there is a suggestion, true in one way but which can be over-extended, that religious belief is one thing and religious conduct another.

TWO APPROACHES TO "PLURALISM" UNDER THE CANADIAN CONSTITUTION

It is important to consider the nature of pluralism in Canada. Like so many terms in our public discourse ("values," "secular," "liberalism," etc.), its common use can mask the fact that it is little analyzed. As such, if there are presuppositions in the term, or an ambiguous usage that is not discovered or discussed, we can be misled as to what is actually being said when the term is used. Pluralism can connote a kind of relativistic approach, as in "because we are a pluralistic society, such and such a moral position cannot have any public validity." It does not have to mean this, however, and in Canada our linkage of a language of pluralism with a firm commitment to group rights, for example, points us to a principled and what might be called structural or shared pluralism, rather than one that is relativistic or, perhaps, totalistic. For this totalistic notion of pluralism views society as moving toward the articulation of only one public policy, and such a view is antagonistic to the notion of plurality and tolerance of diversity. The political condition in Canada respects the modus vivendi, though, as I shall argue with examples drawn from recent legal cases. Whether it will continue to do so remains to be seen, as this foundational aspect is now very much under attack.

John D. Whyte has noted that the Constitution of Canada has not been framed on the basis of any individualistic conception of liberalism but, rather, of one that respects and nurtures each person's communities. Moreover, the two kinds of rights protected by the Charter, group rights and individual rights (which, as with "religion," overlap as both personal and communal), derive from different conceptions of the proper role of the state, both of which are reflected in the Constitution. In his words:

> There are two theoretical models for describing the modern democratic state. One derives from the political philosophy of liberalism, under which society is arranged without a particular conception of the good and in which individuals have claims of right to equal regard and respect. The other might be labelled the organic society, in which the primary focus is not the autonomy of the individual but the importance of nurturing communities or corporate life. Such a society adheres to a conception of the good in the sense that it accepts that the superior condition for individual well-being is not the maximization of personal autonomy but the growth of strong communities formed around common interests. The interest [sic] of individuals are best vindicated not through the recognition of each person's formal equality but through the joining together of those with similar interests to create nurturing, supportive, normative communities. An organic nation is comprised of these various communities each working out a political accommodation which reconciles conflicting interests but which allows as much of the normative role to the particular communities as possible....The truly effective

way to respect life and to achieve a fulfilled life may be through identification with a group and having the assurance that one community or another
recognizes one as having distinguishable substantive value.[2]

Consequently, as Professor Whyte observes:

> It is impossible to discern in the constitutional text either the clear direction
> to promote liberal values as wholeheartedly as possible or the direction to
> sustain communitarian values to the greatest extent possible. The Charter
> reflects the tension. Of course, it gives impetus to the nation's change to
> liberalism, but it does not reveal, in any precise way, where the limit should
> be drawn to protect other political values.[3]

The Canadian model depicted above does not start with the proposition that
either form of right is paramount, or will necessarily converge with or "trumps"
other claims, but instead looks for the proper sphere of operation of each. This
is a form of "structural pluralism" that must be respected. Recent commentary
in the United States has recognized the principles of structural pluralism. James
Skillen has noted that

> a just society is one in which multiple institutions and diverse spheres of
> responsibility can function together in freedom, under protection of the
> law[; so] then part of the legal obligation of a just government is to rec-
> ognize and protect that complex diversity of society. Closely related to this
> principle, and mutually inter-dependent with it, is the principle of religious
> freedom.... [G]overnment should act in accord with the principles of jus-
> tice by treating faiths and faith communities with equal public protection.
> Government cannot do this, however, without respecting the freedom and
> diversity of those faiths.[4]

Claims that are, therefore, totalistic, and which claim to represent in themselves all
of "public policy" where recognition as such effectively delegitimizes other legally
contestable perspectives, must be suspected of overreaching. Such totalistic claims for
"recognition" by any particular advocacy group ought to concern us if we are moving
toward developing a richer respect for structural pluralism that holds together notions
of group as well as individual rights and a plurality of moral perspectives.

THE NATURE OF THE "SECULAR" AND THE ILLUSION OF "NEUTRALITY"

The meaning of the term "secular" has changed over the last century and a half.
The term in general usage now means, typically, free *from* religion, as in "we
ought to keep religion out of the schools because they are secular." This was not
the original meaning, nor is it a definition that recognizes the modus vivendi

aspect of pluralism referred to above or the epistemological reality of moral acts in the lives of all citizens. We are, in short, all believers, and, as we shall see, our courts have recently come to acknowledge that any preemptive exclusion of "religion" from the category of "beliefs" that may operate in society is unfair to and intolerant of those beliefs that emanate from religious convictions, and gives a preferential position to the beliefs or convictions of atheists and agnostics. Such an exclusion is inconsistent with the principles of a free and democratic society. It is not simply a matter of how beliefs are expressed, but of what communities are nurtured and created by our analysis of pluralism that must be examined.

If we start off with the assumption (building it into our use of the term "secular") that religion has no place in the public sphere, then, of course, we shall tend to diminish the role of the religious in civil society. But this is really to adopt implicitly or explicitly the ideology of atheistically driven "secularism", since the term "secular," viewed historically, does not require, though it has come to imply, such a removal of the sacred dimension from the aspects of life it describes. Properly understood, the "secular" (which is better and more clearly understood and examined as the "public") is a realm of competing faith and/or belief claims, not a realm of "non-faith" or "nonbelief" claims. Given the current dominance of the atheistic definitions of "secular" and "separation of church and state," it will take some time for them to be redefined so as to better support the right ordering of freedoms in contemporary society.

Note how, in contemporary usage, "secular schools," "secular government," and so forth are widely understood to mean non-religious or not influenced by religion or religious principles. I would like to suggest that this is because we have adopted the atheistic or agnostic definition of "secular" in which the public sphere is preemptively stripped of religion and not a richer and more properly inclusive conception. The separation of church and state is, after all, a jurisdictional distinction important to both the church and the state. A valid separation should not preclude an equally valid *cooperation* between church and state. Most religious groups in the West, for example, do not in fact want the state to run the church or vice versa.

The historical change in the use of "secular" should be recognized. It is tempting to ignore the change in meaning by acquiescing in the use of the terms "secular" and "religious" as if they described different worlds. But they do not describe different worlds. They describe different functions. What we most often mean by the "secular" is the public or the state, and by "religion," a set of practices within the state. Therefore the separation of "religion" from something constructed as the "secular" serves, usually implicitly and often unintentionally, an anti-religious goal and is neither accurate nor just.

Where the *Oxford English Dictionary* defines "secular," the earliest examples of the use of the word suggesting that the secular is "non-sacred" in character occur as recently as the mid-nineteenth century.[5] This usage was coined by George Jacob Holyoake and popularized by him and those whom he influenced, such as Charles Bradlaugh, who were secularists (atheistic and agnostic in belief). It is from works such as theirs that the current usage derives, in which "secular" is understood to mean "free from religion."

In fact, this more recent use of "secular," which we may justly call the atheistic or agnostic interpretation, is seldom viewed alongside alternative understandings. This is not helpful since an atheistic definition, if used as the meaning for a central term such as "secular," fails to give a proper place to religion in the private and public dimensions of society. The atheistic "secular" becomes, in effect, a blueprint for the naked public square. A more informed historical understanding, built upon a richer epistemological ground, better reflects both the reality of beliefs in society and the principles of freedom that ought to undergird a properly civil society.

THE PARADIGM SHIFT ABOUT THE "SECULAR"

A most significant shift for the future of equality and how we understand accommodation and collisions of rights in law occurred in the case of *Chamberlain* v. *Surrey School District* (which will be discussed in more detail below), and this shift has not yet been sufficiently noted. The term "strictly secular" in the British Columbia *School Act* had to be defined. Did it mean, as held at trial, that "any influence by religion" nullified the "secular" (better understood as "public") nature of the school trustees' role and decisions? When they took into account the concern of local parents on the suitability of certain books as "classroom learning resources" and these concerns in turn were based, as some were, on the religious convictions of the parents, did this run afoul of the "strictly secular" aspect of the legislation? To hold this would have meant that, in effect, only atheists or agnostics had a right to have their beliefs fully respected in the public sphere.

Overturning the decision of the trial judge, Justice Mackenzie for the British Columbia Court of Appeal held that the "secular" must include religious beliefs and not be understood to place impediments in the way of religious believers. Understanding the "secular," public sphere in this way constitutes a shift of tremendous importance; it has relevance in various areas, such as, most recently, the question of the personal beliefs of marriage commissioners in relation to same-sex marriage. A majority of the Supreme Court of Canada subsequently endorsed the holding of the Appeal Court, finding, in effect, that Canada should have a "religiously inclusive" public sphere. In a sense the future requires us to realize that the question is never one of religion and the public, religion and the civic, or religion and law, but of religious belief *within* the public, religious believers and groups *within* the civic, and so forth. The sharp dichotomies of anti-religious secularism should no longer hold sway in our analysis in Canada. This is easy to say, but to do the identification and nuanced analysis required to supplant them is difficult, since it requires rethinking our descriptions from first principles, as we shall see in years ahead.

What inclusiveness demands is making the scope for dissent larger instead of smaller by invoking false dualisms to drive religion into the private and out of the public. Overcoming some of the conceptual confusions of the past in relation to such false dichotomies as I've mentioned must also be accompanied by a re-understanding of "secularism," a term that is almost never used with an awareness of its clearly identifiable anti-religious history. The term is usually employed with no definition at all that elides the history of its origins.

SECULARISM IS ANTI-RELIGIOUS

Secularism, as it is understood in what we may call the English tradition, is a particular ideology. When the term was coined by Holyoake in the mid-nineteenth century, he and those who followed him had an idea of driving religion out of the public sphere. Thus, for the courts to suggest, without analysis or argument on the point, or for academics to suggest, without analysis of the term, that Canada is based upon the principles of "secularism" (as some have done) indicates that they do not realize what they are dealing with.

Equality in relation to all sorts of believers, religious and non-religious, means that we have to think more deeply about the key terms we use to describe Canadian society as we go forward. If we live, as we do, in a society that has no religious establishment and allows public participation by all citizens (the term "secular" as most frequently used obscures these distinctions), it is one that is necessarily religiously inclusive and not one based upon the anti-religious ideology of secularism in which the public sphere is implicitly if not explicitly stripped of religion and religious influence.[6]

The implications of this for our thinking about religious belief in relation to such issues as public education curriculum and sexual orientation claims, or the responsibilities and limits of the role of civic of officials such as marriage commissioners, are obvious. We need a new paradigm to deal with religious belief in relation to equality rights. Even if we look to reconciling, instead of "balancing," in certain areas, as Justice Iacobucci suggested in an article some years ago,[7] we still need to overcome the privatized presumptions or the unrealistic expectations that undergird the false dualisms.

Social recognition is not something the law ought to promise to one side of legally contestable social debates. The law ought to be ensuring the open texture of civil society, not bringing its weight to bear on one side of the matter, for to do so risks tilting civil society against the freedoms that the law in general must protect for everyone.

CHAMBERLAIN V. SURREY SCHOOL DISTRICT: THE MEANING OF "SECULAR" IN CANADIAN LAW

In the years following the turn of the new millennium the nature of the "secular" was very much at issue in the *Chamberlain* series of legal decisions out of British Columbia. There, the British Columbia Court of Appeal rejected the newer atheistic use of "secular" and affirmed that the secular is a realm that properly has a place for beliefs that emerge from religious commitment. Justice Mackenzie, for himself and his colleagues in a unanimous three-justice panel of British Columbia's highest court, analyzed the term "secular" in the following manner:

> Can "strictly secular" in s. 76(1) of the *School Act* be interpreted as limited to moral positions devoid of religious influence? Are only those with a non-religiously informed conscience to be permitted to participate in decisions involving moral instruction of children in the public schools? Must those whose moral positions arise from a conscience influenced by religion be required to leave those convictions behind or otherwise be excluded from participation while those who espouse similar positions emanating from a conscience not informed by religious considerations are free to participate without restriction? Simply to pose the questions in such terms can lead to only one answer in a truly free society. Moral positions must be accorded equal access to the public square without regard to religious influence. A religiously informed conscience should not be accorded any privilege, but neither should it be placed under a disability. In a truly free society moral positions advance or retreat in their influence on law and public policy through decisions of public officials who are not required to pass a religious litmus test.
>
> A contrary interpretation is not only insupportable in principle, it would raise immense practical difficulties. How would it be determined that a moral position advanced from a conscience influenced by religion or not? If the restriction were applied only where the religious conviction was publicly declared it would privilege convictions based on a conscience whose influences were concealed over one openly proclaimed. The alternative would be to require inquiry as to the source of a moral conviction, whether religious or otherwise. Both alternatives are offensive and indefensible.[8]

A leading American scholar on the law relating to religion, Michael W. McConnell, has written the following:

> The beginning of wisdom in this contentious area of law is to recognize that neutrality and secularism are not the same thing. In the marketplace of ideas, secular viewpoints and ideologies are in competition with religious viewpoints and ideologies. It is no more neutral to favor the secular over the religious than it is to favor the religious over the secular. It is time for a

reorientation of constitutional law: *away* back from the false neutrality of the secular state, *toward* a genuine equality of rights.[9]

Consistent with the criticism of the use of the term "secular" presented in this essay, however, observe that while Professor (now Justice) McConnell correctly identifies the "non-neutral" nature of the state, he perpetuates the false bifurcation between "the secular" and "the religious." This, too, must change for there to be a proper delineation of the issues that are at stake in these areas. Still, despite this error, McConnell rightly criticizes the notion that there is a "neutrality" that can be stripped of religious beliefs and claims in such a manner that what is left represents an adequate "consensus" for civil society.

Suggestions that, for example, the use of picture books in kindergarten classrooms to show that same-sex parents are just the same as heterosexual parent couples is "neutral," show that the concept of "neutrality" is incoherent where matters are foundationally contested.

To parents who view respect for persons (as distinct from "recognizing," "welcoming," or "affirming") as all that can reasonably be required of them by civil society, it is rather alarming to be told in cool and dispassionate tones that neutrality requires that their children be taught that what the parents believe to be wrong is, in fact, right. This is what the case amounts to, and it is, in fact, a question of whether genuine respect is shown for religious adherents. The religious parents do not, after all, require that their "beliefs" be affirmed in the public school classroom.

Keeping in mind the nature of the modus vivendi and the danger of a totalizing or convergence liberalism (which assumes that some beliefs will simply slough away over time), it is interesting that the same-sex parenting picture books that were at issue in the kindergarten to grade 2 curriculum of the Surrey school board in the *Chamberlain* case were viewed by a recent commentator as simply "to promote mutual respect and understanding."[10] The author shows no indication that such public classroom promotion that implies the complete equivalency of homosexual/lesbian sexuality and heterosexual sexuality (implicit in being "Mom" and "Dad") is anathema to mainstream religious adherents whether they are Sikh, Hindu, Muslim, Catholic, Protestant, or Jewish.[11]

In giving the reasons of the Supreme Court majority in *Chamberlain,* Chief Justice McLachlin said:

33. Moreover, although parental involvement is important, it cannot come at the expense of respect of the values and practices of all members of the school community. The requirement of secularism in s. 76 of the *School Act,* the emphasis on tolerance in the Preamble, and the insistence of the curriculum on increasing awareness of a broad array of family types, all show, in my view, that parental concerns must be accommodated in a way that respects diversity. *Parental views, however important, cannot override the imperative placed upon the British Columbia public schools to mirror*

the diversity of the community and teach tolerance and understanding of difference. (emphasis added)

Justice Gonthier, in dissent, though not disagreed with by the majority judges on this point, stated:

[I]t is a feeble notion of pluralism that transforms "tolerance" into "mandated approval or acceptance". In my view, the inherent dignity of the individual not only survives such moral disapproval, but to insist on the alternative risks treating another person in a manner inconsistent with their human dignity....[12]

We have seen, above, how some commentators place a requirement of approval on the list of things necessary to respect the dignity of the person, taking a "pick one" approach rather than an "exemption and accommodation" approach. This is an error, since, as I have suggested already, "sexual conduct," like "religious belief," is a matter that should be essentially private, is highly contested, and cannot properly form part of the core notion of civic excellence without driving other conceptions (also perfectly legal to hold) about human sexual conduct into the darkness.

Justice Gonthier added the following trenchant remarks about a kind of "false tolerance":

I also note that language espousing "tolerance" ought not [*sic*] be employed as a cloak for the means of obliterating disagreement. Section 15 of the Charter protects all persons from discrimination on numerous enumerated and analogous grounds, including the grounds of religion and sexual orientation. *Language appealing to "respect", "tolerance", "recognition" or "dignity", however, must reflect a two-way street in the context of conflicting beliefs, as to do otherwise fails to appreciate and respect the dignity of each person involved in any disagreement, and runs the risk of escaping the collision of dignities by saying "pick one". But this cannot be the answer.* In my view, the relationship between s. 2 and s. 15 of the Charter, in a truly free society, must permit persons who respect the fundamental and inherent dignity of others and who do not discriminate, to still disagree with others and even disapprove of the conduct or beliefs of others. Otherwise, claims for "respect" or "recognition" or "tolerance", where such language becomes a constitutionally mandated proxy for "acceptance", tend to obliterate disagreement.[13] (emphasis added)

A more recent decision from the Supreme Court of Canada suggests that a more nuanced balancing of rights is possible than was seen in the original decision and in some of the arguments of the Supreme Court judges in *Chamberlain*.[14] One can only hope that they signal a better approach to future cases in which "Chamberlain"-type conflicts are raised.[15]

NOTES

1. *R. v. Big M Drug Mart Ltd.* [1985] 1 SCR 295 at 336.

2. John D. Whyte, "Is the Private Sector Affected by the Charter?" in Lynn Smith, ed., *Righting the Balance: Canada's New Equality Rights* (Saskatoon: The Canadian Human Rights Reporter Inc., 1986) 145 at 174–175.

3. Ibid. 177–178.

4. James Skillen, "The Theoretical Roots of Equal Treatment," in Stephen V. Monsma and J. Christopher Soper, eds., *Equal Treatment of Religion in a Pluralistic Society* (Grand Rapids: Eerdmans, 1998) 55 at 72.

5. The *Oxford English Dictionary,* 2nd ed., s.v. "secular," "secularism," and "secularity." All uses suggesting a meaning of "secular" that denote an absence of connection with religion postdate G.J. Holyoake, *The Principles of Secularism Briefly Explained* (London: Holyoake & Co., 1859).

6. The trial judgment of Madam Justice Saunders in *Chamberlain,* in which "strictly secular" was interpreted to mean not based upon or influenced by religion, is a good example of a secularistic understanding of the meaning of "secular principles." See *Chamberlain* (1998) 60 BCLR (3d) 311 (SC). For a detailed analysis of this decision in relation to the Court of Appeal judgment which overturned it, see Iain T. Benson and Brad Miller, "Court Corrects Erroneous Understanding of the Secular and Respects Parental Rights," LexView No. 40.0 (2000), available at http://www.culturalrenewal.ca/qry/page.taf?id=64. Accessed August 22, 2011.

7. Justice Frank Iacobucci, "Reconciling Rights: The Supreme Court of Canada's Approach to Competing Charter Rights" (2003) 20 Sup Ct L Rev (2d) 137–167. The argument here is that "reconciling" has advantages over "balancing" as an analytical and practical tool in certain types of cases. The article reviews where reconciliation might be the best approach to what could, at first glance, appear to be a clash or conflict of rights.

8. *Chamberlain v. Surrey School District* (2000) 80 BCLR (3d) 181 (CA) reversing (1998) 60 BCLR (3d) 311 (SC), paras. 28–29 (see also note 6 above).

9. Michael W. McConnell, "Equal Treatment and Religious Discrimination," in Monsma and Soper, *Equal Treatment* 30 at 33.

10. John Russell, "How to be Fair to Religious and Secular Ideals within the Liberal State," *The Advocate* 60, no. 3 (May 2002) 345 at 352.

11. It is, of course, the case that there is divergence within religions as to the acceptability of homosexual and lesbian sexual conduct. This, however, says nothing about the respect that should be owed to communities that define themselves around one side of divergent beliefs. All belief systems imply divergence, and the fact that both feminists and civil libertarians disagree is not an argument against the valid claims for respect that should be owed to feminists or civil libertarians.

12. *Chamberlain* [2002] 4 SCR 710.

13. Ibid. at para. 134.

14. *Multani v. Commission scolaire Marguerite-Bourgeoys* [2006] 1 SCR 256.

15. This paper is part of a longer monograph by Iain Benson published under the same title by the Chester Ronning Centre for the Study of Religion and Public Life in 2010.

POSTSCRIPT

These court rulings deal directly with the question of the legitimacy of using religiously based arguments in debating and deciding matters of public policy. Contemporary liberal political theorists have often been critical of the use of religiously based arguments in political debates. They frequently argue that the modern liberal democratic polity has to be protected from the potentially divisive and destabilizing impact of public religious conflict. To do this, a twofold strategy must be used: politics must be secularized, and religious beliefs must be kept to the private realm, not the public.

Some contemporary liberal theorists take these assumptions to mean that all religiously based lines of reasoning should be excluded from the public sphere. Instead, citizens should employ only "secular" or "rational" positions that are accessible to all. Richard Rorty, for example, argues that in contemporary society it should "seem bad taste to bring religion into discussions of public policy" in his article "Religion as Conversation Stopper," *Philosophy and Social Hope* (London: Penguin, 2000), p. 169. In her judgment, Justice Saunders seems to have gone even beyond this position, contending that even if religious arguments are not employed, any proof that public policy decisions could be rooted in religious beliefs could be a basis for excluding such decisions.

Other contemporary liberal theorists take a less exclusionary point of view. Robert Audi and John Rawls both maintain that such a limiting approach is discriminatory and serves only to silence religiously motivated advocates. They assert instead that citizens may use religiously motivated arguments as long as they also advance other arguments in support of their position that do not depend in any way on religious belief. Governments and courts should rely on these broader arguments, which are open to everyone, as the ultimate basis for making their decisions.

Jonathan Chaplin gives a detailed examination and critique of these issues in "Beyond Liberal Restraint: Defending Religiously Based Arguments in Law and Public Policy," *UBC Law Review* 33, Special Issue (2000), pp. 617–46. Chaplin states that there is little real evidence that religiously based arguments will contribute to greater divisiveness in society, and he sets out his own views on the appropriate role for religiously based argumentation in the public sphere. In addition to Chaplin's article, this special issue of the UBC Law Review on "Religion, Morality, and Law" contains a useful collection of articles dealing with the relationship between religion and public policy. And John von Heyking's "Harmonization of Heaven and Earth? Religion, Politics, and Law in Canada" in this same issue provides helpful background to this debate. See also the useful collection of essays in Douglas Farrow, ed., *Recognizing Religion in a Secular Society: Essays in Pluralism, Religion and Public Policy* (Montreal and Kingston: McGill-Queen's University Press, 2004). In both volumes, articles by Iain Benson discuss the nature of "secular" and "secularism" as an anti-religious ideology. Benson's articles have been cited with approval by the Supreme Court of Canada and the Constitutional Court of South Africa (the latter in its *Fourie* decision of 2005). Iain Benson's article, "Considering Secularism" can be found on pp. 83–98 of the Farrow volume. Readers will also find William Galston's chapter entitled "Religion and the Limits of Liberal Democracy" useful.

Students will also find instructive the following materials on the interaction between religion and law in Canada: Paul Horwitz, "The Sources and Limits of Freedom of Religion in a Liberal Democracy: Section 2(a) and Beyond," *University of Toronto Faculty Law Review* 54, no. 1 (Winter 1990), pp. 1–64; Timothy Macklem, "Faith as a Secular Value," *McGill Law Journal* 45, no. 1 (2000), pp. 3–63; and Albert Menendez, *Church and State in Canada* (Amherst, NY: Prometheus Books, 1996). John von Heyking, who is a professor of political science at the University of Lethbridge, also maintains a useful list of resources covering the relationship between religion and politics. This list can be accessed at http://people.uleth.ca/~john. vonheyking/.

Should Representation in Parliament Mirror Canada's Social Diversity?

✔ **YES**

TIM SCHOULS, "Why Group Representation in Parliament Is Important"

✘ **NO**

JOHN H. REDEKOP, "Group Representation in Parliament Would Be Dysfunctional for Canada"

Canada is a representative democracy in which, every four or five years, we choose certain individuals (members of Parliament) to act on our behalf. We empower them to act as our agents and to represent our interests in the national decision-making process. As long as representative democracy has existed, there has been debate over the exact nature that representation should take.

Much of this debate has focused on how the representative is expected to carry out his or her duties. Traditionally, three different views of representation have been put forward. First, there are those who argue that the representative is to act as a *trustee*. That is, members of Parliament are given a mandate to act as they best see fit on behalf of the interests of the electors. MPs are given considerable leeway to exercise their personal judgment in balancing the interests of their constituents with those of the broader community and in coming up with policies that best serve the common good. While the representatives can exercise wide latitude in making decisions, the voter will hold them accountable by removing them from office at the end of their term if they are perceived to have failed in adequately representing the voter's interests.

Second, there are those who argue that the representative is to act primarily as a *delegate*. According to this view, members of Parliament are to act primarily as they have been instructed to by the voters rather than trusting their own judgment as a guide. Representatives should not stray too far from the explicit wishes of their constituents. A variety of techniques such as constituent surveys, public hall meetings, and even telephone referendums have been used in recent years by MPs, especially those from the former Canadian Alliance party, before voting on a particular issue in an attempt to ascertain what the "instructions" of the electorate were.

Third, representatives have been seen as first and foremost *party members* who act and vote primarily according to the dictates of the party leadership. This perspective assumes that the representatives in a party act as a team and that voters choose which team they feel best represents their interests. Like the trustee model, the electorate must wait until the next election to render a judgment on the success of the representative in representing its interests. The debates that follow in Issues Thirteen and Fourteen address weaknesses of the party model of representation and ways that these deficiencies in representative government can be addressed.

In recent years, the debate over representation has shifted toward a more fundamental question—to what extent do the representatives in Parliament reflect the characteristics of ethnicity, language, and gender that are found in the population at large. On one level, this argument suggests that to be truly "representative," Parliament should be composed of the same proportion of social groups as is Canadian society at large. Parliament, in other words, should be a microcosm of Canadian society. If the population is composed of 51 percent women, 6 percent visible minorities, and 4 percent Aboriginal people, then there should be at least the same proportion of representatives elected to Parliament from each of these groups. A basic premise of this argument is that voters, especially those from minority and marginalized groups within society, will not see the decisions of Parliament as being fully legitimate unless the voters see themselves reflected in the social makeup of the legislature. As the social and cultural makeup of Canada changes, our political institutions could increasingly lose credibility if their composition does not adequately reflect the changing face of the country.

However, this argument goes beyond the question of simply increasing the numerical representation of certain social groups, such as women, in Parliament. It argues that representation is important because, once elected, women will act in the interests of women. They will interpret issues and respond to them differently than a male representative would. Thus, the election of women and minority groups to Parliament would result in substantive changes in the content of public policy, as the views of groups once marginalized and unrepresented in the political system would now be given voice within the corridors of power. Only those who know from experience what it is to be a woman, an Aboriginal person, or a member of a visible minority can truly represent other members of these groups.

In the essays below, we examine in greater depth this view of representation. Tim Schouls sets out the philosophical case for ensuring that the social diversity of Canada is represented in the Canadian legislature. In response, John Redekop examines the implications of this move away from more traditional definitions of representation and questions both the wisdom and practicality of such an approach.

✔ **YES**

Why Group Representation in Parliament Is Important
TIM SCHOULS

An increasing number of Canadians are convinced that the system of parliamentary representation in Canada is unfair because it is seen as unrepresentative of Canada's social diversity as a whole. Parliament has long reflected the regional and linguistic composition of Canada by allocating seats in the House of Commons and Senate in a manner that ensures adequate representation of provincial interests at the national level. But this exclusive concern for provincial and regional representation is now being challenged by nonterritorial groups who demand representation on the basis of characteristics that are not tied to geography. These groups argue that if the full diversity of Canada's population is to be reflected in Parliament, its representative character must be expanded beyond that of territory to include guaranteed seats for disadvantaged groups such as women, Aboriginal peoples, ethnic and visible minorities, and people with disabilities. The belief here is that parliamentary representatives must share central experiences and assumptions with those they represent if those representatives are to understand their constituents' needs and interests. Conversely, these groups believe that they cannot be adequately represented if their needs and interests are not advanced by those who share their gender, Aboriginal status, ethnicity, race, or disability.

The conventional Canadian approach to representative democracy, as represented in the article that follows by John Redekop, is generally hostile to claims for guaranteed group-based representation. According to Redekop's view, effective representation does not depend upon representatives and constituents sharing the same personal attributes. Instead, the effectiveness of representatives is measured by the degree to which they are able to present and advance the concerns and claims of their constituents. According to his line of argument, just as lawyers can represent clients who are very different from them, so too can representatives protect the interests of those whose lives have little in common with their own.

While this article will not take direct issue with this more traditional understanding of democratic representation, it will argue that democracy in Canada can be considerably deepened and enhanced when the composition of the House of Commons substantially reflects the social diversity of the Canadian population.[1] No doubt, MPs can represent constituents who are very different from them, but at the same time, it is not always obvious that this representation has been effective in cases where the constituents in question have been subject to historical disadvantage and marginalization. Of course, not all groups in Canadian society have been marginalized or have suffered disadvantage, but for those that have, their argument that seats in the House of Commons be guaranteed to them is worthy of serious examination. For democracy implies equality, but where conditions of marginalization and disadvantage exist, it necessarily follows that some groups possess greater opportunity, and thus privileges and powers that others do not. In the Canadian parliamentary setting, white males from professional and business backgrounds have historically dominated the House of Commons and Senate, and, as a result, it is they who have traditionally held a monopoly upon the political reigns of power. Conversely, many women, Aboriginal peoples, certain ethnic and visible minorities, and people with disabilities claim that they have been marginalized, which means, among other things, that they have been minimally represented in parliamentary discussions and decision-making processes. This article will argue that where political marginalization of groups has historically existed, active reform to secure these groups seats in the House of Commons is a healthy democratic response. Not only will such reform ensure marginalized groups a greater presence and thus a voice in the parliamentary process, but also such reform may encourage the development of legislation and laws that take more fully into account the views of marginalized groups. In short, an active reform process will counteract the current imbalance in political power and so promote greater democratic equality of opportunity and participation in the House of Commons for Canada's socially diverse groups.

GROUP IDENTITY IN CANADA

It could be argued that to focus exclusively upon demands by marginalized groups for political inclusion within the House of Commons is to largely miss the point of group identity politics in Canada. The range of political differences and objectives represented by Canada's diverse population is extensive, pushing far beyond the kinds of solutions that a politics of inclusion within the House of Commons can offer. To be sure, over the last twenty-five years or so, Canadians have begun to define themselves in new ways, and the politics of parliamentary inclusion is in large part an initiative that attempts to address those changes. For political purposes, Canadians used to identify themselves largely with their provinces of origin, with their use of French or English as their first language, and with their Catholic or Protestant religion. In response, the House of Commons was set up, both in terms of its allocation of seats and in terms of representation within cabinet, to reflect this geographic, linguistic, and religious diversity. In recent years, however, a new set of identity categories has become increasingly salient for many Canadians, categories associated primarily with changing conceptions of ethnicity and with the newfound political relevance of gender. Immigration and demographic trends of the 1970s to the 1990s have made Canada a far more multiethnic and multicultural country, while strong feminist initiatives during this same time frame have elevated the political status of women. New Canadians with origins in the Caribbean, Africa, Middle East, Central and South America, and Asia identify themselves not simply as provincial residents speaking either English or French but, more importantly, as members of ethnic groups with distinctive perspectives and interests to offer to the broader Canadian political agenda. Feminists, meanwhile, point out that the social and political structures of Canada reinforce men's power to the detriment of women. In response, redress of the current structural imbalance of power between men and women constitutes a central component of the feminist political agenda. In short, attachments to geography, language, and religion are receding in their overall political importance. At the same time, attachments to ethnicity and gender are becoming more significant politically. Against these shifting demographic trends, it is therefore not surprising that the conventional geography-based strategy for allocating House of Commons seats is coming under increasing attack.

However, despite the need to address the challenge of representation in the House of Commons for the marginally represented categories of women and ethnic groups, Canadian identity politics is more typically driven by demands for Aboriginal self-government and the recognition of Quebec's "distinct society." Like women and ethnic minorities, Aboriginal peoples and the citizens of Quebec argue that the existing conventions of representation do not grant them standing that is proportional to their numbers in Canada. From the perspectives of their leaders, however, greater representation in Parliament will not guarantee Aboriginal peoples and the citizens of Quebec the kind of legislative power they need to secure their political objectives within Canada. Their numbers are simply too small and their influence too weak to counteract the legislative priorities of the non-Aboriginal, non-Québécois parliamentary majority. Hence, Aboriginal peoples demand an equal partnership with federal and provincial governments based upon the recognition of their inherent right to self-government, while Quebeckers demand at minimum an expansion of their powers within the federal system of government so as to increase their provincial autonomy within Canada. Thus, when Aboriginal peoples and Quebeckers claim that they do not enjoy equal powers within Canada, they typically seek solutions within the realm of intergovernmental affairs rather than parliamentary representation.

When considering the arguments for greater parliamentary representation for disadvantaged or marginalized groups within Canada, it is important to realize from the outset that the demands for political inclusion by Aboriginal peoples, the citizens of Quebec, women, and ethnic and visible minorities are not naturally all of one piece. Aboriginal peoples and Quebeckers demand more autonomy *from* Parliament through self-government and special provincial status (or secession), while women and ethnic and visible minorities demand more autonomy *within* Parliament through elevated levels of representation. In fact in many respects, the demands of the former two groups are mirror images of those of the latter groups. Be that as it may, the demands for equal representation within Parliament remain an important concern for some groups. The intent of this article is to draw attention to only this very small piece of the larger, often poorly interlocking, Canadian identity puzzle.

REPRESENTATIONAL DEFICITS

On the surface, there is an undeniable, indeed, almost irrefutable, logic attached to the demand that the House of Commons reflect the diversity of the Canadian population. At present, for example, electoral mechanisms organize Canadians into geographically bound constituencies. While Redekop is quite right to point out that dividing voters into constituency groups makes sense from a practical point of view, such a division also carries with it the assumption that voters' primary political identity flows from their attachment to territory. MPs are thus linked to their constituents in geographic terms. The geographical division of the electorate encourages voters to think of their varied interests (whether relating to jobs, social security, the environment, etc.) largely in terms of where they live.

Now, while features associated with geography may well shape citizens' identities in some respects, Canadians also possess diverse identities by virtue of their cultural, gender, ethnic, and religious differences, which have very little to do with geography. It therefore stands to reason that along with geographic affiliation, Canadians may want to be represented by those who share their Aboriginal status, gender, ethnicity, or religious identity. There is an intuitive logic attached to the idea, for example, that when legislative initiatives dealing with abortion, childcare, or pay equity are before the House of Commons, female constituents may want to be represented by women who can identify with these issues because they are women. Similarly, when legislative initiatives dealing with reserve-based economic ventures or housing starts are before the House, it makes sense that Aboriginal constituents may want to have Aboriginal people representing their interests. According to this line of reasoning then, there is clearly something amiss when representation within the House is monopolized by a single group (upper- and middle-class males, for example), a group, moreover, that most likely possesses a relatively limited range of perspectives. Indeed, most well-intentioned Canadians would probably readily admit that where underrepresentation of certain groups exists, reforms ought to be encouraged to stimulate a more proportional balance of representation in the House.

While there have been a few improvements, it is undeniably the case that the composition of the House of Commons is only a very pale reflection of the diverse social characteristics of the Canadian population, as can be seen in the following three examples. In the 1988 federal election, thirty-nine, or 13.2 percent, of the MPs elected were women; in the 1993 election, fifty-four, or 18.3 percent, were women; in the 1997 and 2000 elections, sixty-one, or 20.2 percent, were women. This percentage increased only to 21 in the 2004 election. Given that women constitute 51 percent of Canada's population, the severity of their underrepresentation in the House is hard to miss.[2] In the case of Aboriginal peoples and visible minorities, underrepresentation in the House is even more striking.[3] Aboriginal peoples constitute approximately 4 percent of Canada's population, yet they were able to capture only 1 percent of the seats (three of a total 295) in each of the 1988 and 1993 elections.[4] Visible minorities, meanwhile, while constituting 6.3 percent of Canada's population, captured only 2 percent of the seats (six out of 295) in 1988, though they improved their fortunes slightly by increasing their share to 3 percent (nine out of 295) in the election of 1993.[5] Compare these lean numbers to the following scenario. If a proportional share of seats were given to each of the three groups mentioned above, women would be entitled to 153 seats, Aboriginal peoples to twelve seats, and visible minorities to nineteen seats out of the total 301.[6]

The obvious question here is why do women, Aboriginal peoples, and visible minorities persist in being so severely underrepresented in the House of Commons? There is no short answer to this question, for the barriers that inhibit each group from entering electoral politics are numerous and in many respects different from one another. Women, for example, have traditionally avoided political life at the national level because the heavy demands of family life and a political career often strain significantly against one another. Moreover, the challenge associated with securing financing to contest constituency nominations and run campaigns, coupled with the perception that the fierce competition associated with politics is symptomatic of a male domain, has made the political arena at the national level minimally appealing for many women.[7] Aboriginal candidates share with women the structural barrier of limited financing. In addition, as the Committee for Aboriginal Electoral Reform argues, "Canada's history of assimilationist policies has had an adverse impact on Aboriginal perceptions of Parliament and the value of participating within it."[8] The negative feelings Aboriginal peoples hold against Parliament as a colonial instrument of oppression means that many Aboriginal people are inclined not to vote in federal elections. This in turn discourages parties from fielding Aboriginal candidates, as there is little incentive for them to use such Aboriginal candidates in attempts to win a largely apathetic Aboriginal vote. Barriers inhibiting the participation of visible minorities are also readily identifiable. For example, Daiva Stasiulis argues that for many recent immigrants a significant barrier exists in the form of lack of familiarity with Canada's two official languages and with the customs of the British parliamentary tradition.[9] This barrier is compounded in turn by party politics that tend to identify the issues of Canadian politics along a French–English continuum and to engage in the recruitment of candidates by using old, well-established networks that have little, if any, connections to the immigrant community.

Given these structural barriers, it seems but a small step to justify reforms aimed at securing a proportional number of women, Aboriginal peoples, and ethnic and visible minorities in the House of Commons. Moreover, the case for inclusion only gathers strength when we recognize that the primary reason women, Aboriginal peoples, and ethnic and visible minorities are absent from the House of Commons is that they have been ignored and marginalized by the male hierarchy that holds power. Given that men dominate the House of Commons, it only stands to reason that they will have greater opportunity and power to advance their perspectives and legislate their preferences. Conversely, it has been well documented that, relative to men, women suffer greater social and economic disadvantage, a condition that in turn means that women have fewer political resources than men. Aboriginal peoples and ethnic and visible minorities, meanwhile, have long struggled against what Iris Marion Young calls cultural imperialism.[10] In the Canadian setting, cultural imperialism has typically manifested itself in the form of English and French cultures establishing societywide norms. Aboriginal, ethnic, and visible minority cultures, conversely, were traditionally stigmatized as being inferior and in need of transformation to align them more closely with the perspectives and worldviews of the two dominant cultures.

THEORIES OF REPRESENTATION

It is largely in reaction to these structural barriers that numerous calls for reform leading to a more proportional balance of representation in Parliament have been issued over the years. In essence, calls for proportional representation constitute a claim to tip the scales of the currently imbalanced composition of the House of Commons toward a more balanced representation of Canada's social diversity. If the political assumptions associated with white male privilege hamper the capacity of minorities to gain access to the House of Commons, then on democratic grounds surely no effort should be spared to get more minority representatives into the House. Moreover, the urgency that many marginalized groups attach to their claims for inclusion flows directly from the fact that the House of Commons lies at the symbolic heart of representative government in Canada. It is with this state institution more than any other that the primary qualification to become an MP is purely and simply the ability to represent. No doubt, as Redekop points out, many MPs get elected simply because they are better than their opponents in capturing the vote. But in the end, the test of good service is established by the degree to which constituents judge their MP to have been an effective representative on their behalf. This stands in sharp contrast to employment within the judiciary or bureaucracy, for example, where professional expertise and academic qualifications are of first importance. Simply put, legislatures exist to represent the population they serve; this is their central function. It is therefore imperative from the point of view of numerous marginalized groups that, if they are to achieve social and political equality in any meaningful sense, they simply must achieve proportional standing in the parliamentary domain where many of their interests are so regularly considered and debated.

If the case for more proportional inclusion in the House of Commons is so compelling, then why do so many Canadians accept with little trouble the prevailing patterns of white, male-dominated representation? In order to get a handle on this question, it is important that we step back for a moment and examine with some care the conflicting understandings that lie behind the idea of representation itself.

To date, there has been significant agreement in Canada that the practice of parliamentary democracy ought to adhere to a liberal conception of representation. From a liberal point of view, it is the individual who is to be treated as the most important of all political entities. This means that when it comes to representation, each individual is to count equally as one, and no one as more than one. In the context of elections, moreover, this concern for individual equality translates into the well-known slogan One Person, One Vote. What is of principal importance from the liberal point of view, then, is that while group interests can be advanced (given that it is individuals who form groups for the deliberate purpose of promoting common interests), individual interests must not be ignored in the process. Indeed, for liberals, to represent groups exclusively potentially poses two immediate dangers to the individual. First, when MPs represent group interests, they tend to regard those interests as held by all members of the group. However, not all group members may hold the same interests. For example, some women may dissent from a particular daycare strategy, yet if women are treated as a group, MPs may be tempted to regard the endorsement of the strategy by some women as an endorsement by all. Focusing upon the interests of each and every individual gets around this problem of universalizing interests. Second, to focus upon the interests of groups brings with it the possibility that MPs will privilege some groups over others. In this scenario, not only are dissenting individuals within privileged groups left unrepresented, but so too are all members of groups who are not fortunate enough to gain the attention of MPs in the first place.

In the interests of equality of representation, then, representatives are elected to advance the individual interests of their individual constituents. To be sure, the interests of constituents will regularly conflict, and so the MP will be forced to make compromises and secure tradeoffs. The measure of effective representation is determined when, despite being faced by the challenge of conflicting interests, MPs are nevertheless able to take appropriate positions demonstrating that they have taken the interests of all their constituents into account. The issue, then, is not who is in the House of Commons doing the representing, but rather whether the MP, regardless of personal characteristics, is able to get the job done on behalf of his or her constituents. In short, MPs may well possess different social, ethnic, or sexual characteristics from those they represent, but this should not matter if MPs demonstrate a constant readiness to respond in helpful ways to their constituents' needs.

This liberal argument of representation is certainly a very powerful one. But on its own, this liberal theory simply does not do full justice to the political marginalization and exclusion that many women, Aboriginal peoples, and ethnic and visible minorities experience. As Redekop so powerfully argues, men can represent women (much as a male lawyer can represent a female client) if the issue in question is a legislative initiative to which both men and women agree. But what Redekop fails to take seriously is that with respect to many issues, women, Aboriginal peoples, and visible and ethnic minorities will want to be represented by those who are like them because they believe that their identities carry with them distinctive experiences that white male MPs will be hard-pressed to understand. Women, for example, may possess experiences and consequently perspectives that are distinct from those of men with respect to the issues of childbearing and child care, sexual harassment and violence, the division of paid and unpaid labour, and the matter of women's exclusion from significant portions of the economic and political world.[11] Furthermore, with respect to Aboriginal peoples, Ovide Mercredi and Mary Ellen Turpel argue, "As Peoples with distinct cultures, languages, governments, territories and populations in Canada, we must be recognized as full and equal participants in the Canadian political system. We can speak for ourselves and no one else has the political or spiritual authority to speak for us. Canadians cannot speak for us because Canadians are different."[12] What is at issue here is not so much the capacity of MPs to advocate on behalf of their female, Aboriginal, or ethnic and visible minority constituents per se; minorities would certainly endorse any initiative that sees MPs support and advance their political agendas. More directly, what is at issue is the desire of women, Aboriginal peoples, and ethnic and visible minorities to gain a more proportional balance in the House of Commons on the grounds that they have been marginalized and excluded from representing themselves in the past.

At the same time, it is critical to underscore the point that the leaders of marginalized groups do not generally stake their claim for greater inclusion on the grounds that they share common interests–interests, moreover, that they believe only their own representatives are capable of putting before the House of Commons. Such an argument cannot provide the moral foundation for a claim to greater inclusion, because the experiences of marginalized groups are normally too varied to be contained within a single common interest. Women have different perspectives on abortion, child care, and pay equity, for example, while Aboriginal peoples have different perspectives on economic development, land claims, and self-government. Within their respective communities, women and Aboriginal peoples may thus share common policy concerns, but this does not mean that they will also share the same views on how those concerns ought to be handled. Minority groups are not homogeneous, possessing single, distinct policy perspectives. Such images portray far too simplistic a view of the world. Because minority groups do not by definition possess common policy interests, the strength of the argument for greater inclusion in the House of Commons necessarily lies elsewhere.

The argument for greater inclusion in the House of Commons gathers far more strength when considered within the framework of political marginalization or exclusion. The representational claim of marginalized groups is a forceful one because groups want to overcome the barriers of domination that have excluded them from participating in an equitable way in the House in the past. As the argument goes, if the distinct voices and (internally multiple) perspectives of marginalized social groups are not represented in the House, then it is almost certainly the case that the legislative initiatives and policy outcomes of the dominant white male majority will (continue to) prevail. In essence, what marginalized groups are saying is that they have a right to participate in these parliamentary discussions whatever their opinion may be on the matter under consideration. In this sense, the demands for parliamentary inclusion put forward by women, Aboriginal people, and visible and ethnic minorities flow from their common experiences of exclusion as groups, and from their mutual desire to engage more directly in parliamentary debate and decision making. To be sure, as Redekop points out, inclusion in parliamentary debate is not in and of itself enough to guarantee satisfactory legislative outcomes for marginalized groups. Influence can be effective only to the degree that marginalized groups can make their presence felt where power in parliamentary government is exercised—by the majority party and, more particularly, by the prime minister and cabinet drawn from the majority party. At the same time, however, without presence in the House of Commons, there is little opportunity for marginalized groups to exercise any influence at all.

The larger point that the leaders of marginalized groups seek to establish, however, is that because white males have traditionally monopolized parliamentary power, they cannot at this juncture in history take the place of the very groups they have marginalized by standing in as their representatives. As social groups, women, Aboriginal peoples, and visible and ethnic minorities need to be represented by other women, Aboriginal peoples, and visible and ethnic minorities because they share identities, which goes along with having been historically excluded. Thus, for example, men may be able to advance women's interests, but what men cannot do is stand in for women when women want to have all their diversity *as women* represented in the House of Commons. This is a task that only women can perform for themselves. Against historical patterns of exclusion, the presence of women in the House of Commons ensures that all the diverse and quite possibly conflicting interests of women will actually be heard and debated in Canada's central representative political arena.[13]

In sum, the proportional presence of women, Aboriginal peoples, and visible and ethnic minorities in the House of Commons matters because this presence would have the effect of counteracting the current hierarchy of white male power. A more sustained and numerically balanced presence would help to raise the profile of marginalized groups and thereby possibly place their multiple issues more regularly before the House. In this vein, Young argues, "The principle of group representation calls for some means by which the needs, interests, knowledge, and social perspective of oppressed or disadvantaged groups receive explicit and formal representation in political discussions and decision-making. The primary argument for such group representation is that where there are social group differences and some groups are privileged and others oppressed, group representation is necessary to produce a legitimate communicative forum."[14] Proportional representation of marginalized groups in the House of Commons would ensure that the full range of views represented by Canada's diverse population would have the opportunity for expression on a consistent and ongoing basis. This may in turn encourage a situation in which "those who had previously monopolized positions of power and influence might be equally encouraged to recognize their partiality and bias."[15]

OBJECTIONS

In the article following, Redekop raises a number of objections against the arguments put forward thus far. Let me conclude by addressing the three that are most significant.

First, Redekop argues that a politics of parliamentary inclusion based on gender, ethnic, or other minority identities introduces or possibly intensifies divisions between Canadian citizens–divisions, moreover, that arguably may not be of the first importance in the public eye. He points out that Canada has enough trouble as it is building points of commonality between Canadians in Parliament, so why should Canadians further fuel the fire of divisions by paying attention to gender- and ethnicity-based claims to inclusion? Indeed, would it not be far better to encourage citizens to focus on matters of policy instead and try to build alliances across identity differences in support of policy initiatives that all groups can support? To cede to demands for parliamentary inclusion by marginalized groups, argues Redekop, would seem only to add additional stress to an already severely stretched Canadian unity fabric.

There is no easy answer to this objection, for Redekop is undoubtedly right that the demand for inclusion by women, Aboriginal peoples, and visible and ethnic minorities would add a new and potentially divisive dimension to parliamentary politics. However, one way to partly allay these fears of division is to recognize that what marginalized groups are asking for is not to be separated from the structures of Canadian democracy but, rather, to be more fully included within them. Contrast, for example, the demands of Quebec separatists with the demands of marginalized groups and consider which is the more divisive force within Canadian politics. Quebec separatists threaten political unity within Canada because they question the credentials of the Canadian government to exercise any authority over them. Marginalized groups, on the other hand, have drawn attention to their identities only because they want to be more fully included in the political discussions that shape the political identity of Canada as a whole. Thus, although marginalized groups may focus upon the political importance of their social differences, what they are actually doing, as Will Kymlicka puts it, is trying to find avenues for "full membership in the larger society."[16] From this perspective, the demand for greater inclusion by marginalized groups can be seen as an important endorsement of the Canadian parliamentary system.

Redekop's second objection relates to who potentially qualifies for distinct representation within Parliament. If Parliament is to be considered truly representative of Canada's social diversity, Redekop asks, then does this mean that all sectors of the Canadian population should be represented, including, for example, the aged, teachers, students, factory workers, retail sales workers, parents, athletes, and environmentalists? Once we accept the view that the characteristics of people play a role in determining whether they feel adequately represented in Parliament, then we seem to be in the absurd position of having to consider the claims for inclusion by a potentially endless list of groups. Moreover, even if we can establish which groups might qualify for guaranteed representation, Redekop asks, how do we go about establishing who legitimately belongs to which group? Is the attempt to establish boundaries simply too difficult, given that so many people now have what might be called "hybrid" identities (e.g., a person may be both female and Aboriginal)? In other words, on what basis do we distinguish legitimate claims by groups for parliamentary inclusion from those that are not legitimate?

Again, there is no straightforward answer to Redekop's objection, though Anne Phillips points us in a helpful direction. She argues that the case for greater inclusion of women, ethnic groups, and ethnic and visible minorities rests upon "an analysis of the existing structures of exclusion."[17] That is, a system of fair representation does not mean that any or all groups are entitled to specific representation on the basis of some purported principle of equality or fairness. Instead, what we must do is focus upon those particularly urgent instances where the oppression of groups has led to those same groups experiencing a profound degree of marginalization and exclusion from the political process. Proportional representation of groups is thus never simply required but must be determined on a case-by-case basis in reference to these questions: Has this group been historically oppressed? Will proportional representation in Parliament constitute a significant step in overcoming those conditions of oppression? In other words, what qualifies groups for greater inclusion is the likelihood that without guaranteed access to the arena of policymaking they will be unable to overcome their current experiences of exclusion and marginalization. While this approach does not get around the difficulties associated with defining who is and who is not a member of a disadvantaged group, it at least narrows the field of potential candidates who may be eligible for guaranteed representation. Against these more restrictive criteria, women, Aboriginal peoples, and numerous visible minority and ethnic groups in Canada are able to put forward a very strong case.

Third, Redekop argues that the proposal to move to identity-based representation is condescending toward those groups that would benefit from guaranteed seats because, among other things, such representation would relegate them to the status of second-class MPs. If groups can't make it to the House of Commons on their own, in other words, and are thereby "reduced" to relying upon special governmental facilitation to get them there, they will undoubtedly lack credibility.

No doubt, securing seats through special guarantees does constitute a significant departure from standard electoral practice in Canada. But though a departure, these reform proposals are not in and of themselves condescending to disadvantaged and marginalized groups. Here everything depends on one's perspective. Despite what Redekop says, disadvantaged and marginalized groups are not after guaranteed seats because the dominant male hierarchy has told them that such a course of action would be good for them. To accept the directives of the dominant male hierarchy on these grounds would indeed be condescending. On the contrary, disadvantaged and marginalized groups who make the point are saying that they are after guaranteed seats because this is the only way they will be able to break the stranglehold upon power that the dominant male hierarchy now exercises over them. They would stand for office and get elected through conventional channels, in other words, if they could reasonably expect to be successful in this way. The trouble is that their success is minimized because the dominant male hierarchy (which constitutes a minority in demographic terms) has been very effective at retaining its vast majority of seats in the House since it has at its disposal a disproportional share of the party and electoral machinery needed to win elections. From this perspective, the only way to break this cycle of dominance is to make structural changes that directly challenge the male hierarchy. One way to mount this challenge is through a system of guaranteed seats.

CONCLUSION

Redekop is quite right to point out that the practical complications associated with getting a system of guaranteed seats off the ground are considerable. I have no easy solutions to offer. However, there simply being practical difficulties associated with reform should not lead us to abandon the project. Advocates of reform tell us that a system of guaranteed seats is an integral component of their larger project to overcome the debilitating cycle of political marginalization and exclusion they now experience. The question is, what is the best route to heeding this call for justice? There is, of course, safety to be had in steering the ship of democratic practice in Canada into the tranquil waters of the status quo rather than into the rocky waters of reform. The latter route may well lead to significant structural damage to the parliamentary ship as we know it. However, avoiding rocky waters also means that those who now hold power will continue to pilot the ship. The message that the marginalized and disadvantaged in Canada draw to our attention is that this inclination toward "safety" may be less than desirable.

NOTES

1. I will leave aside the question of representation in the Senate, as this would raise issues that lie beyond the scope of this paper.

2. See Jane Arscott and Linda Trimble, "In the Presence of Women: Representation and Political Power," in Jane Arscott and Linda Trimble, eds., *In the Presence of Women: Representation in Canadian Governments* (Toronto: Harcourt Brace & Company, Canada, 1997), pp. 1–17.

3. Ed. note. As of 2007, Aboriginal MPs in the House of Commons numbered only four.

4. See Committee for Aboriginal Electoral Reform, *The Path to Electoral Equality* (Ottawa: Committee for Aboriginal Electoral Reform, 1991), p. 2.

5. See Daiva Stasiulis, "Deep Diversity: Race and Ethnicity in Canadian Politics," in Michael S. Whittington and Glen Williams, eds., *Canadian Politics in the 1990s* (Toronto: Nelson Canada, 1995), pp. 199–200.

6. In the June 1997 federal election, the number of House of Commons seats contested was raised from 295 to 301.

7. On this point, see Lisa Young, "Fulfilling the Mandate of Difference: Women in the Canadian House of Commons," in Jane Arscott and Linda Trimble, *In the Presence of Women: Representation in Canadian Governments,* pp. 85–86.

8. Committee for Aboriginal Electoral Reform, *The Path to Electoral Equality,* pp. 7–12.

9. Daiva Stasiulis, "Deep Diversity," pp. 200–204.

10. Iris Marion Young, "Justice and Communicative Democracy," in Roger S. Gottlieb, ed., *Radical Philosophy: Tradition, Counter-Tradition Politics* (Philadelphia: Temple University Press, 1993), p. 133.

11. Anne Phillips, *The Politics of Presence* (Oxford: Clarendon Press, 1995), pp. 67–68.

12. Ovide Mercredi and Mary Ellen Turpel, *In the Rapids: Navigating the Future of First Nations* (Toronto: Penguin, 1993), p. 36.

13. For an extensive discussion of this point, see Anne Phillips, *The Politics of Presence,* ch. 2.

14. Iris Marion Young, "Justice and Communicative Democracy," p. 136.

15. Anne Phillips, *The Politics of Presence,* p. 152.

16. Will Kymlicka, *Multicultural Citizenship: A Liberal Theory of Minority Rights* (Oxford: Clarendon Press, 1995), p. 192.

17. Anne Phillips, *The Politics of Presence,* p. 47.

✗ NO

Group Representation in Parliament Would Be Dysfunctional for Canada

JOHN H. REDEKOP

INTRODUCTION

Various critics rightly assert that the Canadian Parliament does not accurately reflect Canada's social diversity. They are also correct when they say that Canada's electoral system plays a major role in producing unrepresentative legislatures. What is at issue in the present discussion is not whether the Canadian Parliament, specifically the House of Commons, should be reformed and the electoral system improved but whether the proposal to adopt group representation, as explained by Tim Schouls, constitutes a desirable and workable change.

As I understand it, the proposal under consideration seeks to remedy the alleged major flaw in Canada's electoral system by guaranteeing parliamentary seats for "disadvantaged groups such as women, Aboriginal peoples, ethnic and visible minorities, and people with disabilities." While additional categories are suggested by the phrasing, we will limit this discussion to these five groups; they encompass about 75 percent of Canada's population. We will also limit this analysis to the House of Commons. Senate reform needs to be discussed in its own right.

It should be noted that the proposal emphasizes the need for "political equality," which apparently means "equal representation" or mathematical proportionality. Thus, since females constitute about 51 percent of the population, they would, in the proposed scheme of "proportional parliamentary inclusion" and "proportional presence," be guaranteed 51 percent of the seats in the elected House of Commons. The other four groups would similarly be guaranteed a percentage of seats in this "identity-based" system of representation.

This essay will demonstrate that identity-based group representation in Parliament, with guaranteed seats, as described by Tim Schouls, is neither desirable nor workable in Canada. On balance, I believe, it would not be an improvement over our present single-member plurality electoral system.

One can think of several reasonable and democratic ways in which our present system could be reformed. One way would be to have half of the House of Commons seats filled by our present form of election—which would enable all Canadians to retain the benefits of having their own MP—with the other half being filled by a proportional representation system as is presently practised in Germany, Japan, and New Zealand. Having half of the MPs elected according to the second system would promote unity and goodwill, for example, by allowing a nationally victorious party to have at least some representation from a province where it got a large number of votes but did not come first in any riding. Such was the situation for the Liberals in the general election of 1980, for example, when they received 24 percent of the popular vote in Saskatchewan and 22 percent in each of Alberta and British Columbia but failed to elect even one member in those three provinces. In those three provinces, thus, the Liberals were unrepresented in the national cabinet.

ARGUMENTS BASED ON IDEOLOGICAL CONSIDERATIONS

In part, the case for group representation, as presented in the preceding article, rests on faulty assumptions; we will review seven.

1. **The five groups under consideration are all definable entities with basically clear boundaries.** This assumption is important because we would need to be clear about who belongs to a particular group if we want to assign guaranteed seats to that group. While there is no difficulty in identifying the women in Canada, the situation is problematic for the other four groups. Who should be in the Aboriginal group? Would a person who is one-eighth Aboriginal and seven-eighths French-Canadian—and there are many such people—be part of the Aboriginal group or the French-Canadian group or both? What fraction of Aboriginal blood would be required? Would Aboriginal people be allowed to decide on fractions for themselves? Such kinds of problems are legion. The actual membership and boundary problems boggle the mind. Also, should we include in the Aboriginal group those Aboriginal people who don't want to be part of this racially segregated group but would rather participate in the category of general voters? Would we force them to be racially categorized?

Similarly, who would belong to a given ethnic minority? Would we require some racial tests? And what about the millions of Canadians who identify with more than one ethnic group? To ask the question is to think of enough problems to keep a small army of bureaucrats happy for years. Further, would a Chinese-Canadian husband and his Jamaican-Canadian wife vote for different slates of candidates, and would their twenty-year-old daughter living at home vote for a third slate of candidates? Would she have a choice?

Moreover, which ethnic groups and which visible minorities would qualify for separate and guaranteed representation? If we want to accommodate all organized ethnic groups in Canada, we would have to deal with at least 160 of them. If they each got even one seat—and the larger groups would insist on getting more—then more than half of the seats in the House of Commons would be assigned to these ethnic groups. And let us not wiggle out of this dilemma by suggesting that only the larger ethnic groups would be assigned seats. They already tend to win seats on their own. It's the scores of smaller groups that systematically and regularly get no representation. Perhaps one could argue that ethnic groups could be lumped together, for example, East Europeans, people from the Middle East, Blacks from Africa, and so on. But often the greatest animosities exist between neighbouring groups, such as Serbs and Croats, Jews and Arabs, Taiwanese and mainland Chinese, and so on.

Even agreeing on who in Canada should belong to the group termed "disabled" would be very difficult. Are we thinking only of paraplegics or quadriplegics? Do we include the blind? What about the hearing impaired? What about the mentally impaired? What about those with perpetually sore backs? Do we include those who have AIDS? Would people with chronic fatigue syndrome qualify? And what about the thousands who are terminally ill with cancer or some other disease? They are certainly disabled and permanently so. Should these and others who could be listed all be included? They certainly all have disabilities. Furthermore, how much impairment creates disability? Who would decide? And would it be logical to assume that this diverse spectrum of groups would have a common political agenda?

2. Voters can be represented well only by representatives who share their social traits. Schouls states that "parliamentary representatives must share central experiences and assumptions with those they represent if those representatives are to understand their constituents' needs and interests." I find his argument unconvincing.

If we look at the professions of teaching, medicine, and law, for example, we find that effective representation and service do not require social similarity. I am confident that if members of the five identity-based groups were given the choice, the vast majority would rank competence as more important than social similarity. When people are sick, it is more important that they have a competent physician than that they have one from their own ethnic group. Similarly, people generally look for competent teachers, lawyers, mechanics, accountants, photographers, and other professionals and tradespeople. Why should we assume that it would be different when we turn to the profession of politics? Granted, social similarity is a significant asset, but it is not the most important criterion.

3. Parliamentary input will shape parliamentary output. The Canadian political system grants power and authority to a majority party or coalition, not to minority groups whose support is not needed by governments in order to retain office. Clearly, identity-based minorities would influence what is said in legislative debate, but why should we assume that such minority voices would affect legislative output, the policy decisions? (The special situation with the majority composed of women will be discussed later.) In fact, it would likely be the case that the majority rulers, either one party or a coalition, would be inclined to discount and marginalize the input of identity-based MPs with their narrow agenda because the rulers cannot realistically hope to win them over to the perspective of the governing majority. There is nothing to be gained by acceding to the requests of opposition minorities. Majorities can safely ignore such minorities.

Conversely, if these same identity-based MPs were members of the governing party, or even of the official opposition, they would have some hope of influencing policies and platforms, but only if they were prepared to accept substantial compromises.

As I see it, the error in Schouls's apparent assumptions in this regard is that voice equals influence. A second apparent assumption is that representation in itself, even having one or a few MPs advocating a certain perspective, constitutes power.

Both assumptions, in my view, are faulty. All the eloquence one can imagine and a total sharing of social traits with one's constituents carry virtually no weight in legislative debate if there is not a political reason for the decision makers, generally the cabinet, to take such input seriously. A few eloquent MPs may achieve publicity, even popularity, but generally do not have significant influence on legislative output.

4. Political decisions grow out of parliamentary debate. In earlier times, generations ago, public policies may actually have had their genesis in parliamentary debate, but those days have passed. It is now erroneous to assume that important public policies, the type that the five identity-based groups would like to see enacted, are actually shaped in Parliament and are the result of MPs' input and debate. It seems safe to say that at least 98 percent of public policies in Canada are generated by the cabinet—which may get its ideas from many sources including pressure groups—and are not formed or changed to any significant extent by parliamentary debate. An identity-based group having 5 or 10 percent of the MPs does not mean that it has 5 or 10 percent of the influence on public policies.

Schouls states that "marginalized groups," including the five we are considering, "want to be more fully included in the political discussions that shape the political identity of Canada as a whole." I seriously question whether parliamentary debates play a significant role in shaping Canada's political identity. It seems more accurate to say that these five groups would achieve more success in influencing Canada's political identity if they contributed informed input to cabinet members and senior officials before cabinet decisions are made. In this way they could also, with greater credibility, threaten voter retaliation, if need be, a tactic they cannot employ if the constituency they represent votes in its own elections or at least for its own set of candidates and the decision makers have nothing to gain by accommodating them. A group that is electorally hived off by itself should not expect to gain concessions from decision makers who have nothing to gain by making such concessions.

It could be that MPs who represent identity-based groups would become part of a governing coalition. In such a situation they might be able to influence policy decision but, in virtually all cases, only by making compromises, which is exactly what we have under our present system. In rare instances, such MPs might actually be able to topple a government. Such action would perhaps give the key MPs a sense of power, but it would not bring about the implementation of their political agenda.

5. **Women do not participate in politics as much as men do because the women "have been ignored and marginalized by the male hierarchy."** In earlier times this assumption was valid, but today it has little validity. My experience and observation lead me to conclude that in most situations, political parties, still dominated by males, bend over backward to get qualified women to stand as candidates. They do so for the same reason that they often seek out ethnic and other minority people to stand as candidates—they believe that having such candidates increases their chances of victory.

If we want to find out why women remain relatively underrepresented in Parliament (although the situation is gradually improving), we must probe more deeply. Simply blaming men will not do. Electoral results and various studies have shown, as former prime minister Kim Campbell and many others could verify, that women do not necessarily or even disproportionally vote for women. Most female voters, just like most male voters, tend to vote for the candidate or party that they believe to be the best of the options. People are more sophisticated than to vote, blindly, for a candidate on the basis of which bathroom that candidate uses.

It is also the case, of course, that most of society, including many women, still believes that women can make their greatest contribution by providing a strong home setting. As long as that view is dominant, there is likely to be a relative shortage of qualified women standing for office and being elected. This point ties in with another important reality, namely, that women have babies and men don't.

Any remaining societal barriers hindering political success by women should, of course, be removed. These barriers may include inadequate child care in Parliament, inadequate leave policies for pregnancy, or inappropriate financial policies. We should not delude ourselves, however, by assuming that if we guarantee women a certain number of seats in Parliament we are thereby eliminating barriers.

6. **"The primary qualification to become an MP is purely and simply the ability to represent."** This assumption strikes me as being false. The primary qualification, in our electoral system, to become an MP is to find a way to get more people to vote for you than for any other candidate. Often the person who appears to have the greatest "ability to represent" is not elected. Many explanations come to mind as to why such an outcome is commonplace. For a variety of reasons, a candidate may get a huge sympathy vote. The strongest candidate may not belong to the most popular party or even to a credible party. The incumbent may have done so many favours and created so many IOUs that he can defeat all other

candidates even if they are obviously more capable. And a certain party or party leader may sweep a lamentably weak candidate into office by promising major benefits to the candidate's constituency.

Once we acknowledge the fact that "simply the ability to represent" is not the primary qualification to become an MP, then we realize that there are key factors other than sharing social traits that shape political outcomes and that we should not concentrate primarily on social traits.

7. "The presence of women in Parliament ensures that all the diverse and quite possibly conflicting interests of women will actually be heard and debated in Canada's central representative political arena." For better or worse, such an assumption does not bear up under scrutiny. For one thing, no one can ensure that "all" interests will be presented. The significant subgroups of women, as well as of many other groups, are far too numerous to allow us to accept such an assertion as valid. In our parliamentary system, debate in Parliament will continue to be dominated by differences between government and opposition agendas, not by diverse values and perspectives among men or among women or among Aboriginal people or among ethnic groups. Those differences will, in the main, need to be debated elsewhere.

Moving beyond these ideological assumptions, we need to consider several basic ideological issues:

1. Identity-based representation would increase social fragmentation in Canada. That's exactly the opposite of what Canada needs at present. The biggest question we face is whether we have enough commonality to remain united. The country may not survive the injection of additional cleavages that pit some Canadians against other Canadians. In a free society, having a plethora of organized groups—religious, social, ethnic, economic, athletic, professional, and so on—is a sign of political health. But if these groups are elevated to the point of formal and official electoral competition, then differences tend to overwhelm commonalities.

This country would be dangerously weakened if social differences were incorporated into electoral struggles. We do not need the religious animosities that dominate Irish or Israeli party politics, the ethnic tensions that destroyed Yugoslavia and that perennially threaten Belgium and various other countries, the race-based policies that have bedevilled South Africa and other countries, or a parliamentary division that pits women against men simply because some MPs are women and some MPs are men.

Indeed, I would go so far as to argue that Canada has evolved into a stable, free, and tolerant country largely because our national legislature has not reflected the major cleavages in society and has not let these divisions become dominant in our national political agenda.

2. Identity-based group representation raises insoluble problems of boundary and number. Once we start categorizing people according to their personal traits instead of their possession of citizenship, where do we stop? Groups will quickly realize that to be assigned guaranteed seats is the easiest, indeed, for some the only, way for them to be assured of gaining representation in Parliament. If we guarantee seats for women, we can safely assume that soon homosexual women will want to have the authorities guarantee them a quota of seats because as a small minority group among women, they probably would otherwise not get any.

Quite apart from the long list of groups, especially ethnic groups, that would quickly clamour for guaranteed seats, we would soon see a series of divisions and further divisions within the groups initially assigned seats. This problem raises another key question. Who would decide which groups and subgroups would be guaranteed seats? And would the same authority or authorities decide how many seats each group would get? The whole exercise would undoubtedly generate widespread disappointment, resentment, frustration, and anger.

3. The proposal to move to identity-based representation is condescending toward the five groups under consideration. Today, members of all of these five groups have the right to stand for office and to vote. Increasing numbers do, in fact, stand for office, vote, and win seats. Now, with progress well under way, we are being told that these groups are not good enough to make it on their own.

This proposal is condescending in that it assumes that women, who constitute 51 percent of Canadian society, do not know their own best interests or are too incompetent to vote according to their own best interests. They cannot be trusted to decide which candidates, be they male or female, will be the best representatives for them. They need to be told by the dominant male "hierarchy," to use Tim Schouls's term, that they should vote only for women. That's an insult. Why don't we let them decide for themselves who can best represent their interests? If they want to organize a women's party or if they want to vote for women, let them do so. But surely they do not have to be instructed by men or by our mostly male Parliament what they should do.

The same line of reasoning can be applied to the other groups. It may well be that some categories of voters in some parts of the country will not elect people who are their best advocates. But that's how democracy works. Democracy does not ensure that the wisest and most competent and the most effective representatives will be elected; it can only ensure, generally speaking, that the truly uninformed and the seriously incompetent and the utterly ineffective and those who would seek to destroy freedom do not become representatives in our legislatures.

4. The proposal would create first-class and second-class MPs. Presumably, in an electoral system that incorporates identity-based group representation, some women, some Aboriginal people, some visible minorities, some members of ethnic groups, and some disabled people would still be elected in the open segment of the electoral process in the way that they are elected now. Others would be elected by their own kind to fill guaranteed seats. It seems to me that very quickly a situation would develop in which those who were elected to guaranteed seats would be deemed to be second-class MPs because they were elected with special governmental facilitation. They could not make it on their own the way the others did.

One result of such a development would likely be that those who were elected to guaranteed seats would have less credibility in Parliament. Such a result would, of course, undermine the whole reason for embarking on the exercise in the first place.

5. To a significant extent, immigrants should be assimilated into Canadian society; Canada should not serve only as a receptacle for transplanted societies from around the globe and should not tolerate the transplanting of tensions and animosities that exist in many of those societies. Generally speaking, ethnic groups in Canada should not expect governmental assistance in the perpetuation of their ethnic communities. Analogous to the shifting popularity of religious groups, the survival or disappearance of ethnic groups in Canada is properly the concern of the private sector.

This is, after all, Canada, not the immigrants' former country. Ethnic groups should, as I see it, expect gradual assimilation. In any event, they should not expect the Canadian Parliament to make provision for their segregated survival. Above all, we do not want ethnic cleavages and rivalries built into our Parliament. Guaranteeing ethnic seats would, in my view, seriously increase ethnic antagonisms. Let us assume, for example, that the responsible authorities would guarantee two seats to Indo-Canadians; it could hardly be more, given that half of the total seats would be assigned to women and many other groups would need to be accommodated. Immediately there would be fierce rivalries concerning who should be selected. Should Indo-Canadian Hindus, Buddhists, Sikhs, Muslims, and Christians all be given seats, with the groups taking turns electing their MPs? And what about the growing nonreligious subset?

Would the Canadian government, in trying to be fair, undertake to count the members of the various Indo-Canadian subgroups? It would be a mammoth task to decide which Indo-Canadian groups would get the assigned seats.

Surely it would be much wiser to let Indo-Canadians take their place as Canadians and eventually make their political contributions the way the majority of Canadians do. As a matter of fact, Indo-Canadians have already made important political contributions in various jurisdictions in Canada, even at the cabinet level. The same situation prevails for many other ethnic groups, including Chinese-Canadians and other visible minorities.

What multiethnic Canadian society and its government should promote is the identification and strengthening of areas of commonality. We need all the glue we can find to keep this country united. We do not need an electoral system that emphasizes and reinforces ethnic cleavages and thus also ethnic tensions and rivalries. To put it very candidly, Canadian multicultural policies, in electoral matters and in other areas, should guarantee freedom, tolerance, and respect, but in a truly free society, these policies should not underwrite the political costs of ethnic group perpetuation, and they certainly should not undermine democracy in a futile attempt to guarantee ethnic group survival.

6. It would be very unwise to agree with the proposal that "no effort should be spared to get more minority representatives into the House." "No effort spared" means exactly that. These words may be a popular slogan, but the fundamental idea they convey is a great threat to democracy. Do we want the effort made to ban the nomination of nonminority candidates so that the minorities can win? Do we want quotas applied along racial and ethnic lines for the general elections? These and numerous other efforts should not be undertaken.

7. The term *political equality* needs to be clarified and then to be understood and applied appropriately. I have difficulty understanding what Schouls means by this term, one which seems to be central to his thesis. If he means equality of opportunity, then he is on solid philosophical and political footing. If, on the other hand, he means equality of influence or, even worse, equality of political outcome, then we have a serious problem.

Democracy cannot guarantee ideal outcomes. Freedom of choice means choice, including the right to make unwise or less than ideal decisions. It includes the right to make choices—in politics, religion, economics, and so on—that are not the most advantageous to oneself. It includes the right to make illogical choices. In the area of religion, for example, freedom does not ensure even the survival, let alone the good health or expansion, of any one faith. Concerning ethnic group survival in Canada, guarantees of freedom should only provide a climate of opportunity and perhaps some general tax and other minor concessions. They should not attempt to ensure or guarantee anything more.

With reference to the proposal for identity-based group representation, one needs to ask in what way would minority representation create political equality? It would create minority representation and not much more than that. It certainly would not create equality of influence on legislative outcomes.

8. The liberal approach to representation does not insist that MPs represent individuals only. I question the statement that in the liberal perspective "representatives are elected to advance the individual interests of their individual constituents." Liberalism assumes more than that. Certainly Canadian MPs do more than represent individual interests. Even a brief reading of *Hansard* should correct such a misconception. Individual MPs from both sides of the House and from all parties frequently urge policy changes or initiatives to assist companies, towns and cities, ethnic and other groups, categoric groups such as families, women, taxpayers, or the unemployed, and, of course, the country as a whole.

For me, however, the main issue in this regard is not whether individuals or groups should be represented and promoted—clearly the interests of both categories must be upheld—but whether national well-being is being advanced. With Edmund Burke, I believe that though individual representatives have specific responsibilities to their own constituencies, they should always balance constituency well-being with national well-being.

9. The election of MPs representing identity-based groups would likely produce chronic governmental instability. Most proportional electoral systems have some means, usually a 1 percent or a 5 percent clause, as in Japan and Germany respectively, to prevent the appearance of numerous one-person, two-person, or three-person parties in the legislature. Under the proposal advocated by Schouls, there could be no threshold exclusion clause. In fact, the whole intent would be to have a series of mostly small, special interest groups in Parliament that would be likely to soon become special interest political parties.

Such a situation would, of course, almost certainly produce a series of Parliaments without a majority party, and, therefore, a sequence of shaky and short-lived governments, unless the 153 or more women decided to govern as a bloc. Thus, in trying to address a problem of underrepresentation, we would, in fact, be creating much more serious problems for Canadians.

One of the major reasons for general Canadian political and economic stability, even when separatists threaten to break up the country, is our majority cabinet system with its stability and predictability between elections. If no one party is permitted to field its own slate of candidates in all constituencies in an effort to form a majority government, we might well regularly produce minority governments consisting of numerous groups and parties and, therefore, vulnerable to disintegration in the face of separatist threats or various economic and political crises. We should not toy with such risks.

In passing, we should also note that small ethnic or other groups invited to join coalitions should not expect to make substantial headway with their particular agendas. The larger party or parties leading the coalition would likely have at least several small groups to appease, as best they could, so that each small group would likely get very little of what it wanted.

Such a situation reminds us again that in a democracy, compromise is a crucial ingredient. The desire to implement narrow, doctrinaire agendas is not an important component.

10. **Political accountability is greater when half or more of the members in a legislature are elected in single-member districts.** Single-member districts, as in Canada's present electoral system, tend to create majority governments by disproportionally rewarding that party or those parties that are the most popular. While this system tends thus to distort public preferences, it also tends to produce governmental accountability.

If one believes, as I do, that an effective system of political accountability is a very important factor, then one is prepared to accept the distortion that the system creates. The distortion can, of course, be greatly reduced by the adoption of the dual German electoral system.

Given the broad economic and social scope of governmental activity in our day, it is surely important to know whom to thank and whom to blame. It is much easier to do so if a majority government is in place than if a broad coalition governs. Since most governments tend not to change greatly the general political direction and policies that they inherit when they take office, it seems more important that we should be able to hold governments accountable than that the composition of a legislature accurately reflect the social composition of society.

Furthermore, in the identity-based system of representation being advocated, it is not clear how voters could identify the official loyal opposition, that is, a "government in waiting," the likely alternative to the government of the day. The important distinction between two relatively clear sets of policies and politicians, offering clear alternatives to voters, would become very blurred or even disappear. That would be a serious loss.

11. **Social, religious, or racial fragmentation of society probably constitutes a greater threat to political stability than does the geographical division of the electorate for purposes of electing a legislature.** The proposal makes much of the supposed division of the electorate into geography-based constituencies. Schouls suggests that such a method of dividing voters "rests on the assumption that voters' primary political identity flows from their attachment to geography." As I see it, such an assertion misstates the point. The division of voters into constituency groups is a pragmatic and utilitarian means of getting MPs elected by approximately the same number of potential voters per riding, with special provisions made for sparsely inhabited regions. As I see it, this system does not imply primary attachment of voters to territory or to anything else, although in some cases there is considerable racial or religious homogeneity. It is only a convenient way to divide voters, most of whom likely have nongeographic primary attachments, into groups of the desired size.

Above all, these constituency groupings are not based on social, religious, or other social tests, do not reinforce cleavages or animosities, and do not exacerbate tensions.

ARGUMENTS BASED ON PRACTICAL CONSIDERATIONS

1. The categories and percentages presented in the proposal raise numerous important problems and dilemmas. In the early sections of the article, Schouls emphasizes the importance of the "new Canadians with origins in the Caribbean, Africa, Middle East, Central and South America, and Asia." If, in his ethnic categories, he includes, as he logically should, all ethnic groups, including those not part of the visible minorities, that come from these regions, then the total becomes considerably greater than the 6.3 percent that he cites. Further, when he introduced his five categories, he listed "ethnic and visible minorities" as two groups. What has happened to the ethnic groups that are not visible minorities? Having acknowledged that "numerous visible minority and ethnic groups in Canada are able to put forward a very strong case," Schouls seems to have forgotten about the nonvisible ethnic minorities.

In the scheme before us, 153 seats in the current 301-seat House of Commons would be assigned to women. An additional twelve seats would be assigned to Aboriginal people. Given Schouls's strong commitment to equality, one must conclude that six of these twelve would be given to Aboriginal women. Of the nineteen seats he would guarantee to visible minorities, we ought to conclude that at least nine would be given to women. The result would be that 168 seats would be assigned to women, which means that the male voters, with 133 seats, would be seriously underrepresented. Or maybe the six Aboriginal females would be part of the 153.

The situation becomes additionally complicated if we factor in the people with disabilities, who seem also to have been forgotten somewhere along the way, and, of course, the large groups of ethnic minorities who belong to distinct and cohesive ethnic groups but who, in most cases, are not physically recognizable.

Other complicating factors come to mind. Where would one place an MP, elected to a nonguaranteed seat, who is female, disabled, and Aboriginal? Would she be counted in one or all of those categories, or in none? Even more important, who would decide? And would the number of guaranteed seats be reduced if significant numbers of women and several Aboriginal people and members of visible minorities, or even any of them, managed to get elected to nonguaranteed seats? Surely the authorities could not simply let the number of seats allocated to the "others," the presumably nonvisible minority males, be markedly reduced, or the whole scheme would go out of whack in that direction.

The assigning of individuals to the several voting groups would be a national nightmare. How would one categorize spouses in mixed marriages? How would the authorities categorize the children of these marriages? Would every Canadian have to carry a racial or ethnic identity card, a Canadianized version of apartheid? Presumably so, or the overall registering of voters could not be carried out in a way to facilitate the achievement of the stated percentage goals.

Additional major problems would involve the allocation of the twelve Aboriginal seats to the numerous competing groups, the allocation of the nineteen visible minority seats to at least twenty-five visible minority groups, and the allocation of whatever the appropriate number of seats is to people with disabilities. The challenges and problems boggle the mind.

2. We are not told how the electoral system would be altered to ensure that the guaranteed seats would be filled as intended. This is no small matter. Since relatively well-paid, high-status positions as members of Parliament are at issue, we can be assured that there would be a great clamouring for the occupancy and control of these seats. Who would handle the nominations? For example, concerning the women, would various organizations each be assigned certain seats? Would the National Action Committee on the Status of Women be given a bloc? Would Real Women be assigned a large segment, since they seem to represent a high percentage of nonorganized women? Would the women's organizations be allowed to nominate candidates who would compete against one another? Would there be primary elections? If so, who would pay the costs? What about all of the other women's organizations? Would the guaranteed women's seats be spread across all of the provinces?

And what happens if most of the voters in a given riding don't want to be part of such a guaranteed constituency? Will they simply be told by whoever has the authority to tell them that their MP will be a woman, like it or not? What happens if all of the established parties in one of these ridings refuse to nominate anybody in such an authoritarian situation, but a small women's pressure group manages to nominate a woman? Would that female candidate automatically become that riding's "elected" MP?

And what happens if, in a guaranteed woman's riding, a party nominates a male? Would the sex (or gender) police declare the nomination invalid on account of a candidate being of the wrong sex? How would such a ruling be upheld given Canada's commitment to equality? How could such a ruling or policy be justified given all of the official legislative and judicial decisions, not to mention constitutional provisions, spelling out equality of the sexes?

If, perchance, the assumption is that the guaranteed women MPs, more than half of the House of Commons, would not be elected in existing ridings, then how would they be chosen? Would they be selected by women's groups, or one women's group, such as the National Action Committee on the Status of Women, without any connection to a given territory such as a riding? And how could this be seen as fair in that the women get to vote twice, once in the general election and, presumably, once in a women's election? Or are the 153 "guaranteed" female MPs not even going to be elected? If that is the intent, then how could this be done given the stipulations in the *Elections Act* and the relevant equality provisions of the Charter of Rights and Freedoms?

Furthermore, if it is fair to guarantee a specified number of seats to women, why is it not fair also to specify a number of seats for men? Surely that would be more equitable than giving special guarantees to members of only one sex. Would men be allowed to vote in the women's elections? Would parties still be allowed to nominate women in all of the nonwomen's seats? And what happens if, after all of the ballots are counted, the total number of female MPs comes to 60 or 65 or 70 percent of the House of Commons? That would be a distinct possibility. Would that constitute equality? Would that be more democratic than what we have now?

3. Who will administer the incredibly complex and probably unworkable scheme advocated in the proposal? Somebody will have to make many very controversial, often very unpopular, decisions. Some of the dilemmas would involve policy and others would involve implementation and administration. Is it assumed that the last freely elected House of Commons would try to implement this Orwellian manipulation? Is it assumed that the cabinet would issue an order-in-council or that the legislature would enact a statute, perhaps relying on article 33 of the Charter, the notwithstanding clause, to get this whole venture under way without having it aborted by the courts?

CONCLUSION

Tim Schouls is to be commended for urging that the barriers that many women and other groups face in politics be removed. Unfortunately, guaranteeing seats does not in itself remove barriers. In fact, the proposal being advanced as a remedy creates more barriers than it removes.

Perhaps the major flaw in the proposed scheme is that it fails to accommodate the fundamental principle that democracy cannot, and should not attempt to, guarantee outcomes. Democracy cannot ensure that the ideal will be realized or even that the best option will be chosen. Freedom of political choice, like freedom of religion, includes the right to make wrong choices, wrong as some people or even the majority might define wrong. It includes the right to make choices that are not self-serving, self-advancing, or even well informed.

Throughout history, ideologues have tried to combine idealistic outcomes with democratic means—to do so cannot be ensured and no coercive attempt should be undertaken to try to achieve that goal. Political leaders and common citizens alike must rely on education and persuasion. Either the voters have free choice, within very broad and reasonable limits, or they do not. All else is undemocratic manipulation, even if done in the name of democracy and equality. The French Revolution bears solemn witness to that fact. The proposed plan for representation based on group identity ultimately takes away choice, specifically the option to choose that which ideologues and true believers of various sorts deem to be improper and unwise.

The proposed plan, however laudable its genesis and honourable its intent, must be rejected as both undemocratic and unworkable. It risks the achievements that have been made in assisting the politically marginalized groups, and it undermines the prospect for further democratic progress. We must look elsewhere for the agenda for further success.

POSTSCRIPT

In reading this debate, it is interesting to note the absence of discussion of class issues, especially in the article by Schouls. While he is concerned about increasing the representation of those marginalized in society, marginalization is identified primarily with the identity politics of ethnicity and gender. What role does class play in this analysis? Is the issue of class merely subsumed or transcended by issues of ethnicity and gender? What relevance, if any, does class analysis have to this debate?

Will Kymlicka is one theorist whom Schouls uses to develop the philosophical basis for his argument. See Kymlicka's *Multicultural Citizenship: A Liberal Theory of Minority Rights* (Oxford: Clarendon Press, 1995) for a defence of granting differentiated rights to ethnic groups based on their vulnerability. For an interesting critique of this position, see Brian Walker, "Plural Cultures, Contested Territories: A Critique of Kymlicka," *Canadian Journal of Political Science* 30, no. 2 (June 1997), pp. 211–234.

A number of good references are useful for pursuing this issue further. For two books that deal with the philosophical dimensions of this debate, see Jane Arscott and Linda Trimble, eds., *In the Presence of Women: Representation in Canadian Governments* (Toronto: Harcourt, Brace & Company, 1997), and Anne Phillips, *The Politics of Presence* (Oxford: Clarendon Press, 1995). For a book that tackles some of the practical difficulties of implementing proportional representation for social groups, see Committee for Aboriginal Electoral Reform, *The Path to Electoral Equality* (Ottawa: Committee for Aboriginal Electoral Reform, 1991).

When the territory of Nunavut was being created, an interesting experiment in gender representation was contemplated. The Nunavut Implementation Commission proposed the creation of electoral districts that would elect one man and one woman each in order to create the world's first legislature with full gender parity. However, the proposal received only 43 percent of the vote in a referendum and therefore was not implemented. To learn more about this potential experiment in equitable social representation and why it failed to win support, see Jackie Steele and Manon Tremblay, "Paradise Lost? The Gender Parity Plebiscite in Nunavut," *Canadian Parliamentary Review* (Spring 2005), pp. 34–39.

Jocelyn Praud, who teaches women in politics at the University of Regina, examines some reforms undertaken in France to increase gender parity and discusses their relevance to the Canadian situation. The article, entitled "The Facts Ma'am: Looking to France for Ways to Improve Canada's Representative Democracy?" (May 30, 2002), can be found at http://www.equalvoice.ca/pdf/ Looking%20To%20France.pdf. Also useful is Linda Trimble and Jane Arscott, "Barriers to Women: Why Are We So Far from Gender Parity in Our Legislature?" *Alberta Reviews* (June 5, 2005), pp. 28–31.

In terms of representation of women in the Canadian parliament, Canada still lags behind many countries despite the progress that has been made with regard to women's rights. According to a table published by the Inter-parliamentary Union in June 2011, Canada tied for 38th worldwide, with 24.7 percent of the Canadian Parliament made up of women. The highest ranked country is Rwanda with 56.3 percent. The performance of the United States is even poorer. With only 16.7 percent of Congress composed of women, the United States is tied for 70th place overall.

Are the Media Politically Biased?

✔ **YES**
LYDIA MILJAN, "Political Bias in the Media"

✘ **NO**
PAUL BARKER, "A Bias But Not a Political One"

In his book *Harperland*, journalist Lawrence Martin writes that Prime Minister Harper feels that the Ottawa press gallery (which includes the major reporters on Canadian politics) has little love for Canada's national government. Polls and other indicators show that the public expects the media to report without bias, yet the top politician in Canada thinks they do otherwise, and many close to government concur. The prime minister also feels that the bias is a liberal one—that the media write and speak from a perspective that sees little value in conservative rule and ideas. Here, too, the prime minister receives support. Journalists are supposed to *report* on political events, to be a mirror of reality, but those in the know believe differently. They think, like the prime minister, that governments which favour fewer social programs, lower taxes, and generally a smaller public sector—in other words, modern conservatism—are treated more harshly than governments of a more liberal stripe. In other countries, a similar sentiment is expressed. The media, or at least the mainstream media, report with a liberal slant, which means that the conservative view receives more criticism.

In liberal democracies, the media are assigned an important role. They are supposed to provide information to the citizenry about public affairs so that informed decisions can be made about government policy and elected representatives. The media also act as guard dogs, always on the watch for corruption and wrongdoing by politicians and appointed officials. More generally, they establish a link between the people and their government, a link that is essential to the operation of democracy. Accordingly, the media are important political actors. In carrying out this role, the expectation is that the media will be largely neutral or objective. A biased media might provide distorted information and be too willing to play watchdog with a particular political orientation. People understand that bias can seep into a story (and some media commentators are paid to be political), but this is not supposed to happen too often. But the prime minister says it does, and so do others. There is evidence that shows that journalists in Canada and elsewhere have liberal leanings. They tend to be less critical of politicians on the left side of the political spectrum and support policies that enlarge the size of government. This would be harmless if these leanings had little effect on media offerings, but some show that the separation between personal belief and professional behaviour is hard for the media to maintain: the liberalism of the journalist finds its way into the stories that we read and hear. The liberal bias is sometimes obvious—some cable news networks make no bones about their political orientation—but most times it is more subtle. Nevertheless, even a subtle bias when added up over time has an important impact on the reporting of political life.

The idea of a liberal bias in the media resonates with many, but there are others who insist that journalist practices protect us against too much bias in the media. These practices—which amount to implicit rules—require that both sides of a story be presented, that experts be consulted, and that quotations marks be used to make clear when opinions are being expressed; and then there are the editorial filters that act to catch any remaining political bias that has managed to slip through. When even if this fails, it is suggested that a disinterested media is still possible if they commit themselves to being open to all ideas, to digging deep to locate all the relevant facts, and to reporting the unvarnished truth. It is hard to let go of the belief that the media are—or can be—objective, because without this quality the whole journalistic exercise seems pointless and fraudulent.

For still others, it is impossible to prevent bias because the media are never really reporting; in truth, they are making stories out of a tidal wave of information and thus are engaged in a selection exercise—we need this for the story, but not that. This selecting of what to use could be influenced by a liberal bias, but some researchers believe that the most important bias in the making of stories is a commercial one. In other words, the bias is not oriented toward influencing political developments, but rather works toward creating media products that will attract an audience. This bias acts to craft stories that have entertainment value—simple, dramatic, full of conflict, and with a focus on personalities (as opposed to issues or social forces). The bias creates not a world of liberalism in the media, but one that turns politics into a series of stories, some say soap operas, whose purpose is not to educate or inform but to entertain and draw audiences. This seems an obvious truth, so much so that many dismiss it as being too obvious or not a bias at all; it just describes how the media works. And so the debate continues.

Lydia Miljan, a professor at the University of Windsor argues that a liberal bias can be detected in the media. Paul Barker argues that a bias exists, but it is a commercial bias and not a political one.

✔ **YES**

Political Bias in the Media
LYDIA MILJAN

In the dying days of the 2011 federal election campaign, Liberal Leader Michael Ignatieff urged voters to avoid the media. In a May 1, 2011, clip aired on both the CBC's *The National* and on *CTV News* he said, "I'm saying turn the TV off, turn the radio off, put the papers aside and decide what kind of Canada you want." A day earlier, on April 30, when asked to respond to the news that *The Toronto Star* was endorsing the NDP, he quipped, "Canadians actually make up their own mind. They're not going to be told how to vote by the pollsters. They're not going to be told how to vote by the press." While it is common for the losing candidate to blame the media for their poor performance, there were others who alleged that the media were biased against the Conservatives. Margaret Wente in her May 5, 2011, *Globe and Mail* column noted Conservative Prime Minister Stephen Harper's disdain for the media:

> If you want to understand why Mr. Harper loathes the mainstream media, look no further.... [T]he media demonize the very qualities that have made him a success. They hate him for his micro-managing, control freak ways. But those same qualities have been crucial to his success.... When the Liberals courted new Canadians, it was smart. When the Conservatives do it, it's sleazy.... They were focused and had ground troops who worked hard. For this, they're being accused of running a soulless and techno-cratic campaign. (When Liberals ran things this way, they were called "professional.")[1]

Is bias in the eyes of the beholder? People on the left of the political spectrum are often heard arguing that the media are biased in favour of business, right-wing government, and conservative interests. They claim that because the media are a business they reflect the views of owners whom they perceive to be on the political right. In the same vein, those on the political right argue that the media are biased in favour of left-wing politicians, social dissidents, and liberal interests. The rationale for this argument is that journalists themselves can be placed to the left of their bosses and owners, and the news reflects the journal-ists' predispositions. Who is right? Both sides will feature anecdotal evidence to make their case. For example, there have been some pointed comments made by media insiders regarding Sun TV, the all-news station owned by Quebecor. Some critics, including some well-known journalists, insisted in advance of its launch that the channel would be nothing more than a Canadian copy of the so-called "right wing" Fox News station in the United States. They argue, as Don Newman, retired CBC journalist said, "The reality is that it [Fox News] mainly spews out propaganda that is dangerously misleading and often factually wrong."[2] Despite Newman's assertion about the bias of Fox News, in a study that compared the headlines of CNN and Fox News, CNN was "perceived as more liberal than FOX News, rather than Fox News' headlines being perceived as more conservative than CNN."[3] In contrast, proponents of the channel argue that a conservative news channel will provide much needed diversity of news in Canada, as television airwaves are overwhelming leftist in their approach. The implied and overt declarations made by those who oppose this development are that Canadian news is balanced, accurate, and truthful, with no political distortion. Martin Krossel, writing for the blog site *Frum Forum* claims, "There is a narrower range of opinion in Canadian electronic journalism as a whole than there is at Fox."[4] The fact that Quebecor believes it can make a profit with a right-of-centre editorial stance suggests that there is something lacking in the Canadian marketplace of ideas.

Clearly, there are differences on whether the media are biased toward left or right or whether there is even any bias at all. However, the relevant evidence suggests that the confusion created by the conflicting positions can be resolved in favour of the claim that a bias indeed exists in the mainstream media in Canada (and elsewhere in the developed world) and that this bias results in a media that support liberal views. The aforementioned evidence includes instances of liberal bias in the news but also relies on a consideration of conditions that logically leads to a media slanted to the left.

CONDITIONS FOR A LIBERAL BIAS

Daniel Sutter, a student of media relations, notes that it is difficult to ascertain what kind of bias exists in the media using empirical research. Some will present instances of a right-wing or conservative bias, and others will do the same to support a claim for a left-wing or liberal bias. As a result, he seeks to measure bias through a series of three questions whose answers elicit conditions that provide fertile ground for a liberal bias. His first question is what is the nature of the bias? Is it a demand or supply bias? In other words, do consumers demand liberal ideas more than conservative ones, or do journalists supply them? If the former, a liberal orientation reflects the wishes of readers and nullifies the case for a liberal bias; if the latter, the case becomes strong.[5] In 1996 my colleague, Barry Cooper, and I compared a survey of journalists and Canadians on their backgrounds and values.[6] What we found was that journalists are different from other Canadians. They are more educated; live in urban areas; are predominantly male; have few children; have been divorced; and are not regular churchgoers. In short, they have, what Ronald Inglehart calls post-materialist tendencies.

Inglehart argues that as societies go from periods of want to periods of affluence, they move away from worrying about putting a roof over their heads, feeding and clothing their children, to focus on higher order things such as the environment, human rights, and social justice. This is not to say that post-materialists don't care about their children—only that they tend to have fewer children overall, and that their affluence means they don't need to worry about basic necessities, but can worry about the legacy that they leave to these children.[7]

The argument about why journalists are different rests with post-materialism. By virtue of their status in society, well-educated, affluent, and urban journalists tend to be at the forefront of social change. To test this theory, our survey also looked at what journalists thought about certain issues and how these thoughts compared with the rest of the population. On economic and social issues, journalists led public opinion. Journalists were more supportive of women's groups; they were more likely to support a woman's choice for the termination of a pregnancy. In addition, they also led public opinion on the issue of gay rights. On economic issues, journalists were more likely to support state intervention. In and of themselves, these views should not determine news coverage. Supporters of the press argue that journalistic norms and professional codes of conduct mean that they can put aside their personal beliefs and biases and focus on providing balanced coverage of issues, events, and people. It is true that much of the news does balance or provide neutral descriptions of events. However, when we looked at opinion statements we find that, on average, the opinions presented in the news on economic and social issues reflect the views that the journalists have on those issues. This is despite the fact that, on the economy, for example, journalist views were at odds with the professionals in the field: economists.

What our findings and other research suggests, is that, yes, journalists will provide two sides of the story. However, in their selection of sources, they disproportionately choose the sources that reflect their own prejudices on a subject. The economic subject we examined was unemployment and inflation. According to leading economists there is no tradeoff between low unemployment and low inflation. However, in our survey of journalists, the majority thought there was such a tradeoff.[8] In other words, in the context of the 1990s when Canadians were moving from a high inflation period to the zero inflation policy that we have today, there was great concern that the reduction in inflation would result in even higher unemployment than the double-digit unemployment of the time. This was the tenor of the discussion presented on television news and in newspapers. Even though the majority of economists at the time argued that you could have both, the Canadian media gave disproportionate coverage of the naysayers, even though the pessimists were in the minority when it came to their professional opinion. Therefore, even though on the surface there seemed to be some balance in the coverage in that both sides were presented, the fact that the side in least agreement with the conventional wisdom of the critics was given more attention led us to conclude that, indeed, journalist opinions matter, and they can and do influence the news.

Reaction to these findings was not universally favourable. Indeed, the harshest critics of the study came from journalists themselves. They argued that, whatever their own personal views and backgrounds, there were journalist norms and standards and that these dictated what became the news. While it is true that journalism has normative rules that require balance and fair coverage, content analyses have demonstrated imbalanced coverage. In my own research I have found that on social issues, the coverage emphasizes a move toward more progressive values. On economic issues, bad news is emphasized, and the solutions to the financial woes are often more government regulation.[9]

Is it mere coincidence that the imbalance in coverage is in the same direction as the mindsets of journalists themselves? In other words, are the imbalance and the personal views of journalists unrelated? One part of the theory of journalists influencing the news relates to sources. While journalists may argue that the coverage merely reflects the arguments of the sources in the news, what they neglect to mention is that news is produced. By that I mean news does not simply happen. What people hear on the radio, watch on TV, read in the newspaper, or even download online is a result of a conscious decision to select what is newsworthy.

As mentioned, bias in the media is a difficult thing to measure empirically, but easy to spot anecdotally, and that is why people are quite clear on what is and is not media bias. Take, for example, a rather innocuous campaign story from the 2011 election trail. The headline of the story was "Liberals say they're targets of prank campaign calls."[10] The majority of the story focused on how some people were calling constituents, behaving rudely, and passing themselves off as Liberals. While none of the allegations had been proven, the story ended ironically with the following revelation: "Another riding in the GTA is also making news for its tightly contested race that allegedly prompted one party organizer to take drastic steps. A Liberal campaign worker in Brampton West was arrested and charged last week with possession of stolen property after police allegedly found several lawn signs belonging to the Conservative candidate in the back of his truck."[11] The fact that a Liberal party worker who was charged with theft was neither the main focus of the story nor the headline prompted a furious series of responses by readers who complained of a left-leaning bias in *The Toronto Star*. However, in a similar story, national television news provided even less context than did *The Star*. In the first story aired on *CTV News* on the night of April 24, 2011, the Liberals complained that they were the targets of "politically motivated vandalism." Several Liberal candidates and campaign workers had had tires slashed and cars keyed by vandals. In his "Election 2011" report, Roger Smith noted, "While some local Liberals have accused the Tories, their candidate denies it." Nowhere in the story was there any indication of who actually did the vandalism; there was only the suggestion that there were Conservatives involved. In the story, Bob Rae had to concede one point: "I have a lot of thoughts about Mr. Harper. I don't think for a moment that he slashed the tires on my car. I just want you to know that." Following that statement, Smith added, "But Ignatieff suspects it is politically motivated." Michael Ignatieff was then quoted as saying, "There are people out there who take partisanship to threatening extremes." While Roger Smith acknowledged "all parties have complained about their signs being defaced and stolen," he did not mention the arrest of the Liberal candidate for stealing Conservative signs that had happened a week prior.

Certainly the survey referred to above provides the argument that we are talking about a supply-side bias. The key to the survey was not necessarily what journalists thought about the issues, but that they were to the left of what the general public thought about those same issues. Journalists were more supportive of abortion rights, more sympathetic to Aboriginal rights, and to the left of the public on economic issues.

Even if you accept that journalists are to the left of the public, there still remains the fact that in a commercial media, owners should have the power to influence content. Thus Sutter's second question asks why owners, who presumably are in the business of making money, allow journalists to bias the news in a direction outside their own interests? Part of the answer has to do with the occupational norms and rules of behaviour for journalists. There are two types of rules: constitutive and regulative. Constitutive rules govern what journalists consider newsworthy. Regulative rules, on the other hand, "tell journalists how to produce" the news.[12] Owners and managers may have some control on the regulative rules, such as assigning reporters to cover certain stories, but they have less control on the constitutive rules such as how to write the stories. The constitutive rules are bound by norms of the journalistic profession and allow journalists much leeway in how they pursue their stories.

But this only explains part of the reason. The other relates to the fact that "[c]orporate media owners will be more interested in maximizing profits than pushing a political agenda."[13] Thus, by allowing journalists to slant the news, they could be potentially losing profits. But it is one thing to want journalists to present a more conservative perspective and another to enforce it. As Sutter argues, "liberal bias in the news simply reflects the potential for discretion, just as peer review contributes to a liberal bias in academia." In other words, "the cost of controlling reporters will be high."[14] However, others theorize that bias "does not arise from consumer preferences for confirmatory information, reporters' incentives to promote their own views, or politicians' ability to capture the media. Instead, it arises as a natural consequence of firms' desire to build a reputation for accuracy, and in spite of the fact that eliminating bias could make all agents in the economy better off."[15] In other words, if the journalism pack has a preconceived notion of the accuracy of a topic, the pack's conventional wisdom will enforce the bias, rather than the owners, or even the facts of the issue.

The third and final question Sutter asks is why don't news organizations act to capture the market that isn't being satisfied by a media with a liberal bias? I have argued elsewhere[16] that if you consider all the media outlets at our disposal, Canadians have a balanced media diet. Looking at all the choices for news, we indeed have many options and avenues for information: talk radio, public radio, several newspaper chains, television networks, the Internet, and even bloggers. When scholars and others talk about media bias, they are not examining the overall amount of media that we have the opportunity to consume, but rather national media because of its potential "greater impact on the political agenda than these other outlets do."[17] In some respects, the fact that we have many types of news organizations suggests that some organizations have in fact moved to provide a more balanced presentation of the news. However, if one takes a look at the most powerful component of the Canadian media, national television news, there appears to be a much better sense of how the media overall works like a monopoly or cartel seeking to maintain the status quo—and to keep out competitors who want change by moving to the right. When Sun TV was first announced, CTV's *Question Period* had a panel discussion on the application by Quebecor. The host of the program, Craig Oliver, asked his guest, Ezra Levant, about the viability of such a station. His question revealed much about the network's concern for a new competitor:

> So, Mr. Levant, if you're right that this is just going to be your usual news public affairs network, no different than the other two that exist now, then really who needs it? We're struggling for audiences, we are all of us, we don't need another news channel, I don't think. Why do you?[18]

Sutter argues that more players in a media system, in other words, more competition, allows for increased market diversification. The fact that the *National Post* was launched indicates that there was room in the newspaper market for someone to tap into discontented conservatives who had no voice in Canadian newspapers. When the Asper family purchased the former Southam newspaper chain from Hollinger (which included the *National Post*), they wanted to put their own editorial spin on the national chain. In particular, they wanted the national editorial to run in all the papers in the chain and to have no dissenting voices. The national editorial lasted less than a year. Sutter examines this issue specifically of how the cartel works and its ability to keep out the competitor:

> What prevents a change of orientation at an existing news organization, or how can cartel members punish a cheating firm? Professionalism provides journalists some ability to enforce their practices on news organization through peer evaluation. If the new owners of a television network set about trying to impose a conservative perspective on the news product, other journalists could criticize the compromise of journalistic independence and deterioration of the quality of coverage.[19]

The reason why the national editorial was abandoned so quickly was precisely because of the outrage and dissent heard from journalist insiders and media critics on the outside.[20] Despite the fact that the Aspers held the purse strings, the power of professional norms prevented them from imposing their own editorial stance on the newspaper chain as a whole.

That was the case for a company taking over an existing chain. But what if someone wants to start their own news organization? The same can be said for the entrance of Sun TV into the all-news market. Again Sutter offers an interesting argument about the difficulty of pursuing a new television station and offers insight into the way in which Sun TV was welcomed. He indicates that in addition to the potential barrier of journalistic pressure, there is also the government regulatory environment. In other words, a cartel can only be successful if it has the cooperation of government regulators. In Canada, the Canadian Radio-television Telecommunications Commission (CRTC) limits the number of television stations. Quebecor was denied a category 1 licence, which would give it financial resources and access to a larger market. The CRTC advised Quebecor to apply for a Category 2 licence, which it did obtain.[21] With the aid of the CRTC, the cartel has limited the ability for Sun TV to compete directly with their market. Another way in which the competitors have tried to limit Sun TV's entry into the market is Bell's decision not to allow the Sun TV signal broadcast on its satellite service. Bell is the parent company of CTV. While Sun TV says that Bell is afraid to compete with Sun TV, Bell argues that the reason for not distributing the licence has to do with the fee that Sun TV asked for from Bell. However, had Sun TV been given their category 1 licence, Bell would have been compelled to distribute the channel to its customers. In this way, Sutter is correct that a news cartel needs to have support from government regulators.

AN EMPIRICAL CASE

It is too early to determine what effect, if any, Sun TV will have on the Canadian media landscape. However, even if we don't have a news cartel, content analyses of the news coverage of the 2011 federal election campaign indicates that pack journalism is alive and well. The Media Observatory at McGill conducted a content analysis of newspaper coverage of the federal election campaign. In their most recent analysis, they looked at the eight regional and national newspapers (*Calgary Herald, Montreal Gazette, National Post, Regina Leader Post, The Globe and Mail, The Toronto Star, Vancouver Sun,* and *Winnipeg Free Press*).[22] While they do not provide the breakdown for net tone (the difference between the positive and negative comments) for each of the newspapers, their research shows that, taken together, Canadian newspapers provide more positive attention to Liberal and NDP campaigns than they do of Conservative campaigns. In the most recent election, the Conservative party/leader net tone was consistently below that of the Liberals and the NDP. Despite the fact that, throughout the campaign, the Liberals were losing popular support, their net tone in Canadian newspapers continued to rise or stay the same, at least until the last two weeks of the campaign. In contrast, the NDP led the net tone in terms of favourable coverage throughout the election campaign, with the one exception in the second week when the Liberals surpassed their coverage. The Conservatives were always third. To look at this data one would might assume that the Conservatives were the third place party in the national polls, rather than the Liberals. This cannot be attributed to the campaign dynamics in this one election. The McGill group also found similar trends in the 2008 campaign and, to a lesser extent, in the 2006 election campaign. The McGill group attributes these findings to the fact that the Conservative Party represents the government, and therefore will receive more attacks from the opposition parties. In addition, they note that parties in the lead tend to receive more critical scrutiny because of their potential to become government. The media's role in this case is to help provide due diligence by vetting the campaign platform and the party's ability to form government.

For the 2011 federal election campaign, I conducted a content analysis of national television news coverage. In this study, I examined the two main evening news programs of CBC and CTV. *The National* on CBC and *CTV News* are the flagship programs of the two networks. Each network sends teams of reporters on the campaign buses to follow the leader tours during the campaign. Each also has an all-news channel that devotes considerable time and space to national affairs reporting and uses the same journalists to feed stories into the talk shows. Thus, the main programs on the national networks are informed by much of what appears on the all-news channels and are a good indicator of the overall tenor and focus of the national press corps.

Much like the McGill findings on newspapers, television coverage of the Conservative campaign was more critical of them than it was of any of the other political parties. As can be seen in Figure 1, for each week during the campaign, the net negative evaluations of the Conservatives were always greater than the Liberals or the NDP. The only exception was during the final week, when the Liberals net negative surpassed that of the Conservatives. Nonetheless, in every week of the campaign, the NDP had more positive than negative comments made about them. More significant was the finding regarding the balance between positive and negative evaluations. During the first week of the campaign, the Liberals had the highest frequency of positive evaluations. In the second week, the Liberals and Conservatives were tied for positive evaluations, and the NDP were given very little attention. However, most of it was positive. In the third week, while the Conservatives had the highest frequency of positive statements, they also had a dramatic increase in negative statements, which gave them the highest net negative score. By the fourth week of the campaign, national television news had very few nice things to say about either the Liberals or the Conservative

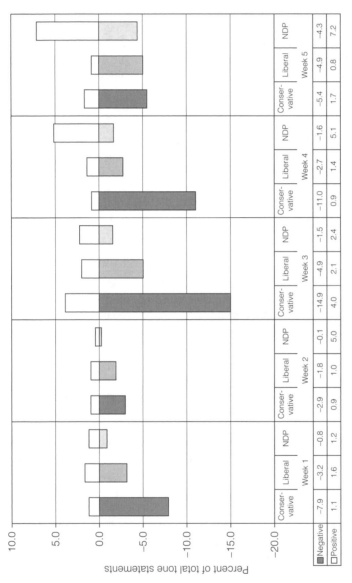

FIGURE 1

TELEVISION NET TONE OF TOP THREE PARTIES 2011 FEDERAL ELECTION CAMPAIGN (CBC AND CTV COMBINED)

Cheryl Collier, 2007.

| | Week 1 | | | Week 2 | | | Week 3 | | | Week 4 | | | Week 5 | | |
	Conser-vative	Liberal	NDP	Conser-vative	Liberal	NDP	Conser-vative	Liberal	NDP	Conser-vative	Liberal	NDP	Conser-vative	Liberal	NDP
Negative	-7.9	-3.2	-0.8	-2.9	-1.8	-0.1	-14.9	-4.9	-1.5	-11.0	-2.7	-1.6	-5.4	-4.9	-4.3
Positive	1.1	1.6	1.2	0.9	1.0	5.0	4.0	2.1	2.4	0.9	1.4	5.1	1.7	0.8	7.2

Percent of total tone statements

campaigns, but a whole lot of complimentary things to say about the NDP. Much of this coverage had to do with public opinion polls, which suggested that the NDP were surging in popularity in Quebec. It is ironic that, while the NDP were surging in Quebec, the media did not turn their focus more sharply on the NDP policies or candidates, both of which had been given precious little attention in the past, but warranted such scrutiny now. In the final week of the campaign, the NDP started to get this needed critical inquiry, and their negative numbers were consistent with those of the Liberals and Conservatives. However, even with the added critical coverage, they also received their highest volume of positive evaluations of the entire campaign.

The other notable finding is that on a weekly basis, the Liberals, who were increasingly losing public support throughout the election campaign, still managed to receive fewer critical evaluations compared to the Conservatives. Though the Liberals did not have the same fawning coverage that the NDP enjoyed, they still were given an easier ride on national television news than the Conservatives. Thus, despite Michael Ingatieff's advice to the Canadian electorate, the coverage of the Liberal campaign was in fact more favourable than that afforded to the Conservatives.[23]

When we look at the news—the type of information that consumers expect to be free from ideological bias—we find an imbalance to the left. We also see that this imbalance is not the result of media owners demanding views from the left but, instead, the internal views of journalists slipping into the news coverage. On a variety of issues and over a large span of time, we have documented how and when the media, in particular, television news, has tilted to the left. This has been the case in economic, social, and electoral news coverage. The ability for media owners to limit or even control this coverage is hampered by the journalist pack and supported, at least on television, by government regulation. It will be interesting to see to what extent Sun TV will be able to provide an alternative voice or whether it will be marginalized by other journalists and licensing decisions of the CRTC.

NOTES

1. Margaret Wente, "Here's Why Stephen Harper Really Won," *The Globe and Mail*, May 5, 2011, available at http://www.theglobeandmail.com/news/opinions/opinion/heres-why-stephen-harper-really-won/article2010333/. Accessed August 23, 2011.

2. Don Newman, "The Absolute Last Thing this Country Needs," *CBC News*, March 24, 2010, available at http://www.cbc.ca/news/canada/story/2010/06/10/f-vp-newman.html. Accessed August 23, 2011.

3. Jeffrey N. Weatherly et al., "Perceptions of Political Bias in the Headlines of Two Major News Organizations," *Press/Politics* 12, no. 2 (2007), p. 97.

4. Martin Krossel, *Challenging Canada's Left-Wing Media Bias*, June 16, 2010, available at http://www.frumforum.com/challenging-canadas-left-wing-media. Accessed May 16, 2011.

5. Daniel Sutter, "Can the Media Be So Liberal? The Economics of Media Bias," *Cato Journal* 20, no. 3 (2001 Winter), pp. 431–450.

6. Lydia Miljan and Barry Cooper, *Hidden Agendas: How Journalists Influence the News* (Vancouver: UBC Press, 2003).

7. Ronald Inglehart, *The Silent Revolution: Changing Values and Political Styles among Western Publics* (Princeton: Princeton University Press, 1977).

8. Miljan and Cooper, *The Silent Revolution*, p. 78.

9. Lydia Miljan, "Balance Is in the Eye of the Beholder," in Josh Greenberg and Charlene Elliott, *Communication in Question: Competing Perspectives on Controversial Issues in Communications Studies* (Toronto: Thomson Nelson, 2008), pp. 52–58.

10. Richard J. Brennan and Kenyon Wallace, "Liberals Say They're Targets of Prank Campaign Calls," *The Toronto Star,* April 19, 2011, available at http://www.thestar.com/news/canada/politics/article/977041--liberals-say-they-re-targets-of-prank-campaign-calls. Accessed August 23, 2011.

11. Ibid.

12. David Michael Ryfe, "The Nature of News Rules," *Political Communication* 23 (2006), p. 204.

13. Sutter, "Can the Media Be So Liberal?", p. 442.

14. Ibid., p. 444.

15. Matthew Gentzkow and Jesse M. Shapiro, "Media Bias and Reputation," *Journal of Political Economy* 114, no. 2 (2006), p. 310.

16. Lydia Miljan, "Balance Is in the Eye of the Beholder."

17. Sutter, "Can the Media Be So Liberal?", p. 431.

18. "Conservative-based Television," *Question Period,* CTV, June 13, 2010.

19. Sutter, "Can the Media Be So Liberal?", p. 447.

20. See, for example, Saleem Khan, "'Unapologetically Pro-Israel' Canwest Imposes National Editorials on Local Papers," *The Washington Report on Middle East Affairs* (April 2002), p. 26; Aaron Moore, "Ownership: A Chill in Canada," *Columbia Journalism Review* 40, no. 6 (2002), pp. 1–11; Dan Luzadder, "Canadian Media and Deregulation Provides Insight into FCC Proposal," July 15, 2010, available at http://www.ojr.org/ojr/law/1054219939.php; Leslie Regan Shade, "Aspergate: Concentration, Convergence and Censorship in Canadian Media," in David Skinner, James Compton, and Michael Gasher, eds., *Converging Media, Diverging Politics: A Political Economy of News Media in the United States and Canada.* (Toronto: Rowan & Littlefield Publishers Inc., 2005), pp. 101–116; Walter Soderlund and Kai Hildebrandt, *Canadian Newspaper Ownership in the Era of Convergence: Rediscovering Social Responsibility* (Edmonton: University of Alberta Press, 2005); Robert Balingall, "Black Consciousness and the Canadain Media's Portrayal of the Third World," *Undercurrent* 3, no. 2 (2006), pp. 52–59; and Paul Knox, "'Not in the Newsroom': Free Expression and Media Concentration in Canada: The Case of Canwest Global," *The RoundTable: The Commonwealth Journal of International Affairs* 91 no. 320 (2008). pp. 503–520.

21. A category 1 licence is a specialty service that provides it digital access privileges; in other words, the cable and satellite distributors are obligated to provide the service. A category 2 licence is not given this assured digital access and therefore the station has to negotiate the fee and distribution with the service providers.

22. McGill Institute for the Study of Canada, "2011 Canadian Federal Election Newspaper Content Analysis," Media Report, May 1, 2011, available at http://www.mcgill.ca/misc/research/media-observatory/eleciton2011/. Accessed August 23, 2011.

23. It should be noted, however, that when one considers newspaper endorsements, Mr. Ignatieff did have a valid point. According to Dwayne Winseck, journalism professor at Carleton University, of the twenty-two Canadian daily newspapers that endorsed a political party for the 2011 election, twenty-one directed readers to vote for the Conservatives. Only *The Toronto Star* endorsed the NDP. His response to this outcome was, "This is not a free press. This is bad for democracy. The fact that a shackled press now stands to an extraordinary degree singing their praises for Dear Leader S. Harper from the same hymn sheet should give us pause for thought and reflection."[24]

Just as reporters are different from the general public in their opinions and orientations toward public policy, they are also different than people hired to express a political point of view. Thus you can have editorials providing a very different presentation and interpretation than the news pages. This does not mean that the two cancel each other out. People look at editorials and columns differently than they do news stories. When we read a particular columnist, we expect to see a stark point of view and we may discount much of what they say because of the knowledge that the source is paid to be biased. However, when we read a news story or see one presented on TV, we have an expectation that the reporter has not imposed their own personal views on the story, but rather has faithfully presented both sides. In addition, the volume of news stories is considerably greater than that of editorials. Thus, overall, we tend to receive a higher proportion of news that favours the left of the political spectrum than the right.

24. Dwayne Winseck, "Politics, the Press and Bad News for Democracy: Newspaper Endorsements Update on Last Day Before Election," *Mediamorphis*, May 1, 2011, available at http://dwmw.wordpress.com/2011/05/01/politics-the-press-and-bad-news-for-democracy-newspaper-endorsements-update-on-last-day-before-election/. Accessed August 23, 2011.

✗ **NO**

A Bias But Not a Political One
PAUL BARKER

During the federal election campaign of 2011, the country's two national news-papers offered readers a variety of images to describe the election. *The Globe and Mail* began with a list of key "battleground ridings" that would determine the fate of the parties.[1] The *Globe's* headlines pursued the metaphor further, claiming that the chances of a majority Conservative government depended on the "battle for the Atlantic" and then the "battle for Ontario."[2] The *National Post* employed the same basic image, but adjusted it to suit the boxing ring, noting that in an important riding, the Liberals had the "reigning champ" in a "[h]eavyweight battle" against a strong Conservative candidate (and the *Globe* quoted the Liberal leader as saying he saw himself as "a fighter who had done a lot of roadwork").[3] Arguably the *Post's* most arresting image was that of the prime minister riding the "whitewater rapids...taking as few risks as possible"[4] (with rapids refer-ring to the leaders' debates). The most popular image was the best-known one, namely the election as a horse race. Early on, the NDP faltered "amid talk of [a] two-way race"; the Conservative Party ran a "frontrunner's campaign" right from the start; the competing parties "enter[ed] the final sprint" in the latter part of the campaign; and at the end the "finish line [was] in sight."[5] The polls, of course, abetted the use of this particular image, something which their creators lamented—pollsters wanted their efforts to be used "to explain the underlying forces that are producing political change." But the plea was to no avail: "[t]he media...are much more interested in the horse-race side of things," said one pollster.[6] The prize for the most ominous image went to the Marxist-like depiction of a "spectre" on the horizon—in this case, a coalition government involving the three opposition parties.[7] With this image, the *Globe* had sought to downplay the possibility of a coalition, but it doubtlessly acted to draw attention to a nagging issue in the minds of voters.

The intent here is not to reveal the aptitudes of the two national newspapers for images, but to do something more relevant: to argue that the media are hardly a purveyor of political biases when covering politics in Canada and elsewhere. (Incidentally, it is also to suggest that the contrary—that the media are free of any bias—is also untrue.) What the initial paragraph reveals is that a different type of bias, a commercial one, influences and shapes the stories, pictures, reports, and anything else the media present to the public on politics. The use of images and the like are part and parcel of the larger attempt of the media to enliven their presentations in order to attract readers and viewers. Radio, newspapers, televi-sion, the Internet—all forms of the media—are in the business of doing business, and the way to do business is to draw large audiences to themselves in order to secure large amounts of advertising. To draw large audiences, such images as battles, horse races, white-water canoeists, and spectres are vital because they give life to a political system that can be dreary and dry. In light of the focus on commercial viability, an attempt to introduce a political slant threatens one segment or another of the market for media products; that is, a political bias makes little sense. In a way, the media resemble politicians wishing to attract all types of views and refrain from offending anyone. When it comes to politics, the media are no longer about public affairs; rather, they are about entertainment, or more accurately a combination of the two—"infotainment."[8]

A LIBERAL BIAS

The issue of bias in the media attracts a great deal of critical attention. "'Bias' refers to any systematic favoring of one position," writes Street, and it is generally felt that such a quality should be absent in the media's presentation of political news.[9] It is granted that the media should be allowed to pursue a profitable existence, but the public also "widely expect[s]" the media "to function in the public interest" and to present a neutral or objective view.[10] Accordingly, any evidence of media bias is unsettling, partly because viewers and readers feel personally betrayed. In effect, there has been a breach in the implicit agreement between the media and the general public. But more important is the fact that in the long run, bias may hurt or damage the healthy functioning of a democratic state. Any first-year student in political science learns that the media offer information to the citizenry basic to the operation of democracy. People rarely gain a solid appreciation of a policy initiative or elect the best leaders if they are without the requisite information. Slanting the news slants our understanding. The assumption in making this argument is that the media do in fact matter and that their offerings have an impact. Without this assumption, bias in the media would be irrelevant; the media might favour one party or candidate, but it would matter little. At times, there has been some dispute about the effect of the media—some have argued that their role is in fact minimal—but the scholarly consensus now appears to confirm the teachings in Political Science 101. At a minimum, the media determine what people will consider important in politics, and they may even have some influence on how people will think about the critical issues. As Taras writes, the media "alert the public about which events are important and...set the context in which those events could be understood."[11]

The two types of biases most often discussed are a right-wing or conservative bias and a left-wing or liberal bias. In a nutshell, the former refers to news reports that support (or even heartily approve) initiatives, party actions, and ideas that limit the role of government, champion economic markets, and preserve the status quo on sensitive moral issues. The latter refers to media presentations that do the opposite—give the benefit of the doubt to government and criticize public officials who rely too easily on markets and slight the need for greater justice and equality. Polls certainly reveal public fears of political bias in the media, and political leaders and members of parties voice the same sentiment. Of the two types, the conservative-bias claim gets relatively little attention aside from the avowedly right-wing Fox News in the United States and radio personalities in the same country. There is also an argument that some owners of the various media outlets force a right-wing viewpoint upon their employees, but this argument holds little sway among most media scholars (partly because the employees—the journalists—can successfully resist such intrusions). It is, however, a different matter with a liberal bias. Anecdotal evidence and polling of public viewpoints furnish much support for a liberal bias in the media, but more important is the scientific evidence. Studies show that journalists tend to hold political views that lie left of the general population, a product seemingly of such factors as their education (relatively high level), religious orientation (more nonbelievers), and economic status (high level, again).[12] For instance, they are more critical of free trade arrangements and oppose privatization in various areas of public policy. This finding, by itself, is insufficient to make the case for a liberal bias—it assumes, incorrectly, that views are automatically translated into news copy—so some studies try to show that journalists and other makers of media content are able to express their views in their work. One such study of the Canadian media shows some correlation between views and stories—the two tend to be left of centre. The liberal journalist emphasizes the bad side of reports on high inflation and low employment, and even when the news is good on the economy, the bad side makes an appearance in the story. A similar dynamic takes place with social issues—the media tends to side with the kind of progressive social change we associate with liberalism.

The case for a liberal bias is strengthened by theory. Inglehart and his colleagues allege that many developed societies are embracing "post-materialism," a mindset which in the area of politics and policy involves a shift "from economic subsistence and the role of the (pre-imbedded) state in the economy to a concern with "higher order" issues, chiefly matters such as human rights, feminism and environmentalism."[13] The cause for this shift from a material to a post-material world is economic growth and its attendant developments—higher levels of education, for instance—that allow large segments of the population to be less worried about jobs and the economy and to be more concerned about progressive issues. Journalists fall into this category and are thus provided with a social foundation for their liberal thinking.

Notwithstanding the support for a liberal bias, many arguments can be arrayed against the proposition. One argument is to fight fire with fire: the empirical basis for a liberal bias is not that strong. In a study of television coverage of the 2006 federal election, Barber found that the "networks presented fair and balanced coverage and held themselves to high professional standards,"[14] and in a further study, Barber (with Rauhala) suggested that the professed vote preferences of news directors "are in line with those of the general population."[15] Even studies that find some trace of a liberal bias are at times almost underwhelming—the case they make could be stronger. For example, journalists may indeed be unlike the general population in some respects, but on arguably the more important ones— for example, voting preferences—the differences are not always that great.[16] These same studies also point to another argument against a liberal-biased position on the part of journalists: namely, that the presence of bias might simply be response to a market demand. The studies note the excessive negativity in the stories of journalists, and interpret this as an outgrowth of liberal views. However, it could just as easily be interpreted as the provision of such a style of reporting to a large and responding audience. In other words, the bias is not a supply-sided phenomenon— journalists acting on their political beliefs—but a demand-sided creation flowing from the preferences of viewers. If this is true, the case for a political bias falls away. There is a further argument against the case for a liberal bias. No one challenges the notion of reporters and journalists having political views. But it does not mean that bias in stories and in reports must follow the bias of journalists as night follows day. Procedures may be in place to prevent this—for example, the stipulation in journalistic practice that both sides of the issue be made available or that experts should be consulted on technical issues. Another obstacle may be the journalist's commitment to providing a balanced story. It was noted earlier that the possible presence of bias unsettles the media's audience. The same happens to journalists—accusations of bias "strike at the core of journalists' self-image."[17]

A COMMERCIAL BIAS

The strongest argument against the case of a liberal bias is that a much more powerful bias—a commercial one—colours media offerings. This argument begins with some logic. The components of the media operate in an incredibly competitive environment and "have a vested interest in producing a marketable neutral product."[18] "Deliberately or even innocently alienating a portion of the market through unfair or biased coverage of candidates and causes would be self-destructive," writes Dennis.[19] Some might counter that journalists are able to fend off the demands of owners for profit, but journalists are also vulnerable to the aforementioned competitive forces. Owners' investments would suffer with lost markets, but so would journalists' jobs (and the upside of this is that journalists can enjoy substantial material rewards—money and notoriety—with a strong demand for their stories). Accordingly, one can agree with Nesbitt-Larking's claim that the "principal factor conditioning the structure of the news is commercial viability" and that "the media have to offer texts that attract audiences and keep them."[20] The media need audiences to survive and thrive, so the logically minimal thing to do is limit the loss of markets. Equally important, the media must not only take action to limit the loss of viewers, but they must also act to generate and increase their audience; and the most appropriate method for achieving this end is to create stories—good stories. These kinds of stories have well-known structure—a start, a middle part, and an end—and they also have qualities that the consumer likes: conflict, drama, simplicity, vividness, novelty, and a host of others along the same lines. The important point here is that these stories do not exist to be discovered and reported by journalists. On the contrary, reality is a chaotic mass of happenings out of which the journalist is required to create a sellable story. Media scholars refer to this activity as "framing," whereby the frame "operates to select and highlight some features of reality and obscure others in a way that tells a consistent story about problems, their causes, moral implications, and remedies."[21] The notion of a "narrative" captures the same idea: that the journalist develops a story line with the aforementioned qualities in order to draw the reader or viewer in. Importantly, the framing is often conveyed by a metaphor or analogy that provides the gist of the story and brings to mind the kind of elements that people find worth reading or watching (recall, for example, the metaphor of a prime minister navigating white-water rapids). The upshot of all this is clear:

> All of the concern with ideological bias has obscured the systematic, consistent biases that the media truly do impose on their narrations of politics and policy. The real media biases favor simplicity over complexity, persons over institutional processes, emotions over facts, and most important, game over substance.[22]

In short, there is a bias, but it is not a liberal bias. It is a commercial bias that reaches into the mind to exploit the human predilection for story (and which possibly satisfies a need created by the media themselves). Critics may bemoan the depth and breath of this effect: that media presentations are awash with stories that are little different from soap operas. This may be true, but the aim of this essay is not to assess the quality of media reports in Canada and other developed countries. Rather it is to reveal the dynamics of newsmaking in the twenty-first century and to expose the fact that media are little different from any other institution and entity in a capitalist state: they must sell to survive.

The support for giving pride of place to a commercial bias and not a liberal bias rests upon three reasons. One has already been mentioned: namely, logic. Some journalists (and owners) may enjoy the luxury of pursuing their beliefs at the expense of career and job, but these are few and far between (this, of course, excludes the commentators on op-ed pages and well-known television and radio personalities who are paid to express a political view). Rationally, the liberal bias makes little or no sense. This logical argument is important because empirical evidence alone is often inconclusive: the latter becomes an instance of duelling studies in which each side is able to come up with some supporting concrete evidence. Nevertheless, the empirical evidence, the second reason for believing no liberal bias exists, should be consulted. As shown, there is some support in the scientific literature (and from the less scientific) that a basis can be made for a liberal bias. But a case can also be made for a bias unrelated to politics. In her study of *The Globe and Mail's* coverage of the aftermath of 9/11, Jiwani observes how the media "frame out certain information and frame in, or give privileged attention to, other kinds of information."[23] In this case, the *Globe* used the emotions of hate, resentment, and anger to explain the attack and ignored the possibility that the events were linked to American foreign policy. Doing the former provided the basis for a story with drama, conflict, simplicity, and emotions—classic elements found in commercial bias; doing the latter meant a complicated narrative that might lose readers (and probably upset more than a handful). Barber's study of the 2006 federal election shows how the Canadian media focused on the front-runners, whatever their political affiliation—few wish to watch a race that gives equal time to all the horses—and Soroka and Andrew in their examination of the 2004 and 2006 federal elections find "the relative predominance of horse-race coverage and the corresponding absence of policy content."[24] In his book, Bain documents a well-known practice associated with commercial bias, which is the media's search for gaffes and mistakes in order to humble or even humiliate politicians and provide a good story.[25] Not surprisingly, this particular practice extends beyond Canada; the chief of staff of a former prime minister of Great Britain (Tony Blair) writes that "[a] type of 'gotcha' journalism has developed where the only aim appears to be to catch the politician out in a mistake and thereby generate a headline."[26] American scholars and observers of the media also provide relevant evidence of this. Entman, for example, documents how the U.S. media often slight any serious consideration of issues in favour of superficial treatments "to attract and emotionally gratify mass audiences."[27] Admittedly, he says one can at times discern a conservative bias and other times at liberal bias, but the only consistency in the reporting is to frame the story in a way that respects the requirements of simplicity, drama, personalities, and so on.

Scholarly studies provide a second reason for believing in a commercial bias, but arguably a more convincing way to demonstrate its presence is to examine a detailed case study—in effect, to watch the bias in motion. A decade ago, the Government of Canada (a Liberal one) financed a set of programs that made grants available to help in one way or another to generate and sustain employment. At the time, an internal audit of the programs—released to the public—suggested that the paperwork and follow-up were incomplete, and hence it was difficult to be precise about the whereabouts and impact of some of the funding. This set the stage for news reports that would incorporate the usual qualities associated with commercial bias: drama, personalities, conflict, unexpected developments, and "preformed storylines" that brook only those facts consistent with the story.[28] The media began their coverage with a rather stunning storyline: "one billion dollars lost."[29] The truth was more complicated—the money was not necessarily lost, only unaccounted for—but simplicity is a requisite for a good story; any cursory examination of the facts revealed that the amount in question fell well short of $1 billion, but again, stories rely on simplicity. The drama developed next. The media reported that some of the money was being used for political reasons, channelled into ridings held by the Liberal government. More incredible, it seemed that just about anyone could get a grant with a little effort and no accountability. The program "was a bank machine that required no card or PIN—just line up and get your withdrawal," wrote a reporter with the *Ottawa Citizen*.[30] A good story always requires personalities, so the media began the hunt for likely suspects responsible for the lost money, and found them in the bureaucracy and in the person of the minister of the relevant government department. The unexpected event also contributed to the story line—the government, reported the media, had initially tried to cover up the problem, and the minister herself had been a victim of her own officials' attempt to keep her unaware of the audit results (which turned out to be untrue). Meanwhile, the government made efforts to rectify the problem, efforts that began to show that the unaccounted money was nowhere near the figure of $1 billion—eventually, it would become $85,000. But the media paid little attention to these announcements; they "framed" them out because the announcements failed to fit into the story of government incompetence and corruption. Conflict is also part of any story line, and the media fed on the conflicts between the government and the opposition, between the minister and her officials, and between the prime minister and the bureaucracy. Eventually, reports by a parliamentary committee, the Auditor General of Canada, and the government itself revealed that the whole matter had been blown out of proportion. Yes, there had been inadequate documentation of the grant process, and yes there had been insufficient follow-up to the initial granting of funds; but the activities of the government department had led to the conclusion that the money involved was far less than the amount initially reported.

The aim of this example is not to reveal that commercial biases always lead to a failure of the media to do their purported job, which is to report factually on affairs important to the population. There are some occasions when the yearning to get a story can uncover corruption and faulty administration in government, so the evaluation of media effects is not the immediate point.[31] Rather, the intent is to show how the media operates. They are not a mirror to the world of politics; they are not a body beholden to their owners; and they are not a champion of liberal causes—they are men and women who simply want to create a page-turning story.

Defenders of the liberal bias appear to place little weight on the notion that storytelling and framing are essential to understanding the behaviour of the media. Efforts to produce stories that are "timely, exciting, entertaining, and so on" represent only "normal constraints" in the newsmaking process. True bias, the defenders continue, "is the result of the explicitly political beliefs and sympathies of a journalist intervening in such a way that the meaning of the spin or a particular story is directly affected."[32] (Interestingly, those who argue for a conservative bias make a similar argument, saying that on the surface there is storytelling and commitment to copy full of drama, conflict, and personalities, but underneath this, the reality is an almost unconscious effort to maintain the status quo in politics.[33]) The arguments of those who stand by their claims of liberal bias may be true, but if we are trying to understand how the media works, then these normal constraints are central to the discussion. Admittedly, one could accept that the commerciality of newsmaking is not really a bias and conclude that the argument against the liberal bias is not that there is a more powerful or important bias, but that the media are basically without bias. With this concession, the argument in this essay is still a no to a liberal bias, but the rebuttal is different—the liberal bias is not trumped by another bias, but instead finds itself powerless against the media practice or requirement of making stories. In some respect, this is a more attractive argument than the one for a commercial bias. By linking the story requirement to the natural order of things, the claim for a political bias becomes even weaker—it goes against what is possible in the world of media and politics. But ultimately this concession or adjustment in argument is unsatisfying. The absence of bias in some hands is too tied to a model of newsmaking that sees the journalist as a mere reporter, taking dictation from reality. A preferable argument appreciates that, at a minimum, the media are about selecting and framing, creating something from the chaos of political life. So we come back to the claim of a commercial bias.

CONCLUSION

"It took me time to get used to the lengths the press would go to in order to obtain a story," writes a former senior official in government, whose garbage—among other things—did not escape the attention of the media.[34] This is a common sentiment expressed by those who deal in the realities of politics. Yes, the media are capable of political biases—a party leader may feel slighted during an election campaign—but this is a sideshow and not the main attraction. When we watch television, read the newspapers, surf the Internet, or do anything else connected to the presentation of political news, it is not the political bias that we note, but the story. Sometimes the two may be linked; a liberal bias may be evident. But sometimes it will be missing. However, always apparent is the story and its attendant qualities: the drama, the conflict, the personalities, the negativism, the distortion, the sensationalism, the simplicity, the visually appealing, the unexpected events. This is the world of modern politics.

NOTES

1. John Ibbitson, "The Big 50 that Will Steer the Country," *The Globe and Mail,* March 25, 2011, p. A11.

2. Steven Chase and John Ibbitson, "The Battle for the Atlantic," *The Globe and Mail,* April 21, 2011, p. A1; and Steven Chase and John Ibbitson, "The Battle for Ontario," *The Globe and Mail,* April 26, 2011, p. A1.

3. Jane Taber, "Ignatieff is Running Hard, Both Eyes on Harper," *The Globe and Mail,* March 31, 2011, p. A6.

4. John Ivison, "The Tories Consolidate Their Lead," *National Post,* April 14, 2011, p. A4.

5. John Ibbitson and Gloria Galloway, "NDP Weakens Amid Talk of Two-way Race," *The Globe and Mail,* April 1, 2011, p. A4; Chris Shelley, "Attack Ads Subvert Tory Strategy," *National Post,* April 4, 2011, p. A5; John Ibbitson, Bill Curry, and Gloria Galloway, "Pivotal Stretch Starts with New Motifs: Health Care, Unity," *The Globe and Mail,* April 18, 2011, p. A1; Campbell Clark, "The Finish Line in Sight, NDP Changes Tack," *The Globe and Mail,* April 29, 2011, A1.

6. John Allemang, "To Poll or Not to Poll, that is the Question," *The Globe and Mail,* April 9, 2011, p. A4.

7. Lawrence Martin, "Smoke, Mirrors and a Harper Majority," *The Globe and Mail,* March 29, 2011, p. A19.

8. Susan Welch et al., *Understanding American Government,* 11th ed. (Canada: Thomson Wadsworth, 2008), p. 149. The text is quoting William Henry III.

9. John Street, *Mass Media, Politics & Democracy,* 2nd ed. (New York: Palgrave MacMillan), p. 26.

10. Robert A. Hackett and Yuezhi Zhao, *Sustaining Democracy? Journalism and the Politics of Objectivity* (Toronto: Garamond Press), p. 1.

11. David Taras, quoted in Shannon Sampert and Linda Trimble, *Mediating Canadian Politics* (Toronto: Pearson Canada), p. 283.

12. See most importantly Lydia Miljan and Barry Cooper, *Hidden Agendas: How Journalists Influence the News* (Vancouver and Toronto: UBC Press, 2003). The following discussion centres on this study.

13. Ibid., p. 56.

14. Marsha Barber, "Getting the Picture: Airtime and Lineup Bias on Canadian Networks during the 2006 Federal Election," *Canadian Journal of Communication* 33, no. 4 (2008), p. 630.

15. Marsha Barber and Ann Rauhala, "The Canadian News Directors Study: Demographics and Political Leanings of Television Decision-Makers," *Canadian Journal of Communication* 30, no. 2 (2005), p. 290.

16. Milijan and Cooper, *Hidden Agendas,* p. 74.

17. Street, *Mass Media, Politics & Democracy,* p. 23.

18. Lance Bennett, *News: The Politics of Illusion* (New York: Pearson Longman, 2009), p. 35.

19. Quoted in Ibid., p. 35.

20. Paul Nesbitt-Larking, *Politics, Society, and the Media* (Peterborough: Broadview Press, 2007), p. 153.

21. Robert M. Entman, "Reporting Environmental Policy Debate: The Real Media Biases," *Harvard International Journal of Press/Politics* 1, no. 3, pp. 77–78.

22. Ibid., 78.

23. Yasmin Jiwani, "Covering Canada's Role in the 'War on Terror,'" in Sampert and Trimble, *Mediating Canadian Politics*, p. 312.

24. Barber, "Getting the Picture: Airtime and Lineup Bias on Canadian Networks during the 2006 Federal Election"; and Stuart Soroka and Blake Andrew, "Media Coverage of Canadian Elections: Horse-Race Coverage and Negativity in Election Campaigns," in Sampert and Trimble, *Mediating Canadian Politics*, pp. 113–228.

25. George Bain, *Gotcha: How the Media Distort the News* (Toronto: Key Porter Books, 1994).

26. Jonathan Powell, *The New Machiavelli: How to Wield Power in the Modern World* (London: The Bodley Head, 2010), p. 204.

27. Entman, "Reporting Environmental Policy Debate," p. 83.

28. David Good, *The Politics of Public Management: The HRDC Audit of Grants and Contributions* (Toronto: University of Toronto Press, 2003), p. 63.

29. Ibid., p. 64.

30. Ibid.

31. For example, the set of developments that came to be known as the "Sponsorship Scandal" in Canadian politics. See the Commission of Inquiry into Sponsorship and Advertising Activities, *Who Is Responsible?* (Ottawa: Author, 2005–2006).

32. Miljan and Cooper, *Hidden Agendas*, p. 41.

33. See Nesbitt-Larking, *Politics, Society, and the Media*.

34. Powell, *The New Machiavelli: How to Wield Power in the Modern World*, p. 200.

POSTSCRIPT

Using Sutter's three questions for determining bias, Miljan does a convincing job of establishing the presence of a liberal bias. She adds muscle to the already strong argument that journalists and other members of the fourth estate are politically left of the average viewer or reader. However, it is always difficult to establish a foolproof case. Miljan says she has shown that the liberal bias in the media is supply bias—a product of journalists—but it is not entirely clear that she has accomplished this end. It seems that one might still argue that, even though the journalists are left of the general public, there could still be a large part of the market that would pay to read or hear items with a liberal bias. Miljan also believes that owners might have trouble reigning in journalists writing with a liberal bias, but it is hard to believe that today's media barons would have such a difficulty. As for the Barker paper, it seems to ignore much of the evidence Miljan puts up to support her case. Over and over again, scholars uncover a basis for a liberal bias, yet Barker sticks with his claim that the media need to make money. Journalists will appreciate the need to survive economically, but they are human beings, and sometimes they will act on conviction and belief. Equally important, journalistic norms and concern for reputation, as Miljan says, may in fact make it difficult for media owners to get their way.

Any student wishing to enter into this debate should first read an introduction to the media. The debate mostly refers to the Canadian experience, so we will concentrate on readings relating to Canada. The following represent good introductions to the media in Canada: Frederick J. Fletcher and Robert Everett, "The Mass Media and Canadian Politics in the Era of Globalization," in Michael Whittington and Glen Williams, eds., *Canadian Politics in the 21st Century*, 7th ed. (Toronto: Thomson Nelson, 2008); Heather MacIvor, *Parameters of Power: Canada's Political Institutions*, 5th ed. (Toronto: Nelson Education, 2010), ch. 14; Jonathan Rose and Paul Nesbitt-Larking, "Politics and the Media: Culture, Technology, and Revolution," in John R. Courtney and David E. Smith, eds., *The Oxford Handbook of Canadian Politics* (Toronto: Oxford University Press, 2010); and Mary Vipond, *The Mass Media in Canada*, 4th ed. (Toronto: James Lorimer & Co., 2011).

The next step is to address the debate. A good place to start is David Taras's *The Newsmakers: The Media's Influence on Canadian Politics* (Toronto: Nelson Canada, 1990). The book is dated, but the first chapter has an excellent discussion of models of newsmaking, which include those relating to political and commercial biases. From here, one can go to more detailed treatments of the topic: Robert Hackett and Yuezhi Zhao, *Sustaining Democracy? Journalism and the Politics of Objectivity* (Toronto: Garamond Press, 1998); Paul Nesbitt-Larking, *Politics, Society, and the Media*, 2nd ed. (Peterborough: Broadview Press, 2007); and Lydia Miljan and Barry Cooper, *Hidden Agendas: How Journalists Influence the News* (Vancouver and Toronto: UBC Press, 2003). For a discussion of bias that goes beyond Canada, John Street's *Mass Media, Politics & Democracy,* 2nd ed. (New York: Palgrave Macmillan, 2011) is relevant. Journal articles listed with the two debate essays are also pertinent.

Other readings pertinent to the debate include case studies and discussions relating to the issue of bias and the behaviour of the media. A useful case study is the one highlighted in Barker's essay, David A. Good, *The Politics of Public Management: The HRDC Audit of Grants and Contributions* (Toronto: University of Toronto Press, 2003). Another text contains a series of articles pertinent to the debate: Shannon Sampert and Linda Trimble, eds. *Mediating Canadian Politics* (Toronto: Pearson Canada, 2010).

Finally, one should not leave this debate without considering that it might be beside the point. Discussions of media focus on the traditional media or the old media—newspapers, established TV networks, radio. But some claim that the new media—networks with a clear ideological slant, websites, and bloggers with notoriety—are what matters. It is argued that any debate about the nature of the media and how they present the news should concentrate on the new and not the old. In the United States, the new media have created what two authors call "Freak Show Politics," so clearly something is up in this new world of media and politics. See Mark Halperin and John F. Harris, *The Way to Win: Taking the White House in 2008* (New York: Random House, 2006).